1970

This book may be kept

THE SHADOW OF HEAVEN

Matter and Stance in Milton's Poetry

The Shadow of Heaven

MATTER AND STANCE IN MILTON'S POETRY

×××

By Jon S. Lawry

CORNELL UNIVERSITY PRESS

Ithaca, New York

First published 1968

Library of Congress Catalog Card Number: 68–16385

PRINTED IN THE UNITED STATES OF AMERICA
BY KINGSPORT PRESS, INC.

Preface

When Hamlet, observing an actor's imitation of grief, demands, "What's Hecuba to him, or he to Hecuba, / That he should weep for her?" he poses a sharp question about the reciprocal relationship of fiction and life. As audience, we can easily dismiss the question. It seems to ask that we reply, "Nothing." However, when Hamlet turns the question upon himself and us ("What would he do, / Had he the motive and the cue for passion that I have?"), we become less certain. If we dispose of the question a second time by consigning Hamlet himself to fiction, not only does Shakespeare's Prospero wait along the way to tell us that we are such dreams as fiction is made of, but Milton, outside of fiction, resolutely approaches to remind us that we and our Christian "fictions" are reality of the highest order. Unless we choose to become the dreams of Hell, he declares, we are the Platonic or "accommodative" shadow of substantial Heaven itself.

Milton pushes the frontiers of fiction beyond the circumference and at the same time into the very center of presumed Christian reality. He, as author in whom "the cause of God and his church was to be pleaded," and we, as audience who share the cause, are the subjects of the true poems we read and the fable of the true plays we enact. Together with some Italian Renaissance critics, Milton soars above the critical Aonian mount that explained and justified fiction as an imitation of intellectual and moral reality, a mimesis. Because his Christian subject is assumed to be true and because both author and audience are directly involved in it, his works open instead into a participative enactment, a *methexis*.[1]

---

[1] Derived from Jane E. Harrison, *Themis* (Cambridge, 1927), pp. 35–44, 125–126, 328–329. The portion of an action that is newly "created" rather

[v]

Although the instrument for participation is of course lyric, narrative, and dramatic poetry, and although traditional devices of those genres are used with great literary self-consciousness, the subject of a work, its human creator and divine Creator, and its audience are all wholly real and wholly active.

These essays propose to extend the *methexis* to include literary discussion with the general reader. Such discussion makes a similar demand upon both the present author and the reader: for the time being, each must accept Milton's general extraliterary beliefs as "given," in order to participate fully in his literary action. It is admittedly an extraordinary demand. We usually suspend our literary disbelief only during the time we are absorbed in an excellent work of fiction. Using a critical shorthand, we may say that we "feel" its pathos and "see" its meaning, but we almost never admit any necessary connection between the literary experience and our beliefs (nor does the pronoun "we" imply the human race—only the supposed readers of the work). But Milton's subject is Renaissance Puritan Christianity, which he believes conveys divine truth. As Wittgenstein sometimes asserted that logic is a mirror of reality, so Milton would hold that his great Argument mirrors—and, in a sense, *is*—reality. His work is to be, not a Platonic imitation of an imitation, but the direct act of revelation. The reader's usual statement that in fiction he "sees" and "feels" will no longer be merely figurative. Instead, the audience will be led to the meditative or incarnative affirmation, "We realize": the awareness of God-with-us. If the devices of *methexis* are as important and rewarding in Milton as I believe them to be, we must surrender our extra-Miltonic theological and metaphysical beliefs as well as our purely literary disbelief during the time that we read him. We, too, can then "see" and "feel" truth—truth that is broadly relevant to God and man, to eternity and time; truth that is not only "about" us or "for" us but even "by" us, as we with Milton enact God's great poem. Such *methexis* in reading and discussion obviously carries no extraliterary imperatives. Even though we live in an ostensibly Christian culture,

---

than repeated continues the miraculous but never mysterious Eleusinian celebration: things invisible to mortal sight will be shown in an *epopteia* by the poet-hierophant.

methexis in no wise presses on us, as though it were Milton's, the personal question, "What would he do, / Had he the motive and the cue for passion that I have?" One no more has to be a certified Miltonic Christian after reading Milton than a worshiper of the Delphic Apollo after reading Sophocles. However, if we are to receive the power of Milton's vast drama, we must at least take care to enter the right theater.

The total *methexis* asks that author and audience to the works, together with the rehearsals and judgments within the works themselves, share the expression both of divine truth in its many manifestations and of human experience in its manifold forms. The poet must be a voice for God, like Moses and David, as well as a humble, fallible servant, like the Adam of *Paradise Lost,* Book XII. The audience, too, must be "zealous servants" among the sons of God singing eternally in the brilliant morning light of Heaven as well as sons of Adam, abjectly mourning in themselves the dark Fall. Nature also will act as Chorus, groaning at the Fall and Crucifixion, rejoicing at the Creation and Incarnation.

Somewhat like the Eleusinian mysteries and certain Christian services of worship, the "saying" (*legomenon*) of poetry is a revealed and prophetic current of truth that becomes action. In "At a Solemn Music," verse and voice can pierce uncreated or dead matter, chaos or Lazarus, and cause it to vibrate in the cosmic hymn and dance. At the least, in such a "saying" subject, sayer, and listener are joined even more closely than they were when Demodocus sang to Odysseus *of* Odysseus, at King Alcinous' feast. In Christian lore, the subject is that which the listener and sayer have done or must do. More important, the poems will possess a direct "doing" (*dromenon*), for the fable must be enacted by the author and audience—not in sympathy or empathy with fictive characters, but immediately within themselves. The song of creation becomes part of the act of Creation. Finally, the new action or continuing meaning of divinity that illumines the human doing and saying can supply a "showing" of things invisible to mortal sight, making the poet a hierophant and the members of the audience direct initiates into holy mystery. It does not matter greatly whether we participate in the divine action at the infernal level, or on earth with its mixed pattern of choices, or in Heaven.

We will see different objects and enact different roles, but they will eventually come to be and to mean almost the same. As Milton says in another context, "All is . . . , / As ever in my great task-Master's eye" (Sonnet 7) .

Such use of *methexis* almost demands the present tense. The eternal moment or the eternal return familiar in primitive ritual becomes a sophisticated eternal act. It also demands the archetype and type in meaning and action. Through typology we will be able to receive the full force of particularity, change, time, and history and at the same time recognize their connection with original creation, the unchanging standards of divine judgment, and the eternal disposition of life or death. The "double vision" asked of his audience by Milton has been symbolized in many ways, most of them suggested by Milton himself—a spiral, intersecting circles and orbits, the ingress and regress of vital forces, the tree of being, a ladder and ramp, and so forth. In these discussions, I suggest the image of a perpendicular. The vertical line is that of divinity—timeless, unchanging, harmonious, infinite. The horizontal line is that implying Hellish and human time, history, cacophony, and change. The lateral line, or flow, seems to those within it to occasion itself, but it is closed rather than infinite at each terminus and depends upon the vertical line for being and meaning. Man can therefore choose lateral "loss," persevere in his own being and meaning, or ascend to any point in the perpendicular, if he will recognize the relationship. Similarly, when God "stoops" to man, it is across no great spiritual distance, for the vertical line unites him to all parts of the horizontal line. If God is Hellenically above man as creator and judge, he is also Hebraically with man, both within history and in man's redemption from history.

In this dynamic, "monistic" relationship, in which matter is not divorced from spirit nor eternity from time, Milton again and again stages the *methexis* which in part constitutes that relationship.[2] If we as audience must fully share the Fall, we may also

----

[2] As Leo Spitzer, in *Classical and Christian Ideas of World Harmony* (Baltimore, 1963) , p. 25, represents the lovely doctrine of music formulated by Ambrose, there will be "a 'performance,' and 'incarnation' of that world harmony about which the Greeks had speculated; and the Church, which was represented in his hymns as echoing the music of the universe, served, actually, as the theater for the performance of these hymns."

fully share the energy of renewal. If men feel within themselves the loss of their conferred harmonious Paradise, they may nevertheless restore a reharmonized Paradise within. Sharing the total Christian experience, men can then discover that the morning song of Genesis and the new song of Revelations and all the vital life that both songs celebrate have always been their own. They will be "breathing instruments" of the great choric psalm that the whole world both is and celebrates.

Milton as Christian poet perhaps dared greatly in hoping to present, more than to represent; to express, not to report; to act, not to relate; to create with, not only to pattern after, divine agents; to do, not to mime. In a sense, that program becomes the great literary "Argument" of his works. As Michael Lloyd has said, to have the Christian vision insists that one preach it.[3] And for Milton, we may add, to preach it or to receive it must also be to enact it.

In these discussions, I have followed Milton in calling his subjects *matter*. The devices of participation within the subject by author and audience I call *stance*. The first term permits a more general conception of Milton's received Christian and classic subjects, together with his own disposition of them in given literary modes, than would more limited terms indicating plot, rhetoric, trope, and so on. It also reflects his sense that a human poet is like the divine creative agency that worked upon chaotic "matter." In Milton, Christian and classic matter tends to compose both the full vertical and horizontal lines of the perpendicular. Action and being in time and eternity are their constituents. Stance, on the other hand, indicates point of view and change of setting, but in a way at once more narrow and more broad than our usual terms suggest. It contains significations of stand, stanza, strophe: physical and moral position, poetic paragraph, and choric place, words, and movement. It often indicates the static or progressive placing of author and audience in a poem—placement as much spiritual

[3] Michael Lloyd, "The Two Worlds of 'Lycidas,'" *Essays in Criticism*, XI (1961), 391. See further the discussion of the imitation of gods in Mircea Eliade, *Cosmos and History*, tr. Willard Trask (New York and Evanston, Ill., 1959), p. 23. For a pertinent discussion of the masque, said to destroy "the barrier between spectators and actors" ("in a sense, what the spectator watched he ultimately became"), see Stephen Orgel, *The Jonsonian Masque* (Cambridge, Mass., 1965), pp. 6–7.

and judicial as physical. Stance writes two important laws in Milton: first, that we as audience participate morally in both the place and attitude of the stance; second, that we temporarily separate ourselves from a speaker, face him, and become his audience when he addresses someone else at length. The consequences of both laws are striking. If we realize, for instance, that our stance in Hell is that of a fallen being sharing the mentality of Hell, we will be less willing to credit the rhetoric of falsehood, whereas if we suppose that we receive Hell's doctrine from "impartial" earth, we may fondly dream of romantic rebels and divine tyranny.

To see *this* matter, for *this* stance, in both of which we ourselves are included, we with Milton therefore enact Adam or the other Son, at Eden or on their high mounts or in their tombs. By our participation, we confirm and recognize act and meaning as both theirs and ours, and also those of all men.

I perhaps should re-emphasize that the discussions which follow are intended for the general reader. For that reason alone, I have limited footnotes to those that offer further assistance to such a reader. The number of my notes stands in inverse relationship to my enormous debts to other scholars.

My obligations to my family, especially my wife Martha, are legion. I am grateful to Professor Merritt Y. Hughes and The Odyssey Press, Inc., for permission to use the Hughes edition, *John Milton: Complete Poems and Major Prose* (New York, 1957), for all quotations from Milton. I am indebted to Ball State University and its English Department for released time and secretarial assistance. My major debt, as great as it is inexpressible, is to the land and people of Greece. During the time that I was writing most of these essays, Greece demonstrated to me that delicate beauty and tragic severity may be joined in one object, and that deep religious feeling and abundant enjoyment of life need not war. Greece is a useful mirror for much of Milton's poetic nature. I regret his sailing back to England without having seen divine Alpheus and the "steep of Delphos."

JON S. LAWRY

Clyde, Ohio, 1967

Abbreviations

Contents

Introduction

In Milton's belief, the individual man and the individual poem derive their existence and value from union with God, the source of being and meaning and beauty. Despite distracting pressures urging that the poet swerve to a lateral line of change and loss, it is his duty as man and as artist to maintain and express that union. That harmony decrees the subject for his work, together with his requisite individual "upright" stance before it and his God:

Thou hadst the diligence, the parts, the language of a man, if a vain subject were to be adorned or beautified, but when the cause of God and his church was to be pleaded, for which purpose that tongue was given thee which thou hast, God listened if he could hear thy voice among his zealous servants ["The Reason of Church Government," p. 666].

Although admitting to himself the possibility of falling into the lateral loss symbolized by Death or by Amaryllis and the shade, when Milton speaks generally of the poet's craft and art, his typical stance and subject are unmistakable even if his attitude is whimsical and "pagan":

You should not despise the poet's task, divine song, which preserves some spark of Promethean fire and is the unrivalled glory of the heaven-born human mind. . . . The gods on high love song and song has power . . . to bind the gods below and control the implacable shades with triple adamant. By song Apollo's priestesses . . . lay bare the mysteries of the faraway future. . . . When we return to our native Olympus and the everlasting ages of immutable eternity are established, we shall walk . . . and with the harp's soft accompaniment we shall sing sweet songs to which the stars shall echo and the vault of heaven from pole to pole ["Ad Patrem" ("To His Father"), p. 83. Prose translations are from the Hughes edition].

In order to express his total subject, Milton conducts the audience to individual stances in as many specific settings and attitudes within the perpendicular lines as are necessary in order that men may see, know, and act within the great divine stance.[1] It is only a little lower than that from which the eye of God [2] perceives both lines:

> Now had th' Almighty Father from above,
> From the pure Empyrean where he sits
> High Thron'd above all highth, bent down his eye,
> His own works and their works at once to view:
>
> . . . . .
>
>   on his right
> The radiant image of his Glory sat,
> His only Son; On Earth he first beheld
> Our two first Parents, yet the only two
> Of mankind . . . ; he then survey'd
> Hell and the Gulf between, and *Satan* there
>
> . . . . .
>
> To stoop with wearied wings, and willing feet
> On the bare outside of this World
> [*Paradise Lost*, III, 56–74].

It does not matter greatly whether this universal stance is called Jove's Court, the seat of Jove, Siloa's brook, Mt. Niphates, or—for God's uses—the temple of Dagon: from its creative source of being and judgment, somewhere beneath the ultimate height of God, all the action of the Miltonic triad *creation, fall, renewal,*[3]

[1] Albert R. Cirillo, in "Noon-Midnight and the Temporal Structure of *Paradise Lost*" (*ELH*, XXIX [1962], 372–373), traces some of the routes by which time and change are embraced within the Christian equivalent of Plato's Great Year.

[2] Among others who have described this pattern, Northrop Frye, in *The Return of Eden* (Toronto, 1965), p. 49, makes an interesting general comparison with the pattern of a fugue: total form revealed through "intricate and energetic movement." In such a form, initial and final resolution can surround a medial "maze."

[3] See Anne D. Ferry, "The Authority of the Narrative Voice in *Paradise Lost*," in *In Defense of Reading*, ed. R. A. Brower and Richard Poirier (New York, 1962), pp. 76–93, for discussion of relationships among narrator, characters, and audience.

expressing God's double gift and man's shame and glory, will take place. Eternal power and being and act are here really one. For Milton and his "methektic" audience,[4] as for all other agencies or manifestations of meaning and action, *hoc opus, hic labor est.*

But as imperatively as he must be a sounding reed in God's cosmic organ, such a poet must be also a shepherd to his own and God's sheep.[5] Although he seeks his individual ecstasy in the early poems, as the later works increase in scope and intensity he accepts stances lower and lower in the vertical line. Finally, both from necessity as a fallen man and from choice, he enters fully into the lateral area, not so much to know it (although he frequently acts as Raphael and Michael to his audience) as to redeem it. If as a young man he had voiced his sense of the lower line in prophetic judgment—"When God commands to take the trumpet and blow a dolorous or a jarring blast, it lies not in man's will what he shall say or what he shall conceal" ("The Reason of Church Government," p. 666) —from the time of *Comus* forward he fashions within the lateral line the pattern creation, fall, renewal for himself and his audience. His reasons are quietly asserted in *Paradise Lost:*

> Taught by the heav'nly Muse to venture down
> The dark descent, and up to reascend,
> Though hard and rare. . . .
> Shine inward, and the mind through all her powers
> Irradiate, there plant eyes, all mist from thence
> Purge and disperse, that I may see and tell
> Of things invisible to mortal sight [III, 19–55].

In order to express his full adoration of God, then, he must find glory not only in creation's nativity and light but in renewal's

[4] For additional discussion of the "mimetic participation" of all creatures within "God's continuous ways," see Arthur E. Barker, "Structural and Doctrinal Pattern in Milton's Later Poems," in *Essays in English Literature from the Renaissance to the Victorian Age, Presented to A. S. P. Woodhouse,* ed. Millar MacLure and F. W. Watt (Toronto, 1964), pp. 173–175.

[5] Lowry Nelson, Jr., in *Baroque Lyric Poetry* (New Haven and London, 1961), p. 139, while discussing other "audiences" within "Lycidas," notes that the audience of readers receives the major address from the speaker. Barbara K. Lewalski, in *Milton's Brief Epic* (Providence, 1966), p. 237, observes that in *Paradise Regained* the narrative voice and that of the Redeemer become one.

prior defeat and darkness; not only in the choruses of heaven, but in the grating cacophony of the pagan gods; not merely outside history, with the Greeks, but inside it, with a Hebraic consciousness. Then the epic *doing* can be the revelation of meditative *saying*. The human word spoken within the moving shadow of history will be inspired from the fixed dynamism of eternity, which it will in turn express. The individual and universal stances will permit the presentation in one poem of the secular wash of time and choice as well as time's full transcendence in reason and teleology. Secular choice can lead to eternal, aspiring *choice of;* social love, to endless *love of.* Even if history should seem to assert that particular things and events aspire toward Satanism, the greater stance will oppose a countervailing divine description and judgment—judgment not only of the types, but of history itself.[6]

After the human artistic choice for redemptive experience within the lateral line has been made, the dynamic activity between Heaven and earth on the vertical line becomes tense and vibrant.[7] Divine act and human act become almost interchangeable on the perpendicular lines, depending upon the absoluteness of the human commitment and the fullness of divine grace. As man falls, Heaven itself and the methektic poem stoop to his aid, even to the extent of sharing his death. As man rises, Heaven itself increases its prospect endlessly, and the poem concordantly moves higher than the sphery chime. Even the fallen subject matter and the stances within folly and loss come to do artistic as well as theological "Errands in the gloomy Deep" (*Paradise Lost,* I, 152) .

The literary consequences of such a subject and such *methexis* are almost revolutionary, even today. We are familiar with Milton's own triumphantly grateful claim that he had created a greater epic and tragedy for the new Christian literary hero and his agon. If we chance to hold that the great classic forms are now outdated and to believe that Christianity can display only monu-

---

[6] See Nelson, *Baroque Lyric Poetry,* pp. 24–25, for discussion of ways in which space and time can be "conquered" in poetry.

[7] Frye, in *The Return of Eden,* p. 50, discusses God's bending to man in song and man's yearning toward God in praise. See also, for the use of type, figure, and form in developing such correspondence, Erich Auerbach, *Scenes from the Drama of European Literature: Six Essays* (New York, 1959) .

ments to dead ideas, we may still concentrate on the "pure" literary effects in *Paradise Lost* and the other poems. They are sometimes "radical," as modern studies both of Milton and of others can attest. For example, a recent study of *Paradise Lost,* one that complements some of the findings of the essays that follow, suggests that Milton's reader is led into his own temptation in order that he may stand as his own judge.[8] We had supposed that only satire would so purposefully "mislead" a reader. Similarly, a recent essay upon the "radical" tendencies of the recent French novel and play all but writes a prescription for Milton's seeking of enactment [9] rather than description (beyond that point, of course, Milton and Sartre radically diverge). We seem to be gaining the suspicion that even his much maligned style has almost as much in common with Gerard Manley Hopkins as with Virgil. The general historical and personal reasons that led Milton to combine the strictly traditional with the personal and exploratory are now reasonably familiar to us. Together with other investigations of the Miltonic use of time and space, of myth, of cross-reflective metaphor, and of structural balance and counterbalance, some concern with his given subject and his manipulation of stances may further illumine that literary substance and that quality which, whether in exasperation or in near-adoration, we call Miltonic.

The matter of Milton's poems is usually of Biblical origin, but is heavily, even dominantly, influenced by Latin, Greek, and Italian literary and philosophical models and by the independent bent of radical Protestant thought. Evidently such an amalgam was necessary to Milton. We know that although the young poet created a winning ode upon the Nativity, he failed in a poem upon the Passion. We usually assume that the matter of the one was agreeable to his talents, whereas that of the other was unwork-

[8] Stanley Fish, "The Harassed Reader in *Paradise Lost*" and "Further Thoughts on Milton's Christian Reader," *CritQ,* VII (1965), 162–182, 279–284. The reader comes to realize that his "responses are being controlled and mocked by the same authority [as] a way to self-knowledge" (p. 166), and that gradually he is educated also to a different sense of time.

[9] Ihab Hassan, "The Literature of Silence," *Encounter,* XXVIII (Jan., 1967), p. 76.

able. If we follow that argument, we first note the Biblical origin of both subjects but then discover major differences. The decisively classical character of most of the Nativity Ode, with its bucolic shepherds, its images of light and purity more applicable to Apollo than to a child "meanly wrapt in the rude manger" (l. 31), and its hope not so much for doomsday as for a golden age, contrasts tellingly with the tortured rejection of such a character and such colors in "The Passion" (pp. 61–63). There, the author exhausts himself in rejection: "These latter scenes confine my roving verse, / To this Horizon is my *Phoebus* bound" (ll. 22–23). We may also infer the militant Protestant's admiration for an agonistically heroic rather than a broken Christ. "The Passion" is almost a definition of the problem Milton faced with any agon that could not yet be understood to be in any way heroic:

> For now to sorrow must I tune my song,
> And set my Harp to notes of saddest woe,
> Which on our dearest Lord did seize ere long,
> Dangers, and snares, and wrongs, and worse than so,
> Which he for us did freely undergo:
>   Most perfect *Hero,* tried in heaviest plight
> Of labors huge and hard, too hard for human wight.
>
> He sovereign Priest, stooping his regal head
> That dropt with odorous oil down his fair eyes,
> Poor fleshly Tabernacle entered,
> His starry front low-rooft beneath the skies;
> O what a Mask was there, what a disguise!
>   Yet more; the stroke of death he must abide,
> Then lies him meekly down fast by his Brethren's side
>   [ll. 8–21].

In these lines striving desperately against paralysis, the only vitality comes from the classical and Protestant heroism that is proscribed by his subject. "Dangers, and snares, and wrongs" are converted almost at once from indications of base humiliation to heroic parallels of those that beset Hercules. The Christ becomes at worst a sacrificial Olympian, not a lamb to be led to the slaughter. It may be that the future advocate of Cromwell finds the parallel of Joseph, disguised in power and resting finally with the patriarchs of Israel, far more appealing than the image of a tortured Jesus himself, much as in *Paradise Lost* the human Jesus will be cast as militant Joshua. Emphasis is directed away from ignominious death to spirited magnanimity.

This choice of matter by Milton seems to have been lifelong, even though the matter itself is later weighed in a somewhat different manner. In the joyous early poems it all but places an Adam in a Marvellian garden with his God. We of course see only what Milton permits us to see of his apprentice pieces, and cannot know of possible exercises on other subjects. Nor can we surely know what may have directed his choice of subjects—whether his father, encouraging schoolmasters and friends, or only his own disposition. Dates of composition of many of the poems are also disputable. However, judging from the poems Milton selected and from the dates of composition now widely accepted, we can extrapolate these forms and subjects in the early works:

(1) Celebrations of Olympian or Elysian images (and Platonic or Neoplatonic ideas) of eternal calm and joy.

(2) Celebrations of divine "vertical" creative power and deliverance, the latter making any "lateral" threat seem illusory or only challenging.

(3) Celebrations of spring and generative power.

(4) Celebrations of friendship.

(5) Celebrations of poetic apprenticeship, poetic habit, and "divine" poetry itself.

(6) Lamentations upon death that shift readily into assurances of eternal life.

(7) Dramatizations of a cycle in which the happy Edenic state is shadowed by a temptation or threat (usually dismissed with ease) that in turn leads to renewal of Eden.

From these subjects, a large sense of Milton's early poetic matter emerges. It is a model or form of the one eternal act, manifestations or disclosures or enactments of which appear in human time. Within that act, every human event—past, present, or future—is seen as a participant or a reflection. Under a mantle of present Olympian calm, made dynamic with the memory or the continuation of Old Testament Creation and with Platonic and

Neoplatonic formulations of Idea, man lives in a joyous and blessed world; then death or threats of corruption enter that Paradise by means that these early poems do not really assess; however, the virtuous human creature remains serene, knowing that death and threat are unreal except insofar as some men choose them, and recognizing that even those who choose error may easily choose renewal or return to a blessed eternity, Christ's divine-human action having pointed the way. The first of the three great tones within Milton's triad—creation, fall, renewal—has been joyously sounded.

Extrinsic weaknesses of several sorts threaten this action, of course. Its greatest flaw, dramatically if not theologically, is a seeming unwillingness to consider lateral evil and death as really existent or meaningful. The "fable" therefore often has to be patched quickly, and whole sections at times are closed off. For instance, Milton wants the story to be universal, but after a time he has to restrict it mainly to virtuous persons; he must cast down death so easily as to trivialize not only general human mortality but also individual human grief; and he is threatened in the early poems with seeing his God become Olympian Zeus, heroic Hercules, the First Cause, Venus genetrix, every Neoplatonic man, or a combination of these. But such threats prove to be minor. Most of the early poems succeed in creating that mysterious, untroubled joy found in archaic Greek statues of gods and men, beings who receive the world of time and experience with objective pleasure which they sometimes express in lithe dance and Apollonian song, but who always see through the temporal world into timeless reality.

This general matter—an almost single-minded celebration of vertical, untroubled creation—commands all the poems that precede *Comus*. Because each of the earlier poems, as well as *Comus* and "Lycidas," is usually considered separately, I have risked displaying their common subjects in quick Homeric catalogue. For the later poems, most of which are relatively familiar, a single witness can carry the same weight of proof as the earlier legions.

The earliest known poem, "A Paraphrase on Psalm CXIV," celebrates Jehovah's easy triumph over Egypt and the power over nature of him "that ever was, and aye shall last" (p. 3). The similar paraphrase of Psalm 136, coining images influenced by Greece, praises the God of "the Golden-tressed Sun" and "The horned Moon . . . / Amongst her spangled sisters" (p. 4). A Latin elegiac exercise strongly Ovidian in tone and subject calls men from slumber with repeated calls of "Surge, age, surge," now that "Lux oritur" (p. 6). An imitation of Aesop contrasts a peasant's skill in creation with his landlord's destructive greed. (The mature Milton may have intended that the poem of his youth bear a statement about the free artist and the official audience that would like to use him officially, but if so, the applicability to his own career appears only in hindsight.) In that poem Milton introduces the sympathetic use of "shepherd," indicating not only an early attraction to pastoral form but also to the literary personages of the form. Elegy 1 prescribes the apprenticeship of a poet preparing, like a Christ in a bucolic wilderness, for the great nationalistic and religious works to come. The translation of Horace's "Ad Pyrrham" rejects amorous enslavement in the rueful recognition that human love can only be impermanent. Milton's obituary for the vice-chancellor, conducted in preponderantly Hellenic images, wishes for the dead an eternity with the blessed spirits in Elysium. The second elegy forces a slow way through frigid conceits to a protest against the death of the university beadle; the conclusion, however, reveals the poem as a clearly recognized apprentice piece, concerned principally with the young author himself ("Let wailing Elegy herself pour out her sad dirge and fill all the schools with its sound").

The five short Latin poems on the Gunpowder Plot are extremely interesting indications of Milton's ability to irradiate actual event with "eternal" meaning. The first attempts are less than triumphant. He employed a conceit that strikes modern readers as either comic or bathetic—the notion that the explosion would propel James vertically into Heaven. However, he later converted the conceit into a Biblical allusion and the threat to James into a parallel with the fiery translation of Elijah. Even in the midst of that correspondence he caused classical references (Tartarus, Styx, Iapetus) to outweigh the Biblical. Not until he reached the long, quasi-epical "In Quintum Novembris" did he begin to work happily within both bodies of literature, Greek and

Hebrew, and the major myths that invigorate them. The sunnier
Olympian myth still dominates the poem, being the less concerned with the problem of evil and the less complicated in its
Elysian theory of afterlife. In the poem proper, James is united
with Trojan Brutus, Satan becomes Pluto (although retaining
some Christian character of evil), England is made into a demi-
paradise, God indulges in Olympian laughter at the flimsy
"threat" to James, and the "Thunderer" dispatches the problem
by sending down "Fame" to stifle the Gunpowder Plot. The poem
inferentially unites the matter of *Paradise Lost* and *Paradise
Regained,* but almost all human and theological tensions are
absent—largely because the Hellenic myth refuses to countenance
them.

Elegy 3, the lamentation for Lancelot Andrewes, considers the
human soul half-divine (*semideamque*) and lends the mourner a
vision of eternal life by means of images still resolutely classic
(*Non dea tam variis ornavit floribus hortos / Alcinoi Zephyro
Chloris amata levi*). The memorial to the Bishop of Ely follows
much the same course but alters agent and agency; what had been
mourner's dream now becomes a swift union of the dead "object"
and the living poet in one direct, oracular voice: "But here I fall
silent, for who that is begotten of a mortal father can tell the
delights of that place? For me it is enough to enjoy them forever"
(p. 25). The extremely powerful effect in the later poems of
uniting object, poet, and audience with God in one eternal action
is here dimly forecast: the "I" of the poem is in part the risen
saint, in part Milton the poet, in part every Christian as reader,
and in part God as the implied immortal father who guarantees
the promise of "forever," eternality being one of his attributes (to
enjoy eternality is to enjoy God).

Elegy 4, protesting English abuse of a Christian soldier,
Thomas Young, is one of the few early poems in which actuality
seems a present threat, but even it reaches an almost
automatic—certainly an easeful—consolation: "But take heart.
. . . Your unarmed breast shall not be violated by any weapon
and no spear shall drink of your blood. For you shall be secure
under the radiant aegis of God. He will be your guardian and
. . . your champion" (p. 29). Milton's God is a Greek protector,

never—so far—the oblique cause of, or confirming permission for, suffering. Apart from its Florentine Platonism, the "Vacation Exercise," with enough accuracy to cause dismissal of some of the attributions of abrupt change in his work, predicts the route Milton's apprenticeship is to follow: he seeks English words that will supply a voice, a logos suitable for the poet-priest, one that will lead him toward "some graver subject" with which the "transported mind" may move to "Heav'n's door"—there to witness not Jehovah, however, but "unshorn Apollo," Zeus, and the secrets of precreation (p. 31). Similarly, "That Nature Is Not Subject to Old Age" joyously rises over apparent change to a vision of eternity: "He has fixed the scales of fate with sure balance and commanded every individual thing in the cosmos to hold to its course forever. . . . Phoebus shines with the ruddy beauty of eternal youth. . . . Thus, in a word, the righteous sequence of all things shall go on perpetually, until the final fire shall destroy the world" (pp. 34–35). These three excerpted sentences contain such certainty about the Christ-figurative Phoebus as to trumpet resurrection even in the moment of death. A semipagan view of the end of earth contains no terrors at all because it is overlaid with untroubling Christian images of the phoenix and the new Jerusalem. (When the phoenix image recurs in *Samson Agonistes,* the preceding drama will have caused it to exercise great pathos.) The early form of Milton's chosen matter is here almost complete.

The myth common to most of Milton's early poems is staged in full in "On the Death of a Fair Infant." In it, wintry Plutonic death apparently snuffs out idyllic human life. In reality, however, the loss was only "imagin'd" because the mother, like Mary, only seemed to suffer loss:

> Think what a present thou to God has sent,
> And render him with patience what he lent;
> This if thou do, he will an offspring give
> That till the world's last end shall make thy name to live
>
> [ll. 74–77].

In this conferred Magnificat arising by the graveside is forecast the patience that will be a dominant theme in the major poems, but here even the patience is exultant. If death can easily be transformed into gift, and loss into assurance of life, the sting of death is indeed slight.

Two spring poems, Elegy 5 and "On May Morning," celebrate vernal desire. In hindsight, however, we can mark the course of that desire toward "wedded love" rather than toward the rout of Comus. Both would restore to a now wretched world, not Venus, but Saturn (or Jupiter) and an age of gold. "On the Morning of Christ's Nativity" (which, with other poems, is discussed in detail below) presents an Apollonian Christ who indicates, even if he cannot yet restore, a perfect serenity that even now is in some measure available to men: "And then at last our bliss / Full and perfect is, / But now *begins*" (ll. 165–167—italics added). That celebrative ode may have led Milton into Elegy 6, which confidently asserts his poetical novitiate: "For truly, the bard is sacred to the gods and is their priest." His subject recently was "the heaven-descended King, the bringer of peace, and the blessed times" (p. 52). Both the stance and the matter suggest Augustus.

There is no profound change of subject with Sonnet 1 or the Italian sonnets. Although they deal warmly with love, like their Italian models they keep in mind the greater reality which human love intimates: "Ah, that my dull heart and hard breast might be as good a soil for Him who plants from heaven" (Sonnet 3, p. 54). Even when human love is considered in itself, its character is Florentine and Spenserian, emphasizing restraint and fixed devotion, "faithful, courageous, and constant . . . , secure against fortune, envy, and the fears and hopes of ordinary men" (Sonnet 6, p. 56).

"On the Platonic Idea" then only half-humorously establishes being—whether involving the human type, such as Adam or Christ, or the human particular in every man—as "eternal, incorruptible, unique yet universal, coeval with the heavens and made in the image of God—in whose likeness skilful Nature has molded the human race. . . . But, though all men have a share in his nature, yet—strange as it may be—he exists by himself as an individual apart and is limited by his own definite bounds in space" (p. 57). That Platonized mystery will be argued differently at a later period, when everyman encounters a fall or the threat of a fall, and the god or godlike man suffers death or the appearance of death. Now, with scarcely a shadow upon belief, the doctrine allows Milton to move forthrightly to Elegy 7, a fervent Ovidian poem which closes with a farewell to "wantonness . . . and a trifling purpose" (p. 61). It is not, however, a "farewell to love," as has sometimes been asserted. Surely the bravado of the final lines is intended to be overconfident, callow, and perhaps Hippolytan: "My breast has been rigid under a thick case of ice, of which the boy himself fears the frost for his arrows, and Venus herself is afraid of my Diomedean strength." It would be a strange rejection that still referred to Cupid and Venus, and a strange compliment from a classical scholar to nominate himself only Diomedean.

"The Passion," as we have seen, tries to mourn, but succeeds only in creating an instant of Herculean heroism. "On Shakespeare" considers a purely literary eternity formed by the "wonder and astonishment" of a poet's readers—a "heaven" the young Milton devoutly wishes, for it matches the Olympian or Elysian Heaven of the early poems far better than that of *Paradise Regained*. The heaven of Shakespeare can be associated with Jupiter, Phoebus, and the age of gold, whereas the Heaven of Jesus is troubling in its demands upon men.

The two epitaphs upon Hobson are so boyishly certain in their affection and consolation that gentle humor leads us to a God who can say of the dead, *"Hobson has supt, and's newly gone to bed"* (p. 64). The "Epitaph on the Marchioness of Winchester" insists that men do not live and die in isolated, temporal particularity but that instead individual life and death are reflections of eternal flame: the apparent death of the marchioness within time is translated into her actual continuing of life in eternal sainthood, even as her seeming particularity is erased by making her one, across time, with Rachel.

"L'Allegro" and "Il Penseroso" continue some of that serene conviction of eternality by following the poet in his untroubled, ascending contemplation. They hold that poetry, approaching the absolute harmony of music, can defeat Pluto; death can be swallowed up in enraptured artistry. Sonnet 7 mounts a famous protest against late productivity but dissolves protest easily into patience in (or with) God. Much in the mood of "L'Allegro" and

"Il Penseroso," "Arcades" transforms a countess into a Faerie Queene and transcends actuality by having a Genius of the Wood salve and heal it, like an unfallen Eve: "And all my Plants I save from nightly ill, / Of noisome winds, and blasting vapors chill" (p. 78). "On Time" similarly deals with the threat of actuality by transforming change into the changeless:

> . . . when as each thing bad thou hast entomb'd,
> And, last of all, thy greedy self consum'd,
> Then long Eternity shall greet our bliss [p. 80].

"Upon the Circumcision" is tormented by desperate conceits, but it permits still one more version of untroubled certainty through holding that, although divine law is just, Christ's love is "more exceeding" (p. 81)—which is a quick happy gloss for *Paradise Lost*, Book III. "At a Solemn Music" expresses once again the common myth in a form nearly complete: although the pure sounds of human voice and verse can join in a divine song through "pure concent," human sin produces discord. The prayer almost assures us that we may "renew that Song" and live "with him, and sing in endless morn of light" (pp. 81–82). Barely concealed is Milton's certainty that his own poetry is divinely directed and is, indeed, itself a form of divine utterance. That claim becomes overt, even if it grows amidst humorous teasing and exaggerated self-justification, in "Ad Patrem": "You should not despise the poet's task, divine song, which . . . is the unrivalled glory of the heaven-born human mind and an evidence of our ethereal origin and celestial descent. . . . You lead me far away . . . beside the Aonian stream, and you permit me to walk there by Phoebus' side, his blessed companion" (pp. 83–84). Surely Lycidas' recompense will include this river and this companion within the Christian Heaven.

Comus too takes as its subject divine song and the divinely celebrated return to it of a human being who in a sense wandered within temptation. In the masque, the only direct threat of mortality is anterior to the action, involving the erstwhile sacrifice of Sabrina, a Lycidian figure who similarly has become a "genius of the shore"; although the Lady herself, together with her Brothers, suffers a kind of Fall, self-renewal is either serenely simple or, because of Sabrina's sacrifice, external to her. Finally, although

Milton's Greek version of Psalm 114 and his epigram "Philosophus ad Regem" both deal with the eruption of evil, the first sees the Lord destroy Egypt and preserve Israel, after which the hills and mountains dance as at the first Creation; the second is an "apology" that finds that the virtue of a good person—an aspect of eternity—is indestructible, even if the life itself is easy to destroy. When a Socrates or a saint is killed by the state, the only real sufferer is the state.

The later poems never wholly abandon this matter, for to do so would mean abandoning the Creator. They resolutely continue to use the matter and the stances of Heaven or Eden. They do not forget the "first obedience" of "At a Solemn Music" even when confronting the "First Disobedience" in *Paradise Lost;* indeed, the conclusion of *Paradise Lost* and all of *Paradise Regained* dramatize a restoration of that first obedience. However, the full triad of creation, fall, renewal begins to introduce the lower range of somber, if more resonant, colors. The altered balance begins in *Comus* and reaches an early phase of completion in "Lycidas." In those poems, the early and buoyant confidence that sprang from trust in a benevolent God and in a world celebrating that goodness, of a young poet's conviction of his merit and power, and of a golden age of received Latin and Greek and Italian thought and literature, gives way perceptibly before shocks to the lateral line. Gradually, subjects expressive of the nature and cost of renovative victory—but never doubtful of its ultimate achievement—become dominant. Divine confidence is now wrought as well as worshiped. The celebration includes the human effort to celebrate, and Milton increases his role as agonist in his own artistic matter. Although the subject of Christian triumph itself does not alter, he increasingly honors the hero who endures and suffers. Perhaps one could argue that the early poems' disinterested "purity," ready confidence, and Olympian calm arising from belief in an Olympian deity were well lost, were it not for their matchlessly buoyant artistry.

When the original matter reappears in the larger field of the later works, it has been altered into these subjects and forms:

(1) Celebrations and justifications of the God who has acted directly toward the human being in creating him, in conferring choice upon him, in confirming the recoil of judgment

upon his errors, and in offering him renewal—all within the pattern of creation, choice, fall, judgment, and renewal (or, if not renewal, the apocalyptic burning away of "dross").

(2) Celebrations not of divine creation alone, but also of human strength manifested either in right choice or in renewal after error.

(3) Celebrations not so much of original generative power as of revival, resurrection, renewal.

(4) Indications for the audience of the oneness of man—one in Adam, in Christ, and in types or analogues that appear in Scripture, history, and contemporary existence.

(5) Solemn asseverations of the divine direction of prophetic poetry, including within the process of poetry itself a re-enactment of the major pattern of creation, fall, renewal.

(6) Major confrontations by Lycidas, Adam, and Samson of the actuality of sin, death, and baffled promise, producing in the works themselves major prayers or demands that God's ways be justified in action.

(7) Epic and dramatic confrontations of human beings with a choice, usually between reason-approving Eden and appetite-approving Hell, in which the struggle turns upon an attempt to prevent or counteract appetite. The contest is fueled immediately by the human will—errant at times, yet stubborn, often indomitable. Ultimately, of course, it is moved by both the original and the renovative gifts of God: life, reason, and grace.

A paradigm of the expansion and change of poetic matter between the early and the late poems is supplied by the late Sonnet 19 and the early Sonnet 7. Sonnet 19 stands as a dark shadow to the brighter poem. Whereas the youthful poem moves quickly to patience, the later one wrestles almost bitterly with God and the severity of an actual blindness. Human patience—not God directly, in either automatic revelation or relief—works the consolation, patience already having become humanly heroic as well as divinely ordained. The suffering, doubting human being reconstructs his position upon which to rejoice. The poem and the methektic audience move resolutely from stance to stance with him in his "reviving motions." Only at the conclusion is there assurance that God's employment of the authorial gift bestowed by God has been justified. Assurance comes not so much from sacred words as from the histrionic human enactment in the poem itself of past "light," present loss, consequent doubt, resultant struggle, and achieved renewal. Finally, whereas the early sonnet rested both will and response largely with God, the later assigns both will and response in large part to the struggling human patience. Even though the result of the agon may never be in question, the sense of struggle itself is instinct with fear and doubt. The later result is perhaps grander, having been won out of greater struggle, than was the trophy so suavely taken by the early poem. The change of coloration permits the later works to deal responsibly both with the early, untroubled Eden and with the later "first disobedience, and all our woe" that is to endure "till one greater Man / Restore us, and regain the blissful seat." The poems will involve and even re-create the conferred Eden; this world of choice, error, doubt, struggle, and faith; and the inward or eternal Paradise that can be achieved.

Theoretically, the matter of Milton's poems might have been handled in many ways. Practically, his aesthetic as well as his spiritual belief tended to ask that it be controlled by placing the author and audience in stances producing a direct realization of the matter.[10] Like that matter, the stances became more complicated as Milton's world view and the traditional genres that he chose to convey it became more complex. If literary decorum asked that the stances be appropriate and true to the audience, theology asked that they be absolutely true—a form not only of knowledge but of salvation.

The stance of the early poems seeks the axis for ascent to Jove's Court. Poet and audience become celebrants, entranced in divine harmony. Man can hardly be other than joyous, vigorous, and untroubled, resembling Adam and Eve in the prelapsarian Gar-

---

[10] For discussion of audience placement for direct realization, see David Daiches, *Milton* (London, 1957), p. 132; Rosemond Tuve, *Images and Themes in Five Poems by Milton* (Cambridge, Mass., 1957), p. 55; and Christopher Ricks, *Milton's Grand Style* (Oxford, 1963), pp. 28–29.

den, filled with a sense of vital participation in the enduring natural and intellectual activity of Creation. The Edenic songs of *Paradise Lost* significantly echo the early songs of Milton's English Eden.

The different disposition of stances in the later poems reflects the descent of the author into his entire subject, including its lateral line. The audience participates with him in his agonic realizations. In *Comus,* such general human awareness causes radical changes of stance from that of the early poems. Now Jove's Court seems to become divorced utterly from the pinfold Earth, and the Lady's sense of nature is divorced from that held by Comus. Stance begins to shift from one polar setting or attitude to the other, finding temporary stasis only in the center of human choice—from which it must again move, by the very nature of choice. The vertical and horizontal lines seemingly can be rejoined only by the sacrificial movement of Sabrina up from the base and by the careful stooping of Heaven down from the summit. The former celebrant himself may restore the harmony if he maintains his vision of the Platonic vertical line, but fraudulent and violent temptation makes it increasingly difficult for even him to persevere upright.

After *Comus,* the necessity for employing several stances in each poem continues, even as the increasing similarity among subject, author, audience, and divine and human agents makes each seemingly separate stance universally meaningful and even harmonious with its fellow stances. After *Comus* finally brings all stances through Neptunic seas to the holy city of Jove, "Lycidas" seemingly once again hurls attention to the opposing side—the fall to watery death and the ultimate imbrutement in a corpse. However, by enactments both of rising self-persuasion and of divine aid, the final stance of "Lycidas" achieves the unexpressive nuptial song by "other streams." Every man becomes involved within all the methektic stances that develop the full matter of reality. In *Paradise Lost,* the great distance between Heaven, earth, and Hell or death is emphasized by stances of almost equal duration. Ultimate Heaven and ultimate Hell are reflected in earth between. There all men, by means of the tutelage of divine agents, cross abysses of time and space to receive knowledge and to enact their own typic choices. In the end as in the beginning, however, the immense distances are simplified into the still point that is also infinity—God. Even the lateral choices of evil, death, and imbrutement are wrought into a vertical power of good by God's infinitely vaster choice. In *Paradise Regained* also, the original harmony gradually is reasserted, creating out of discordant, isolative situations unimaginable union and harmony. In *Samson Agonistes*, a conclusive paradigm is reached. Hero, author, and audience recall a stance of original gift and harmony. We take our stances in the general human fall, however: "eyeless at Gaza, at a mill, with slaves." In particular stances that lead us progressively a little onward, we come at last to the divine stance in which death has been absorbed into deliverance. Because in the person of Samson the first and second Adams and the first and second Lycidases join, and because the Chorus and Manoa embody the experience of themselves and of all other men, all becomes well and fair.

Self-interest alone can lead the Christian audience to its active place within Milton's general subject.[11] Milton's stances place, characterize, and judge characters, author, and audience within the great unitary stance. Perhaps no such confluence of artistic with "actual," of involvement of author and audience within what Aristotle called "action," and of supposed first agents of reality with existent particulars, had ever before, or has ever since, occurred—not even in ritual or in Greek religio-civic drama. It demanded that Milton see his divine subject as real and timeless, yet as capable of being imaged in objects that both share in and intimate that reality; that he see himself as participator, agent of creation, and representative or "model"; and that he conceive of his audience as the entire involved body of mankind. Much has been made of the risks he undertook. They admittedly were enor-

---

[11] O. B. Hardison, Jr., in *The Enduring Monument: A Study of the Idea of Praise in Renaissance Literary Theory and Practice* (Chapel Hill, N.C., 1962), p. 59, notes that for didactic critics, "only when the audience *actually believes* that the events depicted are true will it be persuaded that the poet's moral lessons have practical application." For Renaissance consideration of tragedy within that same framework, see G. Giovannini, "Historical Realism and the Tragic Emotion in Renaissance Criticism," *PQ*, XXXII (1953), 304–320.

mous, but not so great, perhaps, as the rewards possible from breaking down barriers between "imitation" and "action," between author and audience, between subject and act, and between word and deed. Although union between such elements can take place for a brief period whenever disbelief in a fiction is suspended, it is all but certain to occur when belief is triply demanded —called forward from Edenic remembrance, instituted by direct enactment in appropriate "present" stances, and projected upon the future as prophetic certainty. Even had Milton felt no religious obligation to use such a subject, he might have been dazzled by the artistic potentialities. It was, and is, no exaggeration to say that he pursued "Things unattempted yet in Prose or Rhyme." His control of Christian matter by methektic stance went far toward first permitting and then encouraging those attempts.

For Milton, the Word in any of its manifestations—including his own poems—may guide and even help to "save" man, if he chooses to be saved. As the Christian poet's matter is eternal, so is the offering of the Word. Not even the Last Judgment concludes the drama, for it merely demonstrates that the "unreal" always *was* unreal. Milton's revelatory "saying" and "doing" can demonstrate that creation, fall, and renewal, if experienced separately in time, are nevertheless one eternal action in eternity:

> His servants he with new acquist
> Of true experience from this great event
> With peace and consolation hath dismist,
> And calm of mind, all passion spent
> [*Samson Agonistes*, ll. 1755–1758].

[1] "That Undisturbed Song"

Harmony and Its Renewal in
"On the Morning of Christ's Nativity,"
"L'Allegro" and "Il Penseroso,"
"Arcades," and "At a Solemn Music"

To the young Milton, the musicianly son of a musicianly father, music supplied not only an absorbing personal interest but also a traditional description or metaphor of universal harmony. To the Renaissance such harmony was one of the grand explanations and demonstrations of being and Being. It permitted man not merely to envision, but also to inhabit, a timeless "vertical" harmony with all other partial being, and with God. It also allowed him to perceive the "lateral" harmonizing of events in time and history. Their apparent discords (which dialectically possessed hidden capacities for unity) revealed a vast concord. Although the image of harmony has clear relationships with other Renaissance images of being—such as the great chain, and the tree or circle of mutually sustaining relationships—it possessed an inherent comprehensiveness, dynamism, and charm that more static conceptions might lack. If the earth and the heavens and all their creatures glorify their creative God with unceasing dance and song that are part of their individual beings, then all creatural being must forever vibrate with sound and movement even as it remains changeless in form and in the act of praise. If the worshipful essential movement is realized also in expressive words, voice, and melody, all partial being must be engaged eternally in an artistic as well as religious act. If God's glorious creation expresses and reflects God, and to that extent shares divine powers of holiness, creativity, beauty, and reason, then God and his creatures are much more nearly "united" than other images of being had intimated.

In such a view, God shared likeness in exalted degree with the human artist or priest. This sense of correspondence must have been almost irresistible to a prospective artist who had already begun to devote his works and days to the glorification of God. He and his work would be a reed in the great universal organ, a movement in the great dance, a word in the eternal meaning. In giving voice to his own delight, he would also be a voice for all human creatures. His "alternating measures" would be the pattern for their poetic movement. His and their choric word, melody, and action would join with the chorus of spheres, angels, and all other creatures in ever living praise before the central throne of God. In almost all the early poems, Milton's conviction that art is serviceable to both God and men will provide a stance that supplies a joyously confident author, an implicated, participative audience, and their serene but vibrant expression of timeless praise.

Recent studies of the meaning music held for the schooled man of the Renaissance help to explain the power music exerted upon Milton. Although he admired orchestral and vocal music, for him music assumed its loftiest meaning in higher expressions—the harmonizing of human beings, the harmonizing of cosmic intellect, or the ineffable harmony of divine act and being. He was interested primarily in the divine significances and cosmic harmonies that music intimates and rehearses: the one voice of created things harmonizing with each other and with their creator; the "penetration" of divinity downward into the flesh, and of men upward to divinity; the reconciliation of seeming opposites, composing a "symphony" from apparent discord; and the therapeutic tuning or "tempering" that restores a right character to the disharmonious human body and soul.[1] By the time Milton wrote,

---

[1] Gretchen L. Finney, in "A World of Instruments" (*ELH*, XX [1953], 88), reprinted in her *Musical Backgrounds for English Literature: 1580–1650* (New Brunswick, N.J., 1962), quotes the *Parthenia Sacra:* " 'Man is a Harp; the Powers and Faculties of the Soule, the strings; and Reason, the Harper.' "

these and other meanings had combined to form a body of ideas having the authority of belief. Milton uses the tradition with characteristic selectivity, drawing upon at least three past interpretations of music but adapting them to his own poetic statements and practice. (Similarly, most of the discussion that follows considers the interpretations of music within the context of Milton's poems rather than in strict historical description.) With those musical figures, he would set in motion ardent hymns and dances of things, men, spheres, and angels in a harmony of intellectual and spiritual and physical celebration of God.

One of the traditional interpretations of music at times utilized by Milton derived from Platonic, early Neoplatonic, and Augustinian conceptions, most of which were based upon monody, the progressive pattern of single notes within the framework of a mode or kind of key. Its basis was largely mathematical and sequential, its "harmony" consisting in established relationships of tones within time. By analogy, music might contain a model of the universe or a diagram of perfect justice and order. To the Arabs, it suggested the four elements; to others, the pattern of the spheres; to still others, the seven days of creation, the eighth tone indicating a return. Although emphasizing order and proportion, music could also include affecting images of the harmony in the universe (the full order of notes, or diapason), the symphony of such seeming opposites as "low" passion and "high" reason, and the purgation of unhealthy or immoral discords (*dyskrasia*) from the soul and body, as in *Samson Agonistes*.

A second conception of music developed in the Renaissance. From polyphony, in which two or more progressive lines as well as occasional vertical harmonies appeared, were adduced somewhat different implications. To the mainly "pure" monodic relationships were added not only the increased conversation of one musical or creatural voice with others but also the somewhat static vertical relationships of tones within a chord (even though polyphony virtually demanded change within the chordal relationship). In this more baroque conception of music, the sounding-together included both the "vertical" harmonies of Heaven with earth and the "horizontal" harmonies of men within societies and in history, along with the great harmony that was made possible when both great kinds were themselves harmonized. Such an interpretation opened the way for a more active participation by the individual creature. Music continued to reflect Heaven or heavenly rapture, but it also provided a method by which man himself could move to such rapture from his lateral order, thereby involving not only his understanding or fantasy but also his will. Up to a point, men could desire and even compose the rapture. Christians utilized both conceptions of music when they took charity to be a symphonizing agency within man, among men, and between man and God. In a sense, they had chosen "vertically" when they symphonically Christianized Platonic sirens (and sometimes their spheres) into angels, found Orpheus to be one with David, or associated Apollo with Christ, reconciling the seeming opposites of pagan and Christian forms.

Within Milton's own time, Robert Fludd projected upon the monochord of vertical tones or strings yet another sense of the significance of music. The monochord became a vertical model of the relationship of Heaven, the middle regions, and earth, held in static order. For aspiring men, however, the static obviously would become the ecstatic.

These three conceptions of music, which of course were not so discrete as a brief discussion is forced to suggest, offered Milton a wide range of meanings and figures in the early poems. We may guess that they represented beliefs as well, but we receive directly only the analogies and metaphors drawn from such beliefs. The monodic image, quite apart from its attractive intimations of an Apollonian golden age associated with the purity of the lyre and with the artistic and intellectual foundation of humanity, offered an image of sacred notation for the sequential pattern of human history and time, within which harmonic relationships of substance and action move in accord with divine "laws" of harmony. The later polyphonic line permitted a far more complex and subtle, if less nostalgically "pure," pattern for sequences and relationships within history, along with persistent intimations of chordal harmony in the vertical order. The purely chordal analogy involved immediate human rapture and ecstasy, assuring not only the likeness or correspondence of Heaven with earth but also their effectual union. Its music is largely that of an interinvolving, unsequential unity of tone, free of time and change.

Milton adjusts any model to a given subject, of course, but it is clear that the monodic interpretation is somewhat too mathematical (or in "Christian" Pythagoreanism, too rigidly allegorical) for extensive use in the sensuous, dramatic utterance of poetry. The dialectical, counterpoising mode of polyphony is obviously well suited to the structures of *Paradise Lost* and *Samson Agonistes*. The early poems, however, ask a mode suggesting the immediate harmony of Heaven, spheres, earth, elements, man, and human voices and instruments, like that described by Boethius: a "concert" of universal consent, consonance, harmony, in which by involvement or purifying desire the seemingly low orders can "attend" and "penetrate" to union with the highest. The third, or chordal, mode is therefore the frequent handmaiden to Milton in the early poems.

The idea of a chord, however, whether physical or fully "ideal," must remain only descriptive or figurative within the poems. Even the expression of the mode in a poem must sacrifice the static chord to progressive discourse. To Heaven, man may be a "breathing instrument" and his vocal organs a musical plectrum, but in the world, man's music must be composed and played within the flow of time. If the human intelligence were like angelic intuition, the chord composed by God, other creatures, and man might be realized instantly, but because human thought is discursive even in unfallen Adam, any poem—even a lyric— must move sequentially. What is more, even the sunny Milton of the early works does not hold only to the original harmony, the *musica speculativa* of Apollo, but considers also the achieved harmony, the *musica humana* attributed to Orpheus. Although he hastens past the topic, he nevertheless gives due attention to human loss, both individual and general. Human tones in the chord therefore must be tempered in order to achieve "concent." Although the chord may be immediately envisioned, it must be sequentially won.

The early poems thus open characteristically upon an Eden of perfect harmony, chordally celebrated in the present tense; then, realizing that the present celebration of the harmony must in part be illusory because of human distempering in the Fall, they indicate the nature of human discord and of its effect, *angustiae aurium*—the restricting of our ears that produces an inability to hear the primordial, universal harmony. Finally, they either seek or find that harmony again. Through the curative offices of sensible music they sometimes enact the renewed power to hear divine intellective music, returning in rapt "penetration" to man's part in original bliss. The renewed chord continues to tremble slightly with the threat that it may be only conditional or temporary or figurative. For that reason, complicated mazes of polyphony later will be run in order to found harmony more certainly on incarnative or apocalyptic "renewal." It will seem safer then to trust Heaven to stoop concordantly to man than to trust man to rise ecstatically to God.

Although Platonic and Neoplatonic tradition, increasingly Christianized during the Middle Ages and Renaissance, helps to explain much of Milton's literary interest in music, it does not entirely explain or exhaust the influence of Christianity upon musical allusion in the early poems. Leo Spitzer, for example, did not quite see [2] that Christian encounter with the music of creation, of the Psalms, of the angel chorus at the Nativity, of Revelations, and of divine services would have bestowed upon Milton many of the same images and perhaps even some of the same implications as those from the idea of music alone. Although Milton associated Biblical models specifically with literature, considering Revelations, for example, to be a form of tragedy, he noted also the musical nature of Biblical "choruses" and "odes." The Biblical morning stars singing together and the new song of Revelations were grand images of the continuous creative music of God. The joyful noise required by God of his people involved the individual man both before and after the Boethian "human" music might temper body and soul. Musical theory that demanded order as the meaning of music, later insisting also that music itself seek the harmony of reasonable words, had already met a parallel in the tradition of the divinely inspired bard—a

[2] Leo Spitzer, *Classical and Christian Ideas of World Harmony* (Baltimore, 1963), pp. 75–76.

body of literary belief and allusion at least as important to Milton as that of music. He scarcely needed to be shown that verbal meaning and music were to be harmonized like sound, sight, and insight, or that medieval "consonance" indicated not only chord but also rhyme.

In these early poems, Milton is content to emphasize the intellectual, moral, and ontological meaning that must accompany the mere "sound" of music. Later, in *Paradise Lost,* he will insist that the musical instrument, man, is incomplete without the Logos of God: "harmonious numbers" will be moved by thought, and Urania will "govern" the song. For the most part, the poems directly concerned with music take as their matter the celebration of God by means of creative entrance into the meaningful music of eternal harmony. The stance is that of a creatively composing voice within one of the great hymns of praise that are sung and danced around the center of creation. Dynamic in its ardor, the early work strives toward the state suggested by the chordal metaphor. It attempts to resolve any lateral movement (such as that which accompanies loss, or that of the devils in the Nativity Ode) back into the immense monochord. The early poems all but reestablish Eden and sing there the praises of all creatures to the divine master of all music.

"Full Consort" in "On the Morning of Christ's Nativity"

"On the Morning of Christ's Nativity," although seemingly artless and naïve, is harmonized with extreme care and filled with choirs of angels both literary and theological. It everywhere breathes self-confident artistic mastery. The elegy to Diodati shows that Milton was fully aware of its stature.[3] Those who have charged the young author with carelessness not only in form but

[3] E. M. W. Tillyard, *The Miltonic Setting* (London, 1947), p. 34: The poet "sees himself presenting the first-fruits of his new-dedicated muse to Christ, himself, as infant, the first-fruits of the supreme manifestation of the Divine Love." Rosemond Tuve, in *Images and Themes in Five Poems by Milton* (Cambridge, Mass., 1957), p. 43, objects that "O run" is addressed to the muse; however, although the heavenly muse inspires the poem, it is the brilliant poet who presents it.

also in the injudicious admixture of pagan with Christian materials underrate both his critical sense and the empowering belief that in a unified world music harmonizes even the most opposed elements. That he would alter his critical stand slightly and his understanding of the matter quite profoundly during his lifetime is beside the point. If his thought was perhaps as yet unripe, his artistry in the poem is fully developed.

Although the poem deals with a sacred subject, Milton transmutes the ignominious setting of Christ's birth into a charming pastoral scene, sin (as understood by the shepherds) into a forgivable lustihood that is granted the easy charity of "Peace," the long lateral progress of Creation-Incarnation-Apocalypse into one synthesizing praise that triumphs over the feeble dissonances of heathen gods, and—in perhaps the most telling alteration of all—the incarnate Christ into a hero like Hercules or a humanistic god like Apollo. This is not to say that the poem is "pagan." It is rather to insist that the matter of the poem is concentrated in a golden age of light, or an Eden that receives eternal but dynamic effulgence. In such a glorious "time" and "place," a militantly brilliant celebration takes as one the Creation, the birth of Jesus, the present poem, and the Last Judgment. (The ode, that is, is a celebrating gift, but it is also itself a creation in verse and voice.) The creative and heroic Christ as an infant easily strangles the impotent serpent Satan. Milton thus dismisses evil almost as if it were no more than the interesting babble of bassoons and oboes in a tone poem. The poem ends in a great burst of music and light as creation is reaffirmed in the new Adam and the universe continues to wheel majestically from the center of light. Small wonder if readers are impelled to use the word "radiant" in describing the poem.

Professor A. E. Barker's masterly article upon the structure of the ode has all but harvested the field, leaving others little to glean. In brief, this is his characterization of its form:

It . . . consists of three equal movements, held in relation, not by the repetition of a structural pattern, but by the variation of a basic pattern of imagery. The first eight stanzas of the "Hymn" describe the setting of the Nativity, the next nine the angelic choir, the next nine the flight of the heathen gods. The conclusion, the last stanza, presents the scene in the stable. . . . The three movements each present a single modification of the simple contrast, preserved throughout the poem, between images suggesting light and harmony and images of gloom and discord.[4]

Like other readers, I endorse this statement. I will add to it only a particular consideration of matter and stance, thereby coming to a somewhat different emphasis.

In this poem, as in most of Milton's early works, a conviction of the relatively static, chordal harmony of eternity is dominant. The matter will supply an objective recognition and celebration of that harmony. However, if only because a living poet is aware of his mortality and of the congeries of individual choices open to him as he recognizes and celebrates, we must expect some of the pulse and energy of a direct human involvement. Milton's resolution of the apparently changeless with the seemingly change-bound, of the sense of God with the sense of man, supplies the significant action of the ode. The stance expertly accommodates itself to that chosen matter. The poet praises, but is aware that his praise joins that of the morning stars singing eternally together, that of the angels singing "historically" at Bethlehem and at the Apocalypse, and (by implication) that of the present audience chanting its own Christmas music.

To see the structure from this viewpoint, it is necessary to renew our reading of those sections of the ode sometimes classified—and thereby in some measure dismissed—as introduction and conclusion. We then will have five interconnected sections in place of the three major parts properly indicated by Barker. Within the sequential parts, individual contributions to eternal act, or reflections of it, will be celebrated. The sum and meaning of the parts, however, always will reach to the single act outside time.

"FIRST, THY LORD TO GREET": PRESENT *METHEXIS* OF AUTHOR AND AUDIENCE (PRELUDE)

In the first section, the audience is guided to a realization of the exalted matter and of the union of eternity and human moment that illumines the matter. The subject ostensibly is Christ's nativ-

[4] Arthur E. Barker, "The Pattern of Milton's Nativity Ode," *UTQ*, X (1941), 167–181.

ity. That birth might have been considered as a happy but isolated event in history, much as our ordinary Christmas carols
present it; their occasional use of the present tense does not signally dramatize or generalize the birth. The ode, too, would then
have been presented as an individual poem of praise, totally
separated in time from the birth. Instead, a credible dramatic
present tense, together with implications of past and future, appears at once: *"This is* the Month, and *this* the happy morn"
(italics added).[5] Such gathering of historical particulars into an
eternal unity causes the birthday and the day of the memorial
poem to be one. As "events" within the timelessness of eternity,
they are simultaneous. A still higher involvement or absorption of
person and event into Being and eternity occurs when the birth is
recognized as that of the Son descended from "Heav'n's eternal
King." What is more, it is no new act even within man's sense of
time, for in the remote past "holy sages" had sung of the advent,
much as angels later sang and the poet now sings. We now know
that these songs have always been and always will be elements in
the same song, the same eternal chord. Finally, the eschatological
"event"—always implicit in the similar stroke of creation—will
raise man to still another perspective of eternity: "And with his
Father *work* us a *perpetual* peace" (italics added). It is worth
noting yet once more the effect of time simultaneously past, present, and future—that is, eternal—in the present form but future
implication of the word "work," when it is reinforced by both the
original and final promises of "perpetual." "Perpetual" looks
back into God's eternal design and forward beyond human time
to its apocalyptic consummation.

All that rush of contributing parts or reflections toward a central union takes place in the first stanza of the first section. Its
remaining stanzas continue such effects. In the second, Christ
seems, within history, to lay aside his eternal "glorious Form" and
"far-beaming blaze of Majesty" in order to assume a temporal
"darksome House of mortal Clay," but in that act too we are
simultaneously held in our own lifetime, rushed back in historical

[5] David Daiches, in *Milton* (London, 1957), p. 38, notes how sharply the
repetition of *this* commands our attention, enforcing the sense of the immediate present tense.

time, and carried beyond time entirely, to the original creation of man and, in turn, to his Creator. (Adam, Jesus, the poet, and each reader inhabit or have inhabited such a deceptively "mortal" house.) Any seeming defeat of men, by "deadly forfeit," or of Christ, by descent into a tomblike "house of Mortal Clay," is denied by the divine descent "from above," which has already victoriously joined Heaven and earth. The Incarnation is made to occur "eternally" by the residue of action implicit in the infinitive (Christ has descended "to be" with us). The light of God, we soon realize, is never more heroic and militant than in that apparently "darksome" body; we merely await the rising of the Son-Sun.[6]

The third stanza seizes upon that implication at once. The Incarnation is not a suppression of divine light but rather its increased revelation to men, because "all the spangled host keep watch in squadrons bright" for the ineffable light that in a historical sense is still to come (in a descent from Light unsufferable) but that, in the Creation, had formed those same morning stars and set them in their constellations. Their "handmaid" light, like the serviceable angels at the close, anticipates the Bridegroom's blaze of majesty that will radiate from within that "darksome House." Even the lesser light, however, is brilliant enough to draw as worshipers the similarly "Star-led" Magi once, the celebrant poet and audience now, and the angelic choir forever.

The human stance possible or proper before that revelation is established with swift particularity in the third stanza. The stance had been implicit in the present-tense opening ("This *is* the month") which drew speaker and audience directly into the event which in two stanzas was revealed to be eternally, not temporally, "present." Now the participating poet can be more exactly perceived. Inspired by his "Heav'nly Muse," he too must "afford" a celebration. He is to run as one among the shepherds before the Magi, his lips touched like Isaiah's with inspirational, purifying fire from the altar of creation. Because in the poem he will be a Lycidian swain to simple shepherds, he also resembles another

[6] A. B. Chambers, " 'Goodfriday, 1613. Riding Westward': The Poem and the Tradition," *ELH*, XVIII (1961), 46: Christ is *Oriens*, the sun of justice. This signification also insists upon the present tense. See also Miss Tuve, *Images and Themes*, p. 61.

harbinger, John the Baptist. The rigidities of our lateral human sense of time collapse as the seventeenth-century poet joins pre-Christian shepherds, Judaic prophets, and attendant stars in one act. The poet spans both worlds in himself, as well as being joined into them; he must employ his own knowledge of past and present and be the more reverent because of the greater scope of his revelation. Although he may be more humble than the Magi, he must also be more holy, for he fully recognizes what star he follows, what song he hears, and at what altar he worships. From that altar, he knows, proceed both the song of the angels and his own poem. The audience likewise must move with him as fellow "shepherds," worshipers who share the same full knowledge of the flock to which they themselves belong and of the master they know but have not yet fully realized. The birth is "for" both poet and audience: *"our* great redemption" will "work *us* a perpetual peace" (italics added). Both poet and audience therefore act directly in the seemingly new events, or Event: that birth and this poem. By doing so, they too realize the eternal act which each reflects, and join their voices to those of the angel choir. When the poet's "tedious" but serviceable song is concluded, it does not so much end as become absorbed into the unending hymn of Heaven.

"BIRDS OF CALM": CONSECRATION AND NEW COVENANT (STANZAS I–VIII)

As he initiates the hymn proper, Milton all but says of the first section, "That strain I heard was of a higher mood." Its majestic excitement, impelled by the happy universal race to bring celebrative tributes, subsides. The time of the poem apparently alters from eternity to history. The central hymn itself seems almost to descend imitatively from great height, as the Christ will descend into the world of nature among simple shepherds. The chord temporarily surrenders to individuated melody; verbs shift from present and infinitive tenses to the narrative past; and the matter of the poem for a time becomes the isolated rehearsal of the moment of incarnation, as enacted by unsuspecting "fallen" men. Similarly, the stance of the poet (and by implication, that of his fellow "shepherds," the audience) is established within the historical time of the birth. Into that abyss and "Winter wild" must come the life-giving Sun, the greater Pan. *Man* is to be a shepherd of that age, trudging unwittingly toward the revelation on that first occasion. The poem will intimate the greater context, of course, but for a period matter and stance hold to the theophanic moment with considerable tenacity. If we understand the great narrowing of time, vision, and knowledge in this second section, we may give it a better reception than it sometimes has received in the past.

This section, which prepares a consecrative musical rest, a tense stillness into which the celebrating angelic hymn will flood, offers a sense of Nature and Sun as genetrix and paramour—exactly the materialistic and erotic impression that the "Shepherds on the Lawn" (and a Roman lawn at that) might have had of their world.[7] After all, they know of no other meaning, having received no revelation. As yet, Nature is at worst a tomb that awaits a resurrection, at best a bride undergoing purification; the annunciation of the bridegroom and the rapture of the wedding guests are still to come. For that matter, fallen man always begins his spiritual progress in a similar state of deprivation of truth. The audience is not only witnessing a role but enacting it. The Ovidian luxury of the verses may compose a matter and stance temporarily unbefitting shepherds, but the anticipatory moment itself seems intrinsically true: "Perhaps their loves, or else their sheep, / Was all that did their silly thoughts so busy keep" (ll. 91–92). The feeling is right, both psychologically and musically. Martial hubbub is covered over with seeming silence as heroism "above heroic" (and above Augustan) begins to be fashioned, but an expectant pulse beats steadily. Saintly consecration implies no vacuum. Instead, it supplies the heartbeat for the angelic hymn that will swell out in the third section.

The stance of the narrating earthly shepherd is not fixed with obstinate insistence upon the moment, for that would banish all prophetic implications. Nevertheless, he evinces little immediate

[7] D. C. Allen, *The Harmonious Vision* (Baltimore, 1954), p. 26: The dramatic "present" of the poem is the last hour before Christ's birth.

awareness. The descent from "Light unsufferable" has placed a
human child in a rude manger. Although the shepherd knows
that the child was "Heav'n born," his emphasis nevertheless is at
first placed wholly upon the earthly duress. Although he sees
"guilty" Nature assume the veil of a bride (or a nun) in token of
the purity of Christ and perhaps of the immaculate conception of
Mary,[8] he still considers winter whiteness largely as an Ovidian
seasonal myth. The worldwide hush of peace seems in nature to
be mostly an Ovidian event, too; the Creator has sent down a
vaguely erotic dove ("With Turtle wing the amorous clouds dividing" [l. 50]), not yet quite the dove of the ark or of Jordan,
even though it intimates both. The eroticism is figural, of course,
indicating in part the creation of a new "world" from the cathar-
ized abyss.[9] The narrator re-creates for himself the time when he
was one of the waiting shepherds, remembering that they could
not dream that the mighty creative Pan was "kindly" to descend
into their midst, becoming their kind in order to transform humankind. In presenting that time and scene he almost rejoins
them. However, he cannot stop the pulse that beats across the
waiting moment. Relieved of her fear of her own pollution by
means of the descent of forfeit-bearing peace, Nature claims a
pure veil as she awaits a higher bridegroom than the earthly sun.
The sun himself is stilled as he awaits Joshua-Jesus, to whom he is
soon to become "serviceable," even as human kings also await the
supreme king. Other stars, despite the urging of pagan Lucifer-
Venus, will not depart; they are preparing to join an angel choir.
Spears idle from battle indicate that the rout of pagan heroism in
Part III has in effect already begun. The Augustan peace, already
superseded by lovely images of the peace of creative Venus and of
restorative Noah, yearns toward the approaching annunciation of
peace on earth, good will toward men. The rustic Pan is being
transformed into the true Shepherd. Nevertheless, the stillness
that awaits theophany continues to dominate the section.

[8] J. B. Broadbent, "The Nativity Ode," in *The Living Milton,* ed. Frank
Kermode (London, 1960), p. 21, associates guilty Nature with the judgment
of Adam and Eve.
[9] Broadbent, "The Nativity Ode," p. 27: The halcyons promise a second
creation.

"HEAV'N AND EARTH IN HAPPIER UNION": THE ETERNAL SYMPHONY (STANZAS IX–XV)

Quiet is shattered in stanza IX as the third section proclaims the child born into our common "house of mortal clay," in song set to the creative pulse that has been throbbing. The shepherds at once are joined with Heaven, the descent of Christ having simultaneously lifted and transformed them. Necessarily, the matter shifts from earthly apperception to divine revelation, although the "shift" actually only increases our sense of the full chord. No longer is it the normal sun or a star that the shepherds see. It is a "Globe of circular light" (l. 110), a circle of eternity from which resounds the praise of cherubim. Its seraphim, unlike warriors on earth, are "armed" for peace. The shepherds are so far transported that for a time they are rapt in wonder, drawn into the great central harmony of the poem. Earth becomes a sounding board for Heaven, the air as amorously as the clouds of Section I prolonging each lovely tone. The full music has taken "their souls in blissful rapture" (l. 98), even as Nature has achieved her new order through the mystery of spiritual light and virgin birth.

It is time that the fully aware Christian Swain of the introduction step from their ranks, imitating the transformation by means of his own lesser revelation. Even though he preserves the naïve form used for the pastoral stanzas, he must now celebrate his extrahistorical certainty that divine music promises "perpetual peace" *to come,*[10] after Nature's "part was done" (l. 105). He must also recall (or renew his awareness) that the music for a birth and for the apocalypse is also that for (and of) the Creation. At the beginning of the world, too, the great hymn in which the present poem shares had rung out. By taking a fully Christian rather than a time-bound shepherd's stance, the speaker can again personally lead the full audience, as he had in the first section of the poem:

> Ring out ye Crystal spheres,
> Once bless our human ears [ll. 125–126].

---

[10] Allen, in *The Harmonious Vision*, p. 27, notes that the concord of this part of the poem matches the peace of the first part.

"Once" is not conceived as a time or an event within a time, but as the one eternal act for and from which praise rose at the Creation, rises at the Incarnation, and will rise for all other manifestations of divinity that are to come. The anticipated particular manifestation is that of the last days, when entry will be made into the peace forecast as the poem began. Even to think about it is partly to realize it, but the enraptured creative song all but invokes it. The address to the "Crystal spheres" moves quickly to reutilize but to magnify the image of peace after deluge. Whereas the rustic shepherds had witnessed only a dove dividing the amorous clouds or the "guilty" union of nature and sun, the Christian shepherds, assured by the descent of Christ, look forward to the descent of Truth and Justice, returning upon the rainbow. This reminiscently Noetic sign also "divides" clouds of battle and error, putting the material tyranny of devils to rout. In a sense, the earth's "foundations" are now re-established, a "ninefold" harmony having restored earth within the great lyre of Heaven. In that increased vision, Heaven and earth approach the "happier union" which was foreseen in stanza x, was indicated particularly in the experience of Noah, and will be consummated at the end of time. Now it is indicated by the coming of the "bridegroom," Christ, to the newly veiled world. The descent of peace or Astraea is an eternal recurrence, stressed across the poem in conjunction with images of peace and a golden age of unchanging light.

Emphasis hastens toward that which is to come, however. A single act of revelation shows the yawning insubstantiality of Hell's dolorous mansion at the same moment that the "high Palace Hall" (l. 148) of Heaven illimitably throws open its gates to a great nuptial "festival." [11] The re-creative Christ of Easter Sunday and the dead who spurn Hell and the grave at the end of time join in one triumphal act. Similarly, the flight of false gods is a recoil from the arrival of the angelic chorus. The apocalyptic promise has gathered these and all other worshipers of God into

[11] Lowry Nelson, Jr., in *Baroque Lyric Poetry* (New Haven and London, 1961), pp. 46–47, notes the contrast of descending angels and fleeing false gods.

one great hymn—sons of morning, crystal spheres,[12] holy sages, heavenly muse, dazzled shepherds, present poet and audience, and all those who in any way conceive a sense of eternity and are exalted by it.

"THE ORACLES ARE DUMB": PARTIAL DEFEAT OF DISCORD (STANZAS XVI–XXVI)

The poem rose to that crest swiftly and exuberantly across Section III. The strain once again had reached a higher mood, and once again there is a decrescendo. The increasing joy created by consideration of the Last Judgment must be released, for the speaker realizes that such total deliverance is not to be immediate. In order to attain such a consummation, the losses of earth must be redeemed by the "forfeit" of divinity into mortal clay. There must be a descent (a species of Fall) from the eternal brilliance of Creation to human time and the present world of men— graphically, to the world of the shepherds, into which the mortal child will come. Like other fallen men, the speaker may or must sustain his salvation and awareness of God and perhaps a sense of the eternal moment in which the apocalypse will share, but like all men he must also endure the seeming bondage of time and isolated event.

Yet the surrender of the poem to time is only momentary. Almost at the instant that "wisest Fate" postpones the Apocalypse and points to the Christ of Golgotha, the eternal meaning of an event such as the Crucifixion—of the fusion of Creation, Incarnation, and Passion—bursts out again. If time can "run back," it can also run forward. Present descent is paired with future ascents. The suffering Christ, now one with the apocalyptic Pantocrator, will triumph over death. The trump of doom will transform chaotic Hell into a Galilean peace, leaving the insubstantial "old Dragon" within Hell's vacant mansions. The new Sun's light blazes against a hemisphere of rapidly shrinking darkness. All historical discord will be swept away before him, just as war

[12] For a brief discussion of stars, angels, and spheres in the poem, see Ernest Sirluck, "Milton's Idle Right Hand," *JEGP*, LX (1961), 756–757.

had been swept away by the Nativity. What we hear across the fourth section is, in effect, the second and heightened quieting of chaos before Creation, the second purification of nature before the Nativity, and the final purification and elevation of the world (already forecast in stanza x, in which "Nature . . . was almost won / To think her part was done, / And that her reign had here its last fulfilling" (ll. 101–106) ; even here, however, "part" can refer to the eternal song, and Nature's "part" would then not so much stop as be "fulfilled") . In this section, Milton is not so much exorcising pagan devils as causing all partial themes, all apparent discords, either to fall silent, as in Section II, or to resolve symphonically into the majestic harmony heard in the third section. Poet and audience share in that resolution, just as they had before and will again:

> And then at last our bliss
> Full and perfect is,
> But now begins [ll. 165–167].

With that, those gods of the partial Word (the oracles and Apollo) , the gods of nature rather than the God of nature ("the parting Genius" and the nymphs) , the gods of earth and fireside rather than of Heaven and light (the lars and lemures) , the gods of powers of love that only weakly guess at Christ (Baal, Ashtoreth, and Thammuz) , and the gods of terror rather than awe (Moloch and Osiris) , all flee like the shadows or intimations they have always been, before the "rays" of Bethlehem. Their cells, like Hell's mansions, are empty to the "peering day" of a greater Sun. Time coalesces once again when the lightning revelation of Sinai is made one with both the present revelation and the distant Last Judgment, at which time Hell, like these murmuring gods, "itself will pass away" (l. 139) . The heroic spiritual life of the child in swaddling clothes at Bethlehem is contrasted with the damnation to nonbeing of Osiris, lying glumly swaddled in a casket, awaiting the dolorous Hell exposed in the preceding section. All lesser light has again confessed its shame before the greater. The infant blinds the old Dragon's dusky eyes as surely as will the Pantocrator of the Last Judgment. Because attention has become riveted upon the Christ of the Apocalypse (but also upon

the triumphant day of his crucifixion and victory over death),
Jesus is seen as heroic, not weak or suffering. The section urges
allusions to both Hercules and Apollo, as Christ puts down the
Herodic serpent and drives away with light all the ambiguous,
fanciful, half-formed "Fays." Seeming descent into either human
birth or death has proved to be true ascent. The section has
moved by a different, sometimes discordant route, but it has
reached the crest possessed before (in the third section). There is
even a distant—and perhaps unintended—reminder of the theme
of relief from deluge that has appeared twice before: as the
charmingly childlike (but rising) Christian Sun "pillows his chin
upon an Orient wave" (l. 231), the storm of shadows on the
world's Galilee retires.

"WITH HANDMAID LAMP": THE WISE RETURN TO SERVICE (STANZA XXVII)

It remains for the brief concluding section, the final stanza, to
symphonize the poem's several tenses, its stances, and its perspectives upon the Incarnation. It asks first a general return to the
moment of the birth and a general resumption of the stance of
shepherd and shepherd-priest come to worship: "But see! the
Virgin blest, / *Hath* laid her Babe to rest" (ll. 237–238—italics
added). The audience and the poet are then also recalled to their
residual roles in the world of their own lateral experience—
remembering, however, that they have shared an angelic hymn as
well as the present ode: "Time is our tedious Song should *here*
have ending" (l. 239—italics added). But then all the glory of the
light of the first section, the "greater Sun" of the second, the globe
of light of the third, and the rising Sun of the fourth, returns. The
new star of Bethlehem represents the greater Sun "rising" that
day, and the angelic hosts of Section I ("all the spangled host")
await the divine mission: "Bright-harness'd Angels sit in order
serviceable" (l. 244), replacing the unknowing shepherds in their
row. Bethlehem's stable instantly becomes "Courtly" [13]—the
Court of the Sun is now greater than the natural sun, more than

---

[13] Daiches, in *Milton*, p. 48, calls attention to the transverse puns on
courtliness and stability. Miss Tuve, in *Images and Themes*, p. 72, adds that
Nature becomes the greater Sun's court.

his "burning Axletree could bear" (l. 84)—and the steeds become angels rather than Phaeton's coursers. The lusty paramour himself has accepted some of the character of the wise virgin with her "handmaid" lamp.

Light continues to unfold in a seemingly new Creation. In the new Adam, a new substance—half divine, half human, joined in absolute union—is revealed. All forms of creation, ascending or descending, radiate from the potent center, a part of which is now so deceptively housed in "mortal clay." The light of Phoebus is not discarded but exceeded, for the new star in its miraculous appearing is greater than the sun of the semipagan Section II. Classical poetry by the same token is not rejected, but only outdistanced by holy inspiration and holy verse. Similarly, mortal flesh is not mortified, even though it has been called "a darksome House of mortal Clay." It is instead so blessed by divinity that it, too, comes to radiate or reflect eternal light. Nor, for that matter, is the "gaudy trim" of wanton Nature cast aside, but in place of that Eve-like luxury we are given the purity of the second Eve—or perhaps of the first Eve after the judgment by Michael, ashamed that one should "look so near upon her foul deformities" (l. 44). In place of the amorous dove and Venus genetrix, we are offered a consecrated, fruitful Nature marked by the peace of winds kissing the stilled waters of "mild Ocean." The last stanza is both a mortal *berceuse* and an immortal prothalamion.

The myth of the eternal act that guides the poem would be almost arrogantly confident were it not developed in such a combination of simplicity and exultation. As it is, it is intersected only briefly by darting lines from history—the darksome mortal house, the shifting seasons, the distance between wishing human beings and an achieved apocalypse, the temporal change indicated by the departing pagan gods. The typical Miltonic triad of creation, fall, renewal is almost registered, but the fall is quickly orchestrated out of the concert. Instead, we lift our eyes repeatedly from the particular to that which absorbs all particularity, the God suggested in images of light, who so irradiates each individual mote that they all become luminous:

> [The Sun] hid his head for shame,
> As his inferior flame,

The new-enlight'n'd world no more should need;
He saw a greater Sun appear [ll. 80–83].

Earth and men begin to glow like the "Crystal spheres." Probably more memorable to most readers, however, are the suggestions of universal harmony, of the participation of the individual in the whole, conveyed in images of creative music:

Such Music (as 'tis said)
Before was never made,
    But when of old the sons of morning sung,
While the Creator Great
His constellations set,
    And the well-balanc't world on hinges hung,
And cast the dark foundations deep,
And bid the welt'ring waves their oozy channel keep
                                    [ll. 117–124].

In this great concert by the cosmic orchestra, all hymns of creation, incarnation, and celebration join: Heaven and earth cooperate as sounding spheres, "the Bass of Heav'n's deep Organ" forms the necessary base, and the "full consort" of "th' Angelic symphony" (ll. 130–132) almost grants what love has sought—the "age of gold" (l. 135) and sinless concord. That age must be created again in spirit by the heroism of Christ.

Commentary also could become a "tedious song" in celebrating the rich yet simple structure of the ode; it too must here have ending. Despite some controversy that has been visited upon it in the recent past, the poem is a triumphant, if perhaps too carefree, demonstration to the world that its author's claim is just: "the bard is sacred to the gods and is their priest." As celebrant for man and earth, he all but lifts them from shadow to substantial light.

"The Hidden Soul of Harmony": Ascent in "L'Allegro" and "Il Penseroso"

Unlike most of Milton's poems, "L'Allegro" and "Il Penseroso" at first seem to reveal no personal factor. Surely, it must seem, we have here found poems so nearly anonymous that they will escape *ad hominem* praise or dispraise. Far from having resolved all

critical difficulties by a clear objectivity free from aesthetic here-
sies, however, the twin poems seem to occasion as many and as
contrarious descriptions as even *Paradise Regained*. Are they prolusions by the precocious academic poet? *Débats?* Poems of praise?
Are they excessively learned and abstract, or almost excessively
simple and Shakespearean? Do they concern "a man" or an attitude, two men or two attitudes, or Mirth and Melancholy apart
from any individual human attitude? Does each describe a day, or
the ideal day? Are the initial exorcisms serious or parodic? Are the
poems two, or one?

In this somewhat chaotic field of argument, the vernal poems of
our childhood affection can almost disintegrate. Far from wishing
to add to the pressure placed upon them or to multiply argument,
I hope that a brief consideration of the stances, together with
cross-references to other poems by Milton, may contribute toward
a reflective exorcism of some disagreements.

The general stance is that of a votary of the two related virtues,
the true "goddesses" Mirth and Melancholy, both of whom are
good, fair, and humanistic, opposing false Mirth, false Melancholy. Because the virtues are more universal than the individual
human being who reflects or serves them through absorbing their
qualities into his life, they are capable of being personified,
figured, made emblematic. They are nonetheless "involved in
humanity," realizable only in human desire and act.[14] The
speaker in the poems is not only a poet (although the two works
are in part a description for the portrait of an apprentice artist),
but a representative of the virtues. Just as we must be wary of
isolating Mirth from the acting human persons of the poem, so we
must not isolate the speaker from that which he speaks of and for.
Not only do the poems reach out from the representative to other
men, to "us," but also each poem internally, structurally, expresses a wider and wider involvement with humanity. In the
most literal sense, the speaker becomes a master of the ceremonies
of celebration for Mirth and Melancholy. From elements of
human happiness he constructs undiscording song that registers

[14] I disagree slightly with Miss Tuve (*Images and Themes,* pp. 19–20),
when she describes the poems as the registry of mental pleasures only. Because
they have been rigidly screened, Milton's delights of sight and sound are
completely untroubling.

man desiring, man receiving, man reciprocating, and finally—in music—man uniting with that same happiness. In each poem, somewhat after the manner of the Son in *Paradise Regained,* he exorcises a form of falsehood or Hell in order to evoke or reach a form of Heaven. The exorcism is by no means limited to the formal introduction; on the contrary, it acts at every stage of ascent in the poems. In his re-creative way, the speaker stands in relation to the audience as Mirth and Melancholy stand to him. By supplying the audience with delights and by assuring himself of the quality of their reception by the audience, he leads the audience in its ascent even as he has been led by his "goddesses." In the center of each poem, "I" alters significantly to "we." The speaker is therefore doubly the center of the poem, not only presenting the song and thereby expressing the object of the ceremonies, but also leading the audience in its ceremonial responses.

Beyond the union of humanistic virtues with human beings, there are intimations of another level of meaning that is available for a still higher kind of union. Verse and voice continue to express the universe and to gather all creation into one vocal dance. Elements of simple sensuous sound and sight are "tuned" in "L'Allegro." Fiction and music in both poems wed sense and imaginative transport. Elements of contemplation and of union with mind and spirit across time join the diapason in "Il Penseroso." The poems form a progress of man with nature (and its intimated Creator), very broadly conceived and orchestrated: joy and meaning in both man and creation are seen in their mutual delight. In such serenity, any images of death are swallowed up in creative resurrection. Surely it is no accident that both poems echo "At a Solemn Music": "L'Allegro" by insisting that immortal verse can virtually create an Adam or raise a Lazarus (it can "pierce" the meeting soul, rousing the slumbering Orpheus from dream to action), and "Il Penseroso" by causing music to "bring all Heav'n" before the celebrant's eyes and permitting love, in Orpheus, to triumph utterly over time and death. Surely it is no accident either that the two poems stage a Platonic ascent from joys of sense through joys of the mind to virtual union with beauty and Being.

Finally, such recognition of union can profitably be extended to the two poems themselves. It is not necessary, but is useful, to consider them as much more closely related than even "twins." [15] Although each is self-contained, they nevertheless are one in sequence, presenting two stages in an ascent. (It should be noted at once, however, that any particular delight can intimate or even achieve the full ascent at any point.) Together, they form two halves of an achievement like that suggested in the program of studies in "Of Education": a progress from reception of sights and sounds and the sunnier literary forms through Plato and Xenophon to still more heavenly thoughts—perhaps to Heaven itself. In "L'Allegro," Orpheus seems to be but half-roused and Eurydice still only half set free; in "Il Penseroso," Orpheus is manifest and Pluto apparently sympathetically one with the immortal lovers converted from separative death to conjoining life. Needless to say, all past and present poets are associable with Orpheus. In the first poem, the poet is absorbed in secular music that *unlocks* the hidden chains of harmony. In the second, the representative man is *transported* by sacred music to the sacred doors of Heaven, like Eurydice "quite set free."

The speaker and we whom he represents can perceive the works as a Platonic and partly Christian ladder to heaven, to Jove's door. We may choose it over the pinfold earth of *Comus,* here refused in both the initial and the progressive exorcisms. However, time and distance collapse so readily here that the ascent and ladder are not so much sequential as "chordal." Man's tone on the chord of creation can be sounded when he wills. He does not have to "climb," for as a created "tone" he is already harmoniously one with the most elevated notes of the chord. The stance of the author asks that he hear harmonious sounds and join his voice with them. Inferentially, the audience is requested to add its undiscording voice.

"SOFT LYDIAN AIRS": LANDSCAPE, HYMEN, AND MEETING SOUL IN "L'ALLEGRO"

Initial exorcisms and the invocations in both poems are joyous expressions of the routing of discord in order to celebrate, to

[15] Allen, in *The Harmonious Vision,* p. 4, holds that the two poems compose one progress.

"invoke," harmony. In recent years, study of the poems in the context of Milton's prolusions has led us to ask whether the exorcisms are not parodic, too bombastic to be taken seriously. The joy of "L'Allegro" can readily admit that kind of mirth, so long as the effect is not then confused with satire. Some kindly sympathetic fun with an academic exercise in no way circumscribes the major concerns of the works. However, as many of the puns in *Paradise Lost* attest, Milton can be extremely serious with the very materials in which wit and joy appear. I believe that the two exorcisms are quite serious in associating discord with Satan's Hell. In "L'Allegro," "heart-easing Mirth" banishes heart-eating false Melancholy like the old year or the winter to a Cimmerian desert that closely resembles Hell's "frozen continent." Discord there can make its masterpiece of "horrid shapes, and shrieks, and sights unholy" (l. 4). Concord will present the opposite of each as the poem proceeds, but the poem will not entirely forget its escape from "the Stygian Pool" that both it and *Paradise Lost*, Book III, have visited. That is, the poem will repeatedly set Mirth against all that the heart asks Mirth to ease.

The ascent from sensual to higher forms of enjoyment is emphasized in the second of the two suggested genealogies of Mirth. As "some sager" sing, Mirth may have been born from the most innocent springtime union of a Lucretian Zephyr and Aurora in fresh Arcadian dews. Throughout the poem, morning and that dew-drenched, violet-studded nuptial bed are remembered. The "hasting" nymph and the general liberty associated with "heart-easing" joy will make room for the celebrant and *"unreproved pleasures free"* (l. 40—italics added). All illusory pleasures have been banished with false Melancholy.

Much of the poem will supply the simple delights [16] that constitute mirth, most of which will therefore in their way also banish darkness and false Melancholy. They will come in three ceremonial, "harmonizing" displays: innocent natural sounds and scenes in which men appear in increasing numbers, the more imaginative and intellective "sights and sounds" of narrative fiction and

---

[16] J. B. Leishman, " 'L'Allegro' and 'Il Penseroso' in Their Relation to Seventeenth-Century Poetry," *E&S*, n.s. IV (1951), 7: Each poem is a "Catalogue of Delights."

of drama, and the complexly interwoven music that seems both to fulfill sense and imagination and to penetrate to ultimate divine harmony.

The display of sights and sounds is not presented to an only passive consumer, the speaker; he moves abroad to encounter them and to evoke them for the audience. Although he is not involved in them closely, he is "not unseen." He is with this world, if not exactly of it. The mirthful day (no matter whether it be of spring, of fall, or a composite) begins with individual exorcisms of discord, mirroring those of the entire poem. In anticipation of the watch tower of "Il Penseroso," and acting directly against sorrow (l. 45), the lark "startle[s] the dull night" (l. 42) to make way for Zephyr and Aurora once again, and the cock similarly "Scatters the rear of darkness thin" (l. 50).[17] Soon the hounds also "rouse the slumb'ring morn" (l. 54). The "great Sun," having scattered general darkness, accepts clouds as his harmonious companions. Parallel harmonies of sound spring from shepherds and plowmen, the fictional "tale" of the shepherd making distant concord with songs from Theocritus and Bion and therefore looking forward to the sounds within fiction that are to come.

In its own form of ascent, sight is conducted to individual figures in a low-set landscape and from them to increasingly populous upper country scenes. The "secure delight" of liberty offers and rewards a vision of the "upland Hamlets" where young lovers dance while young and old villagers play until nightfall. The whole company then gathers to enjoy simple fiction that internally crosses the valley of the night even while externally preparing for it—the story of how the "Goblin" worked the entire night away for men, to be routed (not unhappily, now) by the "first Cock." Given such a hope after such a day, small wonder that the contented people are lulled to their sleep by the whispering winds—perhaps including Zephyr, still.

The poem seems now about to remove the stance of author and audience to the busy city: "Tow'red Cities please us then" (l. 117). However, the significant Neoplatonic tower image, continuing the progressive ascent, immediately removes us from any

[17] Allen (*The Harmonious Vision*, p. 7), notices that birds in the poems always indicate vigilance of thought.

present city of men. We are to enter instead upon "Such sights as youthful Poets dream" (l. 129), where knights and ladies, like Zephyr and Aurora, can meet within the joy of Hymen. We are only a hint away from sage Spenser. We move from the oral tale of the shepherds through the inwardly seen chivalric narrative to the meaningful enacted tales of Jonson or Shakespeare. Shakespeare's "native Wood-notes wild" (l. 134) remind us of the lark's notes that began Mirth's day, even as they anticipate the still greater, final music in which all discord ends.

Verse and Voice, those two Sirens, appear just behind the lines when Music, the form of harmony itself, comes to be celebrated. The "melting voice" runs through unpreventing mazes like Theseus through the labyrinth, discovering concord (and reminding us that the "eating Cares" of false Melancholy, like a Minotaur, have been vanquished in the course of the poem). Orpheus, "melted" by such love and meaning, can now also "singing startle the dull night" and banish death. He is roused by hearing

> Such strains as would have won the ear
> Of *Pluto,* to have quite set free
> His half-regain'd *Eurydice* [ll. 148–150].

Love and Mirth can exorcise Hell, or better yet, bring it too into the concordant song. In that sense, the last line of the poem may present a sudden and meaningful pun, especially moving because of the nearby reference to the only half-regained Eurydice: "Mirth, with thee I mean to *live*" (italics added). Delight in the living delights of nature and men and the music they form and create is a form of life itself, and Mirth is therefore a vital principle: one of the twins, Youth and Joy, promised in *Comus* by Jove.

"MORE IS MEANT THAN MEETS THE EAR": THOUGHT, DREAM, AND TRANCE IN "IL PENSEROSO"

Exorcism in "Il Penseroso" is at least as serious as it is in "L'Allegro" and similarly intimates the Satan or Death of *Paradise Lost.* Insubstantiality is at best a possible sin, like the dream of Eve; at worst, it is directly like Death. It also closely resembles the toys Christ refuses in *Paradise Regained.* As illusive joys represent a false Mirth, so they are a false vision, a dream, the simulacrum of true inner sight. They are delusive motes in a sunbeam—"gay" enough perhaps, but essentially unreal, both in their insubstantiality and in their attempt to establish substance within fallible human sight rather than in "real" insight. Once they have vanished, Melancholy does not have to be invited to *come*, as was Mirth; she can now be hailed, like the visible "Chastity" of *Comus*. Human sight having been surpassed, we "see" mysteries above "L'Allegro's" delights of the senses. Although Milton does not really carry us into Hermeticism, its metaphors at once appear. In place of Zephyr and Aurora, the parents of Melancholy are Vesta and Saturn. The golden age of the "first" poet-theologians, the golden light beyond Jove's door, and the ineffable light of Heaven—all these appear within the too dazzling brightness of Melancholy. Associated with her will be Contemplation, similarly "on golden wing" (l. 52), and sounds from the Muses singing at *"Jove's* Altar" (l. 48).

As Melancholy might display "looks commercing with the skies" and a "musing gait" (ll. 39, 38), so does the celebrant as he walks into the darkly dazzling night. The poem provides parallels for most of the sounds and sights of "L'Allegro," but, like Melancholy herself, these are quiet and nocturnal. They invite, however, not the satisfied sleep of "L'Allegro," but piercing vision. The nightingale provides music to grant peace to the night rather than to move the day. Similarly, curfew and bellman assure that here, far from the "resort of [false] mirth" (l. 81), there will be no swilled insolence. The presence of human society is intimated in all this care, but each person is serene in his meditative privacy.

Corresponding to the movement to the uplands in "L'Allegro" is a present ascent from the "dry smooth-shaven Green" to the "high lonely Tow'r," higher than the physical flight of the lark in "L'Allegro," [18] more immediately reflecting (and increasing) the upward progress of the mind in "Of Education."

The partly resurrective ascent beyond the "fleshly nook" into the "vast Regions [of] / The immortal mind" (ll. 90–91) can now be completed. If fiction is "sometime" sought, it will be the high-

[18] Allen, *The Harmonious Vision*, p. 17: The ascent is to the soul's acropolis.

est tragedy or epic, perhaps concerning Troy "divine." Melancholy and her votive poet can now figuratively free the great dead, "triumphing over Death, and Chance, and thee / O Time!" Poetry itself, through its voices in Musaeus, Orpheus, Chaucer, and "aught else great Bards beside" (l. 116), elevates beauty beyond the spirit of death, drawing "Iron tears down *Pluto's* cheek" so that Hell will "grant what Love did seek" (ll. 107–108). As Melancholy is too bright for sight, so such poetry will bring no mere flat historical tales of barons and knights, for in its dazzlingly dark conceits "more is meant than meets the ear" (l. 120).

Contemplation can make a proper night by exorcising garish day. When it does, the celebrant will find a paradise in which, although physical creation moves gently around him, the greater and more creative inner vision and songs will come through sleep and its true "vision"—but not entirely a sleep: the Pythagorean bee (recalling the golden wing of Contemplation) is one with "dewy-feather'd Sleep" (l. 146). Emblematic reality and signified meaning become one, much as the creative music he hears after waking may "breathe / Above, about, or underneath" (ll. 151–152); it makes no difference whether he lies above a literal stream, walks in Marvellian paths where creation sings with him in its midst, or soars in the "air" of his contemplative ascent. There is perhaps little more than a transference of that environment when he ascends, not into a holy mountain, but into a college chapel. All the descriptive elements of the "hallow'd haunt" remain. To them is added a great direct concordant celebration of any and all senses and thoughts as, beneath "storied" windows, organ and choir offer Christian voice and verse "in Service high and Anthems clear" (l. 163).[19] Heaven is so completely revealed that it can be "hailed" much as Melancholy had been signaled as the poem began.

Although the ecstasy is complete, it is not yet permanent. His mortal soul has witnessed Heaven, but is not yet unsphered (l.

[19] Nan Cooke Carpenter, in "The Place of Music in *L'Allegro* and *Il Penseroso*" (*UTQ*, XXII [1953], 366–367), associates the active Orpheus and the prophetic speaker with the Son of *Paradise Lost*. See also James Hutton, "Some English Poems in Praise of Music," *EM*, II (1951), 46, for the joining of words with music in a "musical ecstasy" as well as for discussion of music as the one art in Heaven.

88). "Old experience" must continue to supply the mortal base, the present organ point, of man's life. Used wisely, it, like the chant of the nightingale, will guide men into "something like Prophetic strain" (l. 174). In any case, human eyes for a moment have beheld the timeless dawn of eternity. Melancholy apparently will continue to supply the means to renew or retain that moment: "These pleasures *Melancholy* give, / And I with thee will choose to live" (ll. 175–176).

Both poems end with almost the same commitment by the votary. It is partly plea, partly promise, partly imperative: man's voice, joining with Mirth and Melancholy in a hymn beyond discord, enacts the practice as well as the hope "to live." Such pleasures are enough to live for, and, in the immortal sense, to live by-virtue-of.

Having indicated the official character of the speaker, the center through whom all celebration is communicated to the enacting celebrants, our discussion still owes a statement about the speaker within his more restricted role as poet. After all, there is good reason for Professor Allen's describing the poet here as being "lonely as God, sharing his stasis" (see n.7, above), and for Professor Tuve's insisting that the topics of the poems almost ignore Milton's usual universalizing outreach to the audience (see n.3). Because the subject matter of the poems becomes the speaker's material, clearly his to command and to place within the frame of grammatical and actual imperative, and because his is so patently a directorial function as master of ceremonies, the reader is led to see in the two poems a magisterial display of the poetic process. It resembles the greater creative process in the Nativity Ode, where God's disposition of the dynamic universe also causes all materials, even those of discord, to take positions "serviceable" to the disposing mind. In the twin poems, elements from nature and human contemplation are stringently selected for their representative or emblematic properties, and are then set as carefully as the constellations of the ode. It could scarcely be otherwise; more is meant than meets the eye and ear, but the ear and eye still must be considered. Even a prophetic strain or higher significance will take "old experience" as the arch for entry. What is unusual here is that Milton's materials are so nearly free of direction from external myth or ritual. He probably is never again so free to choose and dispose.

Humanity is partly abstracted by the poet into its essence or its most human qualities. It appears in clearly defined kinds and acts: sensuous man and contemplative man; pastoral, literary, and philosophic man; and creative man—the adjective looking back to man's earlier connection with God and forward, through human thought and music, to his temporary reunion with God. Communication among men also emanates largely from the creative mind, whether the form is the rustic fireside tale, the dialogue of Plato, or the song of Musaeus. The large, friendly societies of men intimated in "L'Allegro" are intent upon a kind of supervocal, Thoreauvian communication within art or the mind. In "Il Penseroso," still greater abstraction and simplification bring us toward the form of humanity as these poems envision it: mind, looking down to earth and up to Heaven. Both poems, by setting man within his nature and within his controlling mental position in the universe, demand a prior exorcism of artistic and psychological discord, of formlessness or "eating cares." In both poems, harmony is enacted even as it is invoked. Not the least of their charms is their demonstration that a Neoplatonic ascent to Heaven can be performed by "light fantastic" toes in measure with songs that convert difficulty and distance into gigue or fugue or aria. Even the weltering ocean of "Lycidas" at this time is still only the liquid, relenting tear on Pluto's cheek.

"In Measured Motion": Human search and divine reward in "Arcades"

If the rapture of "L'Allegro" and "Il Penseroso" tended to be highly personal and mainly literary until reaching the "ascent" in music, bringing heaven to grant what love did seek, "Arcades" moves in an almost completely opposite direction until it intersects the harmony of a like ascent. In one instructive likeness to the twin poems, especially if they are considered as one progress, "Arcades" offers first lively matter, then enraptured idea:

> . . . I am the pow'r
> Of this fair Wood, and live in Oak'n bow'r,

> To nurse the Saplings tall, and curl the grove
> With Ringlets quaint, and wanton windings wove.
>
> . . . . .
>
> But else in deep of night, when drowsiness
> Hath lockt up mortal sense, then listen I
> To the celestial *Sirens'* harmony [ll. 44–63].

However, "Arcades" more nearly resembles the past Nativity Ode and the approaching dramatic and dialectical works. It insists upon drawing the audience heavily into the action, while at first glance seeming to remove the author entirely. It also anticipates *Comus* by forming its subject, as the masque form might decree, upon quasi-classical myth. Like *Comus* again, it does not use myth to evade reality, even by constructing allegory, but instead to provide "sacred notes" intimating far more of "reality" than the unpurged ear and uncleared eye might believe possible. The Arcades (nymphs and shepherds from the same pastoral myth as "Lycidas") even here are at once real children in a real setting, actors in a mythical dramatic action, and souls in quest of the contemplative music which, in Christian terms, may represent the state of man and Eden with God before the Fall. Manifestations and idea appear together in rich harmony with myth, which embraces both the real actors and the roles of their particular enactments.

Manifestation and ideal appear together in most of the early poems, the particular appearance from history or myth dancing in a subtle yet close relationship with the thought from eternal being and meaning. Because the later poems increasingly utilize as manifestation a "true" person or event from the Bible, we sometimes slight Milton's sense of the reality of the Arcades, the Lady and her Brothers, and Lycidas. The currents of Florentine Neoplatonism and of the pastoral tradition having failed at almost the same time, we have to reconstitute both: first, perhaps, as metaphor but then (if our vows and wishes approach those of Milton) as beliefs, all extraliterary disbelief having been suspended for the moment. If we do not, our oddly extravagant modern skepticism can combine with too-willing belief in myth, forcing Milton either into autobiography on the one hand or mysticism and aestheticism on the other. Until men choose the Fall, Milton believed, earth is an enjoyable and probably a correct intimation of heaven, and the body is as honorable a part of us as is the soul. However, it is true that "L'Allegro" and "Il Penseroso" in the end gave extreme emphasis to contemplation or idea, seeming to promise (or threaten) movement toward the Herbertian meditative lyric, toward an extended portrait of the artist as a young man, or toward a portrait of the Christian artist-musician in a far more comprehensive sense. The steady appearance of the poet in the first person and his steady reception of the universe as a great orchestra for his conducting supply a sufficient basis for taking the earlier poems to be as self-concerning within a chosen matter as are the statements in "The Reason of Church Government" and "Ad Patrem." Self-concern by such a Christian poet does not imply either selfishness or solipsism, of course, but it does indicate that all statement will tend to and from that strong center.

By choosing the dramatic mode of "Arcades," then, Milton seems to complete a phase. He unobtrusively retires from the visible center of the poem. Although the title might have promised a continuing idyllic pastoral revelation of the singer even within the masque form, the poem instead guarantees that the enactment will be general rather than particular, that it will not be limited to the speaker alone. (As we will see, he does not really remove himself from the poem, but instead now acts from within it; characteristically, he becomes leader of the Chorus as well as poet.) The forms of his own sensory experience and of his own imagination, contemplation, and belief become active in their own right. What is more, they increasingly must operate under the partly external demands of the stage and of Christian doctrine. The matter of the poem and the stance of both audience and poet are concentrated dramatically: words and concerns are supplied by histrionic embodiments that a receiving audience can "see" in apparent action rather than in the recorded realization of the seemingly solitary author. For better or for worse, the world has assumed the mode of action and its creatures henceforward must be celebrated or opposed with a sense of their independent harmony or discord.

The audience, too, will become even more fully participative. Because of the independence of forms within the general subject, the witness of the audience also takes on increased independence. That is not a matter of dramatization alone, of course, for "On the Morning of Christ's Nativity" had also insisted upon the entry of the audience into the poem's celebration and meaning. It is instead a question of the implied number of participants within the creation itself, "I" having often given place to "we," and of whether or not objects and acts are seen by the author alone or by the author, by "independent" characters or agents within the work, and by the audience. "Arcades" marks a change largely because it insists, like most of the later works, that participation and meaning be distributed very widely.

The first and most obvious distribution involves the actors directly in the myths that they enact. In "Arcades," a myth is partly created (but only partly, because pastoral-Christian allusion stirs even in the first lines), then enacted, then witnessed as a ritualistic mystery. Much as the shepherds in the Nativity Ode were at once the historical shepherds keeping watch over their flocks and also members of the audience in their fallen state awaiting consecration, so here Arcadian shepherds and nymphs are "really" members of the house of Derby, but also men in quest of a virtue or realization "All *Arcadia* hath not seen" (l. 95). Milton's Arcades characteristically search for that which transcends Arcadia. They are reflected in the description of the Edenic setting where the quest is accomplished, the shepherds being intimated in the "Saplings tall" and the nymphs in the groves' "Ringlets quaint, and wanton windings" (ll. 46–47). They have come to behold the living countess, but this countess known to Spenser is of course more than merely a noble lady; she becomes a kind of "Faerie Queene."

Almost as if desire had brought all Heaven before their eyes, the young players look into a "sudden blaze of majesty," the end of their vows, wishes, and "solemn search" (ll. 2, 7). The light of the transcendent "Queen" shares the glory of that in *Paradise Lost,* which is associated immediately with God. Greater than Leto, Cybele, or Juno, she too occupies a seat far above the Aonian mount, invested with the virtues of the unfallen Eve, the second Eve, and the spirit of creation. Like the Attendant Spirit of *Comus,* the Genius of the Wood instructs the Arcades, who are fully educable. Arcadian (Edenic) honor penetrates the pastoral disguise of the Adamic young shepherds and of the "breathing Roses" who are like both Artemis and the unfallen Eve. Transcendence from a fallen world is indicated also in the reconciliative union of "divine" Alpheus and Arethusa, who as mortals, before their sea-change, had been so tortuously hostile each to the other. Farther and farther into the ideal the Arcades are led, past tokens of the Genius' Eve-like care of the wood to that which lies beyond "mortal sense." The actors, like the speaker of "At a Vacation Exercise," seem for an instant to "see" beyond the door of Heaven, even to the "thunderous throne." The heart and meaning of creation lie before them: music reveals their own "low world" moving in harmony with the "heavenly tune" that they now have realized. The songs that follow are somewhat daring enactments of that sacred generative melody.

The "warbled string" of Apollo and David will draw the Arcades directly to their object's "sacred vesture" (l. 83). Having accomplished that attentive quest, having brought their realizations to consent, they will remain within that new song. Because this deity is more than Arcadian, at the close they become more than Arcades. (It is one of the oddities of Milton criticism that readers could have converted the injunction "Nymphs and Shepherds dance no more / By sandy *Ladon's* Lillied banks" [ll. 96–97] into Puritan repression. These transfigured pastoral personages have not been forbidden to dance longer: far from it! They have instead been commanded to join Lycidian "sweet Societies / That sing, and singing in their glory move"—in the measured motion of Heaven that is indicated by the Genius of the Wood.) The myth has not only enacted a form of natural epiphany and the rapture of those who witness it, but has then joined heavenly and earthly figures within one joyous celebration.

But the enactment is by no means limited to the Countess and the children or servants. The author, who had seemed to disappear and become only a stage manager, himself places the audience firmly within the mythic action. Its members, too, are led to "enter" the action as nymphs and shepherds. They recognize the transference from manifestation to idea and share the enacted epiphany. The contemporary courtly audience joined the actors as "us" the instant the Arcades rebuked the lavish praise of the Countess: *"We* may justly now accuse / Of detraction from her praise" (ll. 10–11). The present reading audience was absorbed into the action even earlier, when the actors said, "This, this is she / To whom *our* vows and wishes bend" (ll. 5–6—italics added). "Our" is more immediately implicative of a noncontemporary reader than of even the familiar contemporary audience of a masque. We have been impelled beyond the empathic "running" of the Nativity Ode, directly into the center of the stage. We participate as an implied chorus in the action. As for the author, he also will now move forward and take his place as leader of the chorus, the principal voice for the witnesses, guiding their stances with questions and commands: "Look Nymphs, and Shepherds look, / What sudden blaze of majesty / Is that . . . ?" (ll. 1–3). The voice of the Genius of the Wood gradually becomes one with those of actors, audience, and author, all raptly listening "to the celestial *Sirens'* harmony" (l. 63) as it is intimated in the immediate song:

> Such sweet compulsion doth in music lie,
> To lull the daughters of *Necessity,*
> And keep unsteady Nature to her law,
> And the low world in measur'd motion draw
> After the heavenly tune, which none can hear
> Of human mold with gross unpurged ear [ll. 68–73].

Hell again grants what love seeks, allowing at least the momentary restoration of an Eden, the recovery or realization of original harmony, and a form of human redemption. The music is both that of monochord joining earth with Heaven in original harmony and that of monody, restoring the original relationship of the "partial" earth within the grand diapason. The Genius of the Wood, the singing actors, and the songs all attempt both to describe and to enact those "inimitable sounds" (l. 78). In so doing, they seem also to justify the inimitable will of God who, like Orpheus, by means of the "sweet" compulsion of the eternal dance and song of his creation can compel seeming necessity (which now is proved to be only a contingency) and lead the "low" world back to the original height of creation. It is also God, then, who speaks within the voice that charges the questing Arcades, "Look Nymphs, and Shepherds look." His "low" creatures willingly look and, enraptured, see. All that which in "Lycidas" will seem to be lost—the warbled Apollonian string, the unfailing rapture upward to divine majesty, the innocence of the manifested Edenic pastoral, and the source of Edenic being and meaning—are here quickly attained and held.

The myth and its enactment were borne from the form of masque and pastoral through a suspension of disbelief into a ritual of belief itself, showing the audience (and the author, who is histrionically among us) a "better soil" (l. 101) than all our Arcady and a deity better than an earthly Syrinx. Having been drawn at least to the portals of Christian belief, the Christian author and audience become involved in the action in still one more way. Although the myth of "Arcades" bears traces of the far more general Miltonic interest in the pattern creation, fall, renewal, it sweeps almost immediately to the renewal that is an aspect of eternal creation. If the action necessarily had to open upon seeming incompleteness, all those who enact the work are led by Fame (in a kind of gracious anticipation of the "heavenly tune" that draws the "low world") to the end which they have not yet attained—majestic light, transcending sensory experience. They are further told about one in whom they have distantly believed and are reassured by the example of the Genius that shepherdly work on earth (resembling the gardening labor of Eve in Eden) blesses nature. Then—most important—they are shown that they can live in a divine form of Arcady all the year. There need be neither an experienced Fall nor the need for renewal, if they maintain their parts in the great harmony.

Two songs insist that the audience continue to take part in such a realization; the second commands, "Bring your Flocks, and live with *us*" (l. 103—italics added). In such a union, they have come to their "renewal"—or better, to being filled more completely with the original breath of life, the original creative harmony. Their stance has been that of pilgrims in quest of that which they have not so much lost as never yet fully received. They seek a melody they know, but have never quite learned to attend. In the fullness of instruction, which in its way is also a revelation, they realize that the object of the quest has been really with them all the time, just as the kindly Countess at Harefield is visibly with the children who have enacted the Arcades.

"In Perfect Diapason": Renewal of song in "At a Solemn Music"

"At a Solemn Music" is Milton's most perfect statement of the Renaissance idea of music, which, if somewhat esoteric in origin, could nevertheless provide meanings and metaphors of affecting simplicity. It is also partially his farewell to that conception. Although he will use it again in *Paradise Lost*, it will have ceased to be the paradigm and expression of unity, a great concert of theology, cosmology, ethics, and art. The persistent movement toward the metaphor of music has been seen in the Nativity Ode's single great concert of creation, incarnation and apocalypse, in the concluding ecstasies of "L'Allegro" and "Il Penseroso," and in the songs of "Arcades." The movement away from it now will be seen in both *Comus* and "Lycidas," in which metaphors once supplied by the conceptions of music will arise from doctrines of reason and poetry.

Both the sources of meaning are instructively present in the Latin poem "Ad Patrem." As the young poet begins his plea, his metaphors derive from the theory of music. His "divine song" preserves or prophesies something of Heaven on earth, for song not only pleases the gods on high but binds those in Tartarus, and furthermore it will provide the glory of eternity when "we shall walk . . . through the temples of the skies and with the harp's soft accompaniment we shall sing sweet songs" (p. 83). From this stance and matter, reminiscent of those in all the poems considered earlier, Milton then shifts to a more nearly historical stance in which metaphors of poetry almost replace those of music, "song" having noticeably changed from a melodic to a poetic meaning. In the past, the bard "sang" of heroes and gods. The meaning more than the melody of his song mattered. Somewhat teasingly, yet quite seriously, the present poet asks his musician father, "What pleasure is there in the inane modulation of the voice without words and meaning and rhythmic eloquence? Such music is good enough for the forest choirs, but not for Orpheus, who by his song—not by his cithara—restrained rivers and gave ears to the oaks, and by his singing stirred the ghosts of the dead to tears. That fame he owes to his song" (p. 84). As the therapeutic function of art moves to the foreground, bringing with it demands for a statement of Christian doctrine and example, the purely celebrative function recedes to the Edenic past or is removed to the heavenly future. In the present, art must move, redeem, and prepare men for a rapture that, if it is increasingly valued, is also increasingly distant.

It was perhaps inevitable that the shift should take place. The grand paradigm of the universe and its meaning that had been formed from conceptions of music had always presented two major difficulties. First, it could not present a harmonizing "justification" of the fallen world. There, discord not only refused resolution into any order but even tended actively to destroy it. Even the "musical" poems had indicated the difficulty, the Nativity Ode by postponing for men the festival of Heaven, the twin poems by their final resort to the conditional ("These delights if thou canst give"), and "Arcades" by the sense that all was not yet done: the shepherds had not yet arrived at the ideal, but in the *future* were to "Bring your Flocks, and live with us." Second, although music had meaning for the intuitive intelligence of angels and perhaps for the unfallen discursive intelligence of men, its meaning for fallen man might have to be created, not merely attended. Prayer and poetry will have to precede participation in the heavenly Lycidian chorus. Much as the Arcades had needed to follow their "vows and wishes" in "solemn search" before attaining the heavenly tune, so men increasingly must temper themselves or receive divine renewal before they are capable of joining the great concert. In a sense, man has had to move from passive rapture to active pursuit of its conditions. He must labor first to choose, and in that labor the prayer and poetry supplied by an exemplary, perhaps sacrificial, Orpheus become the new major signification of "divine song."

These implications are strongly present in "At a Solemn Music"—not so much in the insistent wedding of voice with verse,

however, as in the stance. It is explicitly that of prayer. Its glorious evocation of music does not conceal the initiating presence
of need. Whereas the twin poems and the Nativity Ode began
with a sense of infinite vitality routing weak discord, this poem
begins with the conviction of discord and the implied absence of
vital strength. Like *Comus,* it registers earth's attributes as dim
and low. The ensuing musical evocation of the song that becomes
possible when the mixed power of voice and verse penetrates
"Dead things with inbreath'd sense" (l. 4) is expressively interrupted by the rueful reminder that men generally had similarly
interrupted the original harmony:

> . . . disproportion'd sin
> Jarr'd against nature's chime, and with harsh din
> Broke the fair music that all creatures made
> To their great Lord, whose love their motion sway'd [ll. 19–22].

With human sin, the music of the world as well as the music of
humanity had become discordant, chaotic; only penetration to the
divine harmony can in any way restore the lesser agencies of that
erstwhile symphony. Some of that penetration now may come only
after death ("till God ere long / To his celestial consort us
unite, / To live with him, and sing in endless morn of light" [ll.
26–28]) . In any case, the stance of the poem asks not so much that
we participate in the music that our "gross unpurged" ears can
scarcely hear, as that we create in ourselves the will for such
participation. Solemn artificial music can evoke the goal. The
"artificial," willed creation of poetry, like the creation of prayer,
can show us the way.

Such a distinction is made clear at the outset when the two
"Sirens . . . , / Voice and Verse" not only celebrate life but in
some measure create it:

> Wed your divine sounds, and mixt power employ
> Dead things with inbreath'd sense able to pierce [ll. 3–4].

The former role of Orpheus as musician and deliverer from
Pluto [20] is here absorbed into poetry and song, the "goddesses"
whom Orpheus had served. We move persistently beyond agent

[20] Hutton, in "Some English Poems in Praise of Music," p. 48, notes that
Orpheus could move dumb things. It should be added that he, like Christ, can
also raise dead or inert things.

toward cause, borne almost to the Creator whose "inspiration" alone, in the end, can make of dead matter a living soul.

"At a Solemn Music" unmistakably accepts the invitation, all but obeyed in "Arcades," to follow metaphor and myth into Christianity. Its ultimate song, desired rather than expressed, is one of "pure concent" (1. 6). It is sung before the sapphire throne celebrated in the Nativity Ode. Although our "high-rais'd fantasy" (1. 5) can receive it as idea and can even in part tune the soul to some correspondence with it, we no longer dance with the spheres and sing with the morning stars.[21] Although the soul may clap its hands and sing at the presentment of past or future "Saintly shout" and martyrs' "Singing everlastingly" (ll. 9, 16) with the eternal music of seraphic trumpeters and cherubic choirs, it is meanwhile sharply aware of its mortal dress. The prayer has asked that Verse and Voice may somehow restore man's place within that great harmony. The audience become somewhat forlorn worshipers who recall the Eden men once knew and the songs their purged ears once heard, resembling those songs both intimated and imitated in "Arcades." Then all creatures had moved like organ reeds "in perfect Diapason" (1. 23). Human discord inflicted a fault of discord across all nature, alienating man both from his earlier "first obedience and . . . state of good" (1. 24) and from his transcendent "celestial consort" (1. 27), union with which, if it is to be at all, is now removed far into the future. Words from *Paradise Lost* bespeaking man's first disobedience and the "distance and distaste, / Anger and just rebuke" of Heaven hover near. In place of that full pathetic sense of Fall, however, there appears a redemptive prayer that can correct that disobedience. It seeks the tempering and "tuning" of human wills toward concert with God's harmonious will, the achievement of an inner Paradise. The darkness of dead things and discord can then be dispelled by a return to the "endless morn of light" (1. 28).[22]

[21] Hutton, in "Some English Poems in Praise of Music," p. 49, discusses the renovative power of music which, like the hope for education in Milton's tract, can restore us to our prelapsarian stance.

[22] John Hollander, in *The Untuning of the Sky: Ideas of Music in English Poetry, 1500–1700* (Princeton, 1961), p. 328, notes that the phrase "As once we did" records blessed history, whereas "O may we soon" is an ultimate hope and prayer.

God of course presents the choice for renewal and the voice and verse that both register and enact the choice, but man must present the choosing. The artist, who can perceive eternity and who with words tries both to intimate and to enact the greater creation, is peculiarly equipped to hear and act rightly and to help others purge their ears and lives. He too possesses the invigorating breath of life that by original creation or by resurrection can "pierce" inert bodies or wills, he himself having been invigorated by it. He both receives (as inspiration) and offers (as poetry) the verse and voice that can impel our human "fantasy" toward epiphany. With his help, the great organ of creation will again be heard as each consenting human being comes to join in "Hymns devout and holy Psalms" (l. 15). Eden or Heaven is only as distant as that moment's choice. When the will is perfected, the song may be directly human, or a reflection or reply to those in Heaven. In that restored worship, all songs once again become the single eternal song.

As the poem closes, its elemental prayer is still only a prayer, not its fulfillment. Increasing ardor among the worshipers has increased the pressure toward fulfillment, of course, and the structure of the poem expresses a harmony beyond that stipulated in the direct statement. The former undiscording melody of Paradise is joined as in a circle with the "future" melody of the Paradise that prayer seems about to restore. The single sentence that is the compass of the poem has moved from invoking the "pledges of Heav'n's joy" (l. 1) to evocation of the consummate "endless morn of light." Similarly, the opening imperative that commanded partial union ("Wed your divine sounds") is answered and transcended by the hope of a greater union, when "God ere long / To his celestial consort us unite."

The inspired celebration forseen in "At a Solemn Music" supplies the fitting conclusion for a discussion of Milton's early poems. If the twin poems seemed to turn inward to the artist, and if "At a Solemn Music" turned outward to some of the external demands of history, the works that precede Comus nevertheless are generally compact and consistent. Their metaphors and myths derive from eternal harmony and light, which themselves are metaphors or manifestations of creation and the Creator. The discords of sin and shadows of death seem only momentary or figurative. Even if man falls out of tune or wanders beyond direct vision of light, redemption by the harmony of his will with God's promises him a renewal of his place within the changeless but dynamic sound and light.

Because the human artist has consented utterly to the creative sound and light, he not only receives them but participates directly in the creative concert. Like Orpheus or the Sirens Verse and Voice, he can help "inspire" dead things—including his own merely human capacities—with his secondary breath of life. The audience, too, will receive from both divine and human creations the evocation of eternal harmony and the redemptive breath that can renew it. In the eternal present, as the Nativity Ode enacted the possibility, "bright-harness'd Angels sit in order serviceable" to the new Sun and the renewed song of creation. The humble ode of human song and prayer also presents its service. Even the discord of sin that seemed to force light and sound from earth is not powerful against them. If the morning of Christ's nativity can supply a general metaphor, the harmony of ascent broken by men has been restored by the harmonizing descent of divinity. Divine harmony ultimately refuses creatural discord. Milton will come to confess a far darker landscape and a more discordant clangor on earth in his later works, but he will never alter this early confidence in the redemptive, because essential, harmony and light of eternity. As *Comus* will assert:

> [Virtue] can teach ye how to climb
> Higher than the Sphery chime;
> Or if Virtue feeble were,
> Heav'n itself would stoop to her [ll. 1020–1023].

[2] "By Due Steps Aspire"
Reason, Appetite, and Trial in *Comus*

Although there is a general continuity of themes across Milton's poetry, a significant local change in theme and stance occurs before 1640. Those who assign the change to 1637 or afterward may delay it too long. The alteration surely begins when lateral shadows of death and corruption first seriously intrude among the early poems' vertical images of light and song, not as interesting musical contrast or as a mere register of the lower faculty of the human constitution, but as a permanent condition—or the persistently appearing illusion of such a condition—that must be opposed lest it assert a disintegrative, Satanic counterforce. If evil has come to seem so unequivocal, at least in its apparent effects within time, it must be acknowledged; perhaps it can then either be cast down or argued into illogic.

It is possible to locate such a basic change of stance and matter within the first speech of the Attendant Spirit in *Comus*.[1] He begins the poem within a stance of light and music, much like the stances of the early poems:

> Before the starry threshold of *Jove's* Court
> My mansion is, where those immortal shapes
> Of bright aërial Spirits live inspher'd
> In Regions mild of calm and serene Air [ll. 1–4].

[1] Noting the day of the performance, J. B. Broadbent, in *Milton: Comus and Samson Agonistes* (London, 1961), p. 10, associates St. Michael with the Attendant Spirit—guardian angels, both. Like the Urania discussed by Lily B. Campbell, in "The Christian Muse" (*Huntington Library Bulletin*, VIII [Oct., 1935], 37), the Attendant Spirit can lift humanity above the stars.

In this partly Odyssean poem, the only Sirens yet present either are Platonic or are those early Miltonic "harmonious Sisters, Voice and Verse." But Circean Sirens rush into their places when the poem must follow the Spirit's gaze downward, reaching an antithetical stance:

> . . . this dim spot,
> Which men call Earth, and with low-thoughted care
> Confin'd and pester'd in this pinfold here,
> Strive to keep up a frail and Feverish being [ll. 5–8].

The shift of stance is painful to the audience because it conveys our own fall, "descent" and degradation. Light gives way to dimness and smoke. The dance of the morning stars surrenders to empty "stir." Although men may still call their wheeling planet by its old name, in it they are less than men: they already have become Circean swine, confined in a "sensual sty" (l. 77), clinging to an existence they know to be despicable. Men thus fallen must labor, must take "Care," with even their despised being. Brought into this stance by the Spirit, the reader must accept this definition of man as a donnée. We must witness, participate in, and even (by changing our perspective from Heaven to earth) consent to a fall as disastrous as that of Satan and his host from the edge of Heaven. They fell as if they were Gadarene swine. In *Comus,* it is men who appear in a Circean sty. From the perspective of the serene early poems, what a fall is there! However, the very presence of the Spirit's voice assures us of the concordant "stoop" of Heaven (l. 1023), which will not cease its harmonious penetration to men, including that of the Incarnation, even though they are fallen.

For the Spirit's definitive statement has not ended with the two stances. He insists upon a reconciling grace in God and a saving will in man by means of which the fall need not take place—or, if it has taken place, need not be final. If it is perhaps a necessary human condition and a certain shadow upon the majority of men, it is by no means irreversible; men may choose to rise, and Heaven will support them in their choice. The poem will close, much as it began, with a descending act of grace. As yet, men need not expect misery—only temptation to luxury. Even on earth, men may "by due steps aspire / To lay their just hands on that Golden Key / That opes the Palace of Eternity" (ll. 12–14), the setting upon which the poem opens. Lest the way seem too hard or exclusive, the verse emphasizes the word "aspire." Its mood is not future, but present: man may choose to "see" and to that extent to inhabit the endless heavenly ring of light now, for it is real, whereas the "dim spot . . . Earth" is finally a temporal illusion. The golden key to *"Jove's* Court" is always at hand and, if the human aspirant weakens in his grasp, gracious "Heav'n itself would stoop" to his aid.

This change in Milton is heralded or accompanied by a major change in metaphoric reference. Heretofore, in the poems initiated with references to music, the imagery was necessarily auditory. Now the metaphor of a circle heralds strong visual and spatial references. The circle formed in *Comus* by human reaching toward God and divine stooping toward men in turn suggests the Florentine Neoplatonic *circuitus spiritualis,* a circling route of love joining men with God. Even the division among men indicated by the Attendant Spirit partly complements the metaphor: although the "bound" human lower soul (*anima secunda*) may seem to remain fastened to the earth even as the Lady is momentarily bound by Comus, the free higher soul (*anima prima*) can freely choose to join the upward circle. Milton's sense of the circuit evidently is far less fixed than was Ficino's—in his Neoplatonism as in his poetry, Milton proposes to soar above the Aonian mount yet again, telling "What never yet was heard in Tale or Song / From old or modern Bard" (ll. 44–45)—but the circle nevertheless suggests the major change of metaphor. The earlier rapture of the lower human "tone" upward to Heaven's highest, most feelingly presented in "Il Penseroso," tended to insist that sight give way to sound, and that even sound seek spirit ditties of no tone. The myth of musical transport exacted certain penalties from poems that celebrated it, limiting the possibilities of description (for the visible world will be transcended), of stance (for it is ultimately fixed in upward quest), and of kinds of character (for, apart from devils, all creatures almost necessarily are concordant pilgrims). "Arcades" is perhaps the consummation of the myth and metaphor from music. Although "At a

Solemn Music" continues the subject of music, its suggestion of polyphony supplies a bridge between the early poems and *Comus*, as does also its suggestion of the circle formed when fallen men are rejoined to the concert of Heaven.

It would be misleading, however, if we were to insist upon absolute metaphorical control of *Comus* by the idea of a circle and its related visual imagery. In the first place, some of the earlier unmoving rapture associated with music remains, appearing whenever the agonists look up from earth to Platonically visible chastity or to divine philosophy. Their human success almost reinstates the confident reference of the monochord; not until there is strong human need will the circle bringing heavenly aid to the needful human creature appear. In the second place, although Milton imagines a grand circle in God's design and demonstrates it in the whole circuit of the Attendant Spirit from Heaven to earth and back to Heaven, neither the visual setting nor the poem's action is basically circular. They instead suggest established platforms in absolute space, with movement between those fixed stations. The distance becomes important to the agon, presenting the human being with cause for doubt and fear, God with reason for pity and compassion, and Comus—who resembles Ficino's *amor ferinus,* insane and bestial love—with swift opportunity. These planes agree more generally with Christian cosmography and Aristotelian ethics than with Platonism. All this is not to say that Milton abandons Neoplatonism, for he makes repeated contacts with it. It rather indicates in *Comus* a general, but gradual, shift to more traditional Hebraic and Christian beliefs and iconology. In any case, although *Comus* utilizes the *circuitus spiritualis* as well as other Neoplatonic images, it partly breaks with them in the agon itself. Parallel planes in part displace both circle and automatically harmonious music, insisting upon aspiration and struggle if the circle is to be inscribed.[2]

The masque form, which came to make a section of opposing antimasque obligatory, also tended to insist upon a division of

[2] William G. Madsen ("The Idea of Nature in Milton's Poetry," in *Three Studies in the Renaissance: Sidney, Jonson, Milton* [New Haven, 1958], p. 224), notices the effect when the Platonic universe of the early poems is altered into the time-involved world of Milton's later poems.

men that is almost spatial—higher opposed to lower.[3] Whereas Neoplatonic tradition might envision a harmonizing debate between two moral choices in which a circle of unity would be achieved, the dialogue that appears from this time forward in Milton's works usually must envision opposing moral positions assigned ultimately to different characters in separate visual planes. (In *Comus*, the Attendant Spirit "permanently" stands above, the Lady aspires from central Earth, and Comus in a persistent recoil explodes downward from godlike similitude toward the beast.) Divine synthesis may be possible, but otherwise there will be little of the former reconciliation into symphony. There will instead appear that antagonism suggested by the prefix in *antimasque*.[4]

In *Comus*, the reassuring images both of the past monochord and the present schematic circle are broken by two hostile conditions, neither of which is wholly consonant with Neoplatonism and both of which are either new in Milton or now receive greatly increased emphasis, darkening the celebration but perhaps increasing its interest. The first is the prior condition or likelihood of a fall beyond either the monochord or the circle. In *Comus* its form is not that of original sin. It is in large measure a kind of Neoplatonic negativity, but conviction that fall is the essential character of the earth and of the human condition nevertheless dominates the beginning of the poem. The second new force is even darker. It asks a sacrifice that will counteract human frailty, thereby intimating the redemptive Christ who was largely absent from the early works. In *Comus*, he is several times removed into myth, it is true—displaced into the guise of the marvelous Sabrina, whose death is turned into delight by swift narrative and melodious song. Nevertheless, death has entered Milton's world, if by a causeway as yet only dimly seen. All we know of it is that its shade is persistent across this poem and those that immediately

[3] A. E. Dyson, in "The Interpretation of *Comus*" (*E&S*, n.s. VIII [1955], 101), discusses the implied ladder in *Comus*—upward to love, downward to the beast.

[4] George Williamson ("The Context of *Comus*," in *Milton and Others* [Chicago, 1965], p. 34), notes the effect of the antimasque in initiating "the same contrast between seductive and repulsive vice that Satan and Sin represent in *Paradise Lost*."

follow, and that it must be confronted with "eager thought" and a new kind of heroism, increasingly like that of Orpheus rather than Hercules.

If in "L'Allegro" and "Il Penseroso" the singularly impelling Orpheus image and Orphic music allowed ready triumph over Pluto, in these more troubled, circling later poems they permit Milton to remake internally the matter of a poem penetrated by death. The stance possible from the myth becomes extraordinarily promising. If a divine singer can transform death into greater life and triumphant song, and if in so doing he becomes a deliverer not only of himself but (virtually or actually) of others, then death and agony can serve beauty, redemption, and eternity. Sabrina, Christ, and, by inference, Milton enter into that stance even in *Comus*. The fall of a feeble virtue can be reversed by charitable action—a sacrificial second "fall" that is also an ascent—which will remove both of the seeming victims into the eternal aspiration or achievement of Jove's Court.

Even such brief considerations as these may suggest why *Comus* often has been considered opaque and difficult. Much of the feeling probably comes from three unexpected currents. First, our ordinary sense of mimesis breaks down almost altogether in the face of the improbable combination of nonimitative allegory with methektic, more-than-imitative enactment by an actor of himself.[5] Second, if the work is considered within the province of art alone, some of the patterns formed by its materials, along with the highly artificial form of the masque itself, make the poem extremely abstract. Its canvas is perhaps more "modern" than that of any of Milton's major works. Its dimension is plane, its mode nonrepresentational, its gestures and characterizations formal, somewhat like those in the Book of Job[6] or Picasso's "Guernica." Finally, partly because its Neoplatonic patterns are as unfamiliar as the

[5] C. L. Barber, *"A Mask Presented at Ludlow Castle,"* in *The Lyric and Dramatic Milton*, ed. Joseph H. Summers (New York and London, 1965), p. 39: The masque could induce "nobility to realize an ideal in miming it." See also Stephen Orgel, *The Jonsonian Masque* (Cambridge, Mass., 1965), pp. 81–109.

[6] C. S. Lewis, in "A Note on *Comus*" (*RES*, VIII [1932], 176), describes the effect Milton gained in revising *Comus* as one of "poetic chastity." It resembles that of *Paradise Regained*.

art is abstract, earlier criticism was led to believe that the Lady was a negative, Puritanical bundle of repressions contesting a healthy, satisfactory Comus; that the masque and its author were obsessively concerned with virginity, not virtue; and that the masque was undramatic (quite a different matter, surely, from Miss Tuve's contention that it is static).[7] Our increasing reacquaintance with Neoplatonism helps to dispel some of the objections to *Comus,* but if the masque is to be more than a faded document in intellectual history, the objections should also be met by contemporary argument. If my contention about *Comus'* abstractness is correct, many such objections can be referred to the structure of the work for reply. My concern is not with the argument as such, Professor Woodhouse having dealt masterfully with that subject not many years ago,[8] but with the disposition of stances and matter in *Comus.*

The masque begins and closes, having described at least a complete framing circuit, in the setting of the heavenly "real," usually invisible to the "blear" human eye. This stance alone is complete and "true." Most of *Comus,* however, takes place in the seeming lateral reality of earth. It is almost literally nonvisible, its smoke and darkness obscuring it to itself and from Heaven. Therefore, when total illusion (Comus) masks itself in pleasing materiality and false glitter, not only Comus but humanity may think it is real, although it is of course the ultimate invisibility. Man may make the same error of identification in the macrocosmic setting or in himself as microcosmos. Verbally and dramatically, the masque begins with the statement and "real" stance of the interested Attendant Spirit, moves at once to the opposite stance and meaning of the antimasque, occupied by the totally night-loving but seemingly light-supplying Comus, and in one sense completes an abstract form by placing the Lady, who sometimes "sees" reality and attends it but who also may "hear" illusion and follow it, in a mediate third stance of choice.

Almost as simply and abstractly, three calls or prayers that

[7] Rosemond Tuve, *Images and Themes in Five Poems by Milton* (Cambridge, Mass., 1957), pp. 112–160.
[8] A. S. P. Woodhouse, "The Argument of Milton's *Comus,*" *UTQ,* XI (1941), 46–71.

reach out from the central human stance toward the other two produce the action of *Comus*. The Lady's plea is answered by the "blear illusion" of Comus; the Brother's resultant plea is answered by the superhuman interest of the Attendant Spirit; the Spirit's consequent command is answered by the sacrificial Sabrina. The correlative stances taken as a result of these pleas almost reverse the original order of stances. The Lady's choice of illusion (Comus) necessitates the Attendant Spirit's demonstration of reality, which in turn leads to a stance of redeemed humanity. Once the human stance has been confirmed in heavenly reality, the original "true" stance triumphantly returns. In and around these three stances in their convergent and divergent dispositions, human doubts, pleas, and convictions are "assayed" against absolute truth and absolute illusion. The three stances for a time also induce three intersecting patterns of movement, all of which are reflected in related dances—the Lady's upward-moving pilgrimage, the gracious circuit from Heaven to earth of the Attendant Spirit, and the dazzling, explosive appearance and recoiling disappearance of Comus. In the end, of course, the one inclusive stance receives all movement back toward itself.

Lest so much emphasis upon pattern and structure suggest that human meaning in *Comus* is absorbed into plane geometry, it should be said at once that three simple and affecting emphases upon the purely human are constant in the work. In the first, the audience is asked to see these patterns as the paradigm of its own "assay." Christian salvation is so heavily intimated in the myth that it dissolves the impression of pure abstractness or aestheticism. In the second, the Lady (and to a lesser degree, her Brothers and even Sabrina) moves through a recognizable, general, moving agon: her "due steps" lead her through a token fall, an ascent toward active allegiance to God's design, and an enforcing redemption—all within a quasi-dramatic segment of time. Finally, the actors of the masque, like those who methektically enacted the Arcades, at times are touching in their embodiments of their roles; the sense of their flesh and blood may be stronger than that of their intellectual or artistic abstraction. Once the principal "assay" in *Comus* is understood to involve those real children who were also the actors, testing not whether technical virginity but whether their humanity can be maintained, the abstractions suddenly become local and familiar. Not only actors and roles but also Heaven and Ludlow Castle, the Heavenly Father and the earthly father, stand in easy correspondent relationship. As the Egerton children stood in methektic relation to the characters and setting, so the audience may stand in relation to *Comus* itself.

And if that were not all, the charm of the verse alone would stoop past even the most heavenly of abstractions, inviting us to join in both earthy "Jigs and rural dance" (l. 952) and the more exalted "trippings to be trod / Of lighter toes, and . . . Court guise" (ll. 961–962) —that "Court" no doubt intimating and including *"Jove's* Court."

"My Unacquainted Feet": Three stances for choice of being

Three great speeches, two indicating ultimate stances and choices and the other the unfailing human imperative and stance of choice, initiate *Comus.* The representatives of opposed spiritual stances, themselves great antagonists, speak in turn, followed by the representative human being who must choose between them—and therefore between ultimate possibilities of human nature. The resulting paradigm is almost as striking as that of *Paradise Lost:*

> . . . and now in little space
> The confines met of Empyrean Heav'n
> And of this World, and on the left hand Hell
> With long reach interpos'd [*Paradise Lost,* X, 320–323].

The Attendant Spirit "necessarily" speaks first and last in the poem, for God's circular design precedes and follows all possible particular and local actions; it is itself a *circuitus spiritualis* that figures timelessness. The first and final stance of the poem is defined by that of the Attendant Spirit. Even though he descends to earth, he essentially exists always at the "starry threshold of *Jove's* Court" (l. 1), beyond which lies "Empyrean Heav'n," both the symbol and eternal site of right human choice. For the audience as well as the characters of *Comus,* this must be held to be the only "real" stance; just as Ludlow Castle intimates Heaven,[9] so do the stances on earth. Like planets (including earth, if it chose) reflecting the great source of light and like complementary angels dancing in praise of God, Neoplatonic "bright aërial Spirits" are here "inspher'd" (l. 3) in stately eternal dance, the first of several dances in *Comus,* all of which tend to be equally expressive. The Attendant Spirit first looks worshipfully to the celebration and its ultimate inspiration. He then somewhat unwillingly considers its opposite.

Far below, most men lead brutish lives on a planet they choose to make terribly unlike those others in the heavenly dance. On their earth, suffocating with the smoke [10] of a Circean pinfold, they have degenerated willingly into swine. Unwillingly, the audience is forced to accept the judgment upon itself if it is to hold the Spirit's stance to be "real" and his words to be "true."

Some few men, however, aware of the "enthron'd gods" instructively circling above them, aspire with "due steps" (l. 12) to join the circle and attain such virtue. The Attendant Spirit, like the doctrinally redemptive Raphael of *Paradise Lost,* points out those simple but ultimate choices to all men. He will "descend," graphically, to aid one representative aspirant, the Lady. He comes from her "native home" (l. 76); with divine aid, both will return to it, the Spirit providing "safe convoy" (l. 81). He will assume the Christlike appearance and function of a "Swain" or shepherd who can "hush the waving Woods" (l. 88) or Galilee. His attitude toward earth, however, reveals him to be more like God or Raphael than Christ, more admonitory than directly redemptive.[11] The perfect and exalted "Jove" (for whom, as is usual in Milton, one can read the Christian God) is more directly benevolent than the God of *Paradise Lost,* however. Although he dwells regally in absolute light, aloof from earth and all save the aspiring few

[9] A. S. P. Woodhouse, "*Comus* Once More," *UTQ,* XIX (1950), 220: "Ludlow, if it is the parents' dwelling, is also a symbol of the Heavenly City."

[10] Erwin Panofsky, in *Studies in Iconology* (New York and Evanston, Ill., 1962), p. 149, identifies smoke and ruins with the Circean Venus in an engraving after Bandinelli.

[11] Cleanth Brooks and J. E. Hardy, *Poems of Mr. John Milton: The 1645 Edition with Essays in Analysis* (New York, 1951), p. 190: "He does not interfere; he is . . . not the *moving* spirit of the play, but the attendant."

among men, his eternal eye is charitably solicitous of merit. He therefore designs to "shoot" the Attendant Spirit down preveniently to aid the typic worthy man. Already the redemptive will of God is strongly suggested. Having established the bearing of God as the loving object (and creator) of reasonable choice and himself as a type of the redemptive Raphael, and having shown man that if wine or any other created gift is gluttonously "misused," man may lose both his sight of reality and his Heaven-witnessing "upright shape" (l. 52), the Spirit retires. His stance insists that the poem and all its considerations begin and end in this absolute light of Heaven.

That "true" stance, in which the Spirit can be in Heaven even while he walks on earth, gives way for the opposite proclamation and stance of Comus. In earth's pinfold, the audience is left alone, like the Lady, with the principle of darkness and smoke. We are forced to attend the antagonist of God and man. Although he inhabits the pinfold and, indeed, is self-imprisoned in the earthly mentality already condemned by the Spirit, Comus' claim to power is great: he is the grand enemy of heavenly light and human dignity. Divine irony of course penetrates his claim, revealing it to be—literally—nothing. At most, he can represent only a bounty misused, as Circe represents at best a degenerative *raptus*. However, because human choice can seem to surrender to Comus the power he does not actually possess, he is not to be underestimated as a pole of choice. The many choose him. His manifesto seemingly is cast in measures as brisk and language as charming as those of "L'Allegro." Milton's success in dramatizing this master of deceit can be judged from the number of readers who have surrendered to this "tipsy" Comus.[12]

However, as the Attendant Spirit's warning against his immoderation indicates, he is not really mere Bacchic generative nature. His speech seethes with Satanic sophistication, envy, and helpless parody of God.

In Comus' stance, evil seeks the dark but tries to dazzle. Comus

---

[12] Charles Williams, in his "Introduction to *The English Poems of John Milton*," reprinted in *Milton Criticism*, ed. James Thorpe (New York, 1950), p. 256, is not seduced: "[Comus] prefers to sit about in sepulchres. Let him, cries the whole lovely dance."

delights in disorder but wants to "imitate" perversely the eternal order of the "Starry Choir" (l. 112). He imagines that he is the grand opponent who lays all Jove's law to rest but, like Satan, half worships God and sometimes imagines all his parodic lies and wishes to be truths. (Similarly, the opponent becomes an implement for furthering God's design; as the Elder Brother will say, "that which mischief meant most harm / Shall in the happy trial prove most glory" [ll. 591–592]). Comus deludes himself into believing his meteoric crew to be of the "purer fire" of the first stance and his "pert Fairies" and "dapper Elves" (l. 118) to be like angels. They are instead like their counterparts, the fallen angels of *Paradise Lost,* Book I. Despite Comus' professed wish, he acts in Pandemonium, not in a midsummer night's dream. Like Satan yet again, he can act only by shadowy reflection, calling himself with little if any conscious irony or parody a vowed priest. His worship, however, is given to the darkly obscene Cotytto; so must be that of any human being who chooses Comus. It is a grave mistake to think of Comus or Satan as irreligious, for they are instead always counterreligious—as the reference to Cotytto indicates. If Orpheus was a Christ figure, a Good Shepherd, and Cotytto one among the savage dismembering maenads,[13] then more than the Lady is under threat. Comus must hope that his ritual "Solemnity" is concealed from the true "telltale Sun" (l. 141)—the greater or lesser light of the Nativity Ode or of Jove and Phoebus in *Comus,* either of which would show Comus' ceremonies to be as empty as they are black. Despite the attractive luxuriousness of the imagery Comus commands and despite his occasionally engaging Puckishness, he is almost as patently Satanic as is the dazzling serpent in Eden. He crows, at the end of his manifesto, that his seductive reason will similarly "hug [easyhearted man] into snares" (ll. 163–164), defeating both human and divine wills. Having established himself as the enemy of God and man and having taken a stance on Earth, not as shepherd but as swineherd within the pinfold he wishes it to be for men, he too retires. The audience has a second in which to recall the other

---

[13] Jane E. Harrison, in *Prolegomena to the Study of Greek Religion* (3d ed.; Cambridge, 1922), pp. 456–457, associates Cottyto with Orphic rites, including the dismemberment of Orpheus.

stance, that of reality rather than illusion, before Jove's Court. With that memory of light it can perhaps offset the wiles Comus has been working on it and will work at once upon the Lady.

Universal human deliberations reaching toward choice now are supplied by the Lady. She hesitates in her stance. Like the audience, she is placed in the choice-demanding, outwardly shadowed wood of human "assay." [14] She should be able to maintain the stance—seeing Heaven (or remembering Ludlow Castle) but aware of earth (and the present dark wood) —with which the Attendant Spirit began the poem. Even if her perspective must reverse the Attendant Spirit's vision and look vertically from low to high, Heaven is, after all, her "native home." But that Paradise, both real and inward, is severely threatened by her outward hesitation. An eternal guide, reason, has been given her as the essential part of her nature, but she turns from it to that "best guide" (l. 171), her ear, for direction. She thereby suffers a temporary Spenserian misdirection to trust in the senses only. The error is underscored by her description of sense as in any way "best," for the first manifesto had insisted that only God merits the superlative. It is stressed again in her conditional but tardy afterthought: "If mine ear be true" (l. 170). Her choice is errant and must produce a fall. Even when her half-choice brings her to hear Comus' rout, even after she recognizes the character of the orgy, she asks despairingly, "Yet O where else / Shall I inform my unacquainted feet / In the blind mazes of this tangl'd Wood?" (ll. 179–181). Milton probably intended us to recall that the Twenty-third Psalm is supposed to inform the Christian's feet and that Christ as well as Contemplation is imaged as guide and lamp. As Raphael in *Paradise Lost* warned, "Perfet within, no outward aid require" (*Paradise Lost*, VIII, 642), and as the Son of *Paradise Regained* might have spoken for her, "Who brought me hither / Will bring me hence, no other Guide I seek" (*Paradise Regained*, I, 335–336).

The Lady then wanders still farther, moving from merely following a false guide to active doubt and despair, fearing that

---

[14] John Arthos (*On "A Mask Presented at Ludlow-Castle,"* Michigan University Contributions in Modern Philology, No. 20 [Ann Arbor, Mich., 1954], p. 31), believes that the plot of *Comus* turns upon "chance rather than sought adventure." The assay itself, however, indicates a directive design.

night can "close up the Stars" of the first stance, they that should give "due light / To the misled and lonely Traveller" (ll. 197–200). Her plaint is ironic in that she is "misled" largely by herself, "unacquainted" only because she is following unreal shadows and not looking to the "inspher'd" stars but instead listening to Comus' circling dance, and "lonely" because she thinks not of her home but only of her "travelling." "Fantasies" and "shapes" and "beck'ning shadows" (ll. 205, 207) like those exorcised in "Il Penseroso" direct her toward Comus through a "desert Wilderness" (l. 209) forecasting that of *Paradise Regained* but seeming now to suggest sadly that she will recapitulate Eve, not the second Adam.

Only near the close of her speech does she recover the "true" stance that will keep her upright. She then contributes, in place of further doubts, a third manifesto, framed for humanity, virtually defining what man is and what he may be. For a moment, she sees again beyond the ambiguous shadows of the senses to the light of either "natural" or divine providence, sun or Son. Emmaus is now almost recalled as she insists that she "walks attended" (l. 211) rather than lonely and misled. She all but returns to the Platonic and Christian realities most relevant to her, Conscience and "visible" Chastity (not Charity—this drama is of the mind, not of society, and chastity is fidelity to both reason and God). Iconically the sable cloud above her at once rolls back to reveal the "silver lining on the night" (l. 222), the eternal illumination that can be seen when the Spirit's stance is maintained. She too voices a personal insight like that which will be revealed by God in *Paradise Lost*—that "all things ill / Are but as slavish officers of vengeance" (ll. 217–218). Her Samson-resembling "enliv'n'd" spirits lead her into the delicate Echo song.

However, her doubts soon roll back upon her. Her major dramatic choice has been insecure, "misled." Her uncertain ear pulls her to Comus and his pinfold almost as strongly as her reason might help her see the "Supreme good" (l. 217). Her song, faintly shadowed with allusions to Narcissus and the nightingale [15] that we associate with Eve, confirms her choice of the sensual Comus.

[15] The suggestion that the Echo song in part betrayed Eve-like narcissism is made by W. B. C. Watkins, in *An Anatomy of Milton's Verse* (Baton Rouge, La., 1955), p. 97.

She who relied on outward sense and accepted its stance is for the moment undone by it. The masque must now proceed to her aspiration for deliverance.

"Eye Me Blest Providence": Three prayers for guidance

The three manifestoes having presented the grand stances and the human who wavers between them as she attempts to hold fast to human being and meaning, a series of three related calls now takes up the structural burden of the masque. The respondents echo in reverse order those of the proclamations: false Comus, true Spirit, persevering human being (Sabrina).

The first prayer proceeds directly from the Lady's speech and from her falling away from the visible reality it asserted. She prays that the darkling woods and noises be other than evil for her. Unhappily, because she gave ear to Comus' rout, the only hearer for the moment is Comus. Although the early poems sought to demonstrate a progress from sound to sight, the metaphor suitable to *Comus* must reject the physical ear as if Satan sat at its entrance. Whereas the Lady's vision is true, her hearing is associated with illusion and fraud; fantasies have calling shapes and seem composed like "airy tongues that syllable men's names" (1. 208). The penetration of sight and reason through material darkness to the plane of true being now becomes the appropriate metaphor, almost reversing the earlier figure from music. Although the Lady is aware that the obscuring clouds are bordered with light and knows also that she does not really travel alone, her call arises mostly from passional fear, including a fear that the Brothers also have wandered "too far" in the darkness that she should doubly see through. As her ear, which conceivably might have heard "audible" choirs of angels, has not been proof against a siren song, so her prayer not only reaches out toward the material Brothers rather than the "glist'ring Guardian" (1. 219) she could almost see, but also is addressed to self-recoiling sound, "Sweet Echo" (1. 230). (Although an echo song was conventional in the masque form, the device is here used dramatically.) "Misled," the Lady consequently finds that her prayer is misdirected; the somewhat sense-encumbered prayer has received a thoroughly sensual echo from Comus.

The second prayer, proceeding from the less doubtful Brothers, is better directed: it calls in the watchful Attendant Spirit. Although Heaven has promised to be servant or champion to man, the Spirit himself is almost as withdrawn and judicial as the God of *Paradise Lost,* bearing a character more of revelation than of direct redemption. In Neoplatonic terms, he stands to the bound Lady much as mind (in *anima prima*) stands to the materialistic lower soul (*anima secunda*). Mind can guide, but mediating reason must free the soul. In the masque's increasingly important Christian terms, the Spirit's promise of redemptive harmony and his reference to the Shepherd Lad, who bears direct analogy with Christ, opens the way to the third prayer. Like Raphael and Michael, the Spirit as "Christian" can only instructively reveal. He must invoke another agent to "save."

The third plea invokes once-human Sabrina. Her past suggests the myth of Philomela, but her typic human role is that of Lycidas, Orpheus, or Christ. "Sunk low, but mounted high" by means of a baptismal "death" by water, Sabrina in her redemptive role lustratively sprinkles the Lady, freeing her for active virtue. A worshipful dance, lauding the achievement of Heaven's design that has been demonstrated in the three prayers and the illumination they reassert, allows the tested human beings now to join the initial radiant dance:

> Heav'n hath timely tri'd their youth,
> Their faith, their patience, and their truth,
> And sent them here through hard assays
> With a crown of deathless Praise,
>   To triumph in victorious dance
> O'er sensual Folly and Intemperance [ll. 970–975].

The Spirit then reveals what must be the true end of the "assay" and therefore of chastity: not sterile isolation and nay-saying, but a sense of union like that in the dance just seen, which truly imitated the movement of the "Starry Choir." Greater analogues of the earthly dance and its circle of union—rising from Venus and Adonis to Cupid and Psyche—intimate the Neoplatonic generative and heavenly loves. Such figures may also suggest the flowering of chastity and virginity into "holy" wedlock and, in Christian terms, the marriage of church with Christ. The three prayers in any case precipitate the line of action that moves from apparent separation, through trial of constancy, to triumphant, active reunion by means of redemptive grace.

"Other Arms and Weapons": A stand against the pinfold

The three manifestoes had established an absolute positive, an absolute negative, and the human Lady who tries to choose wisely between them. The three calls for aid had been interrogative, first imploring and then testing the resultant answer from Comus, the countering response by the Attendant Spirit, and the healing redemptive baptism by Sabrina.[16] Around these stances, the principal matter of the poem shapes into a series of debates (choices, in a verbal mode) that probe or rebut or in the end triumphantly reassert the original proclamation of the Attendant Spirit. Each debate—the initial contest of the Lady with the revealed Comus, of the Brothers with one another, of the Brothers with the Attendant Spirit, of the Lady with Comus in a second encounter, and (in effect) of the Spirit with Sabrina—leads to the center: the choice between the stances of Comus and Jove, and to proper action upon it. The last in the series produces the act of redemption, conferred by Heaven and elective by men.

In the first debate, the Lady's original error of misdirection causes her to choose Comus and his stance, despite his suspect questions and his lying Bacchic description of her Brothers ("I saw them under a green mantling vine / . . . Plucking ripe clusters" [ll. 294–296]). The Heaven he proposes to assist her to is a Circean Hell, but she too innocently asks, partly misled toward his perverse imitation of Heaven, "Gentle villager, / What readiest way would bring me to that place?" (ll. 304–305). (An-

---

[16] Sears Jayne, in "The Subject of Milton's Ludlow *Mask*" (*PMLA,* LXXIV [1959], 533–543), considers the masque Neoplatonically: The Lady embodies Reason; haemony, philosophy; and Sabrina, *Mens.* Although I agree with the justness of that analysis, I prefer the more dramatic reading suggested here.

other verse—"Broad is the path, and easy the way"—quivers at the edge of her question.) Letting her ear again misjudge the sound of his words, she misdeems this swineherd a good shepherd. She is of course near blasphemy. She takes him to be the true Attendant Spirit rather than the diabolic imitation. She concludes the first debate, still in error, still either within a fall or liable to one, with the extremely Eve-like commitment to a wolf in shepherd's clothing: "Shepherd lead on" (l. 330). The path seemingly lies toward both a pinfold and the final darkness of spiritual death.

Almost as if in response to the dangerous direction taken in the first debate, the second opens upon the concerned and searching Brothers of the Lady. They are in the same wood as she and in their own way are meeting the parallel of her trial. They readily represent audience responses to human moral crisis. The Elder Brother, confident in either the Jovian light that must "disinherit *Chaos*" (l. 334) or in its reflection or secondary agency, a "gentle taper . . . / Of some clay habitation" (ll. 337–339), assumes that there is no contest. He rests his certainty upon God the creator or Christ the incarnate agent, believing that chaos finally has been brought into the process of total creation. He is so perfect a Neoplatonist that the Christian Milton must chasten him. He has almost precipitated an entirely new opposition by seeming to offer a new manifesto. If his sister has difficulty seeing visible reality, he has difficulty in realizing the wild Wood. He trusts too readily the human "radiant light" of virtue in its strife with the "dark soul . . . / Benighted . . . under the midday Sun" (ll. 383–384). Such credulousness is very like that of Eve, so much so that for a moment we seem almost transposed into *Paradise Lost* and the scene, time, and overconfidence of Eve's temptation. The problem is not that the Elder Brother trusts God too much, but that he is too confident of man; overconfidence as well as doubt can confirm the human pinfold.

Fortunately, the more cautious and "temperate" younger Brother points out the certain attraction of corruptive vice to virtue, with the implicit suggestion that Comus, defined as "Savage hunger or . . . Savage heat" (l. 358), is at least partly "within" the struggling Lady, representative of that part of human nature that is akin to beasts. He envisions not so much an ideal completed victory of God over darkness as a present realistic contest for the reasonable control and proper use of human passion. He seems to guess that the Lady may be suffering from an excess of noise and parodic devilish lights, not from the vacant "want of light and noise" (l. 369) that the Elder Brother presumes. She endures not solitude but powerfully seductive company.

Because the question has now involved her inward state, the Elder Brother introduces his conviction that chastity is a sure strength against both inner and outer lures. He errs largely in believing that, even "if" Heaven confers strength, it "may be term'd her own." Chastity in the Lady is only one side of an equation that demands a Creator and preserver on the other.[17] It is of her; indeed, it is her spiritual essence, if she is to persevere upright; but it is not hers. Instead, it is a received and guaranteed power which she is to use for a Spenserian governance of her other received energies:

> But if ye saw that which no eyes can see,
> The inward beauty of her liuely spright,
>
> . . . . .
>
> There dwels sweet loue and constant chastity,
> Vnspotted fayth and comely womanhood,
> Regard of honour and mild modesty,
> There vertue raynes as Queene in royal throne,
> And giueth lawes alone.
> The which the base affections doe obay
> ["Epithalamion," ll. 185–196].

If that government is maintained, soul may join with "outward shape" in one doubly visible character resembling that of the Attendant Spirit's plane of reality:

> . . . oft converse with heav'nly habitants
> Begin to cast a beam on th'outward shape,
> The unpolluted temple of the mind,

---

[17] Arthos, in "On a Mask," p. 263, finds chastity and contemplation to be one, within the love of God. David Daiches, in *Milton* (London, 1957), p. 31, considered Milton's "chastity" to include fidelity to the first Christian commandment.

And turns it by degrees to the soul's essence,
Till all be made immortal [ll. 459–463].

If not, the soul just as visibly (insofar as darkness, the deprivation of light, is visible) "imbodies and imbrutes" into animal forms in the pinfold Earth and loses "the divine property of her first being . . . degenerate and degraded" (ll. 468–469, 475). The Elder Brother serenely and somewhat blindly trusts that her "first being" is inviolate in the midst of trial, that she can continually "see" Chastity visibly despite the darkness of Comus.

The Second Brother is won for a moment by the blithe certainty of his elder. It is almost as if the Elder Brother had partially become a Comus; even though we accept the Second Brother's early Miltonic praise of "divine Philosophy . . . musical as is *Apollo's* lute" (ll. 476–478), we must fear that for the moment the musical thought falling so sweetly on his ear is misleading. The Second Brother senses as much, probably, for when noise rings out from the Wood, he does not continue to rely upon his brother's philosophy but cries, with more of prayer than he yet knows (l. 486), "Heav'n keep my sister!" The Elder Brother, still reluctant to confess the seriousness of the trial, retorts (begging at least two questions):

If he be friendly he comes well, if not,
Defense is a good cause, and Heav'n be for us [ll. 488–489].

The "iron stakes" of "old" heroism with which he threatens Comus are as pointless as Odysseus' arms against Scylla; furthermore, the question of *Comus* is never whether a crusader's heaven is favorable to man, but if man, in his inward will, fully aspires to Heaven. Overconfidence and fearful hesitation have made the brothers' debate a standoff because it has not met the central questions. As their sister had feared, they have "engag'd their wand'ring steps too far" (l. 193).

The "hallo" of the Attendant Spirit—who, like Comus, but with a total difference of intention, is in the habit of a shepherd—has elicited a "hallo" of sorts from the brothers, there being in one sense a question who is praying to whom: for the Spirit must act for them only by their own aspiring wish. The Brothers recognize his function as a "good Swain" caring for his sheep but seem to believe his interest is only economic. The Spirit pushes that unworthy question aside. He has come to his "lov'd master's heir and his next joy" (l. 501) because he or his kind has attended Christ in the wilderness. The Elder Brother, still callow in his belief, asks why the Spirit should fear for the Lady. With that, the third debate begins.

The Spirit commands the Brothers to heed the actuality of evil, for in a spiritual sense, at least, chimeras and enchantments and "hell" exist. To think otherwise is to perform not an act of faith but of credulous impiety: such "unbelief is blind" (l. 519). The Brothers as much as the sister, but for almost opposite reasons, are insufficiently knowledgeable about the darkness of this wood. Whereas she wavers toward doubt, they blindly believe, converting belief itself into a species of unbelief. (The issue is not Glanvillian, for Milton would not assert the existence of God by means of that of the devil; instead, the question is of an excess of Protestant human voluntarism, for if the human being can create and save himself, Heaven is needless.) Like the audience, perhaps, the Brothers had expected danger to come in hostile form. They had not known, although the younger Brother half feared, that it would be dazzling and pleasant. Anticipating the several tutors of *Paradise Lost,* the austere Shepherd has to instruct men about the nature of the pleasing serpent, or wolf. That seducer works upon the inviting "sense" of his victim (the trustful "ear" of the Lady, both in her manifesto and in the first debate). Although he and his offers may be chimerical, the seduction away from Being is all the more dangerous and "true."

The demonstration of evil then hastens particularly toward the Lady. All had really been well, that evening, because darkness itself was at first for the Lady "the gray-hooded Ev'n / Like a sad Votarist in Palmer's weed" (ll. 188–189),[18] and for the disguised Spirit a setting for his own "Il Penseroso": he had begun "in a pleasing fit of melancholy, / To meditate [his] rural minstrelsy" (ll. 546–547). The darkness lowers thick and obscure only when the Spirit's psalm is replaced by "barbarous dissonance" (l. 550).

[18] See Tuve, *Images and Themes,* pp. 112–160. The Wood can be a place of holiness and revelation, rather than of riot, much like the landscape of "Il Penseroso."

The only other sound is the sweet prayer of the Lady. Her lone voice in perilous darkness reminds the Spirit of a nightingale, which in turn reminds a classical audience of Philomela.

The younger Brother now stumbles from proper caution into too credulous despair, berating "the confidence" (l. 583) too easily supplied by the Elder Brother. In Milton, these are two familiar sides of one coin—pride. The Elder Brother as a result now recognizes his crumbling position and is led to firmer ground. He places his trust not in the Lady alone but in "that power / Which erring men call Chance" (ll. 587–588), having realized that virtue may be attacked by "unjust force" (l. 590). For a moment more, he follows the truth he has just perceived into a broad vision resembling that of God in *Paradise Lost:*

> . . . that which mischief meant most harm
> Shall in the happy trial prove most glory.
> But evil on itself shall back recoil,
> And mix no more with goodness, when at last
> Gather'd like scum, and settl'd to itself,
> It shall be in eternal restless change
> Self-fed and self-consum'd [ll. 591–597].

He almost voices total divine intention for men and for the earth, including intimations both of a *felix culpa* and of Hell as self-recoiling and self-exterminating dross. However, he relapses from Christian vision into voluntarist heroics, swearing like a Pentheus that he, not God or the tempter's own nature, will "drag [Comus] by the curls to a foul death" (l. 608). The Spirit again has to guide him from that darkness, insisting that not a sword but "other arms and other weapons" (such as those of the Son and the Red Cross Knight) must be taken up against "hellish charms" (ll. 612–613). With that, the debate isolates the only energy that can act finally against Comus.

Externally, the agency described by the Spirit is Homeric—moly, or haemony, like that which protected Odysseus, not against Circe, but against her will to enslave him. (The point will be important later, when the Lady again debates with Comus.) Internally, the agency is seen to be Christian: probably, Christ direct. Certainly it becomes difficult to avoid the suggestion that the "Shepherd Lad / . . . well skill'd / In every virtuous plant and healing herb" (ll. 619–621) who showed the (eternal) Spirit "a small unsightly root" producing a leaf "darkish, and [with] prickles on it," which in another Country bears "a bright golden flow'r" (ll. 629–633), is the redemptive Christ whose "dim," earthly cross and crown of thorns darkly image a heavenly golden flower.[19] The poem has removed trust from an ill to a sure foundation; it now recalls the trust of the Elder Brother in either the heavenly stars or in a mortal Christlike "taper" from a "clay habitation." With its "long levell'd rule of streaming light" it too is a supreme "Cynosure" (l. 342). However, the Spirit, in urging the Brothers into resolute action against Comus, so casts his directions in martial language that the Elder Brother forgets that they must use spiritual "arms and other weapons." He has learned a little, but only a little: he asks Thyrsis to lead, in an exact reversal of the request by the Lady to Comus ("Shepherd lead on"). He can recognize a shepherd, but does not yet perceive the type of the true Shepherd who would give his life for his flock.

Therefore the fourth debate, returning the Lady to direct contest with Comus, must try all that man alone can do. The Lady moves with her forces to enact all that the Elder Brother has too confidently claimed. (In the end, Comus will also enact the emptiness that the Second Brother feared too much.) The nature of the contest is indicated by the setting. Against her will and words [20] are posed the Satanic, sensual "soft Music, Tables spread with all dainties" described in the stage directions, and Comus bearing the glass of a communion not with God but with swine. The setting again seems secret to Comus, allowing full riot of appetites— including the lavish use of her beauty. His first words threaten her

19 Kester Svendsen, *Milton and Science* (Cambridge, Mass., 1956), p. 132: Haemony "blends both the pagan connotations of magical moly and the Christian legend of the Redeemer's blood." Edward S. LeComte, in "New Light on the 'Haemony' Passage in *Comus*" (*PQ*, XXI [1942], 283–298), identifies haemony with the plant called Christ's thorn; Madsen, in "The Idea of Nature," p. 197, contrasts haemony with the "baleful herbs" of Comus; and Joan Klein, in "Some Spenserian Influences on Milton's *Comus*" (*Annuale Mediaevale*, V [1964], 27–47), notes the resemblance of haemony to Marvell's "conscience."

20 Daiches, *Milton*, pp. 67–71: Satanic rhetoric is assigned to Comus, logic to the Christlike Lady.

body with harm—either a kind of death, her "nerves . . . all chain'd up in Alabaster," or (in a vast allusive compliment to himself) inertia after a threat of rape, "as *Daphne* was, / Root-bound, that fled *Apollo*" (ll. 660–662) . His threat to her body is answered from her mind—an answer including the somewhat insulting comment that he is permitted to tempt only "while Heav'n sees good" (l. 665) . (The whole masque suddenly rushes to a center like that of *Paradise Regained:* Heaven has watched all the while, as the first manifesto and the resultant action of the Attendant Spirit have indicated; and Heaven, the ending will insist, has "timely tri'd their youth," making evil the slavish minister of justice.) From that portentous threat, Comus curvets away. For readers of Spenser or "Il Penseroso," his sensual tempta-tion begins to evaporate when he describes his lures, far more accurately than he guesses, as "all the pleasures / That fancy can beget on youthful thoughts" (ll. 668–669) . They are the illusions she "heard" at the outset. However, he conveys her toward such luxurious dreams by references to Helen and her own "dainty limbs." He parodies both the parable of the talents and the Aris-totelian mean, pointing not to proper use but to profligate "spending." The devil quoting Scripture is trapped, however, for the parable alters to that of the prodigal son. All of his doctrine "recoils" when he asks why she should scorn the "unexempt condition / By which all mortal frailty must subsist" (ll. 685–686) . "Mortal frailty" rings away from his question with shocking clarity, recalling the Spirit's original sense of errant man's "frail and Feverish being."

She now sees the Wood with the Spirit's vision. She has been brought not to a dangerous human habitation but to a rather silly palace inhabited by swine. She knows she "fell" because of "credulous innocence," like Eve. She will not be trapped again by her senses, for they have been shocked into perception of spiritual (and consequently of sensory) reality. The senses are not evil, and will not deceive when the spiritual light is maintained. They are pleasures to be "well-govern'd" by a "wise appetite" (l. 705) . The Spirit was partly wrong about Earth. If men choose against the pin-fold, it may be a Ludlow Castle.

Comus, like some of the Lady's critics, mistakes temperance for abstinence and ignorantly berates her for the position that he invented. He falls back again upon the lost argument of profligacy, upon Yeats's mackerel-crowded seas of riotous fertility. He even contrives a Satanic fear of Malthusian strangulation in abundance, if delightful silks, "all-worshipt ore" (l. 719), and the Lady's youthful sexual fires are not consumed feverishly. His remaining arguments use first the already lost ground of the supposed praise of God through abuse of his gift, then a *carpe diem*, then her supposed Eve-like vanity ("It is for homely features to keep home / . . . What need a vermeil-tinctur'd lip for that, / Love-darting eyes, or tresses like the Morn?" [ll. 748–753]). Unhappily for Comus, his final words recoil upon him once more, arguing a position directly contrary to his: there was truly "another meaning in these gifts" (l. 754). Ambiguity undoes him.

The representative Lady answers not so much Comus as the argument, which, like his dressing in shepherd's clothing, is false and must be seen as such. She even uses some of the wit of *Paradise Regained* in the debate. As Jesus at one point recommends that Satan not "obtrude his diligence," so the Lady scoffs at Comus' "Obtruding false rules prankt in reason's garb" (l. 759). She answers the claim that nature must be indulged infinitely by recommending man's care of nature in Eden rather than his postlapsarian gluttony and by urging a broad social diffusion of nature's abundance (a form of charity) rather than greedy individual ravening upon it. In particular, she with the audience recaptures the sense, and perhaps an instant's vision, of the opening stance of the Attendant Spirit: Comus' debased man makes mast of creation, never looking up "to Heav'n amidst his gorgeous feast" (l. 777). Her pun is both witty and judicial. She pairs that judgment with her symbol and enactment of its opposite, "the serious doctrine of Virginity" (l. 787), here associated directly with God: the power of order, control, and chastity is "Sun-clad" (l. 782), like the courts of Jove. But Comus wills not to hear; he has made the choice of "worst."

Ordinarily, the topic of virginity might at this point in our discussion be removed to a footnote, but because in *Comus* the "doctrine" has occasioned great comment, it assumes great importance. If chastity is no longer the central critical problem in the masque, we still may find it necessary to remember what the argument for chastity is and what it is not. First, it is not a personal or doctrinal refusal of sexuality. Milton discards the idea in a famous prose statement of the same period: "celestial songs" will be heard by those "who were not defiled with women, which doubtless means fornication; for marriage must not be called a defilement" ("Apology for Smectymnuus," p. 695) . Insofar as the Lady considers sexuality, she with the author must hold it as a gift of nature to be used properly rather than "crammed." Her general doctrine advocates a temperate mean, not "Sallow Abstinence." The images of union that conclude the poem (Venus and Adonis, Cupid and Psyche) are multiplex in significance but indicate among other things loving harmony or ecstatic union rather than isolation.

Second, even a technical—that is, physical—virginity is correct for the Lady as she is represented on stage. We must risk indelicacy in order to avoid the indelicacy some critics would ask of her. Onstage, she "is" a young girl approaching marriageable age. It would be odd indeed if she were to recommend the license of Cotytto. If it is held that any consideration of the question by Alice Egerton or Milton is coarse, then it must be said that the sermons and parables that they heard and the Shakespeare and Paul that they may have read are coarse. Surely it is a false morality that would allow her to dwell on gluttony but prevent her from considering physical or spiritual "fornication," for that temptation is the center of Comus' attack. He attempts to rape her mind, seducing her to an act of infidelity to her belief, much as in *Paradise Lost* Satan seduces Eve more from God than from Adam. How can she not consider it? Nor is the issue wholly metaphysical. We should not mistake the sexual implications of Comus' speech upon the uses of nature: "Beauty is nature's coin, must not be hoarded, / But must be current. . . . Beauty is nature's brag, and must be shown" (ll. 739–745) . Although he can have no personally villainous designs upon her, any more than Satan has upon Eve, he strongly wants every person to join the herd of Circe. He is not urging her to be a woman, but a heated animal. To some Neoplatonists, his plea obviously would ask that she become not more capable but wholly incapable of love, for her chastity is figured as one among three constituents of Venus and one among three graces.

Third, a poem in either the Christian or classical tradition should be allowed to treat of virginity without rebuke if the Christian can worship a spotless Christ and consider his mother's conception immaculate and if the classicist can treat of such notorious virgins as Athene and Artemis. Fourth, as was noted above, Milton does not assign virginity and its defense only to the Lady, as if she were an earlier Pamela; it is "Sun-clad," a form of divine fidelity "so dear to Heav'n" that Heaven stoops to aid that "unpolluted temple of the mind" with a "thousand liveried Angels." The doctrine is highly reminiscent of that in *Paradise Regained*. That being the case, Comus at once attests its force: "I . . . fear / Her words set off by some superior power," "as when the wrath of *Jove* / Speaks thunder and the chains of *Erebus* / To some of *Saturn's* crew" (ll. 800–805). He thoroughly believes in the power, and dissembles principally to himself when he calls her doctrine "Mere moral babble" (l. 807). Knowing as surely as the Satan of *Paradise Regained*, Book IV, that he has lost the debate, he similarly shifts to a more nearly physical violence in forcing a drink quite the opposite to that of the holy communion upon the Lady.

Readers need not be convinced in the debate merely because Comus is, nor warmed by the Lady's "flame of sacred vehemence" (l. 795). Later eras may well argue that Comus was correct and "the pale Galilean" and Aristotle wrong, but such conviction should not prevent a sympathetic reading of the poem nor encourage the assigning of beliefs to the Lady or to Milton that neither ever held, as her debate with Comus will quickly attest.

Their debate is ended by his violence and by the Brothers' correlative violent attempt at a purely physical deliverance—despite the Spirit's warning that "here thy sword can do thee little stead" (l. 611). The Lady is not so easily delivered from the worldly bondage that has partly imprisoned her reason. It must be remembered that she had doubted as well as trusted even before Comus' attempt upon her and that it remains for her to be freed from her wild Wood to heavenly light. (Those critics who have found her to be negative are in one sense right, for Milton would be the first to agree that on earth she must not merely "see" Faith, Hope, and Chastity but must absorb them so that they are seen in her as well as by her; she must not only contemplate but must also aspire.) Were Comus held to truth, he might free her with "his rod revers't, / And backward mutters of dissevering power" (ll. 816–817).[21] His confession of truth could unmuffle the faint stars. But until the Judgment, at least, it is useless to ask Comus, whatever his sinking inner conviction, to be a redeemer. Instead, in what amounts to a fifth debate, the Spirit turns to a sacrificial fellow being.

"Debate" at such a Raphaelesque level very nearly becomes intuitive prayer and response. It seems to me that in the doctrine of Meliboeus and the figure of Sabrina, the Spirit intimates likenesses, even identification, with God and with Christ (as well as Spenser),[22] just as Comus had quite surely united himself with Satan. Similarly, although the Spirit appears on stage disguised as a shepherd, his real being should not be cloaked from us. He moves into a justification to men of the ways of sacrifice—and therefore, of temptation and even of death. Milton's conception of Sabrina, like his treatment of virginity, has needlessly afflicted many critics. Her significance only begins with the nod to the nearby Severn River. She is a form of the seeming death of the innocent mortal into the hope of resurrection and, as such, is the sister of Lycidas, who also becomes the genius of a shore. If we understand that Lycidas' immortality rests partly upon his temporal enduring example and partly upon eternal Christian promise, we can accept Sabrina with him. But she represents more. Like Orpheus, she has suffered not merely death but terrible slaughter: a "Virgin pure" (like the Lady she may save), she was savagely drowned by her "enraged stepdam *Guendolen*" (l. 830). So far, the conditions roughly parallel those of the Lady's encounter with Comus. But the innocent Sabrina came to an actual death and transformation: Nymphs "Held up their pearled

[21] Douglas Bush, in *John Milton* (New York, 1964), p. 51, discusses Sandys' use of Circe's rod. If it moves from right to left, it enchants; if it is moved from left to right, it restores.

[22] Joan Klein, in "Some Spenserian Influences," p. 31, draws the connection between Meliboeus and Spenser; it is Spenser, then, who directs the Miltonic Thyrsis "to Sabrina."

wrists" like receiving angels and took her to "aged *Nereus'* Hall," where, after baptismal cleansing from "nectar'd lavers," she underwent "quick immortal change" (ll. 834–841). She has become a representative of the Healer, acting against the ills "the shrewd meddling Elf delights to make" (l. 846). Neoplatonically, she, like reason, acts to free the lower soul when it is imprisoned by the determinism of the senses. As a healer, Sabrina, anticipating the Cupid-Psyche myth, removes the Lady from mere passive fidelity to God by showing her how to aspire actively. All shepherds praise Sabrina because, "as the old Swain said, she can unlock / The clasping charm and thaw the numbing spell" (ll. 852–853). Although now immortal, she will help a mortal "such as . . . herself" (l. 856). The severities of temptation and of mortality undergo "immortal change" into sacrifice and resurrection, allowing an Orpheus or a Sabrina to act as Savior, and Milton to deal, if only very distantly, with questions of death and with divine, rather than personal, redemption. If it is objected that Milton removes the matter of the poem too far into myth and too greatly alters the Redeemer into feminine Sabrina (and, in her temptation, into the Lady), it can be answered that his actors and the masque form dictated such a removal. Furthermore, persistent movement to distancing analogy and myth perhaps allowed him to maintain the mostly unaffecting world of his "L'Allegro" and "Il Penseroso." Be that as it may, the "good news" of Sabrina causes her to be invoked as a savior: "Listen and *save*" (l. 866— italics added). For the first time since the Spirit's initial heavenly proclamation, dance and song (rather than isolation, isolating rout, and discord) return: by "the Songs of *Sirens* sweet. . . . By all the *Nymphs* that nightly dance . . . , Rise, rise. . . . Listen and save" (ll. 878–889).

Sabrina all but identifies her "home" with Heaven, "Thick set with Agate and the azurn sheen / Of Turquoise blue and Em'rald green" (ll. 893–894). As spirit, she does not so much rise—except from death—as "stoop" to the Lady, moving like the Genius in "Arcades": "O'er the Cowslip's Velvet head, / That bends not as I tread" (ll. 898–899). She proceeds to a form of re-enactment of her death by water, a purifying baptismal anointment of the frozen lady, freeing her much as Spenser's and Fletcher's Amorets are freed.[23]

The "debate" has produced a conclusion: the baptismal act. Perhaps its empowering doctrine ("now I bethink me," says the Spirit, in beginning the invocation to Sabrina) can help man to achieve virtue when he reaches the limit of his own powers. The Spirit therefore lauds Sabrina (ll. 924–929), uniting a sense of the actual Severn ("thy brimmed waves") and of sacrificial immortal "Genius" ("Summer drouth or singed air / Never scorch thy tresses fair"). Both the characters and the audience are given an impressive vision past the actual into that which it "means" ("a beam on th' outward shape" [l. 460]); with sure indications that wandering, confusion, dialectic, and darkness have finally been resolved by a return to the stance of the original worshipful dances and song, all debates end.

"Your Father's Residence": The renewed circle

The debates—questions, temptations, justifications—end, but not the poem. It marks a return toward the stance of "our first

[23] Northrop Frye, in *The Return of Eden* (Toronto, 1965), p. 125, notes that the argument of Despair (which is somewhat like the immobility of the Lady) is that sin is inevitable, conducing to "indolence and passivity." Ernest S. Gohn, in "The Christian Ethic of *Paradise Lost* and *Samson Agonistes*" (*Studia neophilologica*, XXXIV [1962], 267), describes a similar immobility as demanding re-establishment of order and faith in order to achieve freedom of mind. John Arthos, in "Milton's Sabrina, Virgil and Porphyry," (*Anglia*, LXXIX [1962], 211), considers the freeing of the Lady to be a translation from her enchanted involvement "with the world of matter . . . [from] forgetfulness." Perhaps Spenser's Fradubio should also be called to witness. When the Red Cross Knight meets the rooted, doubt-immobilized Fradubio, this is part of their exchange:

> But how long time, said then the Elfin knight,
> Are you in this misformed house to dwell?
> We may not chaunge (quoth he) this evil plight
> Till we be bathed in a liuing well;
> That is the terme prescribed by the spell.

For a comparison of the bondage of the Lady with that of Adonis in *La catena d'Adone*, see Gretchen L. Finney's *Musical Backgrounds for English Literature: 1580–1650* (New Brunswick, N.J., 1962), pp. 175–194.

Home." In token of their unreality, the scenes of the wild Wood and Comus' castle are "changed" into Ludlow. That which has been intimated throughout is now made unmistakably clear: actor and person, the Lady and Alice Egerton, are one; the home of the human father and divine Father are one; *"Jove's* Court" or the wild Wood is visible in whatever one chooses, and Ludlow, although it properly combines the images of parental and Parental homes, can be the wild Wood or the haunt of Comus, if that is what one blindly chooses and sees there. Similarly, the country dancers at the end intimate or reflect the opening dance of the "inspher'd stars" but, if one sees only a wild Wood, can intimate the rout of Comus. Indeed, all error, threat, overconfidence, and seeming opposition are now revealed to be one, not several, and all will ultimately serve God's (never Comus') design:

> Heav'n hath timely tri'd their youth,
> Their faith, their patience, and their truth,
> And sent them here through hard assays
> With a crown of deathless Praise,
>   To triumph in victorious dance
> O'er sensual Folly and Intemperance [ll. 970–975].

Milton will later be less certain that all can be so easily justified, that God's design and Satan's machinations are so easily made symphonic, and that the triumph can be so painless or so swift. But in *Comus,* he triumphantly ends the revels, not with a sense that actors and stage and audience are such stuff as dreams are made of, but instead that they have been a lens for reality—to which the Spirit now fully returns the audience, even as the characters have been returned to "their Father's state" (l. 35).

Describing the full spiritual circuit, we can now resume the original stance before Jove's Court, having seen the pinfold Earth and the steps by which men may "aspire" from the one to the other. The way is attended with increasingly joyous circles, ever more perfect unions. Reflecting the joyous dance at Ludlow Castle, the graces and hours dance in "eternal Summer" (l. 988). If mortal ears "be true," they can now receive extensions from "the sage / And serious doctrine of Virginity" (ll. 786–787). Here generative Adonis heals his grievous wound by the side of waiting

Venus. Above, in a more rare or purified sphere, circle Cupid and Psyche. In the ascent from lower to higher forms of love, we have risen toward the harmony of cosmic mind and soul, or of Christ and the church. Whatever their implications, the increasingly spiritual unions speak decisively against any doctrine of isolation or refusal. The Lady's future lies in such a union, in proper use of the gifts divinely given and divinely guaranteed, even as Psyche's future will lead her to become, in due time, the "eternal Bride" (l. 1008) of Love and the mother of celebrant Youth and Joy—the youth and joy formerly misclaimed for his crew by Comus.

As the poem comes to a close, having performed a great dance led by the Attendant Spirit who had called, "Mortals . . . follow me" (l. 1018), the Spirit prepares for us a stance looking even higher than that of the beginning. We gaze above the "Sphery chime" of the insphered stars and above Cupid and Psyche in their "spangled sheen," to the source of light. Mortals can learn from virtue how to climb, how with "due steps" to aspire to Heaven. The final line seems to indicate a sudden, almost overwhelmingly gracious alteration of stance: exalted Heaven would stoop to aid any one struggling man in the pinfold Earth we supposed we had left. But of course, the poem has insisted throughout that Heaven is "visible" wherever eyes will see it; and the glory of Heaven is perhaps best demonstrated in its willingness to "stoop," as it did in the agent of salvation—Sabrina (or the Son). The seeming reversal of stance is not literal, however, much as the Spirit's first descent from Jove's court was not strictly a true one. The Spirit, the Lady, her Brothers, and the audience are almost led to say of Ludlow what Mephistopheles, from the pit of an opposite choice, said of the world: "Why this is Heaven, nor am I out of it"—except by choice. In Comus and in Paradise Lost, God desires the correction even of that choice. Human will and divine converge: both are hopeful that a human paradise, the shadow of Heaven, will be maintained.

[3] "With Eager Thought Warbling His Doric Lay"

Stance Achieved in "Lycidas"

In the Ludlow masque, the aspiring human being was aided by the rising Sabrina and the descending Attendant Spirit into freedom from his lateral wild wood and immobility. By means of that aid and his own assay, he in effect climbed vertically "Higher than the Sphery chime" to attain the stance of the Attendant Spirit. In "Lycidas," the apparent distance between the stances of earth and Heaven is increased almost beyond measure. Although the harmonies that unite Heaven with earth are faintly recorded in the initial references to immortal poetry, the speaker for a time turns his back upon them. Although the Muses may speak through him, the words they voice and the stance he takes indicate utter isolation. In this desolate landscape, men are no longer granted even the dubious comfort of the pinfold and the care of Comus. Each is essentially alone before the oceans of eternity. No longer is it possible for the poet to lend his harmonious voice to those of his fellow men and fellow creatures in marveling praise of Being. All that he may do, along with the memorial flowers and the angels helpless in their Heaven, is to offer an epitaph for the man stricken by death, whose name is legion: even his own name is to be written in the whelming tide, not in a book of life. Only a sorrowful and momentary comfort can be taken in the memory of a different stance, that of the pastoral setting and the pastoral flock, for like Eden all of the pastoral landscape seems swept away in the obliterating flood.

This painful stance brings with it the necessity of an agon in which another stance can be reached, lest despair become master of men. The poet who in the Nativity Ode had run almost anonymously with the audience to the epiphany in Bethlehem now assumes the more grim representative voice and stance of men in their knowledge of the world's corruptness and the body's death. The poet's talent of voice and verse, which confers upon him that representative function and supplies him with the broadly representative possibilities of pastoral and elegy, is no longer a gift to be joyfully received and used, for it now must register, harshly and paradoxically, the anticreative, God-defying, life-choking welter of mortality. The conditions for his use of verse and voice are intolerable, as in the agon they are revealed to be untrue. On this occasion, however, no Sabrina can rise to the typical human being's aid, nor does an Attendant Spirit directly stoop to him. Although three trumpet calls of doctrine are remembered and used by him in his agon, no doctrine is supplied him from without. Providence seems a more distant guide than it is to Adam and Eve at the close of *Paradise Lost*. This pastoral poet must forge from his total pastoral material the eternal life and peace that he promises to men even though their lives may be unrewarding and their shrouded bodies "lost." To do so, he records representatively from and in his own consciousness all the "eager thought" that in his agon achieves the stance of Heaven. In large measure, that agon answers the question: Who speaks in the poem? He does, and he could identify all the poem preceding the final eight lines as self-quotation, as rehearsal of his triumphant struggle— including his recaptured voicing of the doctrines of Apollo, Peter, and Michael.

Perhaps Milton as author thought that the phrase "eager thought" (l. 189) would prevent some of the murmurs of misunderstanding that the poem has suffered. He may have believed that the descriptive adjective and the definitive substantive would mark both the process and the essence of the poem. Its mood is to be agonically thoughtful, thought is to be its subject, and mood and subject will be conveyed in language simple, sensuous, and passionate. By means of affective stances and expression the speaker will supply both thought and its passionate experience.

The reader in turn must share the method, procedure, and purpose of the poem. He will then find in the speaker not only a lone elegist but also an "I" who speaks for man and God as firmly as a Jeremiah—or, in the poem, as Phoebus, Peter, and Michael. The speaker will be not only a shepherd mourning the loss of a peer but also the "faithful Herdman" typically practicing his art and the proper care of a flock. In the structure of the poem, he will be not only the unwilling and stricken man crying out, *"Lycidas* is dead" (l. 8), but also the triumphant apocalyptic voice assuring all men that *"Lycidas* is not dead" (l. 166). The thought of both audience and author will move from the enforced "melodious tear" to free, triumphant, eager singing. In its entirety, "Lycidas" will mark not only the dark agony of mortal loss but also the light-flooded celebration of immortal life, almost duplicating the methektic achievement of the Twenty-third Psalm (which Milton probably had in mind as he wrote "Lycidas").

The poem takes three stances. Movement from one to another produces the dynamic structure of the poem as well as the dialectical synthesis of its thought. In their disposition, they closely resemble the stances of *Paradise Lost* and would be reminiscent of *Comus* if the masque had permitted descent into the direct experience of earth's pinfold rather than only into Comus' argument for it. The pastoral sections of "Lycidas" present the stance of an earthly Eden, now seemingly lost except to recollection; across much of the poem, that feeling is reinforced by the use of the past tense. The sections of lamentation and protest descend to a stance of total loss, the irrecoverable end or corruption of being; across the first half of the poem, the present tense insists that this is the enduring, continuing stance for all human affairs. The consolatory sections take stances in immortality, in which tense escapes the "false surmise" of any fixed time but seems to offer thereby no help or comfort to the present. Eventually, the stances will refuse to admit separation into three settings, times, and images, just as the dialectic insists that parts or partialities be drawn into a reconciling third form. The two partial or incomplete stances will come to be seen within that which is ultimately true and real. Seemingly disparate positions will become interrelated and united, partly because Milton's universe is always one when seen through God's whole insight rather than man's limited vision, partly because Hegelian or Socratic "eager thought" has assayed incomplete propositions and, without discarding them, has transcended them. The stance of immortality finally compels the other two so absolutely that they are "answered" in its unifying consolation and reconciliation.

In considering the stances of the poem, this discussion departs slightly from the classic description of "Lycidas'" structure—not from disagreement but for the easier discussion of the poem in its series of stances. It supposes a prelude, three related movements in each of which all three stances are taken, and a postlude. The prelude opposes immortal, God-serving poetry to mortal loss of the poet-priest. Subsequently, each of the three interior movements recalls Eden, falls to the conviction of its loss (made doubly painful by remembrance of the Eden that was, but which now "never must return"), and then, from the perspective of eternity, judges and corrects errors of time and value that must be present in the partial stances.

Stances and dialectic are reinforced by complementary images. The stance of Eden is supplied flowers that may fade, streams that may run dry, and shepherds who can themselves be lost. The opposite stance is a tumult of overwhelming waves and "parching" winds, afflicted with images of drowning, of human sacrifice, and of death's ultimate terror to men, all of whom must in some way "wander in that perilous flood" (l. 185). The stance with immortality transforms dying flowers into the evergreen plants symbolic of both eternal life and poetry, the horrors of the deep into never-failing baptismal still waters, and the isolative terror of death into immortal "blest Kingdoms meek of joy and love" (l. 177). In every case, the stance of immortality accepts the pathetic or terrible image from the partial stance or the incomplete thesis, converting its seeming form in earth's shadow into its true being in Heaven's reality.

The pure ethereal and immortal heavenly stance with poetry and faith, the pathetic vernal joy of a vulnerable pastoral Eden, and the collapse into choking water, chaos, and death—these stances indicate the matter of the poem, but not the manner in which unity is achieved. "Eager thought" must work within them in an increasing completeness of vision and countervision. It must ask with *Paradise Lost* that celestial light

> Shine inward, and the mind through all her powers
> Irradiate, there plant eyes, all mist from thence
> Purge and disperse [*Paradise Lost*, III, 52–54].

Then the parts will reveal not only their proper partial proportions but also their contribution within the absolute. If the "swain" at the beginning could believe that poetry, vital and powerful in the stance of heaven, is truly immortal, his bitterness could drop away. If Camus could see that the flower inscribed *ai, ai* in woe also preserved Hyacinth against direct mortal loss, he would know that an emblem of his dearest pledge revisited Cambridge each spring. If shepherds could possess the vision of the redemptive dolphin rather than that of the destructive Leviathan, they would much sooner cease to weep. But these realizations must be wrought. The poem is the struggle to achieve and maintain the empowering stance for such assurance.

"Ivy Never Sere": Immortal poetry and mortal grief in the prelude (lines 1–24)

Not the least of the pathetic and kinetic ironies of "Lycidas" is that immortality, which should lend relief from the pangs of mortality, at first leads instead into despair.[1] Whereas in *Comus* the stance before Jove's court was all light and musical harmony, here it becomes a new kind of torment to the bereaved typic speaker. His initial gesture is graphic: he as poet approaches the emblematic evergreen symbols of immortality, poetry, and victory, only to turn away in grieving protest against the mortal occasion for this immediate poem. It is as if laurel could now serve

---

[1] D. C. Allen, in *The Harmonious Vision* (Baltimore, 1954), p. 43, discusses the rhetorical forms "that enabled the man of letters to convert the works and days of his fellows into myths like those of the gods." See also B. Rajan, "The Shattering of the Leaves," *SP*, LXIV (1967), 51–64, and O. B. Hardison, Jr., *The Enduring Monument: A Study of the Idea of Praise in Renaissance Literary Theory and Practice* (Chapel Hill, N.C. 1962), p. 113. The poem that begins in protest at mortality becomes the instrument for enacting immortality.

only ironically—in the "Laureate Hearse" (l. 151) of Lycidas.
Yet a second time he comes, this time to invoke the Muses to begin
the poem he has promised as "meed" (l. 14)—but again turns
away unrecompensed as he considers that his death, also, is implicit in the death of Lycidas. What is more, he foresees a fantastic
chain of dying and grieving poets, for as he now mourns Lycidas,
so will a kindred mortal "Muse" soon bid peace to his own sable
shroud. The final verse paragraph of the prelude ends with a faint
savor of remembered Eden, but it is only another reminder that
all this congregation of poets seem equal only in fate, for mortality permits them no renown. If immortal poetry is nothing more
than the stuff of epitaphs that record savage mortality, its essence
and art either are operatively "untrue," or stand meaninglessly or
in cryptic irony before the human experience of human loss. The
opening imagery of the poem also insists that the serene and
Olympian stance of immortality must seem less potent and therefore less real than the oceanic tempests of loss. The speaker finds
torment in either the mystifying relationship or the terrible lack
of relationship between the two stances; and the invocation to the
Muses to "begin" is also a concealed imperative to his own motive
"eager thought." As it is, poetry either is denied by the early
mortality of poets, or its immortality serves only to record their
negating human mortality. To the dedicated poet either position
is unbearable.

We have long since agreed that "Lycidas" is not primarily
about Edward King or John Milton, except as they serve specific
roles as poets and typic roles as poet-priests. On the other hand, it
is somewhat too special in its subject to be about everyman in
quite the way of the Twenty-third Psalm. It is concerned closely
with divine song and the mortal singer. The issue is not narrowly
professional, of course. Milton holds the poet "sacred" both by
classical definition and by Christian analogy. As he had written to
his father:

You should not despise the poet's task, divine song, which . . . is the
unrivalled glory of the heaven-born human mind. . . . When we
return to our native Olympus and the everlasting ages of immutable
eternity are established, we shall walk . . . through the temples of the
skies and . . . sing sweet songs to which the stars shall echo. . . . You

lead me . . . beside the Aonian stream, and you permit me to walk there by Phoebus' side, his blessed companion. . . . Therefore, however humble . . . , I shall sit with the ivy and laurel of a victor ["Ad Patrem," pp. 83–85].

Neither the light tone nor the Hellenic vehicle of the statement should blind us to the seriousness of the definition. "Lycidas," which fears the loss of divine song, is a noble token of Milton's dedication to it. To lose poetry would be to lose one manifestation of the all-creating Word or of Phoebus, along with the great reflective song on earth that should echo or join in Heaven's harmonies.

The major stance of the prelude, then, is before the ancient altar of poetry, "still green with bays" to Alexander Pope. Here divine song originates. Its evergreen emblems of both immortality and poetry—laurels, myrtle, and ivy, "never sere"—oppose mortality's parching winds and certain loss; the laurels of victory also oppose any tattered flowerets of defeat. Vocal muses, close to the deathless Aonian waters, here serve Jove, who in Milton always intimates Jehovah. Those waters are more than Hellenic or even Edenic, for later they will receive the character of Heaven's still waters. The poet is not new to this stance; *yet once more* (for Milton himself, following an encounter in his twenty-third year that evoked a famous sonnet?) he approaches the area of his desiring, although his words suggest that the continuing experience is altogether one of unripeness and constraint.[2] Nor is he making a perfunctory plea for inspiration, but for something akin to doctrinal collaboration:

> Begin then, Sisters of the sacred well,
> That from beneath the seat of *Jove* doth spring,
> Begin, and somewhat loudly sweep the string [ll. 15–17].

In its subject, the poem already has transcended the Aonian mount of pre-Christian elegy. These immortal voices, who with the speaker also "compose" the poem and cause it to be universal and timeless, are truly, if covertly, related to Urania; and she, unlike Calliope, will not fail (*Paradise Lost*, VII, 38). The stream

---

[2] David Daiches, in *Milton* (London, 1957), p. 77, notes that the seasons bring intimations of hope as well as of painful harvest.

is like *"Siloa's* Brook that flow'd / Fast by the Oracle of God" (*Paradise Lost,* I, 11–12). Figuratively, the approaching uncertain singer might even now hear with Lycidas "all the Saints above . . . / That sing, and singing in their glory move" (ll. 178–180). At the close of the poem he will have heard the "unexpressive nuptial song" of ultimate verse and voice. He then will accept his *"Doric* lay" (l. 189) as an undiscording response to Heaven's symphony. Statements (rather than mere intimations) of immortality will be seen to have stood like adamant all across the poem. Above all, the forlorn shepherd will know that the Lord has been his Shepherd throughout—even in the shadows of death. But before the realities and shadows can be plainly perceived, the ears and eyes of the speaker (and of the receptive audience) must be purged.

Despite his suppliant stance, the speaker cannot maintain his stand before the altar of poetry. He is torn from it to either savage protest or leaden despair. In shocking contrast to that immortal poetry to which he appealed, he seems vulnerable, himself weltering in the tempests of change. It is he who is compelled to disturb the season, shattering at least the evergreen leaves of his own poetry before the "mellowing year" (l. 5). The leaves come to seem at best funereal, like a dying wreath. In that way he too is a principle of destruction, not of life. Although his song already begins to partake of immortality—if he does not sing, he or the poet's meed will "surely die," but if he and the Muses sing, the poetry cannot die—his initial human impulse is one of "denial vain, and coy excuse" (l. 18): he is forced to this place not for joyous expression of life but by the terrible, resisted command of death. Elegiac poetry—the only form of expression that seems to remain possible in this compulsively destructive lateral world—must of necessity be damaging, "harsh and crude" (l. 3). Like the stroke of death to the poet of *Paradise Lost,* expression of loss must be bitter and unwilling. Even if the stance remains before the altar of immortality, the speaker's attention is altogether compelled by oceanic mortality, where the dead poet is either hurled by the whelming tide or welters to parching wind. The speaker's own sable shroud is involved in the same loss. So is every other person's, for mortal life seems only a "perilous," obliterating flood. There has been no comfort in the stance of immortality. Its fair promises only add torment to the conviction of loss.

The direct sense of loss is both painful and ironically hopeful, for many of the terms intimate their opposites. The lament, whatever its connections with immortal elegiac verse, plunges to the fear and terror arising from awareness of mortality. The distancing traditional apology is shattered by oxymoron and paradox: "Sad occasion dear," "melodious tear" (ll. 6, 14). The specific poem may be "dear" to immortality yet mortally sad; even the word "dear" shares the meanings "of great value" and "of great cost to the speaker." Similarly, the elegy that may be "melodious" within immortal verse occasions a real tear from the poet, as sternly actual as real death is rendingly inartistic. However, a current of irony also runs against the stance of mortality. When lament says, *"Lycidas is dead, dead ere his prime, / Young Lycidas, and hath not left his peer"* (ll. 8–9), we may half suspect irony of a Christian-comic vein: the seeming death truly precedes the "prime" life of Heaven, and Lycidas truly will not have left his peer, the once woeful shepherd who at the close will weep no more, because *"Lycidas* [his] sorrow is not dead." Even the enforced small "meed" of a melodious tear will be answered by Heaven's vast recompense; then Lycidas will no longer welter on the perilous ocean but be a savior from it. Nevertheless, none of these shadowy intimations and future realizations aid the speaker during the prelude. Somewhat like Samson, he assumes that there can be no prevention of loss nor salvage from it, nor any help to man from immortal poetry and faith. Yet he cannot avoid imploring aid and expression from the immortality which seems impossible or irrelevant to man, if only in order to express that which always chokes helpless man's voice in death.

In this dilemma wherein sacred, life-asserting poetry and destructive, death-assuring mortality seem to wrench the poet with intolerable ironies, there appear other faint possibilities of reconciliation. Not only the close of the prelude but also its general pastoral conventions envision Edenic earthly poetry in which even death can be transmuted into serene verse. Also, the lament that looks to the death of poets also nearly envisions the continuity of singers and divine song. These intimations will be "retrieved" (in

Whitman's sense) as the poem proceeds, allowing the poetic realization to swell into "eager thought."

First, the apparently collapsed Eden of Lycidas' life, as well as
the seemingly revoked possibility of present joyous earthly song,
is offered faint hope of restoration by the mode of pastoral. In
the prelude, pastoral's direct effects are limited to the closing
couplet. Pastoral indicates the possibility that the stance of Eden,
of human life rather than of death on earth, can be continued in
the present, offering not only comfort but encouragement. The
hope appears in surroundings that are sufficiently inauspicious,
however:

> So may some gentle Muse
> With lucky words favor my destin'd Urn,
> And as he passes turn,
> And bid fair peace be to my sable shroud.
> For we were nurst upon the self-same hill,
> Fed the same flock, by fountain, shade, and rill [ll. 19–24].

Although the setting is referred to in the past tense and seems
closed except to memory, it can supply metaphors for unending
faith. The immortal seat and sacred well of Jove, as well as the
groves and streams of Heaven, resemble the earthly "fountain,
shade, and rill." More to the immediate point, the pastoral elegy
as a form within a powerful tradition can lift some of the overpowering sense of mortality into the clear, tragic imitation of such
a sense. Even the traditional name, "Lycidas," suggests such an
artistic transcendence into the poetic tradition, and the traditional gestures all confirm the possibility of achieving artistic
distance from direct loss. The poet already has received the beginning of consolation from the genre of consolation, and intimations of immortality from a long human tradition that has provided
enactments of immortality. Pastoral really should not so have
vexed Dr. Johnson, for it offered the poet one known method
with which to avoid numbering the streaks of the tulip or falling
into the isolated particular grief of those born only yesterday. In
"Lycidas," pastoral makes available multiple contacts with consolatory immortality, even though the speaker does not yet perceive
them or their power.

Finally, if mortality seems utterly to oppose immortal poetry in the prelude, the obverse also is strongly, if less openly, true (and not merely because of definition). The year *will* bring the speaker to noteworthy accomplishment. His harsh fingers *do* also "sweep the string" (l. 17). Even a dead poet *does* receive some meed, some "lucky words" (l. 20). Both Lycidas and the speaker, associated by the sense of loss with immediate watery bier or threatening sable shroud, are nevertheless gathered by their own practice and by both the present and all future elegies into the everlasting stance of poetry:

> . . . he knew
> Himself to sing, and build the lofty rhyme.
> He must not float upon his wat'ry bier
>
> . . . . .
>
> Without the meed of some melodious tear.
>
> . . . . .
>
> So may some gentle Muse
> With lucky words favour my destin'd Urn,
>
> . . . . .
>
> And bid fair peace be to my sable shroud [ll. 10–22].

"Lucky" words are prophetic of the "eager" thought that will be recognized later, even though here the speaker barely touches that hope before plunging again to a vision of his own "destin'd Urn," a burial device like that of the "fatal . . . Bark" (l. 100) of Lycidas. Above all, the poem (as we have seen) derives in part from the immortal sisters of the sacred well, who speak through the merely mortal poet. Invocation to poetry causes even the outcry of mortality and the "denial vain" associated with its poetic expression to change subtly, to abandon part of the conviction of irremediable threat to poets and poetry.

However, in the poem those realizations remain to be achieved. The prelude closes upon an Edenic memory that seems to promise not comfort but final loss. The association of Lycidas and the speaker in a past Eden forces the same association in present death. The last lines seem to establish an earthly setting upon the "self-same hill" (l. 23) of the lost Eden. It is as if a lone man could revisit Eden after the obliterating flood. Loss seems to have been extended not only to him but to Paradise itself.

"In Heav'n Expect Thy Meed": The judgment of Phoebus (lines 25–84)

Despite its seeming despair, the prelude had promised the meed of elegy, a melodious tear, to the fallen Lycidas. The first movement supplies it but leads by direct progression to the infinitely more palliative "meed" (*misthos*—wages, recompense) promised by Phoebus, god of poetry, father of Orpheus and the dolphin-saved Icadius, and himself a model of day-star life. By all the premises of the poem, that stance with immortal poetry—and, increasingly, with immortal, "true" judgment of all being and all men's actions—was certain to be accomplished. Past readers who considered the answer of Phoebus trivial reckoned too little with the agon of reaching it. Although it is not final, it is nevertheless a consoling momentary vision of the absolute, a temporary possession of the stance of immortality. Phoebus by no means disappears from the poem. He is intimated again both in the day-star and in Delphic relationship to the redemptive dolphins (l. 164). He is a guarantor that poetry shall not die.

The movement opens upon the diffident stance in remembered Eden, where human society once was complete. The contrast with the present lonely scene is fixed by the repeated note that the two poets, "nurst upon the self-same hill," were then "Together . . . both together" (ll. 23, 25, 27). They then watched the day-star rise and set with the untried assurance of Eden. (By the close of the poem, the sun's symbolic guarantee will have been assayed and a shepherd's day—that of the poem—will have renewed the seemingly lost pastoral days.) Similarly, they practiced the Herdman's art gaily and confidently alongside earth's Edenic "groves, and . . . streams" (l. 174). Their receptive sheep [3] were then responsibly fed and folded. This innocent Theocritan and Davidian world mirrored Heaven—especially in the shepherd's unconscious, serene acceptance of the world as everlasting, changeless. Even the choirs of "Saints . . . and sweet Societies" (ll. 178, 179) later envisioned for Lycidas in Heaven were here present in natural form; earthly songs joined others like themselves in "Socie-

[3] Michael Lloyd, "The Two Worlds of 'Lycidas,'" *EIC*, XI (1961), 396: "So in Christ meet the two conditions of the Herdman's own resurrection: his death as lamb and his feeding or prophetic function as shepherd."

ties," and an earthly judge "lov'd to hear [their] song" (l. 36). At the close of the poem, all these effects will be regained by being transcendentally magnified, Damoetas' earthly judgment giving into God's heavenly approval, but now they are no sooner presented to our recollective stance than like dying sparks they are obliterated by oceanic tides of loss. Unlike Peter's address to the young swain, who is quietly present at the judgment in the second movement, the living shepherd's address to Lycidas now speaks only into absence ("O the heavy change, now thou art gone" [l. 37]). The Edenic circle is ruthlessly broken. The stance of loss is set with shards and futile fragments on every side: in the speaker, abandonment of his care and flock, even as his "ear" has been abandoned by Lycidas; in nature, the canker-stricken rose, frost-frozen flowers, and needy flocks decimated by the perhaps Satanic taintworm; among men, the choking death of Lycidas, the terrible watery end of the "gory visage" (l. 62) of Orpheus, and the similarly butchering end of human life wrought by Atropos (now become a "blind *Fury*" [l. 75]) with her severing shears; in the heavens, the eclipse of the day-star and the concomitant drowning of the frail "bark" of human life; in art and religion, auditors served not by Christian poets and sermons but only by the discordant pipings of "blind mouths" (l. 119), blankly lubricious poems, and false doctrine; and most generally, all the sad memorial "Bells and Flowrets" that now purple the ground in symbol and token of Lycidas, who in this stance is also the "rathe Primrose that forsaken dies" (ll. 135, 142) —almost no sooner blown than blasted. The pastoral landscape, including its gentle reciprocal affection between man and nature, slides catastrophically downward into the ocean of helplessness, or death.

After the sense of mortal suffocation passes, returning the stance to that of "sere" mortality in the loneliness of the present, we occupy the "self-same hill" of Eden, now defaced and obliterated after a Flood. Nothing in the pastoral landscape was of avail. Nature's helplessness before mortality includes her inability to aid poetry and the poet. No longer can she respond to Lycidas' own responsive "soft lays" (l. 44). Like Calliope with the archetypal poet Orpheus, she was helpless to prevent the death of "her own enchanting Son"; as at swift Hebrus, so at the companion stormy Hebrides (ll. 63, 156). At best, like the bereaved speaker she can only lament, for loss of Eden seems to include loss of its poetic being. Conventional elegiac appeals to pastoral deities are overwhelmed and ended by despairing lamentation resembling that for the lost priest in the following section. The supposedly saving pastoral nymphs are gone, especially from the relevant British landscape. Like the lost setting of Cambridge itself, nature and motherland would have been helpless before reality: "Had ye been there . . . what could that have done?" (l. 57). Although his rueful recognition—"Ay me, I fondly dream" (l. 56)—in part rebukes the shepherd's several despairing surmises as he gropes toward eager thought, the admission directly abandons any hope of "natural providence." Therefore from the stance of individual hopeless loss arises a general protesting lament for lost poetry and priesthood:

> Alas! What boots it with uncessant care
> To tend the homely slighted Shepherd's trade,
> And strictly meditate the thankless Muse? [ll. 64–66].

Loss leads the speaker to turn away from the Muse, as he had in the prelude, in despair of its preventing or assuaging death and loss. His grief must lead him to call priesthood and poetry thankless, empty of recompense. The poem's stances make his protest almost inevitable, for along with Lycidas and Orpheus the Edenic possibility had seemed to fall. What is more, all such falls appear to reveal complicitous human wills: a representative hideous rout had slain the representative poet-priest, Orpheus.[4] Orpheus, too, seems doomed to a poet's destined urn. The Fate of death joined by the blind Fury of earthly corruption combines Orpheus' execution and the stroke of the abhorred shears. Therefore the question of the loss of poetry, not only from death but also from the world's misuse and misjudgment, arises painfully, much as it will arise for the priesthood in St. Peter's section, leading now to the protest that Fame, the meed of the poet, necessarily will also be lost. With the loss of due fame fall justice and judgment.

In response, the poem now retrieves its initial stance—that of immortal faith and poetry anticipating, looming above, the troubled human suppliant. Through the agency of Apollo the healer,

[4] Allen, in *The Harmonious Vision*, p. 63, associates Orpheus with Christ. I am indebted to Mrs. Margaret Iliff for the specific associations of "laurel" with "Laureate Hearse," and of Hebrus with Hebrides.

who thrillingly touches the mortal speaker's "ear" that had been attending only the loss of Lycidas' voice, we return to the "seat of Jove" (l. 16), to learn that true fame appears only in that stance, where "all-judging *Jove*" (l. 82) within eternity will return proper wages for the "homely slighted Shepherd's trade" (l. 65), in whatever temporal Eden it was practiced. We should not fail to remember this guarantee, for the conclusion of "Lycidas" supplies the promised reward: "There entertain him all the Saints above" (l. 178) —in Heaven, where Lycidas hears and joins the "unexpressive nuptial Song" (l. 176), even as the present speech is bearing restored harmonies within the divine order. An ocean of death remains to be crossed before the poem attains that realization. Milton is aware that the melodious singer who transcends reality must also be its victim. However, if Calliope is helpless, Delphic Phoebus can "waft" the hapless youth to immortality. Orpheus can be recalled later in the resurrection assigned Lycidas, because the Thracian poet also mystically triumphed over water; and at that point, both will be joined by "him that walk'd the waves" (l. 173). When poet and lament are fully seen from the stance of Heaven, reconciliation will occur. Not only fame but poetic being itself may be "no plant that grows on mortal soil" (l. 78). The seeming mortal extinction of the "sudden blaze" (l. 74) of poetic fame is denied by Apollo,[5] who thereby serves to unite the pastoral daylight of the two poets with the day-star who eternally "flames in the forehead of the morning sky" (l. 171). The return to the heavenly stance has allowed us a moment's eternally clear vision of Helicon, redemptive Phoebus, and the seat of Jove, in place of parching wind, helpless Calliope, and the blind Fury.

"The Golden Opes, the Iron Shuts Amain": The judgment of Peter (lines 85–131)

The immortal place appropriate to Phoebus' statement, lofty but not yet finally consoling, is abandoned again as the poem

[5] Daiches (*Milton,* p. 83) holds that Apollo's answer lends the speaker cold or distant comfort. It seems to me that Apollo's answer is in no way vacant. Although it deals with only the speaker's protest concerning poetry, it meets that demand completely.

descends to the pastoral stance variously caught between past Eden and present death; Apollo's lyre having fallen silent, the forlorn "Oat proceeds" (l. 88) following that brief burst of music from the higher, nuptial song. The return to the past Edenic stance is not hopeful, for it seemed unequal to the thrust of reality. Nevertheless, the stance will achieve a portion of reconciliation, if not yet of consolation. To correct the speaker's earlier violent outrage with the "watery bier," "parching wind," and "remorseless" ocean that either destroyed Lycidas or seemed implacable to him even in death, Nature (through Neptune) now pleads that the ocean was peaceful and the winds calm at the time of death. The stance of mortality must accept corrective evidence from the past into its present grief, discovering that nature of itself has been Edenic, not hostile. Nature and man, as well as the times of past Eden and present grief, approach reconciliation in relieved innocence. Because the winds and seas are not of themselves parching and weltering, one tempest of protesting grief has been stilled. Only the human contrivance, "fatal and perfidious" (l. 100), destroyed Lycidas.

The poem intimates far more than meets the ear in that ascription, implying that original sin and Satan, not nature, are the causes through which death enters the Edenic world. However, the innocence of land and water and of their pastoral representatives in no way relieves their impotence, even though it helps the speaker to move closer to the proper judgment of "all-judging *Jove*." The next water figure, the Edenic Camus, can only descend again to the sense of the mortal whelming tide: "Ah! Who hath reft . . . my dearest pledge?" (l. 107). That Camus does not realize the immortal connotations in the ecstatic "rapture" of Lycidas nor in the hyacinth figure (as shown in Milton's own "figuring" of the emblem in "On the Death of a Fair Infant") is only so much more proof that pastoral is helpless before loss. There is as yet no stay in Eden. Its stance quickly gives way again, and this time the fall seems even more hopeless. We must plunge through mere oceanic loss into an abyss of fatality and falsehood, entering the metaphysical Hell rather than a merely natural death in the earthly setting.

Into that seeming end, where the "sacred" (l. 102) head of

Lycidas (like the gory visage of Orpheus) is sunk low, moves the final water figure, Peter, who as a human fisher had also been threatened once with sinking "low" into Galilee (Matt. 14:29–31). Through the example of Peter, Lycidas and the speaker and methektic readers may find ways in which those who must sink low can nevertheless also "mount high" into the eternal being of Heaven—perhaps similarly to hear a voice ask, "O thou of little faith, wherefore didst thou doubt?"

Before that victory can be reached, corruption and inattention by the world must again be faced. The poem accepts the lowest stance. *This time, however, it is not the doubting poet but the divine judge who presents the protest.* The difference in effect is striking. Whereas in the first movement the plaintive poet was answered by Phoebus, the divine judge and voice for poetry, with the two stances remaining separate except as the poet received the divine instruction, in this second movement both the protest and the judgment proceed from the agent of God. This does not diminish the expression of loss and corruption in any way. The protest is all the more vigorous for having been assigned to Peter. The seemingly particular loss and grief of Lycidas and the speaker are thereby made typic, all-involving. The lower stance increasingly anticipates the stance of Heaven. However, the lamenting poet by no means disappears from the protest. His human voice instead begins to join undiscordingly with the divine protest and sequent divine judgment, both of which can lead to human and divine consolation.

Within the mortal stance, Peter quickly laments the loss to Eden (virtually the loss *of* Eden) when it is "reft" of Lycidas—and of the speaker, who, because of grief, seems no longer to batten his flocks but to say, "Ite domum impasti, domino iam non vacat, agni" ("Go home, my lambs, unfed; your master has no time for you" ["Damon's Epitaph"]). If the faithful Herdman is dead, grief-stricken, or ignored by a corrupt world, then false shepherds will usurp the fold, much as the place of the slighted shepherd of the first movement would be taken by the "others" who wrote lyrics for Hell. Whereas Lycidas' flocks and those of the swain in the present had once been battened with the fresh dews and rural songs once had assured them of joyous care, now false shepherds feed only themselves and "grate on their scrannel Pipes of wretched straw" (l. 124), to the loss of needy flocks. The proper "Oat" of "Lycidas" is itself the proper substance from a true Herdman, but the speaker cannot yet recognize his and the Muses' present service. Instead, everything that had characterized the recollected Edenic stance seems perverted into its opposite. Even as Peter describes this Fall, however, immortal judgment moves upon the false living shepherds and their seemingly undue meed. The whole speech has addressed Lycidas in his state of eternal recompense, whereas the speaker earlier had addressed him only as "gone," in death. The language itself also expresses the most forceful present praise of the good shepherd and condemnation of the bad. What might have been mere controversialist vituperation if lodged with the speaker is direct, eternal judgment when given to Peter. The language of mortal protest has become synthesized with divine assay.

The heavenly stance appears explicitly only with the reference to the "two-handed" (l. 130) engine of final judgment, when the thunder of doom for false shepherds will be opposed by the final "nuptial Song" (l. 176) for Lycidas, eternally confirming the present [6] judgment of Peter. In the conviction that present and future judgment can unite, however, the heavenly stance in the second movement was reached more quickly and maintained far longer than it had been in Phoebus' speech in the first movement. Increasingly, present mortal time and stance merge with timeless immortal stance. In a striking instance, Peter's address begins by stressing the mortal loss of Lycidas and the corruption of his flock by lewd hirelings. However, he addresses the time-freed Lycidas in Heaven ("How well could I have spar'd for thee, young swain" [l. 113]) even as he judges his past death and the present false shepherds. The poem has very quietly attained an anticipatory glimpse of Lycidas and Orpheus within the *misthos* (meed) of

---

[6] Isabel G. MacCaffrey, in *"Lycidas:* The Poet in a Landscape," in *The Lyric and Dramatic Milton*, ed. Joseph H. Summers (New York and London, 1965), p. 72, notes that the sense of the past in the speeches of Apollo and Peter is absorbed into the "now" of "the speaker's meditation."

eternity. It is not yet ready to command, "Weep no more" (l. 165), but the unredeemed temporal causes of grief are gradually being absorbed into the inalterable joy of eternity.

This second forging of consolation in the poem remains promissory. Reality, however, has been proved not overwhelmingly hostile to men. Eden has begun to recover some claim to the present tense, and mortality has found that immortal judgment can qualify its tyranny of the present. Transferred into the light of Christian and poetic faith, gradually receiving the shepherd and fisher as Shepherd and Fisher, the pastoral materials of Eden can reappear within a reality no longer wholly antithetical to them. Triton, unable to aid those in mortality's tides, will be transformed into Christ, the savior who walks the waves, stills them, and makes them baptismal. But the full transformation and unifying reconciliation must await the third assay. It is not yet this agon's Easter morning.

"O Ye Dolphins": Fallen human surmise and rising divine recompense (lines 132–164)

The hopeful change within the stance of Eden is registered as the third movement begins. The stream Alpheus, shrunk by the "dread voice" (l. 132) of St. Peter, returns to its Edenic proportions to re-establish the stance. (By the way, the stream surely was not dried up by Peter, but merely seen in reductive perspective from the "higher mood" and higher stance.) Alpheus joins the fountain Arethusa, which had been the vehicle for the previous return to Edenic stance. The mythical Alpheus and Arethusa, after metamorphosis beyond reality seeking mysterious union across "the bottom of the monstrous world" (l. 158), are themselves a principle of reconciliation. Even Alpheus alone suggests such meaning. Although he had joined himself to criminal lust in mortal life, he underwent a transformation whereby he achieved pastoral beauty. In seeking union with Arethusa, he intimates the "unexpressive nuptial Song" that is to come.

The speaker, however, still alone in the vacant Edenic stance with his "frail thoughts" (l. 153), cannot yet see that such pastoral figures offer transcendent consolation. Instead, under a dark star the paradisal "valleys low where the mild whispers use / Of shades and wanton winds and gushing brooks" (ll. 136–137) are sorrowfully asked only for memorial flowers rather than for immediate intimations of other groves and streams. Even if their fading hues may interpose the "little ease" of color, the flowers also insist upon grief and death, as had the merely floral hyacinth and the shattered evergreen leaves of the prelude. Their purpling of the ground again suggests the spilling of blood. Both emblematically and in their fading beauty, they can only reflect the surrender of immortality: "Bid *Amaranthus* all his beauty shed" (l. 149).

However, a change begins with the weeping daffodils, for theirs are the last tears remaining in the poem. The increasingly judicial speaker, who had once received judgment from Phoebus and had shared judgment with Peter, now moves to judge his own "frail thoughts" and "false surmise" (l. 153). If his human emotion expressing his sorrow for lost Eden and present death is still partial, as "false" in surmise as similar emotions in the preceding movements, his resolute judgment, divinely bright like that of Phoebus and Peter, may nevertheless be taken as eternally true. That his judgment begins in doubt is not strange, for Peter's judgment upon false priests had also begun with extensive notice of the world's corruption. The speaker first reconsiders the flower section, recognizing that the "little ease" of floral tribute was "false surmise," not eager thought.

His judgment then moves forward, at first stumblingly, toward truth—first, that of the human body (Lycidas' corpse obviously cannot really be where "the Laureate Hearse" [l. 151] has visibly lain, nor will that of the speaker necessarily so await a gentle muse): almost as soon as the despairing early image of the remorseless deep returns, it is altered to include at least the implication of a Jonah, who experienced not only a form of death but also one of birth-resembling resurrection at "the bottom of the monstrous world." That first providential hint permits a swift extension of thought to Michael's care. By associating Lycidas with a specific guardian geographical location, the poem anticipates his becoming Genius of the shore. He may sleep at Cornwall in a form of memory, but, far more importantly, he may live there in spirit as exemplary poet-priest, thereby sharing in that "great vision of the guarded Mount" (l. 161). He is already joined with others in a heavenly society. The formerly helpless British sites now have become charged with the potency of eternal meaning and being; if heretofore the speaker cried, "Had ye been there—for what could that have done?" he now sees powerful presence and recompense. If fame does not grow on mortal soil, mortal soil can nonetheless receive its meaning. If it can receive Michael's temporal and eternal vision, it can also receive the double significance of Lycidas, "on earth as it is in Heaven." The angel looks "homeward" (l. 163) for a moment in the grief appropriate for the loss of a champion. A second disclosure of truth reveals that Heaven itself stoops toward mortal grief, in another great bond of reconciliation. Once Michael's ruth joins the singer's melodious tear, the Christlike and Apollonian dolphins [7] (resembling the angels at the close of *Paradise Regained*) can waft the fallen Lycidas to the shore of Britain as to the shore of Heaven. Unlike Calliope, the Delphic day-star Phoebus can "do" transcendently for his "enchanting son." Then the tears can be wiped "for ever from his eyes" (l. 181) and those of the audience, releasing mortal men from the "bitter constraint" (l. 6) of death.

The direct coincidence of the speaker's judgment with the higher voices of Phoebus and Peter and with the vision of Michael asks that we look for a moment beyond the close of the third movement. It has been assumed that in the postlude the poem turns to a stance squarely opposed to that of the prelude: that in place of bitter constraint, we find eager thought; in place of the statement *"Lycidas* is dead," the insistence *"Lycidas* your sorrow is not dead"; and in place of a "loss to Shepherd's ear" (l. 49), the

---

[7] Lowry Nelson, Jr., in *Baroque Lyric Poetry* (New Haven and London, 1961), p. 146, discusses the convergent relationships of Apollo, natural "history," Christ, and the images of resurrection in the dolphin passage. See also Lloyd, "The Two Worlds," p. 398: "Apollo himself in the guise of a dolphin rescued his drowning son Icadius, and carried him to Mount Parnassus." The image recalls the salvation of Peter on Galilee, thereby anticipating the similar service to Lycidas of the "dear might of him that walk'd the waves." Apollo is also father to Asclepius, the healer.

confident "Weep no more, woeful Shepherds weep no more" (l. 165). So much is true, of course, but the belief that there is a complete turn causes the end of the third movement to seem obscure or too swift. In the postlude the speaker proves the validity of the two judgments he approached in the third movement. In the first, the sympathetic providence of Michael reaches across men's sense of time and space to help "waft" Lycidas to "other groves and other streams," where heavenly societies, melting in ruth with Michael but like him offering supreme consolation, "wipe the tears for ever from his eyes." The "dear might of him that walk'd the waves" has removed the fear that Lycidas' body is physically lost amidst shores and sounding seas. Similarly, Lycidas' now sun-like, sacred "head," once drooping like those of the flowers, has been repaired. The opening eyelids of the morn will now indicate theophanic assurance. In the other sphere of judgment, the fear that Lycidas' voice is lost because of inattention from poetic public or pastoral flock and therefore also hurled far away, metaphorically, is resolved into confidence that he is "the Genius of the shore" (l. 183), continuingly "good / To all that wander in that perilous flood." In his turn, he supplies some of the "dear might of him that walk'd the waves" (l. 173). So large is his recompense that he is not only saved and comforted but also continues his earthly service of salvation and comfort. The word "recompense" firmly suggests both judgment and reward; the third movement has neared the Heavenly judgment as offered by the speaker himself. It remains for the postlude to confirm it.

"Weep No More, Woeful Shepherds": Consolation and recompense in the postlude (lines 165–193)

That Milton intends the consolation of "Lycidas" to be general is indicated by his shift from the poem's initial singular *shepherd* to plural *shepherds* [8] and by the implication that if a salvation has been wrought for Lycidas by his own faith and works, a salvation has been wrought for the speaker by his "eager thought," which

[8] See Nelson, *Baroque Lyric Poetry*, pp. 67–144, for a study of the subtle interweaving of several different times and the speaker in "Lycidas."

now becomes available to still other shepherds.[9] There will be not one but two geniuses of the shore, opposing the fearful bier and urn of the prelude. As Lycidas becomes legion by metaphoric association with the infinitely "dying" and rising day-star and with the other saints preserved "through the dear might of him that walk'd the waves," so the comforted shepherds themselves are distantly associated with the Heaven of Lycidas. As the sweet societies have wiped the tears forever from the eyes of Lycidas, so that comfort reaches to the restored society of speaker and shepherds (and those greater Shepherds, Apollo, Peter, and Michael), and "Lycidas" all but unites with Psalm 23. Also, if those Heavenly hosts now act as consoling shepherds to Lycidas, practicing the "faithful Herdman's art" (l. 121) above, they also extend pastoral care to the earthly society by showing that it too should "weep no more." In a balancing recompense, Lycidas, the day-star, will be "good" to his new flock, those who welter in the perilous seas of mortality. A circle has joined Heaven and earth, first in consolation, then in forms of salvation, and finally in divine celebration. All stances join as the Edenic day-star seems to sink "beneath the wat'ry floor" only to recover with "new-spangled Ore," coming full circle into the forehead of the morning sky. "So Lycidas."

The divine singer at the end of the poem may seem to have contained all this in his mind and spirit. It is true that the dialectic, with appropriate accompanying stances, has been under his total direction. However, as stricken man and threatened poet-priest, he was so variously involved with the matter of the poem that stance could not possibly have been restrained to that of one shepherd singing across a day to sibylline oaks and fountains. The inner paradise he has gained is as universal as that which later will be envisioned by Adam. As "uncouth Swain" (l. 186) in the postlude, the poet represents in one being the mourning shepherds gazing into terrible mortal loss, the recalled shepherds of Edenic Cambridge, and the high Herdmen of divine service both on earth and in Heaven. In "warbling his Doric lay," he represents not only the drowned poet Lycidas and the sacrificed

[9] Lloyd, "The Two Worlds," p. 393: This victorious shepherd guarantees the succession of shepherds.

singer Orpheus but also the eternal choirs celebrating the "unexpressive nuptial Song" in Heaven, the traditional source of all music. As priest, he has enacted the ritual of human loss and divine renewal, and with the blue mantle of hope (Speranza) [10] can move gaily to increased service. Even within his own dialectical eager thought, at the close of "Lycidas" he is in full command of the stance of Eden as well as that of mortality, because both are seen within their originating and transforming third, that of eternal Heaven. The heavenly stance has conferred upon both poets an immortal wreath rather than mortality's fading flowers.

Although its goal is not doctrine so much as metaphor, "Lycidas" succeeds remarkably in revealing some of the ways of God to men. The recompense to which Lycidas is led is similar to those achieved by the speaker in the sonnet "When I Consider . . ." and by Samson in his agon. As for the divine singer, he gains a striking meed in spite of sorrow: not only has he sympathetically shared in the recompense of Lycidas, but also his own agon has restored his Eden in the waste wilderness of mortality. The fresh woods of the close are those of Eden, rehabilitated and reinhabited. The day has witnessed his full renewal in service. With this poem he has once more battened his "flock" as in the evenings of Lycidas' other life. The setting sun is a leave-taking of this setting; it will rise in, and on, a new birth. The coming dawn promises both author and audience first the complete renewal of Eden, then its expansion. If in the beginning it seemed only vulnerable, a new cause for sorrow because Eden could be so swiftly and terribly lost, it now reasserts a strength that transcends mortality. One aspect of Lycidas will be maintained in the heavenly stance of divine "groves and . . . streams" where the isolation of death is revoked:

> There entertain him all the Saints above,
> In solemn troops, and sweet Societies
> That sing, and singing in their glory move,
> And wipe the tears for ever from his eyes [ll. 178–181].

[10] D. C. Allen, in "Symbolic Color in the Literature of the English Renaissance" (*PQ*, XV [1936], 84), records that Spenser's use of blue also indicates "truth in love."

From that achieved stance, the earlier complaint, "Such, *Lycidas,* thy loss to Shepherd's ear," is gently rebuked. With the assurance of a Heaven of absolute recovery, the speaker can confidently inhabit the fields and pastures of Heaven's earthly shadow, guaranteed that, like the day-star, he and his flocks will (with some divine irony) measure things in that Heaven by those on this earth: "Tomorrow to fresh Woods, and Pastures new" (l. 193) —whether by the Cam or Heaven's other streams, for to either of the recovered good men, Lycidas and the present singer, one site is always virtually the other. The ostensible dirge has been transformed into a hymn to earthly and heavenly life, and the opening words "Yet once more" have been converted from timely protest to eternal assurance.

[4] "Most Reason Is
That Reason Overcome"
Choice in *Paradise Lost*

Despite its magnitude, *Paradise Lost* is probably the simplest of Milton's major poems. Its very size permits the full expression and resolution of matters that in other works must be developed only partially. It can demonstrate the Boethian simplicity of God and his cosmic design. The multifarious conditions of human (and angelic) existence can be reduced to the single requirement of choice. Disparate cultures and genres, even opposed astronomies, can supply centripetal images. The infinitely divergent patterns of eternity and human history may come to reveal so many correspondences that they approach identity. Creation, choice (with the option of a Fall), and renewal (with the penalty or promise of a Judgment) can merge into one eternal act. The audience, by methektic absorption into the central energy and meaning of God's design, comes to realize, through Satan's attempted parody, gracious angelic instruction, the action of the two Adams and the two Eves, and the typological recurrences of events throughout the corridors of time and eternity, that divine and human action must ultimately be one. If the amplitude of *Paradise Lost* presents God's overwhelming plenty, stretching illimitably beyond the alpha and omega of human time, space, and knowledge, it also reveals an ultimate dynamic simplicity.

In that clear, direct vision the audience learns to surmount the familiar "various bustle of resort" of itself and its world, for, as the Elder Brother once noted, such a lowly perspective prevents

wisdom and contemplation. As the poem itself seeks a continuing
Godlike stance "above the Aonian mount," and as the poet would
perceive the entire moral cosmos and respond to it with the
undiscording form of his own poetic order,[1] so the audience is
asked to enter an action leading upward from Hellish or Edenic
confusion to the serene light of an inward Paradise: [2]

> He that has light within his own clear breast
> May sit i' th' center, and enjoy bright day,
> But he that hides a dark soul and foul thoughts
> Benighted walks under the midday Sun;
> Himself is his own dungeon [*Comus*, ll. 381–385].

The action of *Paradise Lost* produces this revelation through
what at first appear to be opposed designs of *fall* and *renewal*.[3] We
are first made forcibly aware of fall and of its reflection in the

[1] Joseph H. Summers, in *The Muse's Method* (Cambridge, Mass., 1962),
p. 16, emphasizes the direct involvement of author and audience in the
settings and agon of *Paradise Lost*.

[2] Jackson I. Cope, in "Fortunate Falls as Form in Milton's 'Fair Infant'"
(*JEGP*, LXIII [1964], 665), considers the reader as a *ritrovatore*, a retriever of
allusion; Milton's reader is asked more generally to be a "retriever" of Eden.
William B. Hunter, Jr., in "Holy Light in *Paradise Lost*" (*Rice Institute
Pamphlet*, XLVI [Jan. 1960], 12), shows reason why the poem and the author
can be considered within the province of the Logos. Jackson I. Cope, in *The
Metaphoric Structure of Paradise Lost* (Baltimore, 1962), p. 121, notes the
author's function in the prelude to Book VII as microcosmic mirror of the
general action. J. B. Broadbent, in *Some Graver Subject* (London, 1960), p.
68, shows that Milton associates himself as poet with the creative power of
God. As Knowledge and Wisdom create the world in Book VII, so their lesser
manifestations create the poem.

[3] B. Rajan, in *Paradise Lost and the Seventeenth Century Reader* (New
York, 1948), pp. 43–49, indicates at length the reflective patterns of creation
and destruction. John M. Steadman, in "Miracle and the Epic Marvellous in
Paradise Lost" (*Archiv*, CXCVIII [1961], 302), contrasts Satan's "lying won-
ders" with the true miracles of God. Roy Daniells, in *Milton, Mannerism and
Baroque* (Toronto, 1963), pp. 81–82, describes Satan as on the wrong end of
a drive shaft but inseparable from it: "He can do nothing but press directly
up against an axis that thrusts him directly down." A. S. P. Woodhouse, in
"Pattern in *Paradise Lost*" (*UTQ*, XXII [1953], 114–116), shows the pattern
as both static and developmental, a comedy to God even though a tragedy to
man. H. R. MacCallum ("Milton and Sacred History: Books XI and XII of
Paradise Lost," in *Essays in English Literature from the Renaissance to the
Victorian Age, Presented to A. S. P. Woodhouse*, ed. Millar MacLure and
F. W. Watt [Toronto, 1964], p. 152, n. 8), believes that Milton saw history as "a
rhythm of fall and reformation."

lateral design of time and history, emphasizing a pattern of rebellion, loss of Heaven or of Eden, chaotic tides of experience, and alienation of the human creature into ignorance and isolation. The immediate vehicle for fallen time and history is the chronology of epic: initiation *in medias res,* the recovery of precedent events by means of interior narrative, the completion of narrative time in both a direct and a prophetic span. Because this sweep of time seems at first to hurtle causally from fall to fall, the intervals of renewal seem almost accidental. Although in the narrative Hell is followed by Heaven, destruction in Heaven by creation of earth, and the double falls of man (in Adam and in history) by double renewals, nevertheless the seemingly routine, inevitable movement to error and folly yields the hopeless cycle foreseen by Michael:

> . . . so shall the World go on,
> To good malignant, to bad men benign,
> Under her own weight groaning [XII, 537–539].

Acting as blind bard to the audience,[4] as Knowledge to Everyman, or as Michael to Adam, the narrator tolls out changes of setting that reinforce the fallen impulses of chronology. Heaven and Paradise come to seem lost indeed.

However, as even the details of the lateral line frequently disclosed, the poet has another function,[5] the audience a more hopeful if more demanding participative agon, and the epic action a meaning that is drawn from eternity rather than time. Although it touches the lateral design of *fall, renewal,* this "vertical" design creates within it an eternal act of creation and renovation. It joins all the characters typologically by drawing this epic—and, indeed, the whole earth—into Heaven's meaning, either directly or through the theory of accommodation.[6] All the seeming acts

[4] See Anne D. Ferry, *Milton's Epic Voice* (Cambridge, Mass., 1963), *passim,* for discussion of the narrator's voices as those of soaring bird and blind bard.

[5] Louis L. Martz, *The Paradise Within* (New Haven and London, 1964), p. 106: "The bard emerges at the center of the action, Satan's human antagonist"; p. 109: "The bard himself seems . . . to be guided by the revelations of the action as he explores the way toward Eden."

[6] C. A. Patrides describes the accommodation of divine meaning to human terms in "*Paradise Lost* and the Theory of Accommodation" (*TSLL,* V [1963], 58–63). He notes that Milton's God, conceived anthropopathically, is comprehensible to the active reason of men.

within fallen time are removed into creation and judgment within eternity. Somewhat to its surprise, the audience finds itself, together with the poetic voice, sharing in divine foreknowledge and forewarning. As God's foreknowledge includes all human history, so our human knowledge includes not only past history (as related in Books XI and XII) but also a prophetic sense of the future history into which the "the World [shall] go on" (XII, 537).

The ultimate design forms *Paradise Lost* into three parts of four Books each. To the chronological changes indicated by the lateral design are added timeless choices that reach into the vertical line. When errant creatural choice commands the fall from creation to corruption, creative grace erects Eden again, even in the resultant waste wilderness. That insistent pull by the vertical not only justifies God's ways to men generally but also informs the otherwise gloomy pattern emphasized throughout the epic—fall, renewal. That pattern appears in the first four Books in Satan's choice for Hell and the Son's for Heaven. In the second, surrounded on both sides by reflective assays of Adam and Eve, it appears in the account of the destructive battle in Heaven and the renovative creation of earth. In the final section, the pattern appears first in the fall and regeneration of Adam and Eve, then in the historical fall to the Flood and the renewal in Christ-types and Christ. It reaches from that point forward to all humanity, including that of the seventeenth and twentieth centuries after Christ. In Johnson's terms, all these are choices for eternity. But there is a height in the vertical line beyond even these choices. It reveals God, the creator of the choice, the gracious instructor against error, the judge who necessarily confirms the self-destruction wrought by wrong choice, and the source of merciful grace even to those who have knowingly erred. From this height, which is the assumed perspective for much of *Paradise Lost*,[7] Satan's

---

[7] Rosalie Colie, in "Time and Eternity: Paradox and Structure in *Paradise Lost*," (*JWCI*, XXIII [1960], 131), points out usefully that "God's point of view always dominates: it is through God's eyes that we first meet Adam and Eve." See also Daniells, *Milton, Mannerism and Baroque*, p. 97, on the Father's "omniscient view," and B. A. Wright, *Milton's Paradise Lost* (New York, 1962), pp. 118–119, on the divine stance as witness for the entire landscape of assay in Paradise.

destructive lateral Hell and death are opposed by the Son and creative life, Satan's discordant battle in Heaven with the Son's harmonious formation of the earth, and Satanic-human hatred and loss with divine and human compassion. Within this height also appears the creation of a new "paradise within . . . , happier far" (XII, 587), for representative Adam.

The essential oneness of the designs and the action is emphasized by controlling metaphors for Satan, the Son, and man. For Satan, "recoil" identifies a warlike and war-engineering pride that must return destructively upon its inventor's head, thereby identifying sin as a form of suicide and Hell itself as a perverse and helplessly vacant reflection of Heaven.[8] For the Son, a creative or sacrificial "raising" of man from the dust of earth indicates both the creator and the redeemer. For man, a fallen or an upright position illustrates his alliance with either destructive recoil or vital aspiration upward. He is also imaged as the mariner on a storm-wracked or night-shrouded sea. He may be misled to the delusive "island" of warring Satan and be destroyed, or lulled to peaceful inattention in a hellish harbor (II, 284–290). On the other hand, he may be delivered by either his own clear light or "the dear might of him that walk'd the waves." In still another form of judgment, the entire vertical design ironically judges Satan's pretensions and the illusions bred in his lateral, processive order of time. If the audience fully receives the images for choice and the judgment that plays in and upon them, the epic will almost have justified God's ways methektically to men.

Two matters having to do with choice remain. First, choice, though illimitable, is not blind or licentious. Although in a sense God must choose whether to be God or Satan, at such a level—and it is to such a level that *Paradise Lost* mounts— "choice" cannot dream of equality of objects or attraction. To choose the evidently and indescribably inferior, the nonexistent, is so mindless that it ceases to be choice, degenerating instead to blundering mistake and inanity. Reasonable "choice" instead is almost certain to be the confirmation, after free "assay," of that

[8] M. M. Mahood, in *Poetry and Humanism* (London, 1950), p. 186, sees Hell as a concave mirror for Heaven. C. S. Lewis adds that Satan can exist only in reflection (*A Preface to Paradise Lost* [London, 1942], p. 94).

which previously has been valued. It will be continuous and dynamic so long as one admires—"chooses"—the object or even the quality of the choice. To such choice, Milton allows noun and verb to bend in adjectival tribute. His formula "Reason . . . is choice" (III, 108) becomes doubly or triply analytical: reason consists of choice; that which is most choice—most worth choosing—is reason; and reason perpetually confirms itself in choosing that which is choice. In the end, reason comes to be grace as well as choice. Second, the audience probably must unite with the vertical design its literary choice of which characters to believe in. One of the undiagnosed, unacknowledged difficulties in much Milton criticism is the enormous disparity in degrees of credibility that readers assign to the several characters of *Paradise Lost* and *Paradise Regained*. Although many readers can accept Adam and Eve mythically, they want to reject Milton's angels outright or banish them totally from human history or myth. Although the historic Jesus, supposedly made human flesh, should be near the audience, it may nevertheless choose God and Satan as being more "real" or "relevant," because if considered symbolically they exert felt pressures upon human life. Oddly enough, the hated God is often more fully "believed in" than is Satan, if only because readers judge his judicial mercy for them more harshly than Satan's avowed homicidal hatred. Milton, however, considers all the beings who choose, like their choices, to be essentially one.

Paradise Lost therefore has no one hero and no one villain. Instead, it has a heroic choice, faced several times over and judged for recurrent consequences. In Adam the human choice is clearly central, but it is framed on both sides with the massive choices of Satan and the Son. Around those choices coalesce the other encounters with the same issue, such as those of Abdiel and Beelzebub, Abel and Cain, Joshua and Judas. The literary unities of epic, slightly transformed, come to reflect and reinforce the sweeping unities of this cosmic Christian subject.

The poem will intimate such revelation of unity from the outset and accomplish it for both Adam and the reader in the conclusion. In the interim rests the reader's great assay in these choices and this design. The matter for our way forward must continuously engage the "wild Wood" of our lateral experience—a world so familiar that only shock will reveal it to audience eyes—along with painfully "true" judgment upon it. It is a clever mistake to believe that Milton was of the devil's party without knowing it; on the contrary, he wants us to know, fully, that it is we who have been of the devil's party without knowing it. The relationship of Milton to us resembles that of Michael to Adam. We must experience choice, including the choice of error, and recognize the portion of Hell that is where *we* are [9]—for Milton's Hell is often similar to the City of Men at its best. We therefore begin our agon with Satan as he magniloquently justifies his ways to himself. Unlike our first stance in *Comus,* that of *Paradise Lost* forces us to accept the extremely limited perspective of the fallen. We must share Satan's prideful sin and fall before we, as fallible human creatures, can properly comprehend the approaching "great Argument" of divinity.[10] Perhaps it was not Miltonic irony alone but rather grave poetic and theological necessity that caused the first fall of the poem—that in the invocation—to be suffered by the reader. Lacking an Attendant Spirit or a Virgil, and for the moment bereft even of authorial guidance, the reader plunges from the invocation's total light to a darkness only faintly "visible." There we enter into the archetypal form and act of disastrous choice that is also the initiation of our lateral time.

Although even our guide upward from Hell is ostensibly Satan, Book III offers us participation in realms of light and in belief flatly opposing that we received in Hell. In place of Hell's warm tyranny we are given a cool challenge to liberty, to an almost total consignment into our own choices. If Heaven seems to utter non-

[9] Northrop Frye, in *The Return of Eden* (Toronto, 1965), p. 106, considers Milton's Hell to model perverted forms of our society, both in state and church.

[10] Stanley Fish, in "The Harassed Reader in *Paradise Lost*" and "Further Thoughts on Milton's Christian Reader" (*CritQ,* VII [1965], 162–182, 279–284), takes much the attitude of these essays toward Milton's implicating his readers in action which they must come to judge. His essays and mine were developed independently. See also Anne Ferry, *Milton's Epic Voice,* p. 46. I disagree that the narrator's blindness necessarily separates him from the audience, for it brings him closer to audience insight. In any case, like Adam in Book XI, the reader has to judge his own faculty for understanding modes of address and revelation as they progress.

sense in attempting to discriminate between uncausative fore-knowledge and foreordination, it at least tries; Satan had smudged all such issues, collapsing necessary distinctions, even categorical opposites, within the strong absurd cries of his ego. Even though the Son manifests the pity and redemption that are projected from God, the reader still is likely to feel a freezing sense of solitude as he faces that demanding liberty. He may agonically resent the cold air of Olympus after the exciting red Brocken of Hell.

When the stance is removed to central Earth, even before man is introduced the paradigms of hellish and heavenly choice "colonize" the planet, as if to insist that Heaven and Hell will in part be wherever choosing man is. The formerly separate, opposed stances now join. The theater is to be earth, the conflict that of reason caught between wise and foolishly destructive choices, and the principal actors human representatives—Adam (and the Son) in the direct action, the audience in a participative literary action. With Adam, we enter the major prevenient tutelary section of the epic. Having wrought an elective argument by intellectual man in *Comus,* Milton here returns to it—but with a major difference. Whereas the Lady spoke from a lateral wild wood of "experience," upright Adam speaks from the innocent center of an earthly light that preserves its vertical connection with Heaven. Therefore, a gift of redemptive (because preventive) reason precedes his trial. The third manifesto in *Comus,* delivered by man, had stated the position for man. The equivalent statement in *Paradise Lost* is given by Raphael, a divine agent and form of *gratia praevenitia,* for man. It is as if Sabrina, given the power of revelation to maintain the light of reason for the Lady, had preceded Comus and thereby obviated the need for gracious redemption. The entire central portion of *Paradise Lost* is entirely devoted to that divine instruction. It is conveyed by the absolute examples of original destructive or creative choice in Lucifer and Christ. Parallels for such instruction exist in Scripture and in all exposition of sacred knowledge—including, in its way, this poem. Prevenient tutelage is a part of man's having been made sufficient to have stood the demands of choice.

The archetypal human choice against reason and judgment

follows. In the now bright wood of human assay, Eve, despite full instruction, falls. The audience is made to recognize that human error recapitulates Satan's stance: pride, jealousy, and greed; a dizzying sense of great height and then of great fall; finally, darkness and the threat of imbrutement. We now know, however, that the Son's chariot "is" always sweeping to the defeat of error. His means is the conversion of negative to positive, of loss into benefit. Adam and audience are then held to witness and judge the double result. First, the lateral choice is to recur continually across history. When the choice is erroneous, it will continue to open Hell's gates, freeing Sin and Death. On the other hand, as for Abraham and Elisha, judgment (right choice) can sustain a form of Paradise so that there is no absolute need for a redeemer. Second, if men will in any way permit it, God's eternal design will intersect and reform even the erroneous temporal choices of men. Grace within history is shown in God's saving Noah, in his delivering the Israelites from even their own error, and in his greatly promising all men a second Adam, a new root of spiritual being. The reasonable instructions of the center are almost repeated at the end of *Paradise Lost*—not this time for Adam in Paradise, but for Adam and man in our world. The epic closes, shadowed with sadness but also newly illuminated with serene confidence, upon man's entrance into the wider arena of judgment and choice:

> The World was all before them, where to choose
> Thir place of rest, and Providence thir guide [XII, 646–647].

Even so is providence the guide for Milton and audience in the epic ("Instruct me, for Thou know'st; . . . What in me is dark / Illumine, what is low raise and support" [I, 19–23]).

Our general experience in *Paradise Lost,* concerned with creatural choices within time that in turn involve eternity, thus encounters two mythic poles of choice; sees new-made but typic man supplied with preventive judgment, with enough light of creative and tutorial reason to maintain himself upright; witnesses his time-damning choice to fall, which is also a choice that Eden end; sees with him the release of Sin and Death upon himself and all his children but also sees some men (including the penitent Adam) choose justly despite sin; and foresees Christ as a second

Adam, who on the same mount of temptation will elect life in essential love of creation and who within time will defeat time's errors. Even more simply, the design of the epic asks us to witness free choice for or against God and his countering pity for vulnerable humans when wrong choice brings ruinous consequence. The plot that gives body to the design does not begin with Adam, nor does it end with him. It reaches back to the "first" great negative choice by Satan and ahead in time to the "historical" figures of Books XI and XII (including Jesus), then beyond them to the "last" positive redemptive choice of the apocalyptic Christ. It seems to end there. Within time, however, human history will continue to supply its embodiment as it had down to 1667—and also within the twentieth century, if our literary *methexis* holds. Furthermore, "other worlds" may in other ways or times manifest the eternality of reason and choice that is conferred by the Creator upon his spiritual creations. "True" both inside and outside human time and history, the plot of *Paradise Lost* offers the typical Miltonic pattern of creation, fall, renewal, although greatest emphasis rests upon the last two forms. The pattern is unified through vertical creativity and judgment, thereby including the widest possible implications of theology, history, and human meaning.

"Measuring Things in Heaven by Things on Earth": Typic choices and related stances (Books I–IV)

Although from one point of view *Paradise Lost* properly begins *in medias res*, from another it can be said to start with two new creations: Hell and earth. Although both partake of eternity in divine foreknowledge and design, both were potential only, unformed and uninhabited, until Satan's errant choice—an anticreative creation—legislated his fall from Heaven and eternity. In opposition to timeless eternity, his doom of time comes to mean the threat of ending for every particular being. In opposition to Heaven, Hell means spatial divorce from the source of being. Despite its having been the consequence of time, Adam's Paradise is capable of being free of time and at one, spiritually, with

Heaven. Satanic choice, on the other hand, can plunge earth and its creatures into doomed diabolic time and spiritually separated place. Both "new" creations, when seen from the generative nimbus of Heaven, move uneasily toward the ticking of clocks and the too swift passing of days in places rushing away from the center of light—if time-condemning choices reject eternity.

The lateral line of the epic, then, "begins" when errant choice has determined that Hell, heretofore merely a possibility, be filled with those who chose that Hell be. That line is intersected by a vertical ascent to Heaven, where we are reminded that no creation need be damned by time. Nevertheless, the resumed lateral progress demonstrates sadly the doom that most men on earth will choose—"till one greater Man" (I, 4) restore that which diabolical time has lost. It will observe fleetingly the abortive result if choice of neither God nor Satan, neither eternity nor the world's time, is attempted. The first section then concludes with the elective human beings entranced in their abundant prelapsarian world, there also "to choose / Thir place of rest, and Providence thir guide." Providence will not alter its guidance, even though they may refuse its light.

Our participative discussion will follow that lateral line and the stances of its enactment but will look also to the vertical line of creation and judgment that supplies "God's ways to men" (I, 26).

"TO FALL OFF FROM THIR CREATOR": HELL'S TYPIC CHOICE OF
IGNORANCE AND NONBEING (BOOKS I-II)

The invocation to *Paradise Lost* promptly impels audience and author into a methektic plunge downward to "all our woe" (I, 3).[11] It stresses man's first disobedience against self and life, opening therefore into terrible perspectives of resultant sin (the agent of "all our woe"—II, 872) and death. Next, a swift upward

[11] Isabel G. MacCaffrey, in "The Meditative Paradigm" (*ELH,* XXXII [1965], 399), indicates that even as the poet is guided, so he guides the audience; he "plays the parts *both* of Dante the pilgrim and of Dante the maker." Partly for that reason, as Douglas Bush notes in "Virgil and Milton" (*CJ,* XLVII [1952], 179), the invocations are not so much epic conventions as prayers.

movement draws us to a second choice running restoratively counter to all the motions of the first and, in a sense, terminating
them: "till one greater Man / Restore us, and regain the blissful
Seat" (I, 4–5).[12] Although the promise specifically engages the
historical Jesus, it can embrace also the vertical inward paradise,
"happier far," to which the representative man, Adam, will be
restored. To that extent, Adam himself, like any similar person,
becomes a "greater Man." The countermovement having soared
as high as God's covert or open design, we come to momentary rest
"above th' *Aonian* Mount" (I, 15) or any one of earth's high
places, a perspective from which man can see the time-encounter-
ing world and be seen from timeless Heaven. The "Heavenly
Muse"[13] that reached down, descended, to tutelary Moses and
redemptive Christ when they, reaching up, ascended into a high
place, is invoked once more to form the contact. This time it is the
present author—a poet-seer, and an expression of eternal
Word—who asks Urania's and the Creator's aid in achieving a
Christian end more exalted than that of authors of epic whose
expression was not directly Christian. He will sing the new song of
Psalm 33. He will also in his way explore a promised land, "restore us, and regain the blissful Seat." The readers of the poem
participatively stand with him. For both readers and author,
reason both human and divine is invoked. It is to move the "great
Argument" (I, 24), part of which, like the secret top of Sinai,
must remain above the reach of human words. It will instruct the
author, and through him the audience, even as within his poem
holy wisdom in the persons of Raphael and Michael instructs
Adam and Eve and their sons. Such wisdom knows (I, 19) that
the "light" which once wrought form from chaos can now illumine the poet's mind and raise him—and, with him, the audience—from the fallen world to the radiant high place of received
and enacted knowledge.

[12] Arthur E. Barker ("Structural and Doctrinal Pattern in Milton's Later
Poems," in *Essays in English Literature from the Renaissance to the Victorian
Age,* p. 184), reminds us that in Milton's time "till" implied " 'during the
time in which' or 'while.' "
[13] Lily B. Campbell, in "The Christian Muse" (*Huntington Library Bulletin,* VIII [Oct. 1935], 44), notes that the Christian dove soars above Pegasus
and that Milton's muse exceeds that of Greece.

Like the stances of the epic as a whole, the invocation had swung quickly from the depth "Of Man's First Disobedience" (I, 1) to great height and returned, through the person of the author, to the earthly center where human choice is conferred and made. The poem proper again describes much the same movement as it takes its first major stance. It asks the eternal voice of knowledge to explain how our typic "Grand Parents," placed idyllically in a middle position but in far more continuously direct contact with God—"Favor'd of Heav'n so highly" (I, 30)—could fall off. In answer, we—Milton's assumed Christian audience, the readers who I assume will suspend a priori disbelief in Milton's fiction during the time that they read—immediately plunge as low as the Edenic, earthly Serpent (who will be discovered again in Book IX, vainly eating the fruits of temptation forever). In him, we register our own guile, envy, revenge, and pride, all of which defy God and seduce our better energies as they did Eve. In another instant, leaving the original arc, we are flung still farther, far past the merely human fall; we must see that archetypal consequence of erroneous choice, the First Fall.[14] We scarcely notice that the immediate image or metaphor for Fall is that of war and "Battle proud" (I, 43), but it is well to fix that sense: any erroneous choice is direct warfare against both creativity and eternity, as well as a suicidal antagonistic "recoil" against the chooser. For the moment, the participative audience is impelled beyond history and human thought over the flaming cataract, in the original expulsion from a kind of Eden. Two "paradises" are lost in the epic, but if men's instruction is effective, they may regain the greater. As our first enactment in the myth, the "matter" of the epic, we suffer a dizzying headlong plummet into the "fiery Gulf" (I, 52). The narrative past tense gradually gives way to the methektic present: "for *now* the thought / Both of lost happiness and lasting pain / *Torments*" (I, 54–56—italics added). Knowledge of the loss of eternal reason and of clinging timelessly instead to an occasionally produced but obdurately maintained choice of folly is one definition of this Hell.

Because the myth pulls us so irresistibly toward making Satan

---

[14] Isabel G. MacCaffrey, in *Paradise Lost as "Myth"* (Cambridge, Mass., 1959), p. 117, sees the total geography and the total spirit of Eden as one.

its sole subject, we should recall that both our stance as readers and the chosen initial matter of the poem insist that we, also—not merely the Infernal Serpent—experience the fall. As the good man Virgil conducted Dante first to the Inferno, so the good man Milton conducts us first to Hell, insisting that we taste these ashen fruits as well as those of the Paradise to come: "O taste and see!" The narrative is *of* a myth but is *for* us. We must bear witness fully to the fatality and folly of an archetypal choice and consequence, and so—as Raphael says in his similar "epic" recounted to Adam—"beware . . . [because] to stand or fall / Free in thine own Arbitrement it lies" (VIII, 638–641). At best, we can then joyously avoid self-imprisoning error. At worst, we can sadly accept divine aid in escaping the prison. We will then know that for Milton man is both better and wiser than the finally fallen Satan.

With utmost instructiveness, then, our stance rests first with the type of perversely chosen necessity, in consequence made absolute: to Satan "hope never comes / That comes to all" *men* (I, 66–67), because he will not be instructed by reason nor permit himself to reverse an error. His necessitarian fixed mind is a form of Hell. He is "baleful," doubly: his principal target is himself. The extent of his "reasonless" self-entrapment is imaged by the "darkness visible" (I, 63) rather than by a "dark with excessive bright" (III, 380) through which he now moves, and by the bold attitude of his address to Beelzebub, publicly so sure but in private first fumbling pathetically then "falling" into the conditional: "*If* thou beest hee; But O how fall'n! how chang'd"; "*If* he whom mutual league, / United thoughts and counsels, equal hope" (I, 84, 87–88—italics added). We will hear such words again from Adam when Eve falls in a typic repetition of Satan's fall but, significantly, Adam will not have to use the "reasonless" conditional. Unlike Satan with Sin, he will know the inflamed creature by his side and how it came about that she is similarly "Defac't, deflow'r'd, and now to Death devote" (IX, 901). Nor will he entirely bewilder himself as Satan does.

Because of his pride of mind, Satan is unreasoning, unreasonable. It is a grim pity (but high methektic art) that Satan has succeeded in confusing or tempting sensible readers as well as himself. If he is not to be dismissed as an ass, neither is he to be embraced as a democratic oracle. In his first essay in reason, a recoiling parody of Logos (because devils can only simulate, not counter, God), he trumpets that he will not "repent or change, / Though chang'd" (I, 96–97). He proclaims that his mind and the minds of his followers are fixed, even as he acknowledges that their changing has wrought their fall. He cannot hear the insistent note of folly as he says that his adverse power opposed God's "utmost power" (I, 103). Although he supposes he has said that he nearly won, he instead has acknowledged God's power to be absolute over even what devils perform in Hell. When he imagines he cannot end, the error strides back upon him, causing him to repeat his first terrible error of "outshining" pride: already he too is "how fall'n! how chang'd / From him, who in the happy Realms of Light / Cloth'd with transcendent brightness did . . . outshine / Myriads though bright." It sometimes has been held [15] that Milton so celebrates his devils in their speeches that puritanically, but in a form of self-betrayal, he then must condemn them in the narrative. It is true that Milton describes Satan as "vaunting aloud" and "rackt with deep despair" (I, 126), but in view of Satan's revealing speeches, a more judicious objection might hold that such narrative recapitulations are "wrong" only because they are tautological.

If reason is choice, we as audience participating in the ensuing consult in Hell look steadily into that unreason which is error. In their way, Books I and II compose a Dunciad as well as a prophecy of the ways of men in Books XI and XII. The choice for negativity and destruction is a logical trap, for one thing; the divine possibility of converting negative to positive does not admit of the reverse convertibility. When Satan counterlogically tries to oppose God's design of bringing good from evil, "out of good still to find means of evil" (I, 165), his own despair at once betrays him into the conditional: "If I fail not" (I, 167). Increasingly, the conditional is the only sign of Satan's boasted intellectual capacity—the lingering ability to doubt his own pronouncements. However, if we complacently try to separate ourselves from the villainously destructive fool that Satan is becoming, our stance in Hell quietly recalls to us that Satan was our first guide hither

[15] A. J. A. Waldock (*Paradise Lost and Its Critics* [Cambridge, 1947], pp. 75–83), believes that Milton as narrator reduced the stature of the devils created by Milton the dramatist, in creative treason.

and what he intends for mankind "hence." Because Milton gives the devil his dramatic due, we are to give Milton's devil our critical attention. For us, now he is much what he was for Eve in the garden or for Jesus in the wilderness—a seeming dismal toad, a dazzling serpent, or a murmuring shade, according to our will. (Even in epic simile, he is not valorous; predicting the form in which he awaits the reader, he is already serpentine and "monstrous," like the *"Titanian . . . that warr'd on Jove,"* Typhon, and Leviathan [I, 197–201]). The rhetoric of temptation—including that of self-temptation—is unmistakable in Hell unless we will to mistake. If the reader credits falsehood either attentively or inattentively, that vacant falsehood, like the vacant bestial forms taken by Satan, is granted the same kind of operative substantiality that it has for Satan: evil, be thou our good.

Any Satanic farewell to "happy Fields" (I, 249) is acceptance of the lot of Tityos over Achilles' Elysium. If we sympathize with the speciously heroic Satan now, that is a part of our methektic fall; our recovery fortunately will lead us to the new and greater heroism announced in the invocation to Book IX. It should also lead us from the brutal, parodic forms of God and the Son that we meet both in history and in Hell to intimations of the real—past Moloch, demanding not Christian compassion but blank violence, whose deadly worship in human time will turn "The pleasant Valley of *Hinnom*" into "the Type of Hell" (I, 404–405); past Baal, whose freeing of lust parodied Christian agape but who was driven by Christ-figural Josiah "to Hell" (I, 418); past Astarte, who becomes a type of the lustful sway of sexual passion over reason in Adam, Solomon, and even Satan himself; past Thammuz, who might have been figural of Christ or Orpheus but who instead, like Adam to Eve at the Fall, became sexually infecting to *"Sion's* daughters" (I, 453); past Osiris, Isis, and Horus, half-respected for meaning but ridiculed for taking Satanic brute form; past Belial, the "god" of false priests, apostates, and atheists, those who parodically worship a negative; and past the Titanic and Olympian gods, who are false dawns at best. All such are both types and consequences of error, shamefully instructive to men both inside and outside human history.[16]

---

[16] Rosalie Colie, in "Time and Eternity," pp. 136–137, demonstrates the correspondence of human history with Milton's account of Hell.

Because the fallen stance of the first two Books has led readers to mistake "semblance" for substance and to accept Satan at his own valuation, ignoring the treacherous self-contradiction of his speeches, we must attend the ironic vertical line of judgment. All Hell is its own self-exploding recoil. In Satan's re-enactment in Hell of his choice in Heaven, we see plainly how even when in Heaven he made a Hell for himself. The legions of Satan in Hell, far from being absolutely under God's tyrannic sway, are in all particulars free to do exactly as they wish. If the host of devils is "raised" by error that is only seeming reason, it must again fall. The ensign of these parodically non-Christian soldiers glows like a *falling* meteor. Satan's shield shows mainly an eclipse. Their battle tears "Hell's Concave" (I, 542), frightening Chaos and Night because it so nearly resembles the anticreative, negative birth of Death from Sin. The music may be like that which moved human heroes to battle, but Satan has already determined upon stealth and guile; Dorian flutes at best send him only to his station like a toad at Eve's ear. His spurious tears may be angelic in substance but not in motive, welling as they do only for unsuccessful folly. And most damaging: if Eve's reasoning in Book IX is feminine, he now becomes effeminate, arguing in a vapid jingle that "[God] tempted our attempt, and wrought our fall" (I, 642). The conclusive irony develops around his cry, "This Infernal Pit shall never hold / Celestial Spirits" (I, 657–658). Although it will not hold the celestial Christ, it must entomb infernal Satan, for such is his obdurate choice.

Our stance in Pandemonium is yet more instructive to us, for here we see the type of our world almost as clearly as we see it with Adam in Books XI and XII and as the Son encounters it in *Paradise Regained.* Our general, typical experience in Book II of blind anger in Moloch, seductive ease in Belial, and riches in Mammon precedes but parallels our historical experience of Cain, the tents of Cain, and the cities of the plain in Book XI. Human representatives in history recapitulate types from myth or Biblical "parahistory," for our human typology for the spiritual world can be matched by a spiritual typology for historical man. However, there is one major difference between the representatives of earth and the types of Hell. If Hell, like earth, can build vain monuments, its vanity is more transparent: Pandemonium rises "like an

Exhalation," perhaps a sigh (I, 711). Even its insubstantiality, however, is not its own. Like Mulciber who also fell headlong flaming, Satan was sent "with his industrious crew to build in hell" (I, 751) —somewhat as if to dig their own chosen graves. We listen to the devils move "with the hiss of rustling wings" (I, 768), hearing serpents and ephemeral locusts, not angels, and watching unnatural distentions and collapses rather than substance. These fallen creatures are like the plague that served God against Egypt—themselves, in absolute servile recoil, being both the plague and the present Egypt.

By participation, the audience, "greatly instructed" (XII, 557), should now know what a fall is. Hell is a pridefully relentless demonstration, however. We next must attend a catastrophic parody, Hell's "free" assembly, which may resemble history's parliaments but which contrasts vertically with the consults of God in Heaven and of Adam, Eve, and angels in Eden. The obdurately faithless swear "union, and firm Faith" (II, 36). Satan, tellingly "uplifted beyond hope" (II, 7), asks Hell to believe a self-bewildering claim which parodies the "Fortunate Fall": that the fallen creatures are now "Surer to prosper than prosperity / Could have assur'd us" (II, 39–40). Unreason towers and crashes in these unwitting, shuttling quibbles and puns. We also receive the varieties possible to general political unreason: Moloch, attacked by both fact and anticlimax, claiming "descent and fall / To us is adverse" (II, 76–77); Belial, in defiance of his own self-analysis, claiming "intellectual being" even as he knows that his "thoughts . . . wander through Eternity" (II, 147–148); Mammon, in Hell as in Heaven hoping for fortune but finding only the fall, grubbing destructively for God's light and something "prosperous of adverse" (II, 259) among the gems and gold of Hell.[17] (He likens God's "obscure" glory to Satan's, and Heaven to Hell; his folly contains truth, for Hell, like earth, is always in some form a shadow of Heaven, as parody after helpless parody reveals.) The crowning perversion of reason remains for

[17] For a consideration of the devils as epitomizing pride, envy, and revenge, see Robert C. Fox, "Satan's Triad of Vices" *TSLL*, II (1960), 261–280. In another representation, Mammon's attack on the floor of Hell resembles that of the hellhounds on Mother Sin.

Beelzebub, who concludes the free assembly by saying, "War hath determin'd us" (II, 330) : wrong choice is not left open to the correction of reason but instead congeals into fate. Although he asks that they hatch no "vain Empires" (II, 378), irony immediately retorts that Hell has no fecundating Spirit for its vast abyss. However, if we are tempted to smile when Beelzebub, skirting comedy, complains that God shows little liking for devils, a chill like that of the Black Mass removes his corollary statement far from comedy: he is sure that men—including us, the men attentive in the audience, *his* audience—are "to be created like to us" (II, 349), the devils, rather than in God's image. Even though he still fancies himself to be an angel, the words strike the audience as potentially true. We are as little comforted by the recoiling assurance that their eruption into the world will in truth hatch a vain empire rather than create or serve a world.

Finally, when Satan answers his parody of Isaiah's "Whom shall we send?" by dictatorially volunteering to "harrow" Hell only by escaping it, and says, "Long is the way / And hard, that out of Hell leads up to light" (II, 432–433), we should carefully attend his only real knowledge. To devils, he promises only an abortive deliverance, because he adventures not to find light and substance but to extinguish them. On earth as in Heaven, all that his choice can offer is death; however, even his choice—ironically, like that of the Son in Heaven impelled by God—is ultimately directed to God's counterdesign. To men, he demonstrates choice become necessity and consequence become prison or tomb.[18] Any remaining supposititious "freedom" in Hell is doubly denied devils and audience in this stance, first by the hinted roll of thunder and second by the "awful reverence" (II, 478) of the salaam to dictatorial, fatal Satan.

With another reminder that the audience should measure things in Hell by things on earth both through reflectively intensifying the stormy extremes of temperature on fallen earth and by noting that even devils can rise above human mutual war, Milton ends our stance in Pandemonium. He sets us then a double jour-

[18] J. H. Adamson, "The War in Heaven: Milton's Version of the *Merkabah*," *JEGP*, LVII (1958), 700: In Milton's adaptation, "unity with the Divine Will brings freedom whereas separateness inevitably brings servitude."

ney. Before we are through learning of Hell, we must encounter it in the "old" heroism that is earth's vanity—the vain heroism of godless Olympiads, the vain chaotic rage of brute strength seeking no more than its own exercise, the vain, self-pitying, "epic" complaints of devils against their chosen fate, vain philosophy that refuses light,[19] and vain physical exploration of Styx and Acheron. Beyond, there rages a correlative disorder, monstrosity, and vanity of elements hurling upon one another. Into this lower chaos, but following Satan rather than a Virgil, the audience takes its second journey. Having listened long to the rhetoric of the Fall, we, together with the archetypal destroyer, must now experience its ultimate consequence. Like Adam in Book XI, we must witness the typic anticreative birth of Sin and Death.

Satan's thoughts, again almost sexually "inflam'd" (II, 630), as they were in Heaven, lead him to the Sin he then lusted after but who, although he will not recognize it, now mirrors the Serpent he is to become. Sin is born again in every utterance of Satan but recoils on him as destructively as Death turns upon her. Mental and moral disorder appear in Hell's narcissism, forgetfulness, incest. All too humanly recognizable and of prime threat later to Eve, narcissistic selfishness leads on to its objectification in the form and power of Sin and to the lustful use of that form and power in breeding Death. However, in psychotic, self-deluding repression, the extreme form of selfishness, each of the persons forgets all of his self-created event, thereby insuring that precisely the same cycle must recur. Such ignorance cannot perceive choice. It instead guarantees determined fall, erasure of knowledge, and repeated fall.

Milton criticism has moved far from Dr. Johnson's objection to the personification of sin and death—so far that we sometimes see Sin as a comic diva and the story of Sin with Death as an allegory of human neurosis, rejecting love for self and self-images. A new danger forms in that too timely acceptance. Sin and Death should serve the major audience, at least, as reflections of fatal choice—that is, of self-elected judgment—even as Satan and God present

[19] David Daiches, in *Milton* (London, 1957), p. 174, finds that the arguments of Hell anticipate the sophistic arguments of Athens that are rejected by the Son in *Paradise Regained*.

the conditions or fields of choice. Although allegory is in one sense used expressively for the progeny of Satan, stressing the insubstantiality of their own "being," the point is not really to develop their character and relationship to Satan, but to us. Significantly, the second journey had positioned us in our stance, the setting with Sin and Death, before Satan reached it. He acts as our chosen spokesman, but it is with "our" sin and death that we must reckon.

We should first assess the newly experienced trinity of devilish choice, consequential sin, and determined death against the "vertical" original trinity, which can be as freely chosen. Second, we should anticipate the form of Sin that Satan will take with Eve (and with her children) : attractive to her waist, Sin is hideously serpentine in her incestuous and insatiable lower parts. Excepting one son, her progeny never really grow (for she is "fruitless") , but at threat retire to the originating womb in recoiling incestuous disorder. As chaos may prove to be for Nature, the origin of evil must also be its grave. Sin's parodic son, her "wages," is Death. He is conclusively negative:

> The other shape,
> If shape it might be call'd that shape had none
> Distinguishable in member, joint, or limb,
> Or substance might be call'd that shadow seem'd,
> For each seem'd either [II, 666–670].

The audience, sharing the stance and the repressive ignorance of Satan, at first finds nothing to fear in this blank void. Like the despairing Samson, Death seems only "carelessly diffus'd" (*Samson Agonistes*, 118). With Satan (whose words when uttered by another Son will recoil upon him), the audience valorously cries to this son, "Retire, or taste thy folly, and learn by proof, / Hellborn, not to contend with Spirits of Heav'n" (II, 686–687). This son critically answers his general father: "Hell-doom'd" (II, 697). Death considers himself to be sole king and lord; ambitious father has sired ambitious son. Catching up the audience in its toils, this universal competition of pride whirls on, each insubstantiality swelling venomously against the other in grimly parodic "recognitions." If evil choice always emanates Sin and Death, and if Death consumes that which it is nourished by, Milton's audience is forced to watch, sickened, as the type of human concupiscence wars with its consequent mortality. Between the contenders steps the parodic mediatrix, Sin. She declares, but cannot make herself remember, who directs all three of them. The blows of devil and Death are in reality struck by

> . . . him who sits above and laughs the while
> At thee ordain'd his drudge, to execute
> Whate'er his wrath, which he calls Justice, bids,
> His wrath which one day will destroy ye both [II, 731–734].

They are God's ordained executioners and self-executioners. Because Sin is one aspect of the knowledge that invests choice—she is what Satan chose over God, and what the audience in its complicitous *Wasteland* stance must see as its possible choice against life and God—for a grim second she sees the whole of God's vertical design for the unholy trinity. She characteristically omits seeing herself, of course, but her reasoning insists that Sin, too, must anticipate (as she has already experienced) self-destructive recoil.

With Satan's and the audience's choice having halted before Sin in order that men might re-experience that first self-reflecting, disobedient bent to sin, there follows a questioning parody of the epic invocation itself ("till first I know of thee" [II, 740]), then a flat statement of the revulsion of choice from its elected consequence ("I know thee not, nor ever saw till now / Sight more detestable than him and thee" [II, 744–745]). Satan's disdain is severe lack of self-knowledge,[20] anticipating Adam's revulsion from Eve after he, in his way, similarly assisted her to fall: self-recognition of sin must always say, "If thou beest . . . ; But O how fall'n!" Sin's birth in the unreason of Satan's mind—"likest to thee in shape and count'nance" (II, 756)—is not only a grotesque parody of Athene but also, if Adam wills it, a parody for the loving, God-given (but "sinister") birth of Eve from the "wound" of Adam; the concupiscent image of the father may appear all too clearly in the daughter-wife. Satan typically must see his own nature in the objectified sin: "Thyself in me thy perfect image

---

[20] James H. Hanford, in *A Milton Handbook* (4th ed.; New York, 1954), p. 95, emphasizes the loss of light to both Satan and Adam.

viewing" (II, 764) . The audience becomes aware that its possible sin would be a Satanic image, just as its conferred goodness is a Godlike image, and that within itself a chosen sin can *perfect*— that is, bring to an ultimate manifestation—the idea that nourished it. The rape and incest of this unholy trinity contrast heavily with divine and human love yet bear unhappy comparison with the rapacious sexuality of Eve and Adam after the Fall. In Sin, any seeming creation or procreation serves only insatiable destructiveness, poorly perceived because blindly conceived. Sin's blind fear that Death may afflict Satan is dead wrong, however, for Death is nothing; instead, it is the living Son whom they must dread. Nor is she aware of the shattering irony in her description of Satan's armor as "temper'd heav'nly" (II, 813) , but we know that the whole of God's design flames through her lines.

Once more familiar to Satan, his ignorant Sin is ignorantly acknowledged in words not only prophetic of the Fall but also descriptive of its originating ignorance. His words are therefore of vital diagnostic importance to the audience:

> . . . my fair Son here shows't me, the dear pledge
> Of dalliance had with thee in Heav'n, and joys
> Then sweet, now sad to mention, through dire change
> Befall'n us unforeseen, unthought of . . . [II, 818–821].

Having made a Hell not of Heaven but of himself and having therefore abandoned divine foreknowledge, Satan as little foresees the consequences to him of the lustful rape he intends upon a new world and its "upstart" (II, 834) creatures. (In Heaven both the Son and God had also seemed to him "upstart," exalted.) The audience can cherish no such obscuring ignorance. A witness to evil choice, it now becomes victim to that choice: like Death, the audience becomes its "Son." It is more dismayed to see the consequences of evil choice join the attack, as eager as fledgling harpies. It is with our own world that Sin and Death "shall be fed and fill'd / Immeasurably, all things shall be [their] prey" (II, 843– 844) .[21] Although Death's macabre grin will "recoil" upon him when he is vanquished by the other man-God Son, who as one of

---

[21] Summers, *The Muse's Method,* pp. 52–53: The earth is introduced through the lens "of these absurd, 'non-existent' horrors."

those "upstart" human beings will be much too life-possessed to rest in Death's maw, any human comfort in this stance must be short-lived. Typic pride and rebellion break out again from Sin, who (like Eve) claims herself to be "heav'nly-born" (II, 860) — merely because Satan chose her Hell in Heaven. Limited truth becomes general falsehood, which is the only semblance of reason available laterally in Hell.

Harsh thunder, reminding us of Satan's scarred fall and foretelling further retribution, attends the parodic opening of the gates. The audience, dimly aware of the "freeing" of all its enemies and of its own complicity through its own sins that release first lust and then death, retains the stance in Hell for a period, as Satan, already familiar with the discordant warfare of "hot, cold, moist, and dry" (II, 898) in the confusion that is Hell, is impelled across the precreative drift of Chaos. It is little relief to realize that so far as man is concerned, Satan will come to a self-consumed "end" like the dregs or refuse of chaos. The stance is taken up from Hell in order to force the audience to watch, with greater horror, as the typic choice for evil now enters earth. Like the stance, Hell itself attempts transference. Even though Satan typically falls once again down the "vast vacuity" (II, 932) that in part intimates his essence, he lifts again toward the chaos that gave the world body [22] and toward the night that is one aspect of human experience, moving closer and closer to the substantiality of earth and men.

Much as Sin and Death expect a spiritual glut, Chaos and darkness are promised a material glut from a dissolving, falling earth. Satan's facile asphaltic "broad and beat'n way" (II, 1026) between Hell and this "frail World" (II, 1030) is intended to join earth so firmly to such destruction that the golden chain above cannot hold it to creative goodness. However, the reader is now delivered, "restored," from the true but most limited and partial perspectives of Hell. If our human origin is in part from Sin, our birth into the light beyond it is now also recognized. Hell is not the entire cosmos; God and good angels will support elective men against its unholy trinity. As the new stance near Heaven is taken,

[22] Hanford, in *A Milton Handbook*, p. 208, sees the victory over chaos as greater than that over the rebel angels.

earth is made to seem both inalterably majestic and yet minute and vulnerable, grandly chosen by God yet capable through human choice of tinily opposing both God and itself. The description descends from great to little:

> . . . fast by [Heaven] hanging in a golden Chain
> This pendant world, in bigness as a Star
> Of smallest Magnitude [II, 1051–1053].

The source of being and example of nonbeing choose this world even as the world chooses between them. The chain and the ramp indicate the possibility of double attention as of double route. The vital cosmos is of a piece. That is why choice is so important, as man's coming injury to all nature will attest.

If for a time stance seemed to weigh earth objectively like God's scales, at the close of Book II, Satan seizes our stance once more. It is past his gigantic cormorant shoulder (he, too, is a fisher of men) that we look upon a world that should remain pendant from Heaven but is dangerously free to fall to chaos. Only attachment to Heaven supplies strength to the world. Below Heaven lies terrible dissolving weakness that now has been fully experienced by the ascending audience. The typic choice for error and for ignorantly chosen result has been demonstrated in manifold ways, most prominently in the self-realization of Satan and in the presences of Sin and Death. The reader, whom verse and stance have brought to share in the plunge, knows Satanic choice. He may have been made ready to see—and "choose"—the opposite.

"THE MIND THROUGH ALL HER POWERS IRRADIATE": HEAVEN'S TYPIC
CHOICE FOR REASON AND BEING (BOOK III, LINES 1–417)

A hymnic second invocation gloriously redirects poet and audience from Hell to a radically opposed stance and to the matter of heavenly choice. Having left Satan staring balefully at both the world and Heaven, the invocation now prepares for us a place in Heaven—*revisiting* it, returning to the original site stipulated within the grand invocation to the entire epic. We are reminded that this divine station supplies the total perspective and the one ultimate position of *Paradise Lost*. If Satan leads us to the world, he in turn is always seen and led by God. We are also given a direct pattern of the paradise within, happier far, that Adam will attain. Although the sightless poet agonically laments the loss of his own earthly visual Eden, he is reassured that despite such Adamic loss, such a seeming Fall, the ultimately real "Celestial light" can

> Shine inward, and the mind through all her powers
> Irradiate, there plant eyes, all mist from thence
> Purge and disperse, that I may see and tell
> Of things invisible to mortal sight [III, 52–55].

Already resembling "*Tiresias* and *Phineus* Prophets old" (III, 36), he will fully become the new prophet forecast in "Il Penseroso."

In such creative light (which reflects the first creation and is reflected again in this very poem), God now is virtually made manifest. Like Adam on the mount, the audience takes a stance from which it can perceive, if not attain, divine perspective: "from the pure Empyrean [God] bent down his eye" (III, 57–58). The shared downward vision rests first upon God's son, who is to be the "second Adam," then upon our "Grand Parents," "reaping immortal fruits of joy and love, / Uninterrupted joy, unrivall'd love" (III, 67–68), instead of one grim mortal apple. Finally, divine vision takes note of the intrusion of Satan, that other son now become an Absalom.

The suggestion of time or sequence in such vision fades as the audience increasingly enters mentally into the "vertical" design. The invocation had celebrated our renewed contact with eternity:

> . . . before the Sun,
> Before the Heavens thou wert . . .
>
> . . . . .
>
> Thee I revisit now with bolder wing,
> Escap't the *Stygian* pool [III, 8–14].

The divine agency of absolute doing, saying, and showing in part dictates this reflective poem, even as the human mind in part becomes a fountain of received light and knowledge. Even the tenderly affecting lines upon his blindness lead Milton toward the same sense of union:

Shine inward . . . that I may see and tell
Of things invisible to mortal sight [III, 52–55].

Increasingly the epic will reveal all action to be not so much a
series of sequential, lateral episodes as one pattern of choice. Each
agent or actor will supply a part or type of one general response to
God-given creative liberty, an aspect of which is reinstituted in
every creatural choice.

The new stance of the reader, he who is one among God's
material "own works and their works" (III, 59), is uncomfortable
and demanding in comparison with that of Hell. Although the
approach to Heaven offered marvellous "Opal Tow'rs and Battle-
ments adorn'd / Of living Sapphire" (II, 1049–1050), even they
were seen first with Satan's jealous eyes. Once inside, Satanic
restlessness is likely to set in. The quick, furious, time-ridden,
ultimately destructive activity of Hell is replaced by the timeless
throbbing dynamism of creativity of Heaven, on the surface far
less volatile and exciting. The grandiloquent rhetoric of Hell gives
way to almost Socratic plainness of question and response. In
place of the gaudy splendors of "darkness visible," the audience
must bear Olympic clarity, the "unapproached Light" (III, 4)
that is an aspect of eternity. It is possible that like "the Sanctities
of Heaven" the audience should also receive "Beatitude past
utterance" (III, 62) from God's light, but it is probable that it
may resist strenuously; the history of man and of Milton criticism
suggests as much. Modern readers often feel Heaven to be literarily and spiritually both dull and terrifying. If even the stance of
Heaven seems unpleasant, what shall be said of God as against
easily chosen, easily choosing Satan?

Some critics suggest that Milton should not have permitted God
to speak at all; [23] if it is true that no human words can suggest his

---

[23] Perhaps the suggestion by Douglas Bush (*John Milton* [New York, 1964],
p. 154) that we think in terms of Greek *Dike* (justice) rather than in the
Christian tradition alone will be of help. Merritt Y. Hughes ("The Celestial
Dialogue," in *Ten Perspectives on Milton* [New Haven and London, 1965],
p. 122) points out how much of God's speech derives not from Milton alone
but directly from the Bible. John M. Steadman, in "The God of *Paradise Lost*
and the *Divina Commedia*" (*Archiv*, CXCV [1959], 279), suggests that Milton's anthropomorphic God, not less than Dante's, must be considered to be
symbolic, subject to the general policy of "accommodation."

wisdom, it is held, then human words are likely to express the opposite—dry platitude at best, or the viciousness of an almighty executioner at worst. Perhaps a God of vague terror or vague beauty could have remained shrouded in mystery, but that is not Milton's God. This God is to be justified as reasonable, as reasoning, as reason, even if man cannot comprehend it.[24] Ultimately, such a Word in part "is" God. As the Word, he cannot be encompassed within the words of this poem. Milton openly insists that all his poem, including its base of Biblical narrative, can only shadow forth reality. In the second place, God is here presented within severe limitations, largely as a choice that man can make. Unlike the industrious and familiar Satan, the God of Book III is abstracted almost into simple description of man's gift of creation, both original and redemptive. His words often are inquiring rather than commanding. They concern men, the human creatures who will choose, rather than God, who is not to be reasoned about in human terms. Although for dramatic convenience the voice is called that of "God," it is more exactly an intimation of only the extremely slight portion of divine attention that concerns man. Even this voice seems cold and difficult. It must oppose Satan by presenting an argument for severe justice, from which the Son will come to understand the need and the way of redemptive love.

I believe, therefore, that there is methektic method in this literary madness. If Satan (like Faust's Mephistopheles) seemed to us approachable, easy to describe and comprehend, surely it is Milton's direct purpose that we confess our warm attraction to Satanism, warm as our passional human blood, much as in the poem we first experienced Hell rather than Heaven.[25] Similarly, we must confess our hostility to God and to the clear light of free reason, much as Eve confesses her preference of narcissistic softness to Adam's reason. Then we as audience can discover that it is we, rather than God, who are spiritually as cold as the north of

[24] John S. Diekhoff (*Milton's Paradise Lost* [New York, 1946], p. 83), in describing the difficulty of the role of God, holds that he must be considered the most trustworthy of the witnesses.

[25] J. B. Broadbent, in *Some Graver Subject*, p. 124, considers the reader's route to Heaven as his exorcism of Satanism.

Hell. Whatever the literary dangers (and it may well be that Milton forced his readers dangerously beyond their natural sympathies), there can be little doubt of Milton's methektic genius in his causing us to experience instructively not only our pleasurable swerve toward vice but also our offended yaw from virtue. It is one of the significant anomalies in Milton criticism that readers, although displeased with God's foreknowing illimitable design for men in spite of its grace, mercy, and promise of renovation, are content with Satan's limited foreknowing design in spite of its sure sense of fate and mortality. Surely we witness more than mere resistance to the ultimate power of God or mere disbelief in Satan. From our own resistance to God we learn why Satan and Eve wandered into disaffection, thereby realizing within ourselves the springs of inanity and hatred.

The first words assigned for God stand resolutely against those of Satan.[26] The light of reason is not yet so very harsh. God voices love rather than hatred for a Son, together with absolute knowledge as against Satan's ignorant question, "Whence and what art thou, execrable shape?" Sure knowledge of time now forewitnesses Satan within his vast recoil. Satan is so persistently caught in the toils of that metaphor of armed self-punishment which also is divine design that it becomes almost an epithet. What is more, it supplies at least a poetic justification of those notorious cannons in Heaven. "Recoil" is implicit in rebellion. Although rage may swell Satan beyond loss for a moment, it must again "redound / Upon his own rebellious head" (III, 85–86). The purpose of the argument is not, however, to reveal the future of Satan but of man. Man too will try to "rise" rebelliously, like a puffing adder, will fall, and will then suffer fatal recoil. Unlike Satan, man always may choose truly to rise, whether beyond his own rebelliousness in the first case or beyond his recoil-dooming grave in the second.

God has been charged with being defensive and legalistic. If his words were a calculated defense of himself or if they alone constituted Milton's promised "justification" of God, the accusation

[26] Rosemond Tuve, in "George Herbert and *Caritas*" (*JWCI*, XXII [1959], 303–331), emphasizes that natural man does not and will not like God's plan.

would have merit. They instead are meant for man. Up to a point, they are even produced by man. The human creature is now to consider the epic's thematic question of his "first disobedience." He must therefore take God's perspective, if not his divine stance. ("To justify God's ways to men" also means to adjust men to God's ways, to alter man's means of measuring so that he may judge from the perspective of eternity.) The audience has already experienced Satan's fall and his eruptive attack upon the world. It also realizes as part of its own history that men similarly fell: "So will fall / Hee and his faithless Progeny" (III, 95–96). (Emphasis probably should rest upon *faithless,* for the term is exclusive rather than inclusive.) Because of its own participative realization, the audience fully comprehends both falls.

The query of the invocation must now be faced: "Whose fault?" (III, 96). Demanding light now increases, magnified until it is blinding but free of all shadows, hesitations, or ambiguities. It is the audience as much as God that replies, "Whose but his own? ingrate" (III, 97). Man now must accept the terrible, reasonable gift of freedom within the stance of Heaven, just as he had shared warmly in the folly of Hell. Reason (he is reminded) is choice; but the choice does not operate from chaotic chance or anarchic confusion of values. The human creature, like his angelic brother, was made "just and right" (III, 98) and free. Had he not been free, he could not have praised God but only served him, as Satan is mindlessly served (and ironically praised for destructiveness and loss) in Hell. The light of Heaven rests with unremitting clarity upon Milton's ultimate dynamic condition of human existence: freedom.

Milton's argument for God is not without flaws, of course. It moves by conditions already canceled (man prophetically "has" not persevered upright) and subjunctives already become indicatives. However, it resolves into two eternal considerations unaffected by the knowledge of change. First, the essential gift of reason, inherent in man's definition, is powerful enough to help him persevere within that definition. Second, the free choice attendant upon the gift of reason permits man the decision whether or not he will use reason and maintain his posture. His only determined act is choosing for or against reason, life, and God. If like Satan he elects to fall, he probably will then concoct a reason other than his own evil choice. Milton seems here to echo the complaint of Zeus in the *Odyssey:* in their good fortune men praise themselves, but in their evil choices they tax the gods. This argument too might be repellent if it proceeded only from God's illimitable will but is creditable enough when it is positioned for man, as Milton intended that it be: God is not directly author of the events men choose. In their complaints against their own choice, men will resemble "ingrate" Satan, who, although not the author of his being, is nevertheless the creator of his direct history wherein freedom was converted into fate. Similarly, man is free in politics, spirit, and intellect—until, like Samson in Milton's tragedy, he enthralls himself.

The issue remains unwaveringly centered in choice. The first "sort"—Satan and his angels—fell by their own "suggestion . . . / Self-tempted, self-deprav'd" (III, 129–130). Books I and II indicated that self-temptation continues for them and for men without abatement, and later Books will reinforce that truth repeatedly. As almost all of his private musings reveal, Satan can still choose not to be Hellish, but he causes the question to be academic: he will not so choose. The host of devils also makes gestures of freedom but readily surrenders its choice to Satan. Choice does not remain quite so open as its original conditions would suggest, however. One terrible effect of choice of error is the consequential "swerving" imbrutement, which must involve the deterioration of original reason. Volitional democracy then collapses into the hard simple necessitarianism of dictatorship. The second "sort," man, should recognize this threat. To help him, as Adam or as audience, God supplies long procedures of instruction. But because man has received active pressure toward wrong choice and because he is removed physically from the Heaven that Satan had directly enjoyed, if he falls, God will then "create" pressure countering the "swerve" (V, 238) and with mercy (as yet not particularized in the Son) will both help him in his original choice and also try to lead him back from self-depraving error.

The later specific charge to man will re-emphasize the conditions under which man's choice is made. In dispatching Raphael, God tells him:

> . . . such discourse bring on,
> As may advise him of his happy state,
> Happiness in his power left free to will,
> Left to his own free Will, his Will though free,
> Yet mutable; whence warn him to beware
> He swerve not too secure: tell him withal
> His danger, and from whom, what enemy
> Late fall'n himself from Heaven, is plotting now
> The fall of others from like state of bliss;
> By violence, no, for that shall be withstood,
> But by deceit and lies; this let him know [V, 233–243].

The field of human choice is so open that man must realize the dangers in freedom. If free will is abandoned, the will is made "mutable," slipping into determinism; if man is ignorantly self-confident in his liberty, he may swerve into a fall. He will also have to exercise Milton's difficult new heroism of patience rather than the old, easier heroism against "violence . . . that shall be withstood." Milton's God is revealed to be not so much the law-giver as the guarantor of continuing free will. Satan, on the other hand, is not so much a destroyer of men as he is the principle of their self-deceit, of the error by which men, like Satan, may "swerve" outside happiness. As readers, we can err by too great concentration upon both Satan and God as "characters." Although the epic conceived them as theologically true and also cast them in dramatic roles, its major attention rests upon their function as types of human ethical and religious choice.

The Son, on the other hand, is in part a great agent of both creation and choice, in part a typic man with human "character." In the first function he faced the same possibilities in Heaven as the angelic Satan but chose reasonably, meritoriously. If at times during the narrative when we see Satan alone the "Adversary" seems to be a force equal to God, it is only Satanic illusion or dramatic concentration, never a condition of power or theology. Whatever the degree of the Son's divinity, in Heaven he and Satan both were sons of God, "brothers" in the matter of choice, if not in creative power. All activity that the audience witnessed in the "present" time—that which was initiated when Satan first spoke in Book I—is a continuation of Satan's choice and the Son's choice, for like Satan, the Son continues choosing without abatement, eternally.

It is the Son's role as typic man—as one form of Adam—that most commands our human attention. The great oracular voice for God has spoken. From God has come the promise of "new joy" (III, 137), a new creation from which we will understand how God's Son, mercy, and love come to be "substantially express'd" (III, 140). It is at this moment that the redemptive Son is in one sense "begotten" (III, 80). For the first time in the poem we now receive from a dramatic personage an open *human* response, both in the narrative and in the dialogue. (Much of Satan's speech and of the narrative that accompanied it was perforce a much-doctored account of Satan's choice and its consequences; even though the narrative carefully chose ironic metaphors and disclaimed the truth of Satan's often nonsensical statements, the dramatic presentation was impelled almost to abet the father of lies in his lies, even as the taking of a stance with Satan forced the reader to experience Satan's fall.) The Son, who will be the means of the promised grace, fixes his attention altogether upon man's need and God's supplementary aid—grace. Doubly a son of God, he "unites" himself at once with "Man / Thy creature late so lov'd, thy youngest Son" (III, 150–151). He, rather than the supposedly Promethean Satan, is our better representative and voice.

It is the Son who supplies the first prayer for man, which is also the type of prayers by Adam and Abraham. However, the reason for his ensuing Abraham-like protestation that God should not let man fall—"that be from thee far, / That far be from thee, Father" (III, 153–154) [27]—has at times been misunderstood. It has been assumed that a severely condemnatory God is gradually forced to relent from his harshness by the eloquence of a more gracious personage. To correct the assumption, we must remember the nature of the Son in Milton. He is not divine Reason; he merely *has* reason. In contrast to his agon in *Paradise Regained,* his present effort is not to reject earthly knowledge and power but

[27] For the Son's allusive use of Biblical speeches by Abraham, see Mother M. Christopher Pecheux, "Abraham, Adam, and the Theme of Exile in *Paradise Lost,*" *PMLA,* LXXX (1965), 365–371, and James H. Sims, *The Bible in Milton's Epics* (Gainesville, Fla., 1962), pp. 202–204.

to attain active divine wisdom. He is led by Socratic propositions (ironically resembling those of the brief epic) into responsive protests and questions; God himself brings on "such discourse" as he later will suggest to Raphael. Biblical narrative had suggestively presented Christ asking similar questions—primarily that terrible question asked both by Adam and Christ, "My God, my God, why hast thou forsaken me?" The Son's present question approaches or echoes that: "shall the Adversary thus obtain / His end, and frustrate thine?" (III, 156–157). The point is not that a judging God is forced by a young public defender into fair judgment. It is instead that a type of our human reason is responding to the unalterable conditions of choice and the consequences of erroneous choice, attempting specifically to comprehend the "grace" and "Mercy" (III, 131, 132) just promised by God and even now operating in the very questions being asked. Christ's question (almost a prayer for creative realization) here is not fundamentally different from those that will come from Adam, for God and the Son in part predict Raphael and Adam. Both the one and the other "human" questions illustrate the wholly proper exercise of reason. It is only when such exploratory questions cease and dogmatic personal proclamations begin that Satanic immobilization within error, usually signaled by gorgeous rhetorical declarations, occurs.

Like his first great "foreseeing" attestation, God's rejoinder to the Son's questing speech (which tried to understand God, not to contest with him) has been widely misunderstood. When God says that the Son's speech has spoken "as my thoughts are, all / As my Eternal purpose hath decreed" (III, 171–172), those discontented with Milton's God have been confirmed in their suspicion that the judge has now usurped the young public defender's program, passing it off as his own. Instead, the Son, possessing (or having chosen) reason, has just manifested it: to God he is *now* "My word, my wisdom, and effectual might" (III, 170), in active form. Creation is of course of God, but by Christ; so are the realized creative actions of "word, . . . wisdom, . . . might." So, in its turn, must reason be recognized as being of God but, in its workings in the human being and in human history, by men. The promise that follows is not extracted from an unwilling God.

Instead, it comes to be perceived by the Son of God and son of man, even as in *Paradise Regained* he comes to understanding by the means of hard assays.[28] Care is needed still once more when God seems to offer a gift only in order to withdraw it:

> Man shall not quite be lost, but sav'd who will,
> Yet not of will in him, but grace in me
> Freely voutsaf't [III, 173–175].

Disaffected readers are again sure that they detect not only niggling second thoughts but a towering, totalitarian assertion of jealous omnipotence that refuses to permit the human will any power to act toward its own salvation. It is a grave misunderstanding of the proffered aid of grace. Obviously, Christ's will, as demonstrated during this dialogue, is perfect. Not so that of "foreseen" man, for it will have heavily "swerved" in error. Man cannot by himself "will" away the swerve or the possible Satanic pressure of evil, for the Fall will have surrendered some of that free exercise of reason. After the Fall, the first Adam may try to possess eternal life and a Paradise within but cannot erase the loss of earthly life and Eden. A foreseeing God envisions for him the mercy and grace made manifest in a second Adam, who with them will help needy men to "regain that blissful seat."

Much of our difficulty with *Paradise Lost* arises from our failure to view lateral human history from this ultimate, eternal stance. We usually isolate only one or another segment of time and event and rest all our sense of God's meaning with it. We should instead utilize the stance of Book III in order that we place any particular segment within the general perspective of Heaven, which is also that of the epic. First, Adam will fall in a choice freely made, but God has already promised gracious counterpressure. In *Paradise Lost,* that aid is the prevenient instruction by

---

[28] To the same point, see Hughes, *Ten Perspectives,* pp. 111–112; Barker, "Structural and Doctrinal Patterns," p. 185 ("The purpose is to call the Son in a way which invites him to a free act of participation in the Father's will and of confirmed free agency"); Daniells, in *Milton, Mannerism and Baroque,* p. 101, who sees the Son's will as deriving from that of the Father; and Irene Samuel, in "The Dialogue in Heaven: A Reconsideration of *Paradise Lost,* III, 1–417" (*PMLA,* LXXII [1957], 601–611), who sees that the Son receives far more mercy for man than he has requested.

Raphael, subsequent instruction by Michael, and the promise of a redemptive Christ to come. Second, *Paradise Regained,* as well as the Crucifixion, is dimly intimated when God promises:

> . . . once more [man] shall stand
> On even ground aginst his mortal foe,
> By me upheld, that he may know how frail
> His fall'n condition is [III, 178–181].

As *Paradise Regained* will insist, it is not Christ alone but God through him, or the choice for God by him, that sustains him in his battle with error. At first glance, the reason—"that he may know how frail / His fall'n condition is"—seems yet again jealous and petty, but is in practice a gift of instruction. When Satan thought he knew, he fell, and because he will not recover a truth that even he at times perceives, he remains fallen. If man considers his personal powers to be sufficient, particularly in the postlapsarian future now being "foreseen" by God, then he surely will fail. Weak overconfidence in human powers—a fault that will be pitiably demonstrated by Eve on the day of the Fall—is almost a guarantee of their loss. For God to be kind and man wise, Montaignesque man must know himself. Similarly, God's statement that man will owe his deliverance to "none but me" (III, 182) is not the jealous guarding of prerogative but a statement of obvious truth. It must be remembered that rebellious Satan will claim to Eve that he instead offers salvation, and that for this reason the historical Christ will have to retire into the submissive "not my will, but thine be done."

It is perhaps unfortunate that Milton's God must make statements that in a human being would be arrogant or offensive, but this God is not a person; he is an absolute, and only by absolutes can his being and his will be suggested. He is "all in all." He will not here answer in those sometimes pleasantly human, because shadowy, certitudes of the Son in *Paradise Regained.* Unlike the Son, he knows, absolutely, on a scale far removed from human question and clouded intimations.

We have not even yet done with our own justifying of the proclamations of Milton's God—especially of the manner of their phrasing. God shortly proclaims one sort of election, seeming thereby yet once more to assert divine caprice or tyranny. Milton's is no narrow doctrine of election. Nearly everything in *Paradise Lost* declares that man, not God, chooses man's immediate and eternal destiny. Therefore, when God says, "Some I have chosen of peculiar grace / Elect above the rest; so is my will" (III, 183–184), we must give close attention to the conditions, for this "election"—the first somewhat ambiguous demonstration of divine love—is not so much to special salvation as to special service. The condition of election most clearly operative in *Paradise Lost* is, I think, the historical one (if we understand "historical" in only the sense of a lateral unfolding of events) : by virtue of a greater wisdom, the Son is elect over angels as Adam is elect over Eve. In the historical review in Books XI and XII, Enoch and Elijah are so elect (in part, of course, "electing" themselves) . If God "elects" them, they obviously can refuse the election. The second condition is a Biblical memory: "Many are called but few are chosen." In his fiction, Milton would gloss that text, I suspect, as "self-chosen." The final condition involves a question of emphasis. The lines insist that the "election" appears only in the "peculiar grace" conferred upon the chosen men. They are not elect to salvation or eternal bliss, for that election rests mainly in their own choice. Nor has God signally "chosen" them in any way other than an extraordinary endowment with peculiar grace. That "peculiar grace" carries with it extraordinary demands for service, even agony: the elect and exalted "Only begotten Son" is being prepared for the offer of despised and humiliating sacrifice the Son will choose to make. Milton no doubt recognized in himself a similar "election" to a peculiar talent, along with a parallel demand for service and suffering.

For all the rest of mankind (no persons are damned before the fact of their own choice, in Milton's doctrine) , God will warn and "clear thir senses dark" (III, 188), supplying Raphael to Adam and Eve before the Fall, Michael afterward, and the Bible, sermons, hymns—and *Paradise Lost*—far more generally. His mercy is so extensive that if men even "endeavor" to "bring obedience due," he promises, "Mine ear shall not be slow, mine eye not shut" (III, 190–193) . What is more, he will send to all men not only a comforter but a champion—"My Umpire *Conscience*"—

who, if they choose to attend, will help them to "Light after light well us'd" (III, 195–196).

Although divine doctrine is not yet quite complete, for the manifesting Son has not yet made his great offer, the terms of the proclamation are clear. A beloved creature, showered with harmonious gifts of creation, will find among those gifts his own freedom to choose discord and deprivation. Because of the pressure of selfish passion typified by Satan, Adam will first choose erroneously. So may many (but not all) of his progeny. The Fall and some recoiling self-punishment will ensue. However, a countervailing "grace" and "mercy" are freely offered all men, among whom some few are supplied "peculiar grace" (which they are of course free to reject, as angelic Satan had refused his portion). A Johnsonian choice "for eternity" always remains open.

All this is fair and promising, but one great creative act still remains to be realized, and the Son must freely choose to be its agent. Therefore, God seems once again to "retire" into the harshness and severe legalism that induce choice. The first of his conditions is tolerable, for in observing Satan we have already witnessed the reason for it: those who "neglect and scorn . . . , [the] hard [will] be hard'n'd, blind be blinded more, / That they may stumble on, and deeper fall; / And none but such from mercy I exclude" (III, 199–202). Although a Biblical whisper suggests that God deliberately increases the refusal of these who, like Pharaoh, refuse him, Milton's doctrine throughout suggests that it is instead the rarely obdurate creature, whether man or Satan, who fixes his mind and hardens his own heart, who refuses all the warning and light; such beings therefore can be said to have "themselves ordain'd thir fall" (III, 128). The second condition seems much worse and is signaled by the peremptory "But yet all is not done" (III, 203). God insists that the first Adam, disobeying Heaven, "Affecting God-head" as Satan had, must die: "Die hee or Justice must" (III, 210). This notorious equation has set the teeth of generations of readers on edge. Once again, we must look carefully to the conditions of the statement. We now know that it is the prelude to a great call for a savior to free men from death. First, divine "foreseeing" of course knows that death will come to postlapsarian Adam and all men. The barest historical wisdom, to say nothing of omniscience, would contain such a truth. Furthermore, the reader of *Paradise Lost* must himself recall that he has seen Death initiated in erroneous choice in Heaven and hastened to full maturity in Hell; he can then contribute his particular narrative knowledge to the understanding of the condition stated by God. *Both* God and man, to say nothing of the audience that participated in Book II, have no choice but to know that Death is born to men. "Die hee . . . must," by the same knowledgeable justice that condemns a suicide who leaps from forty stories and by the history that records the event. If God is absolutely just, he cannot undo the self-recoiling injustice of men nor reverse with tyrannical caprice the death men themselves elected. If God is absolutely good, he cannot allow evil and death a place within his goodness, even though he pities the men who chose them. If man sins without consequence, the goodness into which he is created is revoked or set aside. In sum, the seemingly horrible sentence, "Die hee or Justice must; unless for him / Some other able, and as willing, pay / The rigid satisfaction" (III, 210–212), is at base little other than a statement of the law of noncontradiction, here taking this form: if the created object chooses to be other than the nature of its creation and creator, it will move to nonbeing, general alteration, death.

The manner of statement, however, involves yet another question of the nature of God. Although the equation really contains not rigid justice but the great act of mercy that is being prepared ("death for death," when applied to God's agent, Christ, seems to be not terrible law but overwhelming love) , its direct interest is in inciting the choice of the Son to be a savior. Its severity is one way of creating compassion. The confirmatory "sentencing" of man to his chosen physical death (despite all the promises that those who seek eternal life will find it) is intended to activate the compassionate pity of the Son, which will cause him to share the sentence. Totally unlike the rigged, self-electing maneuvering of Satan in Book II that was concealed under the fairest of rhetoric and most "glozing" of lies, divine "statement" has been directed toward persuading the Son to a free choice. *It has immediate parallels in the "harsh" statements of Michael that will bring the first Adam to a similar compassion for men.* After Michael similarly says,

"Adam, now ope thine eyes, and first behold [Death]" (XI, 423),
he "wept . . . compassion quell'd / His best of Man, and gave him
up to tears / A space" (XI, 495–498). Earlier, of course, he, like
Christ, had wished to bear all the suffering for the sin he had
chosen: "On mee, mee only, as the source and spring / Of all
corruption, all the blame lights due; / So might the wrath" (X,
832–834). The voice of God, either directly or through Michael,
and the answer of man, whether from the first or the second
Adam, are the same in both cases. Apart from its being an absolute in itself, "Justice" is used to impel love; it is the sharp right
profile of Mercy.[29]

The Son volunteers as savior. It must be emphasized once more,
however, that in doing so he enacts the idea of God. The "fulness
. . . of love divine" (III, 225) dwells in the Son but does not
originate with him. God's "word" for grace, "unprevented, unim-
plor'd, unsought" (III, 231), moves in him much as the poetic
words for justification supposedly move in Milton's own "unpremeditated" verse. Divine grace is already in process as the Son
moves to choose it; he is not really reminding an unwilling God of
a previous commitment when he says, "Thy word is past, man
shall find grace" (III, 227), but instead is realizing in himself the
means by which the promise may be fulfilled.

Now the promise intended in "death for death," but concealed
before, is made creatively manifest. In mortal communion, the
Son chooses its full implication: "Life for life / I offer" (III, 236–
237). "Account mee man," says the fully living god-man, who
cannot die:

> . . . thou hast giv'n me to possess
> Life in myself for ever . . .
> Though now to Death I yield, and am his due
> All that of me can die [III, 238, 243–246].

Now we are returned to the point of doctrine which the Father's
severity had seemed to revoke. "Account mee man" heralds much

---

[29] C. A. Patrides, in "Milton and the Protestant Theory of the Atonement"
(*PMLA,* LXXIV [1959], 13), concludes an illuminating article with Robert
Frost's sometimes Miltonesque "A Masque of Mercy" and the comment that
"it took another poet to discern the importance" of Milton's "Mercy first and
last shall brightest shine."

of Milton's doctrine, for as only the bodily portion of Christ will die, so death can never claim a greater portion of any man—unless the man so wills. As man, the Son is to enact what any postlapsarian man can choose. He of course acts also as the great apocalyptic champion, triumphing over Death, returning to God's presence "wherein no cloud / Of anger shall remain, but peace assur'd, / And reconcilement" (III, 262–264); but then every man, like Noah within the Flood, can be in his own choice a champion over death, even though like the Son he will suffer its physical effects. The Son has offered himself up freely, a life for a life, as Isaac will freely offer himself:

> . . . as a sacrifice
> Glad to be offer'd, he attends the will
> Of his great Father [III, 269–271].

The divine response is instinct with pride and love:

> . . . well thou know'st how dear
> To me are all my works, nor Man the least
> Though last created [III, 276–278].

Rather than permitting men by choice to degenerate into a lower order of being, God will preveniently insure that through Christ they share the divine "image" yet once again. They will receive a reinfusion of creation: "so in thee / As from a second root shall be restor'd, / . . . And live in thee transplanted, and from thee / Receive new life" (III, 287–294). Their doubly conferred life, in short, will precede their elective death. As the poem in Books I and II reflected acts of loss and death, so it now has enacted both creation and resurrection.

The whole epic threatened for a moment to turn sharply toward the second, renovative Adam, and to the apocalyptic associations proper to his being humanly judged, to his "dying" in his human part, and to his being raised (and with him all his "Brethren")—but the shift was only momentary. We instead return to the divine offer (and command) that man choose. The operative word in the passage below is *still,* italicized to show its insistence that choice by men is as timeless as God's idea of man:

> So Heav'nly love shall outdo Hellish hate,
> Giving to death, and dying to redeem,

> So dearly to redeem what Hellish hate
> So easily destroy'd, and *still* destroys
> In those who, when they may, accept not grace [III, 298–302].

Even Christ is Christ partly by choice rather than by God's will alone: he has "been found / By Merit more than Birthright Son of God, / Found worthiest to be so by being Good, / Far more than Great or High" (III, 308–311) . For such goodness to "counterfall" in sacrifice is only another form of its exaltation, and for such a being to assume his glory is only to indicate that he fully exercises his own compassionate, new-heroic goodness, "far more than Great or High." All creatural choice can be foreseen in its final form when "Bad men and Angels" (III, 331) are judged and sealed in the Hell of their own choice and judgment forever, while, phoenix-like, the earth purges its dross in fire and all forms of separate being merge into the great One:

> Then thou thy regal Sceptre shall lay by,
> For regal Sceptre then no more shall need,
> God shall be All in All [III, 339–341].

Man by this promise can ascend to a more spiritualized form of existence; Christ, like all other secondary substances, is here promised the ultimate ascension.

In contrast to the martial clangor heard in the stance of Hell, the audience hears the hosts of Heaven with humble reverence respond to the proclamations and offer of service, celebrating the amaranth of timelessness that man is on the point of refusing. Heretofore, the reader had been permitted to stand below Heaven in order to receive instruction. The stance suddenly alters. Instead of merely observing divine celebration, the audience, in a movement almost like that of the Nativity Ode, is drawn directly and irresistibly into the hosts of worshippers. Milton had properly withheld such absolute methektic assent in Hell. Now each reader's voice and the authorial words join in the consent and concord of Heaven, addressing as "thee" both the gracious Father and the participative Son, exalting the latter as both spiritually begetting "Adam" and as brother:

> *Thee* Father first they sung Omnipotent
>
> . . . . .

Thee next they sang of all Creation first,
Begotten Son, Divine Similitude,
In whose conspicuous count'nance, without cloud
Made visible, th' Almighty Father shines
                [III, 372–386—italics added].

In praising Christ, man, who also has a "human face divine" (III, 44) , for a moment sees Hell in proper perspective as a place of "fierce vengeance" (III, 399) by God, not against God (as Satan fancies it to be) . He also defines God not as tyrant but as "Father of Mercy and Grace" (III, 401) . Although never quite reaching Christ's stance, the audience briefly sees as he sees. The Son recognizes himself as an extension or manifestation of God, chosen of God even as he chooses God; therefore, the love realized in his mortal participation with man is ultimately God's love. In an ebb and flow of ambiguity, the verse itself hesitates whether to assign the creative sacrifice to Christ or to God but resolves the question by directing it finally to God, who in the beginning and end of history, as of definition, is "all in all."

"SUSPICION SLEEPS": VANITY AND CREDULITY AS ACCESSORIES TO ERROR (BOOK III, LINES 418–742)

The epic has reached to the depth, then to the height, of human choices, taking participative stands with each, powerfully initiating the lateral pattern of fall, time, history, and death, even while envisioning the vertical pattern in which fall and death, through judgment and grace, are transformed into their opposites. From this point forward, the stance becomes that of the human world and human knowledge. The great poles of Hell and Heaven have fixed that world and its knowledge within the vast stretches of eternal choosing and eternal choice. The human world is to be the theater for the new enactment of choice, but there is always a doubled sense of divine (and diabolic) audience and of divine composer beyond. Not only will the drama re-enact timeless choices, running all the way back to Lucifer and forward to the choices ratified by the apocalypse, but also each seeming individual choice will be revealed as individual neither in provenance nor in ultimate consequence.

The perspective of Heaven is closed, for the time being, by human separation from the heavenly hymn. Audience stance descends, leaving "them"—the hosts of Heaven—in the empyrean, "above the starry Sphere" (III, 416) where *Comus* originated. It enters "*this* round World" (III, 419—italics added). Earth resembles other spheres but will be particularized with human events. The outer limit of this world, its moral periphery, is significantly open on one side toward Chaos but, just as significantly, is open on the side facing Heaven to a gracious "small reflection . . . / Of glimmering air less vext with tempest loud" (III, 428–429). Toward this pleasant golden fruit Satan speeds.

Before entering mortal Eden, the poem considers one further possibility of choice—in that which is none. The final movement in Book III recapitulates the pattern *fall, renewal* just prior to the full descent to earth. When Satan's chosen insubstantiality appears, a form of human chaos and nothingness, the limbo of fools, is objectified near him. Often misunderstood, that limbo is necessary to Milton's (as to Spenser's) belief in the human will. It is better almost to be damned than idle, evasive of the dust and heat of the race. Like Pascal, Milton might insist, "But you must wager. It is not optional. You are embarked." Limbo possesses those who will reject even denial, the heat of which can even germinate hope (for men, if not for devils). Limbo seems to offer a third "pole" for human choice, but like the mechanical absurdity of that notion is necessarily vain. Anticipating Books XI and XII and human history, it will hold the empty shells of men who hoped for final glory from the vanity of things and the "praise of men" (III, 453). In one way it is hellish, being caught in a violent superstitious swerve [30] from true religion and the true Heaven it vainly imitates. Its choices were perhaps rightly begun but later were so severely misdirected as to dissolve reason into intellectual chaos. To such a house of mortal fame Milton, in a marvellously poetic but scornful juxtaposition, assigns "Embryos, and Idiots,

[30] Frank L. Huntley, "A Justification of Milton's 'Paradise of Fools' (*P.L.*, III, 431–499)," *ELH*, XXI (1954), 111: "The apparently disparate concepts of perverted sex and strong wind unite the symbol of the vulture," thus associating the cormorant, perverse sexuality, and wind with Limbo, Hell, and the Fall.

Eremites and Friars" (III, 474). It is to this emptiness that Satan would mislead the Son of *Paradise Regained*. Limbo is not so much positively Satanic as negatively Prufrockian, recalling the image of "wandering" by the philosophers of Hell. Having chosen eternal chaotic nonsense, these "fools" are provided a corresponding image and place, a negative parody of the "placelessness" of the omnipresent God. It is fitting that the audience should discover Limbo with Satan who, when he is not immobilized in his own prideful fate, almost admires God and hopes for Heaven— vainly. As in pride he is king of Hell, so in vanity of desiring he is also perhaps first in the parodic and prophetic Paradise—of Fools.

For his self-torment, Satan is permitted to observe the renovative stairs of Heaven, so unlike his chosen asphaltic ramp to Hell, along with the bright sea of jasper that shames the roiling tumult of Hell's ocean. For a second Satan's perspective is neutral—is indeed ours—as he, with the audience, takes a stance just above earth. He looks "with wonder . . . / At sight of all this World beheld so fair" (III, 542, 554). His helpless admiration almost moves him to a hymn of praise, but then foolishly, characteristically, it buckles into hateful egotism. Although Jacob here saw the gate of Heaven, Satan permits his gate to read only "Abandon hope." He elects Hell again, for he is both more and less than a mere fool. He hurls himself toward the sun, which is a typic image or metaphor for God and the angelic spheres that dance before him (and for Meredith's army of unalterable law):

> . . . they as they move
> Thir Starry dance in numbers that compute
> Days, months, and years, towards his all-cheering Lamp
> Turn swift thir various motions, or are turn'd
> By his Magnetic beam, that gently warms
> The Universe, and to each inward part
> With gentle penetration, though unseen,
> Shoots invisible virtue even to the deep [III, 579–586].

This sun also is in part the image of creative and "Celestial Light," so much so that heliocentrism threatens the specific sense of the sun as star. Metaphor begins to suggest that creative spiritual light within the blindness of the poet is like the coming of form to chaos, and that prevenient warmth raising an inward paradise is one with generative physical warmth in the calving and breathing dust of earth. Those dangers or promises are evaded, however, with the doctrine that the sun itself is here "matter new," silver and gold and "radiant light" (III, 613, 594).

Within the sun, Uriel, both an angelic inhabitant and an ethical meaning, stands deep in thought. His reason will present the first direct earthly articulation of earthly choices, in that opposing decisions made here for and against light, God, and the new world will be geographically typical for the human choices that are to come. Wishful Satan stages an aërial temptation recalling that in Heaven and foretelling those on earth. As Hell had decided, his strategy is no longer one of violence but of stealth and disguise. He tries to perfect in advance the weapons he will use against credulous Eve. In this transitional angelic encounter, fall again precedes renewal. Uriel is an abrupt warning to the human audience, even though he also eventually achieves instructive right choice. Right choice for men or angels asks, not dewy innocence and credulousness, but exacting skill and caution, somewhat like that uncomfortable divine standard of judgment encountered in Heaven. The readers, uneasily sharing Satan's perspective during the encounter, patently must judge with terror Satan's assurance that earth is his "journey's end and our beginning woe" (III, 633). Like Milton in Book IV, the audience can only wish for an apocalyptic voice with which to warn Uriel, who like Spenser's knight is "too simple and too true." The Adversary makes his insubstantiality simulate the substance of a cherub. Here, as in *Paradise Regained,* he takes for his disguise his own notion of the likeness of the tempted object. He complementally glozes his words, even though open ironies and secret self-temptations writhe within them. Much as he will address Eve later, he temptingly nominates Uriel as "first" in doing God's will (displacing Christ) and as "interpreter through highest Heav'n" (ignoring Christ as Word [III, 657]). He all but promises Uriel an Eve-like honor in the new World. As for man, Satan, like the angel, admits an "unspeakable desire" to know this creature "alone thus wand'ring" (III, 662, 667). His dreadful "secret gaze" is bent upon

"all things" (III, 671, 675) else made by God; for the newborn
world, he acts as a Herod inquiring after the child Jesus.[31]

Readers sometimes have objected to Milton's assertion that evil
can enter the mind of angels and of God. Uriel supplies the
overpowering reason why it probably should enter the mind and
be "known" in a preventive sense lest it enter the body and spirit
irredeemably. Nearly as foolish as Limbo's refusal to choose is the
credulity that chooses blindly:

> . . . oft though wisdom wake, suspicion sleeps
> At wisdom's Gate, and to simplicity
> Resigns her charge, while goodness thinks no ill
> Where no ill seems [III, 686–689].

Uriel is such an unguarded sleeper, for he takes Satan's professed
desire for knowledge to be praiseworthy. The wiser Raphael later
will have some properly "suspicious" words when such a wish is
voiced by Adam. Uriel invites Satan and the audience to witness
the new world in its position of choice:

> Look downward on that Globe whose hither side
> With light from hence, though but reflected, shines;
> That place is Earth the seat of Man, that light
> His day [III, 722–725].

We should recall the countervailing beatitude that is God's physical light (resembling his manifested Son), even as we observe the
dark seeming success of the first earthly temptation. Furthermore,
a comparable spiritual beautitude in Uriel now "rises" to oppose
Satan's victory. The full pattern of fall, renewal forms when the
credulous angel recovers into confident and active choice for the
general design of God. He closes the exchange with an unwitting
condemnation of Satan to his chosen fall—"Thy way thou canst
not miss"—and a renewed confirmation of his own allegiance—"me mine requires" (III, 735). Once again as solitary as
pride except for the methektic presence of author and reader,
Satan alights on Mount Niphates. There he will stage the tempta-

---

[31] James H. Sims (*The Bible in Milton's Epics*, p. 174) finds Herod to
reflect Satan. The same kind of star rises over both.

tions of both the first and the second Adam. By type, they are all men, as Niphates is all places of earth.

With that placement of Satan on earth, the great preparatory stands of *Paradise Lost,* closely resembling the first stances of *Comus,* are ended. The stage lies waiting for the image of the Creator on earth, he who must elect creativity or sterility, sympathy or isolation, charity or pride, life or death, Being or nonbeing.

"WHERE AND WHAT I WAS": PARADIGMS OF CHOICE AND DEFINITION FOR ORIGINAL MEN (BOOK IV)

In the economy of *Paradise Lost,* Book IV is excellent and indispensable. It was necessary that a transition between the enactments of Heaven and Hell and those of earth be formed, and that the two great polar choices for man be present as man is ceremoniously introduced in Paradise—for we will never see our kind in isolation, but always within a "happy State / Favor'd of Heav'n," as well as in the shadows of a "foul revolt" (I, 29–30, 33). The towering paradigms must supply the moral motivations and the proscenium of Eden. Milton converted what might have been necessity alone into a poetic crucible wherein all the elements of *Paradise Lost* meet and are synthesized.

Lateral and vertical designs here come into perfect equipoise. God's design, evident both in creation on earth and in the attendant guardianship of man by angels, is intersected by Satan's somewhat lesser rebellious-servile design. As in Books I and II, Satan's doing, although reaching well beyond human sense spatially and temporally, is nevertheless time-confined. He is intent now upon subverting the new world and the new creatures who restore the void of love that he had caused. If men choose him, they too will fall from God's time, through Satan's, into the human time later witnessed by Adam. Book IV recapitulates epic progress to this point, as well as the pattern of fall, renewal, by bringing Satan and Satanic mentality first upon the stage. The opposing claim of reason, paralleling that of God in Book III, is now courageously voiced by man. The likelihood of fall is also present, in the dreaming, questioning, fleshly possibilities of Eve. The eye of God sees all, and man is on this occasion safely returned from danger to a love of his kind and of the angelic heavens. Angels, no longer credulous, discover Satan and repeat their contest on earth as it was in Heaven, until the scales of God show all of Satan's lateral movements to be vain. Satan's murmurous flight into the shadows predicts his apocalyptic end as "chaff." Not only, then, does this microcosmic Book prepare that which might be, for man, by showing him originally persevering upright amidst his choices; it also fixes what will be accomplished by means of God's design, regardless of the swerving particular actions of Satan or man.

Even our initial entrance into Eden, heralded by the pained prophetic outcry of the author in his merely human function, is attended by that balance of design. Although the speaker at first presents not a general agonic invocation but instead strained personal human pity for the entering human actors, he is immediately identified with another John who watched terminal malice stoop on mankind, and thereby becomes himself almost a "first" John of Patmos:

> O for that warning voice, which he who saw
> Th' *Apocalypse,* heard cry in Heav'n aloud,
> Then when the Dragon, put to second rout,
> Came furious down to be reveng'd on men,
> *Woe to the inhabitants on Earth!* [IV, 1–5].

Now such victorious announcement of the routs that begin and end Satanic time is joined with the pain, suggesting in turn that John's voice is also a manifestation of eternal grace and deliverance. Now adding a sense of prophetic revelation to its "saying" and "doing," the poem in itself, with Milton as hierophant, will supply a "warning voice" from Raphael across the entire center of the epic. Nevertheless, human compassion for Adam and Eve, like that to which Adam and Eve will themselves arrive, is the immediate, narrow effect of the exordium. As audience, their children must sadly realize that "all our woe," stressed in the beginning of the epic, is the prior condition chosen by man for man's beginning. In Hopkins' words, "It ís the blight man was born for, / It is Margaret you mourn for." The effect is unsparing and severe. Time at once shifts toward the present, engaging the woe as ours: "for *now* / *Satan, now* first inflam'd with rage, came down" (IV,

8–9—extra italics added). As the credulousness of Uriel in Book III gave warning, the choice for this blundering evil can be made far too casually; the distant ironic recoil of the Last Judgment upon Satan is the ultimate demonstration. However, it is not now an ultimate choice but instead the first human disobedience that must be enacted before the sorrowing audience—and within it.

Because of the general pattern of fall and renewal and the complementary order of the preparatory stands in Hell and Heaven, the typic threat rather than the promise in man's open choice is enacted first, duplicating the epic's grand strategy within which we saw Hell before we saw Heaven. Its form is the self-destructive passion that "boils" hellishly in the "tumultuous" breast of Satan (IV, 16). God's design, as well as Satan's own self-inflicted punishment, is again expressed in the image of a cannon, the apocalyptic "devilish Engine [which] back recoils / Upon himself" (IV, 17–18). Hell is Satan's choice and he is never out of it, climb toward Heaven or earth though he may: the truism is demonstrated at once in his soliloquy. He all but worships God and the sun, yet recoiling ambition always wars with his reason and egotism always defeats praise. All future human hesitations and choices are prefigured in his questions, which, whipping backward and forward and rending themselves, are of the nature of Hell. Ambiguity and perversion of argument rush him to the unreasonable (which for him are nevertheless true) conclusions, "Be then his Love accurst, since love or hate, / To me alike, it deals eternal woe" and "Evil be thou my Good" (IV, 69–70, 110). Eve will bend to much the same kind of fantastic utterance but will lack Satan's secret conviction that God is good. She therefore will escape Satan's knowledge-defying "hardened" heart. The recurring fall of Satan is typologically the fall of man, as like passions "dim" his face (IV, 114). In a counter effect, sadder and wiser Uriel penetrates the "darkness visible" of momentary hypocrisy. Like Eve later, Satan had supposed foolishly that if he were alone he would be unseen.

The unwillingly complicitous audience now must follow the Adversary into the center of the bountiful gifts given man as Satan enters Eden, wrought artfully in the image of a grander golden age but made to breathe the spices of a present Araby. Like a showy schoolboy, he vaults over the protective wall, but his intention shifts the metaphor: he has hurtled like a wolf on the fold, or like those seventeenth-century Lycidian "lewd Hirelings" that climb into "his Church" (IV, 193). More threateningly, but perhaps necessarily if man is to choose, he rests vulture-like within the Tree of Life. This "middle" Tree in the Garden bears analogy with the future "tree" of Calvary, because it will prove to be paradoxically "next to Life / Our Death" (IV, 220–221) for the first Adam but the opposite for the second. Satan is the full prohibition, in a sense; as himself, he is disorder, and as father of Death, he is its fruit or consequence. Although Eden is mounted upon poles of choice, it can be maintained as both a luxuriantly fertile and a quietly Horatian "happy rural seat of various view" (IV, 247), dear to classical and neoclassical hearts. Milton's contemporary audience must have felt the loss of this Eden keenly. The verse, too, finds Eden to be threatened as it compares Eden with Enna, or with the abandoned or forsworn grove and spring of Daphne and Apollo, or with Comus-haunted, Bacchic Nysa. These intimations increase the audience's fear as it awaits the entrance of man. The apprehension is warranted, because it must see man first within the malevolent stance of Satan, who "saw undelighted all delight" (IV, 286).

Upon their entrance, Milton bestows a description of creative Phidian splendor [32] upon our free "grand Parents." In Adam's "large Front" and "Hyacinthine Locks" beauty and intelligence meet, bearing "the image of thir glorious Maker" (IV, 300–301, 292). Man generally is defined within his original reflective gifts from God—"Truth, Wisdom, Sanctitude"—and his consequent "filial" relationship (IV, 293–294). Although created as filial, he is free to become prodigal. He has only to break the natural creative order of gifts:

> For contemplation hee and valor form'd,
> For softness shee and sweet attractive Grace,
> Hee for God only, shee for God in him [IV, 297–299].

This hierarchical order of the sexes, repugnant to many of Milton's readers, is not really tyrannical, for it can be broken all too

---

[32] Sister Mary Corcoran, in *Milton's Paradise with Reference to the Hexameral Background* (Washington, D. C., 1945), p. 45, records that the description of Adam is in part based upon portraits of Christ.

easily—in the upshot, we see how easily. Nor is it "unfair" to Eve, for if Adam is a reflection of God and shares God's "contemplation," Eve is a second reflection, sharing both God's grace and man's love. She was the first, as Christ is a second, gracious offering to man. As yet, Edenic order prevents one of the terrible, divisive by-products of sin, "dishonest shame / Of Nature's works, honor dishonorable," for by antagonistic sin shame entered the world and brought with it the immodest need for separative "modesty" (IV, 313–314). There is now only ideal, complementary union of reason and truth with love and beauty.

Because of the fear induced by Satan's presence, our first vision of Adam and Eve is already elegiac, already haunted with the great similarity between our first and last glimpses of them in Paradise. In Book IV, with a tremulous insistence on the past tense for Eden,

> . . . hand in hand they pass'd, the loveliest pair
> That ever since in love's imbraces met,
> *Adam* the goodliest man of men since born
> His Sons, the fairest of her Daughters *Eve* [IV, 321–324].

At the end of the epic, we know the two visions to have been one, as

> They hand in hand with wand'ring steps and slow,
> Through *Eden* took thir solitary way [XII, 648–649].

Our concern now might have been reduced, for Adam and Eve gradually blot Satan from the edge of our vision. But he, too, is their audience, and persistent references to his pressure and their coming fall frame the scene.[33] A prophetic verb appears in the first description of their appetite: "to thir Supper Fruits they *fell*" (IV, 331—italics added). The happy pastoral scene of peaceful animals at play is shivered with the reminder that the beasts of history are "since wild" (IV, 341). The serpent seems to play before them, "his fatal guile . . . unheeded" (IV, 349–350). Fear for our representative parents mounts as we are returned to the Satanic mentality that may afflict their minds and therefore become universally human. Milton dares what is in part a joke, in

---

[33] Mahood, in *Poetry and Humanism,* pp. 180–182, considers our knowledge of corruption to be our gateway for return to Eden's "womb-like security."

part a total revelation of accursed choice, with Satan's first words as he considers Eden in this second soliloquy (IV, 358) : "Oh Hell!" His peculiar savoring of beauty and God again brings him to the edge of worship for both creatures and Creator, "whom my thoughts pursue / With wonder, and could love, so lively shines / In them Divine resemblance" (IV, 362–364) . But by his perverse choice, resembling that of Eve later, love becomes Sin and any embrace that of Death. His loved image of man fades to that of a grinning skull. He pleads not divine freedom but "necessity, / The Tyrant's plea" (IV, 393–394) . Furthermore, "freely" (so he supposes) he sinks into the forms of brutes for concealment, while his unwitting but complementary imbrutement proceeds. The poem's imagery permits its readers no respite in their initial experience of Satan among men, for it likens Satan to a tiger who "by chance hath spi'd / In some Purlieu two gentle Fawns at play" (IV, 403–404) . This is the brace seen fleeing Eden at the end of *Paradise Lost*.

As we draw near to listen now to Adam and Eve, we can for a time forget the Satanic fate they may choose. Some time-honored questions rise around them: When exactly did they fall? Could they consider evil before the Fall? Is not their mentality more interesting and their spirituality more active after the Fall? The well-meaning questions show little perception of Milton's Paradise. Although, unlike the methektic reader, Adam and Eve in their beginning are not fallen, they are full-grown from the start, possessing the same choices, the same free contemplation of all things whether good or evil, and the same mentality (though not the same spirituality) before as after the Fall. They differ from us only in possessing immortality, unfading youthfulness, and all useful knowledge. The coming temptation should be "fruitless" to them, because they already possess everything except change and death. Notably, they are precisely like us in having no option of avoiding free choice. It is their only "necessity." Like Hell to Satan, the choice of Eden is wherever and whenever they are. If we have forgotten paradigmatic Satan, Adam's first words recall him; Adam elevates Eve as dangerously as Satan had "raised" Sin. He addresses her as "Sole partner and sole part of all these joys, / Dearer thyself than all" (IV, 411–412) . Filial order and

divine love threaten to alter into appetite. However, even as that
choice seems to threaten, the voice of grace and reason opposes it.
Adam tells Eve that they are

> not to taste that only Tree
> Of Knowledge, planted by the Tree of Life,
> So near grows Death to Life, whate'er Death is,
>
> . . . . .
>
> The only sign of our obedience left
> Among so many signs of power and rule
> Conferr'd upon us, and Dominion giv'n [IV, 423–430].

They lack negative knowledge of Satan and death, it is true,
but they possess the fullness of its divine opposite, a power "As
liberal and free as infinite" (IV, 412–415). Beyond their life-de-
voted present knowledge, even greater grace and reason virtually
promise the fallen men of the audience resurrection within the
very image of creation: God "rais'd us from the dust and plac't us
here / In all this happiness" (IV, 416–417). For the present, however, reason, as voiced by its particular human agent, Adam,
makes them sufficient to have stood.

We uneasily notice that for our generating parents human
self-definition begins in peril of Satanic pride. As Adam has perhaps unduly elevated Eve, so Eve places Adam in a position not
only of superiority to herself but to any divine creativeness: "O
thou for whom / And from whom I was form'd flesh of thy
flesh, / And without whom am to no end" (IV, 440–442). Although she now loves Adam, her love of mankind tends toward
the narcissistic, neglecting union with God. All vital human questions rush to a head as she recalls her creation, "much wond'ring
where / And what I was" (IV, 451–452). In one respect Adam and
Eve are very modern indeed: they must choose what they will be.
Even their names suggest the imperative of choice, with its possibilities of virtue or vice. Regardless of God's originating idea and
of his "life" in their substance, they can elect their own definitions
in process. Satan already has elected his definition. Rigid self-im-
prisonment possesses his memory and prophesies "what he was,
what is, and what must be / Worse" (IV, 25–26). But for Adam
and Eve, a free first choice and the guarantee, by grace, of a
second will be held open.

Guiding the search of the audience, Eve's first quest for identity is not promising. Opposing Adam's preceding stand, it is a form of fall, the first of three such separations from Adam and God. Narcissistically,[34] she half falls in love with her own image in a pool. As self-love had undone Satan and given birth to Sin, so it openly threatens mankind through our great mother. A reasonable voice directs her from self to Adam (as at the Fall an unreasonable voice will lead her back to her sole self), but the analysis of her first conscious response to reason gives double cause for fear. In the first place, she is easily led and can therefore be misled easily. On this occasion she asks helplessly, "What could I do, / But follow straight, invisibly thus led?" (IV, 475–476). Such obedience looks suspiciously like swift surrender into Satanic fate. Also, her original reaction to Adam, closely paralleling that of the audience to God in Book III, is one of resistance to godlike virtues; she desires instead that which is more "winning soft . . . amiably mild" than his "manly grace / And wisdom" (IV, 479, 490–491). As Satan's chosen "perfect image" was sin, so hers is self; she already all but renounces her having been created in the general image of man, who was created in the image of God. Dangerously, her first gesture had been one of flight from superior being, divine or human, choosing instead the isolative "worse." She had moved from that fall to proper choice, instead, of his "grace / And widsom, which alone is truly fair."

Although their finely frank, innocent, and renewing love is placed under immediate threat when Satan and the unwilling, but participatively implicated, audience view them with voyeuristic and fallen "jealous leer" (IV, 503), the greater threat comes from Satan's renewed fall. Again—but in Eden!—the audience is forced to share the process of deception and the rhetoric of falsehood. While Satan deliberately converts love into the "fierce desire" (IV, 509) of hatred, he begins to mumble over again the very words which continually lead him to sorrowful choice, and which will in turn successfully mislead Eve (but fail with Jesus). He tempts himself again before he approaches man. Although he had denied the revelation of his own will to the denizens of Hell, he

[34] D. C. Allen, in "Milton's Eve and the Evening Angels" (*MLN*, LXXV [1960], 108), finds the fallen angels, like Eve, to have succumbed to narcissism.

now tells himself that forbidden knowledge is "suspicious, reasonless" (IV, 516). He is sure that Edenic innocence is ignorance. He
again thrusts himself (and the audience, if it chooses with him)
into the primal sin by believing that "Knowledge might exalt
[men] / Equal with Gods" (IV, 525–526). If the realistic, destructive side of him knows that in such a wish men will "taste and die"
(IV, 527), his cunning ignorance prevents his seeing that the sentence also involves him and his tasting of the ashen fruits of Hell.
Unreasoning, increasingly degenerate delusion appears when he
sentences them to death while saying, "Live while ye may"
(IV, 533), assuming that it is he who gives or withdraws spiritual
life, and also when he turns his "proud step . . . scornful" but
with an ignoble "sly circumspection" (IV, 536–537). The audience may be relieved when he withdraws again from stage center,
but his presence remains. In token of it, Eden's sun sinks, pathetically.

If Satan had been opposed before by the words of Adam, during
a night reminiscent of that in *Comus* he is opposed a second time
by attendant spirits. Displacing Satan in the audience vision is a
tower reaching "with one ascent / Accessible from Earth" (IV,
545–546) toward Heaven. Upon it Gabriel mounts a watch rival
to Satan's watch upon men. Near the angel race the Homeric-
astronomical victorious "unarmed Youth of Heav'n" (IV, 552
—unarmed in Homer's sense, but no doubt armed spiritually
by Paul). Metaphorically a second guardian because his descent
resembles that of the Attendant Spirit, Uriel like a "shooting
Star" helps the benighted sailor avoid Leviathan: in a double
sense such a light "thwarts the night . . . and shows the
Mariner / From what point of his Compass to beware / Impetuous
winds" (IV, 557–560). His typic mission is to warn Gabriel, for
man, of the passion now exerting pressure on man. Gabriel somewhat too easily assures angel and man that if Satan enters Eden,
it is not from Satan's will but with God's permission. As guardian,
Gabriel believes he will surely know of any intrusion and provide
warning. He is right, but like the Elder Brother in *Comus*, he is
overconfident of man.

Before the paradigmatic opponents come into open confrontation, the epic takes one last stand in original Eden. A gorgeous

nocturne tuned to the nightingale's song leads Adam and Eve to mutual love—her imitation from the Song of Songs becomes an ode to Adam—and to human questions. Against Adam's reasonable image of man's duty to "lop [the] wanton growth" (IV, 629) of otherwise too luxuriant nature, Eve opposes a selfish question indicting God of waste or of having included passionate, appetitive superabundance in the nature of things, almost as if to anticipate not only her prelapsarian greed but also her postlapsarian suggestion that all procreation cease: "But wherefore all night long shine these, for whom / This glorious sight, when sleep hath shut all eyes?" (IV, 657–658) . Adam replies that light illumines all the world on alternate hemispheres, "Lest total darkness should by Night regain / Her old possession" (IV, 665–666) . He rebukes nascent human egotism by reminding her that man is not the only inhabitant of earth: "Millions of spiritual Creatures walk the Earth / Unseen" and provide "Celestial voices to the midnight air" (IV, 677–678, 682) . (Adam incidentally marks those heavenly hosts, angelic and spheric, that in time will announce the second Adam's birth.)

Having dangerously questioned but perseveringly come through doubt, the Heaven-choosing pair are returned to their human love, which in Milton's description is sacramental. The poem invests Eve triply with Christian love: as virgin, bride of the Son of God, and mother. Although a sad analogy with Pandora haunts Eve, in their vesper hymn our first parents again choose rightly within God's abundance, recognizing that, whereas Satan would prevent human love (IV, 749) , God has promised them "a Race / To fill the Earth" (IV, 732–733) . Milton perhaps touched the words faintly with prophetic tragic irony, indicating the grave which Adam and Eve will "fill" with their race, but the principal meaning is clear: they forego their own questioning of God's abundance, "understanding" him joyfully rather than merely questioning without thought. The same kind of reasonable understanding of natural gifts bursts from the epic narrator, who now asserts his choric role with the audience in the hymn "Hail wedded Love" (IV, 750–775) —with which the fallen animal-coupling of Book IX contrasts so shockingly. He is quick to honor not only the body but the spiritual, quasi-Platonic (and Puritan) virtues that are associated with proper love in the body. Orderly human choice of wedded love drives "adulterous lust" down into "bestial herds" like those of Circe and Comus, permitting the proper expression of marital love in "Reason, Loyal, Just, and Pure" that in turn produces the social love of "Relations dear, and all the Charities / Of Father, Son, and Brother" (IV, 753–754, 755–757). The capitalized words in "Father, Son, and Brother" half insist that the love between God, the Son, and the altogether human "Brothers" of Christ is based in such a generative "mysterious Law." This is not to say that Milton veers toward worship of Mary or a Lucretian Venus, for God will of course remain "all in all," but he sees in the image of "wedded love" the sense of oneness in love and will that can bind the Church to Christ, Christ to God, and men to one another and to God.[35] It totally opposes the isolation and forgetfulness involved in the "love" of Satan with Sin and Death, and makes ready the great cosmic love that motivates the Creation in Book VIII. The choric voice creates a vast pity for man, in whom author and audience are so heavily involved. For a second, the poem repeats the lament that initiated Book IV as it cries, "Sleep on, / Blest pair; and O yet happiest if ye seek / No happier state, and know to know no more" (IV, 773–775). They will "know more," of course, for their questions have already sent them exploring; but in hindsight we can pity the hard knowledge that they gain, and gain for us. Human entrance after the Fall into "a paradise within . . . , happier far" (XII, 587) will come only through massive, continuing human suffering.

Meanwhile, as the pair sleep, the opposing choices again confront each other. To the relief and instruction of the audience, Heaven typically "stoops" to man. Gabriel sends Uzziel, Ithuriel, and Zephon scouting for interlopers in Eden. The intruder is found, already degenerate lower than the serpent, like "a Toad, close at the ear of *Eve*" (IV, 800). Like Comus attacking at the ear of the Lady, into which both reason and unreason can pour, Satan

---

[35] William Haller, in "'Hail Wedded Love'" (*ELH*, XIII [1946], 97), concludes that marriage is at the center of *Paradise Lost*, as containing in embryo God's plan on earth, divine order, and the entire human society. It is therefore a prime target to Satan, the prime antihumanist.

intends to lead Eve from reason into "Phantasms and Dreams" (such as the sight-entrancing dream of herself) or "animal spirits" that can lead to his own kind of recoiling "distemper'd, discontented thoughts, / Vain hopes, vain aims, inordinate desires / Blown up with high conceits ingend'ring pride" (IV, 803, 805, 807–809). In place of the fit and mystical generation of "wedded love," he intends that his familiar horrors—isolation, sin, and death—will be generated from her "head" (that is, from her reason and choice) as they once were from his. Ithuriel, a type of the victorious Son (and of patriots victorious over Guy Fawkes), prods Satan with a spear, revealing his true form. That form is assaulted also with ambiguities, perhaps now unrecognizable to Satan. Because he has degenerated, his demand, "Know ye not then, . . . / Know ye not mee?" (IV, 827–828) comically recoils upon him. He intends it to strike present terror in the angels and to recall to them his past power in Heaven. Instead, it reveals him to be all but a toad. To both the question of identity and the Delphic injunction, he might now say of himself as he first said of Beelzebub: "If thou beest hee; But O how fall'n! how chang'd / From him . . . in the happy Realms of Light!" Zephon has to tell him that which his pride chose but cannot often admit: "thou resembl'st now / Thy sin and place of doom obscure and foul" (IV, 839–840).

For an instant Satan understands "what he is" and again suffers the hell of loss. He nevertheless chooses yet again in a prideful taunt to God. The verbal contest is strikingly reminiscent of those in *Paradise Regained,* and like them is extremely witty, although even if we ignore their implication of Adam and Eve, his obduracy prevents their being comical. Satan tempts his own terrible pride by saying:

> If I must contend . . . ,
> Best with the best, the Sender not the sent,
> Or all at once; more glory will be won,
> Or less be lost [IV, 851–854].

Here then are no enigmas of forevision, as in the witches' speeches in *Macbeth,* but only the illogical, pride-driven boasts of the fool. The angelic answer better fits cases:

Thy fear . . . ,
Will save us trial what the least can do
Single against thee wicked, and thence weak
[IV, 854–856].

Unhappily, perhaps, Zephon's response is better accommodated to
the trial of the "least" Son of *Paradise Regained* and to his
historical crucifixion than to the trial of "single" Eve. However,
even Eve's least effort is under protection, for Satan is then compared with a vainglorious steed "champing his iron curb" (IV,
859) of divine direction. Some of his chosen direction is also indicated in a double-meaning description by Gabriel. That leader
says that "in his look defiance low'rs" (IV, 873). It both lours and
lowers—lowers him, in a perpetual Fall. In his supposed wit,
Satan promptly demonstrates that Fall. Gabriel having asked why
Satan has transgressed here, Satan taunts him for his angelic
ignorance. The joke is on Satan, who of course has knowledge
only of Hell. He also reveals his willful ignorance in yet another
unwitting admission. To Gabriel, he says, flight from Hell is "no
reason" (IV, 895). There was no reason in the choice for Hell, and
the flight is undone and without reason if, as Satan has already
said, Hell is where he is. That realization, so easily forgotten,
plagues his contemptuous statement that, if God directs all, he
should have bound Hell more tightly. The self-chosen bonds of
Hell have not parted, even for a moment. Those who have found
the Satan of *Paradise Regained* a comically poor sophist should
look also to his failure of reason in *Paradise Lost*. Once his
original choice is set upon unreason, Satan does not fall progressively; the plunge is absolute. When his words seem most clever,
their self-condemning ironies are most savage.

Gabriel answers truly but most bitingly, playing Satan's chosen
word "wise" through as many ironies as Antony plays Brutus'
"honor" in *Julius Caesar:* "O loss of one in Heav'n to judge of
wise, / . . . whom folly overthrew" (IV, 904–905). He also indicts
Satan for that which might long since have been obvious: that
Satan's "sacrificial" eruption from Hell really was desertion of
his suffering legions—exactly the opposite of Christ's projected
sacrifice and ascent from Hell. Nor does Satan's response save
him further hard truths, for Gabriel sharply points out the

unreason in everything said by the Father of Lies: "To say and straight unsay, pretending first / Wise to fly pain, professing next the Spy, / Argues no Leader, but a liar trac't, . . . Army of Fiends, fit body to fit head" (IV, 947–953). And Satan is forewarned (if he could hear) of the Last Judgment, when divine hosts will complete for him once for all the "death" he chose. Fiery red anger, like the flames of that final punition as well as of the eventual punition of Eden, colors the angelic hosts. In the same eschatological sense, they threaten him with a harvest in which grain is forever separated from chaff, sheep from goats, substance from dross. He tries to raise a spear and shield in defiance and to offer danger once more to Heaven, but at that moment still another apocalyptic signal of lasting judgment affrights him. Eternal scales appear even now in the sky, showing not only Satan's present power but also his future evaporation into dross. With that, the contest of "is" with "seems" concludes, recapitulating the close of the Battle in Heaven. Like the parallel Son there and in *Paradise Regained,* Gabriel quietly says, "I know thy strength, and thou know'st mine" (IV, 1006) —and adds that both strengths came, and will continue to come, only from God. All of Satan's "ascent" into arrogant claims, secret agony and secret guile, and noble defiance collapses flimsily upon that enduring rock. Satan flies murmuring from this knowledge like an insubstantial shade of night. As is frequent in Milton, literary simile suddenly becomes analytical statement, indicating both Satan's present identity and his eschatological fate.

With this ignominious flight of Satan, resembling that of locusts, Egyptian armies, or the leaves of Vallambrosa, and with his supposedly proud voice reduced to a "murmur" (IV, 1015) that suggests the inarticulate hissing of the serpent he is to become in his final degradation, the first great section of *Paradise Lost* draws to a close. Man, with his particular portion of blessed creation and already dangerous freedom, has barely appeared upon the scene. The epic has instead stationed around him a vast panorama of eternal freedom of choice and the two absolute poles to which that choice can move: joyous participation in creation and hate-filled rejection of it in favor of seemingly "free" (but in reality, most imprisoning) destructiveness. The freedom in no way suggests that chance rules the universe. God's design is absolute, including his conferring of choice upon all rational creatures. It is angels or men, not God, who determine whether or not the design shall be honored by them. A quibble must begin at just this point about foreordination and foreknowledge; some doubt may remain whether the latter does not impel the former, despite Milton's best efforts to remove it. However, a certain freedom rests in either apparent determination, for foreordination is lessened not only in that man may choose again another day (only Satan refuses choice) but also in that God will offer grace to help him choose. What is more, God will re-create the race through a second Adam in order at least to balance the "original" faulty choice of the first. In that sense, God's design continues to be creative, to arrange assistance in advance of the need, and to "stoop" to man.

To man's eyes, such aid may seem to create a dilemma: either the aid must be occasional and God therefore changeable, or else man's choice must be illusory, having always been lodged somehow in God's design. Milton hints a possible Boethian answer but leaves its particular terms open or suggests, fideistically, that although the answer is certain, human powers cannot entirely conceive of it. Rather than drive the poem into interminable discourse upon the point, he returns to demonstration.

Because Satan has already shown us the self-condemning and ignorant choice of Sin and Death, and Christ the God-realizing and self-fulfilling choice of love and life, the later episodes in the first part are able to reflect and reinforce those acts. First, when faced with the new world and its obvious appeal for admiration and love, Satan chooses again to deny himself such pleasure. Second, Adam and Eve, when faced with the same appeal, raise hymns and doubts in almost equal proportion, indicating that the field of choice is already fully—perhaps threateningly—open to them. As we have seen with Satan, Hell or Heaven exists in part within the choice and the chooser. Heaven may be the object of man's distant prayers, but a personal Hell can be the object of his direct choice. Finally, the past "war" of Satan in Heaven is almost repeated in the present man-concerning contest at Heaven's and earth's rim. Because Satan's choice of insubstantiality remains constant, this war not only recalls that of the past but foretells that final defeat of Satan when human time will close. Hell will never cease, exactly, but Satan and his hosts will assume in full the chaffy insubstantiality to which they have wished to "fall."

Only Satan foreordains an imprisoning absolute choice. God's knowledge in a sense acts against such reckless, binding, thoughtless foreordination. With Satan's prophetic retreat, light rolls across the epic once more, as it did when our stance was taken before the throne of God. The epic is now ready to assume a long stand with the human creature before whom such elemental choices rest. Most of the stand, however, is lighted by God's prevenient grace, which through Raphael warns, instructs, and persuades men toward the full use of reason. That reason can instantly affirm the one alternative over the other does not really destroy choice. It instead exercises and affirms reason as humanly essential —and, in every sense, as "choice."

"Thrice Happy If They Know Thir Happiness, and Persevere Upright": Instruction for choice in Eden (Books V–VIII)

The four medial Books of *Paradise Lost* shift the mode of action from direct doing to tutorial narrative. Providence offers to man's representative and progenitor, Adam, admonitory and exemplary accounts of the archetypal fall and the earth's creation. (Book XII will similarly move to narrative after the dramatic "vision" of Book XI.) These Books concentrate the effort to define for man the essence of Paradise under the aegis of choice, balancing the postlapsarian definitions of man and the world in Books IX–XII. Adam will now enter into methektic experience like that of the audience for Books I–IV by receiving the pattern *fall, renewal* in the narratives of the battle in Heaven, creation of earth. Much as the audience in the first section (and through Adam, in this central portion as well) was continually made aware that the plot was "for" itself, Adam and Eve should know that in their present experience they move within a like pattern of choices. Indeed, Adam and Eve supply a complementary frame for the narratives. Before Raphael's accounts stands the frame of Eve's falling dream and Adam's rising exploration of the human essence; after them stands the frame of Adam's choice for Eve and the troubled judgment of Raphael upon the uxoriousness that affects man's choice. Although Milton could have been expected to use exemplary Biblical narrative, and although a staging of the hexaemeron was almost obligatory, he not only binds them within the total pattern of *Paradise Lost* but charges them with immediacy by having Adam and Eve directly reflect the pattern of the methektic narratives. If for Adam and Eve it becomes pleasantly difficult aesthetically to tell the dancer from the dance, the audience in its doubled *methexis* may find it a further immense illumination of unity.

Because God, through Raphael, leans to man throughout these Books with open prevenient assistance, yet once more "creating" in him sufficiency to stand,[36] all four Books in one sense concern the Creation. Even the humorous exchanges on human as compared with angelic love bear upon God's triple gift to men—original being, creative reason, and a model of creation itself in man's capacity to generate new human life. The principal emphasis of the section, however, is upon the gift and choice of persevering reason, for it determines whether or not the original being shall be maintained above imbruting choice and whether or not human reproduction shall, by choice, taint all of man's physical order with original sin. Raphael cautions Adam that man must duly honor Eden and his being:

> Be strong, live happy, and love, but first of all
> Him whom to love is to obey. . . .
> . . . thine and of all thy Sons
> The weal or woe in thee is plac't; beware.
> . . . stand fast; to stand or fall
> Free in thine own Arbitrement it lies.
> Perfet within, no outward aid require [VIII, 633–642].

Even fallen man retains the capacity to stand and ascend, although for the audience much continuing education will now be necessary to "repair the ruins of our first parents by regaining to know God aright, and out of that knowledge to love him, to

---

[36] D. C. Allen, in *The Harmonious Vision* (Baltimore, 1954), p. 78, describes the instruction by Raphael as "intelligential lessonings" for Adam.

imitate him, to be like him, as we may the nearest by possessing our souls of true virtue, which being united to the heavenly grace of faith makes up the highest perfection" ("Of Education," p. 631). The postlapsarian audience therefore joins the stance of prelapsarian Adam in the divine school supplied by grace. Like Raphael to Adam, the narrator will act to us as a second to "that Shepherd, who first taught the chosen Seed, / In the Beginning how the Heav'ns and Earth / Rose out of *Chaos*" (I, 8–10). To that end, Eve's dream of chaos and Adam's praise of reason are equally instructive with the Easter battle in Heaven in which evil is expelled, and the six-day creation of the earth in which the necessary choice for evil is admitted.[37]

And that is a note which tolls us back to our lateral experience in loss. Adam and Eve refused preventive knowledge. The great narratives are in large measure lost on them, as is Raphael's other tutelage and judgment. It is well to remember that Adam's final voicing of the *felix culpa* in *Paradise Lost* is not the hymn that might have been, but only a limited rejoicing that the Fall could be divinely wrought into some degree of mercy and restoration. Even the possibility of a postlapsarian inward paradise, "happier far," is beyond measuring less than the ascending glory that had been promised. The audience cannot help mourning that which "might have been"; lest the center of the epic seem to us no more than mythology on an antique tapestry, we should recall our own methektic involvement in the agon. If Eden is what might have been for Adam, its type has appeared for all men in the days of their innocence. We are not permitted romantic nostalgia for a remote golden age vanished long ago, *in illo tempore:* it soon becomes our own direct loss that must be mourned. However, as the narratives and the judgment continue to indicate, the choice for loss need not be final in either Adam or in his sons. Infinite exemplary hope "to be," opposing the finite exemplary loss of "what might have been," is restored with the second Adam. Placed at the nexus where all Adams must choose, the audience

[37] Irene Samuel, in "*Purgatorio* and the Dream of Eve" (*JEGP*, LXIII [1964], 441–449), indicates that Eve could have learned by means of the vision as Adam learned by means of Raphael's instruction, and thereby have averted failure during trial in Book IX.

can rest in neither grief nor consolation. The two radii of choice command that we also choose between our own further, individual falls and our possible cooperative renewal.

"THIS WAS THAT CAUTION GIVEN THEE": FREE CHOICE FOR THE DREAM
OF SIN OR THE REALITY OF REASONABLE BEING (BOOK V, LINES 1–560)

In Book IV, the two great paradigms of choice had surrounded entrant man and supplied the stances of the epic. Because Book V initiates the great central section of instruction to men, the order is reversed. Men's thoughts now reach out from earth toward the great paradigms, seeking through those polar possibilities to understand men themselves. Although the conditions of Hell and Heaven are never distant from man even before the great colloquy of Adam and Raphael takes place, the stance demands that we now perceive the world with human vision, likening things in Heaven to things on earth. As introduction to the grand lesson, Adam and Eve so look out upon themselves and their universe. Their characteristic roles are stressed as types of the general human being and of his natural impulse to choice: Adam shows strength and reason, Eve softness and fancy. The central section begins with Eve's virtual human fall, which partly makes necessary the "renewal" in Raphael's creative revelation.

Eden is opened to them as the East—symphonically Ovidian, Homeric, and Christian—sends rosy-footed Morn scattering creative corpuscular pearls of light like manna before men. Within this paradise that is itself one kind of choice, choice awakens with new humanity. Adam greets the dawn in healthful joy, for he has so chosen, so governed his appetite, that he is almost as ethereal as his sleep was "Aery light" (V, 4). Eve, on the other hand, has been earthily restless, her cheek "glowing" and her hair "discompos'd" (V, 10). He calls her with an archetypal song of songs, offering procreative love like that of the fructifying Zephyrus to the receptive Flora and warning her, prophetically, that they "lose the prime" of the day to such sleep (V, 21). Awaking, she again casts on him a "startl'd eye" (V, 26); as Penelope resists the eagle of another dream and as Eve herself had resisted Adam in her first dream of self, so she again is impelled to choose her isolative fancy over his reason. All this while, the addresses of the pair to one another continue to elevate the human being dangerously, threatening to displace with human love "Him whom to love is to obey" (VIII, 634). Evil choices have not yet been made, but the possible "swerve" toward them is powerfully present.

Eve's "chosen" dream—like most (but not all) Miltonic dreams insubstantial, half-true but half-false, never to be confused with reason—strongly marks the swerve toward pride and disunity. As Sin entered the head of Satan in Heaven, so "offense and trouble" (V, 34) have insinuated themselves into her mind in Paradise. In her dream, she had credulously believed the only voice in the garden to be Adam's (and so the voice of the Satanic toad *could* have been, for choice may find in any object or any words its objective correlative). Sensuality rather than peace had risen in the "love-labor'd song" (V, 41) of the bird. In the darkness, Eve had asked Satanic questions about the full use of God's gifts and had considered man, not God, to be the focus and definition of love. Her words, celebrating Astartian night, luxury, and self, are unhappily close to those of Comus and Satan—they who also rejected the clear divine light:

> Full Orb'd the Moon, and with more pleasing light
> Shadowy sets off the face of things; in vain,
> If none regard; Heav'n wakes with all his eyes,
> Whom to behold but thee, Nature's desire,
> In whose sight all things joy, with ravishment
> Attracted by thy beauty still to gaze [V, 42–47].

Alas for Eve. "Ravishment" indicates the bestial loves Milton and Spenser associate with the animal Jove rather than the governed human love asked by Adam, and forecasts almost too pathetically Eve's coming "ravishment" by her own senses. She prophetically dreams of herself as separated from Adam and reason. Her fancy plays idolatrously upon the tree of knowledge, making it fairer, more tempting than by day. Into her imagination, steadily drifting farther from Adam and God, there comes a being who looks like an angel, even as Comus once appeared in shepherd's clothing and Satan in the guise of a cherub. They gaze together at the tree. In advance of Raphael's beneficent tutelage, Satan supplies for her the words that begin her speech—a complaint against God's "unreasonable" bounty, the wasted fruit ("knowledge") of the tree. Eve's infected, "impregnated" mind races with him toward sophistical self-delusion, first questioning God ("is Knowledge so despis'd?" [V, 60]), then belittling him into a creature envious or fearful of man. With a dangerous "swerve," Satan's voice (or hers, or Adam's) rebels: "Forbid who will, none shall from me withhold" (V, 62).

It is an amazing scene. We see Satan falling once again, but for a moment the glamor of his seemingly Promethean courage is reborn. It fades as he perhaps unwittingly parodies the coming sacrifice of Christ and death of Eve ("O Fruit Divine, / Sweet of thyself, but much more sweet thus cropt" [V, 67–68]). Like Adam at the Fall, Eve shivers when she feels Death sweep as near as her choice: "mee damp horror chill'd" (V, 65). However, Satan sets ambition raging in himself and Eve, calling her angelic, already a goddess, indeed capable (by such disobedience) to "Ascend to Heav'n, by merit thine" (V, 80). In Eve's account, a hug of grinning sexual temptation follows: "he drew nigh, and to me held, / Even to my mouth of that same fruit held part / Which he had pluckt" (V, 82–84). Her account increases audience fears, though not her own knowledge. The fruit, she says, quickened her appetite so that, fatally, she "could not but taste" (V, 86). His words have had their ravishingly compulsive effect not only upon her physical but also her spiritual appetite, for in her dream she impels his temptation for her to ascend to Heaven into actuality, flying with the devil and "wond'ring at my flight and change / To this high exaltation" (V, 89–90). She enacts a prideful parody of Mary's Magnificat and Christ's temptation on the temple. The dream had ended with her "sinking down"—paradoxically, not in the image of a spiritual fall but of a return instead to spiritual equilibrium, the original state of her creation, after her too heady flight. It may be that modern readers do not see in full the pre-Freudian implication of her dream. Not only does she adopt Satanic thoughts and ready herself for both the "fall" to appetite and the accursed "ascent" to pride, but also she has flown with Satan. Some of Milton's readers might have detected in Eve a perilous likeness to a witch.[38] Judging from Milton's surprisingly

[38] See John M. Steadman, "Eve's Dream and the Conventions of Witchcraft." *JHI*, XXVI (1965), 567–574.

impassioned indictment of Adam and Eve in *De Doctrina Christiana,* he might sanction the association. In any case, she has listened agreeably to feigning words that are essentially diabolic.

Dream, fancy, and appetite have brought Eve toward unreasonable, because unthinking, choice. To counter this token fall, "sad" (V, 94), tutorial Adam supplies restorative balance, a first countermovement to renewal, by judging the "wild work" of this dream much as the second Adam will judge the kingdoms of earth. He calls the dream "uncouth" (unknowing [V, 98]) and counters it with a humane ethic based upon classic political analogies. Rightly used, Eve's vision of evil on earth can be as instructively preventive as Raphael's coming narrative of evil in Heaven. Reason should command the chaotic impressions that "fancy" has received from experience, for those impressions are true or false only as Reason (Light, the Word) confirms and chooses them. The choice is of a creation that arises from chaos or a chaos that has degenerated from creation. If reason, like Eve, sleeps, then fancy, like Satan, assumes control, letting impressions conjoin in monstrous shapes—perhaps like those of Sin and Death. Uncontrolled fancy is as dictatorial as Satan, either fleeing or misjoining realities. Eve's dream itself strongly suggests the birth of Sin.

Adam takes pains, however, to declare that no evil intrinsically infects the senses or fancy. Nor does it arise from Eve, "created pure" (V, 100). It is born in the failure to use reason as governor, arbiter, and, by analogy, creator of the formless, chaotic images reported by the senses and fancy. Consequences that follow such mutations may be evil in themselves, but the materials used by reason are not harmful: "Evil into the mind of God or Man / May come and go, so unapprov'd, and leave / No spot or blame behind" (V, 117–119). Eve has not fallen; she has only experienced the way in which chaotic fancy might lead her from reason to a fall. Nevertheless, the tears of Eve that fall in Eden, like the tears of Satan in Hell, may hint at regret. Until the Fall, Eve's pity is likely to appear only for herself and her seemingly secondary role in Eden. The night in Eden therefore threatens to recapitulate Satan's fatal night in Heaven.

The possible choice for error having been corrected by Adam's reason, the audience vision now is shifted from Eve's dangerous dream to the renewal that each day offers in Paradise. The audience cannot avoid a lingering fear that the reconciliation of Adam with Eve has been too quick when the narrative confidently says, "So all was clear'd and to the Field they haste" (V, 136), for all pastures new bring only repetitions of choice. However, if night offers a serpentine Satan, it can also offer the great watchful eye of God. Our human progenitors accordingly return from the voice of self, fancy, or Satan to a second great renewal, that with Heaven, in their *benedicite, omnia opera*. Like the poem itself, they sing that earth intimates Heaven, creation the Creator. A great circling dance and hymn resembling those of the Nativity Ode absorb Adam and Eve with the audience into the union of stars, light, all creatures, basal elements, dim mists and exhalations (that can be made hellish if they resist light but are beneficent if they serve earth), and the hills and valleys of earth: each particular being makes a pattern and is within a pattern of *Paradise Lost,* as renewing "light dispels the dark" (V, 208). Creative dawn and dance have replaced Eve's nighttime insubstantiality.

The praise of Adam and Eve, which is much like the Lord's Prayer itself, even as Eden is a type of church, is answered at once in yet a third surge of renewal. To the choice-involved human beings, now rejoined in love like the vine and the elm within the order of the rest of the Garden, God sends Raphael, a kind of divine "gardener" of excess in human thought. Soaring above the classical Hermes, Raphael brings not merely messages, but Gospel-forecasting "good news." Using instruction in ethics and dialectic, he will perform preventively, like Pico's physician. He will speak as divine friend (and agent of the Word) to human friend, fulfilling the promise that concluded *Comus.* As conveyor of God's inner light to mankind, he is the first agent in *Paradise Lost* to enact the invocation's promise that God's ways will be justified to man.[39] Man will then possess a portion of the divine foreknowl-

---

[39] Arthur E. Barker, in "Structural and Doctrinal Pattern in Milton's Later Poems," in *Essays in English Literature from the Renaissance to the Victorian Age,* p. 187, says, "Even Raphael learns much in his effort to respond adequately to his call." I myself attach a greater sense of historical "truth" to the Battle in Heaven and of divine verity (rather than of creatural achievement) to Raphael's instruction. Anne D. Ferry, in *Milton's Epic Voice,* pp.

edge of God. Like God, he will partake no foreordination; if man is to fall, man must freely ordain it. Because the area of contest is our human reason and will, Raphael is directed to follow God's strategy of persuasion in Book III:

> . . . such discourse bring on,
> As may advise him of his happy state,
> Happiness in his power left free to will,
> Left to his own free Will, his Will though free,
> Yet mutable; whence warn him to beware
> He swerve not too secure [V, 233–238].

Raphael is a type of Christ and of any other descending spiritual or physical agent of God directed to man's aid.[40] The pitying renovative "fall" of such beings to earth, in part an enactment of sacrifice, is in direct contrast to the destructive "rising" of Satan. Each struggles to influence man's choice, but Raphael's descent is corrective; it intends to supply spiritual counterpressure that can "restore" an Eden threatened by appetite. He is one in the great chain of instruction—God to angels, angels to men, Adam to Eve, the narrator to man. He will sketch for Adam the immense pattern from prehistory, even as the epic itself has drawn it for Adam's sons. Coming from light during the day, the phoenix-like Raphael contrasts tellingly with the night-bound cormorant Satan. The one would aid man's reason; the other would pervert his fancy, attacking men not with violence but with ignorance and lies. The angel stoops to the human pair at the blaze of noon, in divine choice that tries to anticipate and oppose Eve's aspiration in another noon.

Because the entire section strives to see the great paradigmatic forces in human terms, the stance is made resolutely domestic.

155–156, attributes a pastoral framework to Raphael's narration. If so, it is expressive of the divine wish to maintain Eden and of our fallen human wish to regain its fertile innocence.

[40] Irene Samuel, in *Plato and Milton* (Ithaca, N.Y., 1947), p. 115, notes that Raphael is first in *Paradise Lost* to inquire of the ways of God to men. Kester Svendsen, in *Milton and Science* (Cambridge, Mass., 1956), p. 148, associates Raphael's descent with that of the solar bird—eagle or phoenix. Because of his redemptive function, he also resembles the Christian dove.

The audience is placed with Adam and his freedom to inquire. The verse itself alters somewhat from that of the earlier Books, becoming in every sense colloquial. Our tacit voices are freely involved in the questions of Adam and his empowering dramatist, Milton: both are intent upon justifying God's ways to men— partly through doubt, partly through eager celebration.

Human questions reach ahead of Adam's actual colloquy. Intimating a now familiar question in place of the earlier *benedicite,* the verse notes that the creative sun illimitably warms the earth to fertility in her "inmost womb" (V, 302), supplying far more heat than man alone needs. The Satanic objection to divine economy and the equally Satanic identification of Providence with man's own needs or wishes alone are suspended, however, as Raphael approaches. A roll of classical names and an allusion to Alcinous cause Eden to outsoar Greek paradises. Adam's first, harmonious act recapitulates the praise of God as he offers "our givers thir own gifts" (V, 317). Instinct with order, his offer is both a courtesy and a token of divine and human union. Renewal has all but restored sometimes isolative man to the total purity of his first concord with Heaven.

Man's first questions had turned toward God, whether in praise or in doubt. Increasingly, his subsequent queries turn to man in his experience and judgment of matter and spirit. Although Raphael's accounts of Creation, including the creation of sin, involve much more than man, all issues of the colloquy incline toward the central questions of man's essence: what is man? and what was he, and what may he come to be?

On this first occasion of instruction, Eve—at Adam's hospitable wish—goes out alone to prepare food for her angelic guest. (Later, rebelliously, she will go out in isolation from Adam and God to serve her own private will and appetite.) If perhaps more like the busy Martha than the attendant Mary of Bethany, she is nevertheless all generous care now, "more lovely fair / Than Wood-Nymph" (V, 380–381) or any imagined pagan glorification of woman. She demonstrates her essence. Adam similarly realizes his essence by being, in his kind, as magnanimously and clearly noble as Raphael himself—like the angel, possessing "in himself . . . all his state" (V, 353). When properly "himself," the first man clearly opposes the false heroes of human history as well as the specious heroism of Hell.

A first consideration of human essence asks about earth's relation to Heaven. Adam considers Raphael at first to be remote, if Christlike, in leaving distant Heaven, but Raphael denies any scale of difference in value or merit between earth and Heaven. In token of Heaven's proximity to earth and its esteem for man, the angel greets Eve with "the holy salutation us'd / Long after to blest *Mary,* second *Eve*" (V, 386–387). The Christian reader may be too sadly aware that the second Eve must suffer agony because of the appetite of the first, but he will thereby miss the implication of the Ave. The human essence in both is magnificent. At this early moment, despite shadows of sensuality and ambition, Eve promises essential majesty and infinite love in her role as mother of man.

The same double implication is assigned to Adam, by Milton fondly saluted as "Our Author" (V, 397). He gives us our being, but he also causes it to be removed to the post-Edenic wilderness; he is the "Author" partially both of Paradise and its loss. He is now the enduring voice of human reason, supplying the human word in dialogue with divine Word, even though he later will elect the voice of unreason. His still humble question to Raphael inquires concerning God's ways to man. In remarking the angelic "descent," he not only points to a general union of material being with the Creator but also intimates the sacrament of Communion:

> . . . please to taste
> These bounties which our Nourisher, from whom
> All perfet good unmeasur'd out, descends,
> To us for food and for delight [V, 397–400].

His courteous intent is only to ask if Raphael can eat earthly food. (Lesser "gods," of course, could not; they lived on nonhuman ambrosia and nectar or the smokes of sacrifice.) However, the invitation brings with it leading questions about God and man and all being, even as it indicates the proper use of the fruits of Eden.

To the implied Delphic question, Orphic Raphael answers that man is in part spiritual and in essence rational, admitting no impediment between his nature and that of more "intelligential" (V, 408) beings. He then likens all being (except, perhaps, that of ultimate divinity) to a great interdependent chain, in which the humble serve and sustain the exalted. This chain is of course reversible in Christ, who from his exaltation "sustains" the meek and lowly. The principal analogy, however, is more nearly biological or microcosmical, like that of the approaching image of the tree of being: the humble "roots" gather sustenance which partly supplies the more ethereal "leaves." The image of the return of gifts to the Giver recalls the morning prayer of men to God. In witness to unity in creation, Raphael eats paradisal food with real hunger, and the food is instantly transubstantiated into his being.

Word and deed have demonstrated to men that angelic being is not greatly different from theirs. Man may participate in the unity far beyond his given mediocre level, for with "due steps [he can] aspire" to still greater likeness. He needs no artificial stimulus of a tree of knowledge to encourage his aspiring questions. Adam's mind "sudden . . . arose" (V, 452); the words suggest again his capacity to choose, for the metaphor suggests both Sin arising from the head of Satan and also Adam's own persevering "upright." Human and divine Word "unite," as they will again in the human Christ, producing now the third great consult of *Paradise Lost*. In it, reason and reasonable decisions are wrought concerning not Satan's or the Son's actions toward man, but man's service to himself and God. Adam returns to the humble, earthly half of the vast question: "What compare" between Heaven and earth? In reply, the angel supplies the great monistic image of the substantial tree of being, "one first matter all" (V, 472), in which body, either generally or in a particular form, may work up (aspire) to spirit, much as vegetables, when used in human sustenance, take on energies "vital," "animal," "intellectual" (V, 484–485). In man, similarly, life and sense feed fancy and understanding, which in turn serve and even, in one sense, produce the soul. The existence and essence of Miltonic being is reason—usually intuitive or vertical in the "intelligential" angels, usually "discursive" (V, 488) or to some degree lateral in man, but differing only in disposition, not in kind. Because "discourse" best suits Adam's mind and ours, the "great Argument" continues, after conferring upon human choice its great prospect or promise of ascent:

> . . . from these corporal nutriments perhaps
> Your bodies may at last turn all to spirit,
> Improv'd by tract of time, and wing'd ascend
> Ethereal, as wee, or may at choice
> Here or in Heav'nly Paradises dwell
>
> . . . . .
>
> . . . Meanwhile enjoy
> Your fill what happiness this happy state
> Can comprehend, incapable of more [V, 496–505].

Adam is not slow to grasp the promise. He immediately applies it to the already established image of a tree of being, aware that "in contemplation of created things / By steps we may ascend to God" (V, 511–512). *Here was the proper tree of knowledge, a Jacob's ladder freely offered men.* Men already have moved somewhat "nearer to him" (V, 476) who made them, as Adam ardently confesses: "Thy words / Attentive, and with more delighted ear / Divine instructor, I have heard, than . . . / Cherubic Songs" (V, 544–547). Until this time, he had not realized that "both will and deed" (V, 549) were created free. His instructed sufficiency to stand involves also increased capacity and appetency to rise. This true offer opposes Eve's specious, witch-like dream of ascending. Man's possible choice for ascent must be registered in any assessment of the Fortunate Fall. By God's design, the Son's sacrifice, and Adam's affirming recognition of both, the Fall became in one sense fortunate in that it was not unmitigable disaster; however, there is never any question, from the first three lines of the poem to the last, that a choice to aspire, to "persevere upright," would have been infinitely better. The Fall should not blind us to what the ascent can be (or could have been), whether we look to the first or the second Adam. For the audience, the choice for ascent need not be ended, even though sin causes its conditions to be radically transformed.

Raphael's prospect contains a glorious definition: earthly and heavenly paradises are the same, except in degree of corporeality. It also bears a warning: man is to take Paradise as a plenum, complete although dynamic, surging with innocent sustenance and "countersustenance" among beings. If he seeks more, he vainly or destructively seeks that which either does not exist or is not apprehensible by his faculties. The angel hints distantly that if man seeks other than his dynamic aspirations within a perfect system of creation, he will find only folly or death.

Adam responds with comprehension, supplying his own image of being: center and circumference, all one. He does not understand the need for a warning, for he agrees that humanity has "to the utmost measure . . . what bliss / Human desires can seek or apprehend" (V, 517–518). His image, however, may reveal his danger. An earthly tower, ladder, or tree to intellectual Heaven presents the scheme of being as Raphael intends it. Man might safely "climb" within that tree, rather than in the disastrous tree of knowledge he later seeks. Adam's image of a circle [41] can present not only an acceptable sense of unity but also a greater potential wish for equality, a suspicious Satanic increase of the sense of oneness with God not only in kind but in degree. It can also become a circle fruitless as the mazes of Hell.

Raphael commands attention, by which Adam, son of God and man or of "Heav'n and Earth" (V, 519), halfway up the scale leading from greater corporeality to greater spirituality, may learn the proper energies, even the proper differentiation, of God and man. As doctrine had insisted in Book III, God made man happy. Adam and Eve have thought happiness a static condition. They must now discover, partly as a result of Adam's expanding question, that instead freedom (and hence change) is and always has been their environment.

This crucial scene asks a participative "discovery" by the audience as well. It is from this position that two major adverse criticisms of Milton's composed epic universe often are launched. First, it is sometimes claimed that, despite Raphael's present introduction of change, Eden was static both physically and morally, as boring in its easy climate, easy diet, and easy companion-

---

[41] A circle can represent unity of being with the divine still point but can also be an image of egocentricity (Northrop Frye, *The Return of Eden*, p. 37). However, C. A. Patrides, in *Milton and the Christian Tradition* (Oxford, 1966), pp. 40–41, sees the figure as "sacrosanct."

ship as it was enervating in its absolute, perfect spiritual inertia. As a corollary, it is charged that Adam and Eve are puppets in Paradise, manipulated wholly by God's will, thus bearing out Satan's charge of God's tyranny and his claim that rebellion is a release into personality and its vital self-directing energy. Second, a closely related claim has it that the Fall was "necessary"—that man could not stand still, whether because of his own exploring mind or God's command that he choose, and the only "change" possible, partly because it was "foreknown," was that which indeed occurred. It then proceeds to a Nietzschean celebration of mankind's Fortunate Fall into humanly fulfilling energy.

If the argument is confined to *Paradise Lost,* the two claims ignore Milton's open and clear statements. First, almost from the moment we see man and hear his voice, we see choices ranging before him and note several suspicious shadows of turning—in human addresses to humans, in human considerations of self, and in human dreams. Currents of change disturb the still waters almost before we have had a chance to praise Eden and our "Grand Parents." Not only have possibilities of "swerve" veered toward becoming probable, but also the shade-driven serpent even now infects the night, typically adding the pressure of ambition, appetite, and self-willed ignorance to the already kinetic human considerations of humanity, nature, and God. Those of us who may associate *Angst* with man's animal and spiritual health will find almost a superfluity of concern, even though it is unfocused, in and about Eden. Nor can it truly be said that Adam and Eve are mechanical or involuntary, whether physically or spiritually. Although they have not left Eden nor involved their lives with death, the currents by which they may fall away are open and compelling, as Eve attests. Her removal into control by fancy instead of reason starkly shows how freely she may choose, and does choose, to think un-Edenic thoughts (for she phrases them, "thinks them," in words after having dreamed them). Consequential actions are always only a voluntary instant away. Finally, *Paradise Lost* no doubt agrees that man must "move." Its insistence upon creativity, hymns of praise, and the ordinary delights of the body in both angel and man dispels most notions of stasis. The only question is where man *may* move. He may stay where he is, *in full movement,* as the stars and angels dance and have their being. He may choose a fall, as Satan has done and as Eve's dream indicates that she and Adam may do. But the movement offered by God is that of ascent,[42] so long as it takes place as aspiration rather than attempted usurpation—a twice-defeating usurpation, for if man, who is one form of extension from God, attempts to usurp God's place, he must also usurp his own "place" of being, choosing one or another form of self-destruction.

All this continual vibration of choice or change is made manifest to Adam. God's doctrine in Book III reappears, but it now conveys pitying assistance, not legal condemnation. It shifts from the imperative to the inclusive first-person plural, including angel and Adam, Milton and audience, God and man:

> That thou art happy, owe to God;
> That thou continu'st such, owe to thyself,
> . . . therein stand.
> This was that caution giv'n thee; be advis'd.
> God made thee perfet, not immutable.
>
> .   .   .   .   .
>
> . . . freely we serve,
> Because we freely love, as in our will
> To love or not; in this we stand or fall:
> And some are fall'n [V, 520–541].

To maintain his divine similitude is man's practice of "obedience" to God; to live as a man, loving the human form and function, is man's love and obedience to man. But no man is forced into obedience; he may depart from both of its forms. Adam meets the realization with a too readily "delighted ear," for however "attentive" to Raphael, and however "sad" over the dream of Eve, he does not really sense the possibility of fall. His innocence, like that of Shakespeare's Miranda, possesses some inattentive ignorance to his "Cyropaedia." Perhaps for that reason, he is not content to stop the discourse but wishes to hear more still of God's ways in Heaven. Significantly, Raphael hesitates.

[42] Paul O. Kristeller, *Eight Philosophers of the Italian Renaissance* (Stanford, 1964), p. 44: To Ficino, love and will are more necessary to Neoplatonic ascent than are intellect and knowledge. Adam has little opportunity for stasis. If he loves God, his Neoplatonic love demands that he aspire.

Not only must he, and Milton with him, insist that the narrative and explanations to come can be only shadowy intimations of divine reality, dim parables and symbols that only accommodatively liken "spiritual to corporal forms" (V, 573), but also he must question whether Adam's search for knowledge remains good. Although questions about God are infinitely admissible, questioning of God is not, for reasons that Satan has demonstrated at length. Only the motive determines whether the tree of knowledge is used well or attacked destructively. As the upshot reveals, Raphael did well to hesitate.

"DEEP MALICE THENCE CONCEIVING": SELF DEFINED AS THE SEED OF SIN, RECOIL AS ITS WAGES (BOOK V, LINES 561–907; BOOK VI)

As Adam with his sons enters into the tutelary narrative, a Virgilian "contained epic," treating of Heaven as it was "chosen" by Satan and the Son, and of the consequent new-created earth, it is necessary to consider Raphael's probing identification of earth with Heaven. Milton intends that we deal wisely with the question, "What if Earth / Be but the shadow of Heav'n, and things therein / Each to other like, more than on Earth is thought?" (V, 574–576). The image of the tree of creation has prepared us to accept the unity and continuity of being. We must allow Raphael's interior epic narrative at least a symbolic or figurative truth as it involves actions entirely apart from man, for Milton believes any part of reason-endorsed Scripture to be true in a literal, almost "historical" sense. The Battle in Heaven and the Creation will therefore contain some theological truth apart from man and human-directed meaning. Also, we are to receive the narrative individually as divine story reflects the truth that involves the life of each man, even as we receive the endorsing greater epic, *Paradise Lost* itself. Types of a sort exist in Heaven as they do on earth. The theory of accommodation therefore works in both directions; as unseen spiritual realities can be intimated by concrete parallels, so the material parallels can lead upward to significant human abstractions and arguments—in short, to discursive intelligence about Heaven. Finally, the narrative will supply an anagogic myth for the existence and meaning of all man's spiritual experience and contemplation, his alpha and omega. With these arguments, then, the divine bards Raphael and Milton solicit our affirmation: that in terms of spiritual reality, earth is a Platonic shadow of Heaven; that man's individual experience can be seen within the stories of election, fall, and creation; and that the myth of great choice for mankind is both actual and meaningful. In the upshot, the Battle in Heaven will resemble the "reality" of fallen earth much too closely.

That correspondence of myth with man begins in God's exaltation and election of his earlier Son, the prototype of Adam, nearest his wisdom. It anticipates the similar creation of the first Adam, just as it evidently initiated the counterbirth of Sin. We should remember Beelzebub's report: man himself was so elect, "favor'd more / Of him who rules above; so was his will / Pronounc'd among the Gods" (II, 350–352). God's creative gift and grace are much the same in both "elections," and the narratives of both Heaven and earth begin with the begetting of a son. The son is worshiped by angels, not in subjection, any more than Eve should worship Adam in subjection, but "united as one individual Soul" (V, 610). As he has been told, Adam can aspire to such Heavenly height. God warns that choice against his order, unity, and light is a fall into hellish or brutal "utter darkness, deep ingulft" (V, 614). Heavenly praise thereafter composes dynamic, complex harmonies that are orderly within seeming eccentricity. The design of praise and being, like God's, is always more subtle and active than a quick mortal glance would indicate; and such praise is as little static and dull as the eager but ordered life of Eden.

In the first "begetting" of a Son, divine circumference and the center of light have been maintained, but so has the movement within them. On the day of the "begetting" of the Son, Heaven's unity and peace resembled that of present Eden. The correspondence of Heaven with Eden does not end there. Night, which in Heaven is only a "grateful" (V, 645) twilight, gives angels, as it gives men, rest. The "unsleeping eyes of God" (V, 647) watch on while angels, like the devils in Hell of Book II, construct tabernacles and shelters in Heaven. However, the comparison of Heaven with Eden is far more immediate, for in Heaven's timeless night, as in Eden's—choice being free in both sides—a serpent of ambitious malice appears. With it is born the doom of hellish time.

In narrative, the audience revisits the mentality of Hell but now steadily perceives it from Raphael's represented stance in Heaven and from its reflective immediate meaning for men.[43] We watch with Adam the downward toppling of a spirituality that refused to persevere "upright." (The double experience of the audience furthers its own justification of God's ways to men, because it sees the amplitude of Heaven's preventive aid.) Like Eve, Satan is not forced to possess the evil he contemplates, for it may enter and depart his mind without harming him. At the instant of his choice, however, circumferential being has risen in envy of the central creating Son, believing itself "impair'd" (V, 665). In this planetary image, Satan discovers an ironic truth, for later he will be described as in self-chosen "dim Eclipse" (I, 597). Similarly, in Eden Eve already has begun faintly to resent Adam's governing intelligence, even as in Eden Satan also will be envious of God's "second" begotten son, Adam. Like Eve, Satan withdraws into egoistic isolation. His mind conceives and brings forth the monster, malice, which also is called Sin. He attempts at once to disseminate Sin by night in Heaven as he will attempt to propagate sin in Eden's noon by means of Eve. Indeed, the dream of Eve is almost rehearsed in this narrative as a warning from Heaven to its shadow, earth. Already employing the uncreating word, Satan leads his faintly feminine, faintly Eve-like "Companion dear" (V, 673) to resent new laws by setting up his own antagonistic "new" minds and "new" counsels (V, 680, 681). Satan's consult unwittingly prophesies the "new" creature who will replace the apostate angels—man, who like the Son is involved in the description of "one and . . . his image" (V, 784). Present men who duly inhabit the shadow of Heaven observe, however, that the likenesses of Satan in Heaven with Eve on earth

[43] B. A. Wright, in *Milton's Paradise Lost*, p. 137, notes that Book VI supplies God's perspective upon the events of Books I and II. Arnold Stein, in "Milton's War in Heaven—an Extended Metaphor" (*ELH*, XVIII [1951], 201–220), believes that the whole narrative is suitably accommodated to Adam's reason; hence, it is also available for our own human understanding. (Stein's essay appears also in *Answerable Style: Essays on Paradise Lost* [Minneapolis, 1953].)

steadily increase in number and relevancy. Pride swerves Satan's mind toward fall when he rejects the present council in Heaven in favor of the (future) consult of Hell. Similarly, pride in the dream of Eve supplied to her in place of Adam new forms, new counsel, new "exaltation." As Satan infuses bad influence into his associate, so Eve will influence Adam. Satan has been the morning star, she the fairest morning flower. Even as Raphael's account proceeds, isolated Eve is in danger of Satanism, and prophetically she is not long alone within the possible swerve. If Satan foolishly contends with the Son in *Paradise Regained,* Adam even now in Paradise moves dangerously close, "in thought," to questioning God's power and his right. With pressure from Satan, Eve will of course hazard the way beyond mere "thought."

In earth as it is in Heaven, then, pride's gravitational swerve away from life is enormous. The Son supplies a heavenly analysis for Satan or for man, if either will hear: creatural will against order and creation, against God's design and love, will inevitably hatch "vain designs and tumults vain" (V, 737), plunging the rebel into nonbeing or nonmeaning.

Demonstratively, Satan sets up a mountain rivaling that of the Son's consecration, lavishing on it Eastern "Pyramids and Tow'rs" (V, 758) suggestive of Babel and, of course, prophetic of Hell. Guile like that of Judas, rather than his own professed heroism, causes Satan to call the disaffected together to murmur treasonably of "the great reception of thir King" (V, 769). Like Eve at the Fall, he charges that service is servility, "knee-tribute" (V, 782), submission of the neck to the collar (and, unknown to him, to a self-released guillotine). Sophism and unreason, along with a will to tyranny that is cloaked under a pretense to democracy, spring from him, as they will from Eve, with Orwellian transparency: all angels, he says, shall be, "if not equal all, yet free, / Equally free; for Orders and Degrees / Jar not with liberty, but well consist" (V, 791–793). As his rhetoric wheels still more splendidly, reason flies from his words, leaving only prideful fancy. This is the voice of evil, already heard by "our Mother" Eve in Paradise and by each man in his pride of being.

Representative man and a methektic audience have now seen the original anarchic rebellion against creation, the cause of the

Fall of Book I. At once, Raphael instructively presents an opposite choice for renewal. The Christlike Abdiel stands alone in the confrontation, but then Satan, too, frequently stands alone with moral questions. The angel's choice is a type of that available to men even during the oppressions of history. He indicts the speech as "false and proud" (V, 809), as attempting to dictate laws to God while protesting law, as denying God's patent wish not to humble his creatures but to exalt all of them in their way as Christ was exalted in his, and as trying to make creature equal with creator.

Like the earlier discussion of Raphael and Adam in Paradise, the argument in Heaven advances to the human or diabolic sense not of social or political place but of being itself. Pride now tells Satan, "We know no time when we were not as now; / . . . self-begot, self-rais'd / By our own quick'ning power" (V, 859–861). Resenting God, the rebellious try to assume his attributes, much as Eve will try to equal or surpass Adam. They do not realize that a concession of ignorance about the time and manner of their creation concedes failure in the signal attribute of knowledge, to say nothing of creation.

Abdiel answers with an inclusive type of judgment upon evil, embracing the condemnations that evolve in human history across Books XI and XII, that appear at the close of the Battle in Heaven, and that will come in the "future" Last Day. Because he forsook good, Satan is forsaken of it. He has alienated himself from the law of God's goodness and pity, and now must accept as his own the other "law" of his rejection of goodness. He has chosen that God's "Golden Sceptre" become an "Iron Rod," which like the future human heel will "bruise and break" his attempt to destroy life (V, 886–887). Milton's personal voice bears the poem for a moment as he applauds the preventive or self-redemptive choice against disobedience to freedom, intimating openly that Abdiel's mythic or typical choice could have shown the first man how to prevent the "First Disobedience" and other men, that later and perhaps even less comprehensible "disobedience" of 1660:

> Among innumerable false, unmov'd,
> Unshak'n, unseduc'd, unterrifi'd

His Loyalty he kept, his Love, his Zeal;
Nor number, nor example with him wrought
To swerve from truth, or change his constant mind
Though single [V, 898–903].

Raphael, reader, and Milton in their stance apart look anxiously to the listening Adam. Has the word "swerve" recalled God's warning to man, "Swerve not too secure"? Has the example of constancy before temptation reached the second son? Adam, perhaps including the Adam in all of us, listens joyfully, smiling, full of delight. Theological and political argument has been accepted fictitiously, not mythically; the story has been enjoyed more than believed. Narrative therefore marches directly on to the more empathetic battle. It is almost as if *Hamlet*'s dumb show had been displayed before a Claudius innocent but vulnerable to temptation; if it did not catch his conscience, a more completely imitative form must be used.

A further brief interior epic is therefore produced for Adam, beginning reminiscently with that morning's rosy-fingered Homeric light but proceeding at once to the more openly divine golden "Morn" which already has banished "Night" (VI, 12–14), even as that morning's light in Paradise and the third day's Easter light in Heaven, intimating also the Apocalypse, cause Satan to cower away into shrouded blackness. Almost as if he were its typological source of good during the time he opposed evil, Abdiel takes the first new-heroic stance of this interior epic. Receiving the "meed" of divine approval much as Lycidas had in the earlier triumph, the "new" hero Abdiel returns to the fold of the faithful. Like that of Christ, Abdiel's "Word" has triumphed over the power of physical evil and death, because evil and death are the direct choice of those "who reason for thir Law refuse" (VI, 41). For an instant, God threatens to be absorbed into human right reason, but the interior epic then exalts him in the heroic position of the Creator dispatching Gabriel and Michael against Satan. Violence must redound upon the heads of the violent. The audience recalls, however, that as with Abdiel their best weapon is reason, the Word. So will it be for Adam; so would it have been for Eve, had she not "wandered."

The metaphors that attend Satan and the Son are intimated in

Satan's "recoiling" three days' crucifical battle against life. The divine Judge permits Hell the Hell it chooses (VI, 50–55) , even as at the close of *Paradise Lost* he will let Eden become the Hell men chose. The trumpets of Good Friday's hellish attack (that will alter into trumpets of resurrective victory) call Satan's "Powers Militant" (VI, 61) to the North, which figures not only Hell but the dark Cimmerian desert of "L'Allegro." Satan, given divine light but disdaining it, has tried to exercise its dim parody (a "darkness visible") , even as Abdiel now confidently exercises both light and its proper power:

> His puissance . . .
> I mean to try, whose Reason I have tri'd
> Unsound and false; nor is it aught but just,
> That he who in debate of Truth hath won,
> Should win in Arms, in both disputes alike
> Victor; though brutish that contest and foul,
> When Reason hath to deal with force, yet so
> Most reason is that Reason overcome [VI, 119–126].

Redemptive reason having failed to persuade the suicidal will, the recoil of force is surrendered to the violent. In the process, reason yet once more overcomes unreason. Much of *Paradise Regained* and *Samson Agonistes* is contained in Abdiel's speech. Much of *Paradise Lost* is intimated in his ensuing statement that God could have destroyed all of Satan's attempts in a moment. It is therefore clear that the contest in *Paradise Lost* does not really involve God's will nor his power, but only those of his creatures. Abdiel clearly tells Satan that the battle is only with a "Sect" of his own kind (VI, 147–148) . However, he counters Satan's familiar charge of God's tyranny with a swift index of the components of freedom, extending the sense of God into physical and political significance. Much as Pope will later say that classical and natural are one, Abdiel now says that nature (including essential human nature) , although it is not God, will not contradict Him, and that it must be understood to present intimations of Him:

> Unjustly thou deprav'st it with the name
> Of *Servitude* to serve whom God ordains,
> Or Nature; God and Nature bid the same,
> When he who rules is worthiest, and excels

> Them whom he governs. This is servitude,
> To serve th' unwise, or him who hath rebell'd
> Against his worthier, as thine now serve thee,
> Thyself not free, but to thyself enthrall'd [VI, 174–181].

Again, the knowing and experiencing audience anxiously observes Adam. Is exemplary tutelage being wasted on him—and on Eve, who already has shown those restless signs of similar rebellion against her "worthier"? Has Adam observed that in the last verse, Abdiel has narrowed the area of definition to one man, not "men," and has Adam found that "servility" is ultimately not an external but an interior condition, so that the cry "Myself am Hell" may be only a moment's personal choice away? Has he seen that the gathering angels know and retain their essences even as he knows and in that measure confirms the essences of the birds to which he gives names (VI, 73–76)?

For Adam's sake and ours, it might be better if narrative had slowed to a pace that required contemplation. It might have dwelt upon Abdiel's swearing, "O Heav'n" (VI, 114) in contrast to Satan's oath, "O Hell!" (IV, 358), and upon God's sense that the battle of the Word and will is infinitely harder than that against violence, thereby intimating the truths of *Paradise Regained*. Instead, it rushes to the typological personal victory of Abdiel and to that "recoil" of Satan which once more fixes the whole design of *Paradise Lost*. Ironically cast in the position of worship, Satan falls to his knee, as he will later drop into the forms of serpent and chaff. Paschalian, typological *"Hosanna to the Highest"* (VI, 205) greets the new-heroic victor, but in the pre-earthly battle an imaged earth "to her Centre shook" (VI, 219) in anticipation of the hour of the Son's great human battle. Rebellious war, which is a type of Hell, the "dreadful combustion" (VI, 225) into which all the diabolic hosts fell, then returns. The type of the Christian warrior, who acknowledges his Leader yet who protestantly "on himself reli'[s]" (VI, 238), is made representative; like Abdiel's, however, the primary force of this attack is that of reason (although the too human Adam sees mainly the more brutal power of arms). Satan is forced by the apocalyptically "inflam'd" (VI, 261) Michael to confess that misery, evil, and war—the very war Satan now suffers, "hateful [and] heaviest by just measure on thyself" (VI, 264–265) —are his own creations, wholly unlike the creation he opposes and which must "cast [him] out" (VI, 272). Satan answers, in almost human ignorance, that what Michael calls evil is a form of the earth's old heroism in Books XI and XII, "the strife of Glory" (VI, 290), which must either triumph or make of Heaven a hell.

The involvement of the human Adam and human reader in the action is enforced in still another way when Raphael and Milton remind their human listeners that not even the tongues of angels can put heavenly events into "conspicuous" (VI, 299) earthly likenesses. Although the disclaimer draws us away from overliteral attention to physical battle, it also serves to recall Raphael's hint that the likenesses actually are great because creation is one and that Milton has announced his intention to soar, *with divine illumination,* to the full height of the great argument. A typological likeness between Heaven and earth appears immediately. Satan now knows the pain of truth. In that penalty, Satan "[writhes] him to and fro convolv'd" (VI, 328) like the serpent he is to be in the Garden and in Hell. He falls, stained; but his chosen ignorance does not permit him to know, for long, that far from contesting with God, he has fallen before an angel. Unlike Adam and Eve after their stain and defeat, he cannot recognize failure. Nor can the devils—Moloch, Adramelech, Asmadai, Ariel, Arioch, Ramiel—who, in the first glimmering of a historical sweep of false gods, are routed by the Israel-resembling Abdiel, Uriel, and Raphael. "Recoil," the persistent image of self-inflicted defeat, inflicts "first" fear and pain upon all the rebellious host.

As night closes this first day of the War in Heaven that immediately resembles not only the Easter war of the Son but also the initial situation of the epic (Satan in Heaven "first" displays the sin of disobedience), Heaven watches in light. Satan recoils into physical and mental darkness, counseling vainly that the host of fiends attempt not only liberty but "Glory" (VI, 422), boasting (with no awareness of the unremitting ironic "recoil" in his words) that God now "seems" (VI, 428) fallible, but hoping at the same time that their own confessedly ignorant "minds, and understanding" can find ways to defeat whatever "hidden cause" opposes them (VI, 444, 442). Mental as well as physiognomical clouds plague the "aspect" of his confederate, Nisroch, who, nonsensical in all things save irony, hails Satan as "Deliverer from new Lords, leader to free / Enjoyment of our right as Gods" and says that hellish heroes' pain "overturns / All patience" (VI, 450, 451–452, 463–464). The irony and nonsense alter into rending pathos, however, when the reader realizes that the words and deeds prophesy those of Eve during the coming terrific blaze of noon. Satan significantly hails the nightlike "dark Nativity" (VI, 482) of anticreativeness rather than the glorious light of creation. Such a chaotic place, he adds in unwitting prophecy, "shall yield us, pregnant with infernal flame" (VI, 483) the materials of gunpowder. That notorious gunpowder,[44] often the occasion of ridicule and merriment, is now being recognized as a powerful metaphor. It is the choice to convert the beings and materials of Heaven into those of Hell. Recoil now becomes a palpable presence, projecting and describing the fearful births of Sin and Death. The devils are the destructive infernal flame in which they themselves burn; so may man be. Their increasingly materialistic thinking brings them to think of even themselves as corporeal. Milton forced the description near or past the edge of pun when he caused "pregnant with infernal flame" in part to modify the word "us." The Spenserian Mammon of Book II meets here his master, who finds in this matter capable of injury not only natural chaotic powers but his own nature; the flame in his being makes him in that sense almost as "self-begetting" as he has wished. Book I had said as much: in Hell "torture without end / Still urges, and a fiery Deluge, fed / With ever-burning Sulphur unconsum'd" (ll. 67–69); similarly, hellish and sinlike Aetna possesses "combustible / And fuell'd entrails . . . conceiving Fire" (I, 233–234). Also, Milton vividly remembered the Gunpowder Plot, which had offered him matter for an earlier, minor *Paradise Lost*. A whole era of misapplied science—indeed, from Milton's

---

[44] Frye, in *The Return of Eden*, p. 35, speaks cogently upon Milton's expressive uses of gunpowder.

point of view the upsetting of much that had once been intimated in the word "science"—is reflected here. Gunpowder is as conclusive a metaphor in Heaven as it is in Swift's Brobdingnag. Milton's immediate audience of seventeenth-century Adams was asked to take due note:

> . . . haply of thy Race
> In future days, if Malice should abound,
> Some one intent on mischief, or inspir'd
> With dev'lish machination might devise
> Like instrument to plague the Sons of men
> For sin, on war and mutual slaughter bent [VI, 501–506].

Nor does the warning end with the narrative of Heaven. The earth, all Adams are told, has exactly such black material, which can either feed the life of plants or work "mutual slaughter" among men; man will choose which, as Cain will demonstrate in history.

The second day dawns upon the full use of the chaotic subterranean fuel. In purely Christian terms, it intimates the grave. Satan, the anti-Word, unleashes fiery death, his secret weapon, his Trojan horse, in one "deceitful" pun after another: "Heav'n witness thou anon, while we discharge / Freely our part: . . . / Do as you have in charge, and briefly touch / What we propound, and loud that all may hear" (VI, 564–567). He cannot realize the fearful image of recoil that has continued to mount all the while. At first, his angelic opponents fall. Like Odysseus' men before Scylla, having armed themselves with the corporeal rather than the spiritual, they fall corporeally. There is ponderous rejoicing among the Hellish, as if on Easter Saturday. Like Eve later—but, in a recoiling ambiguity, beyond all "doubt" of victory—the hosts of Satan become pridefully "highth'n'd in thir thoughts" (VI, 629).

Then Milton produces a second scandal, almost literally piling Pelion on Ossa. Having risked gunpowder in Heaven, he now risks angels fighting devils with mountains. At first glance, not even recognizing the imitation from Hesiod will help matters; the war in Heaven seems to have turned wholly against Milton. Typologically, however, the episode has profound meaning. Not only does this material destruction reflect the devilish desire for chaos; on the Last Day, the verse also intimates, sinners will call for such mountains to hide them from judgment. Perhaps they will justly receive them, as Satan's hosts now do. The material earth and Satan's rival mountain ironically recoil, pressing the rebels, not Christ, into a form of "grave":

> Thir armor help'd thir harm, crush't in and bruis'd
> Into thir substance pent . . . ere they could wind
> Out of such prison, though Spirits of purest light,
> Purest at first, now gross by sinning grown [VI, 656–661].

Despite Satan's losses, the primordial disorder created by rebellion seems to disrupt all created Heaven much as it had disrupted Hell itself in Book II. It threatens to create "wild work" in Heaven like that of Sin, Death, and Chaos upon earth in Book X. Our stance shifts radically in order to replace that "seeming" with redemptive reality. Standing with God, we see that he has permitted all this (but not more) within his design. He calls attention to a proleptic victory in three days ("two days are past, / Two days, as we compute the days of Heav'n" [VI, 684–685]) that can refer both to the historical death of Christ and to the great "days" in human history of creation, trial (like that of Books XI and XII), and final judgment which concludes all human time. The pattern of Christ's volunteering in Book III is repeated or, in strict sequence of action, anticipated. Again, God does not force sacrifice but marks that the contest will be a stalemate ("no solution will be found" [VI, 694]) unless the Son heroically acts in the third day. Then in a typic sense Christ can "end" the contest, showing his power in both Heaven and Hell (by its harrowing).[45] The Son "falls" into submission that is highest realization, a form of union with being like that promised to Adam: "Thou shalt be All in All, and I in thee / For ever, and in mee all whom thou lov'st"

---

[45] J. B. Broadbent, in *Some Graver Subject*, pp. 219–230, scoffs at the Battle in Heaven, not quite seeing that Milton prophetically pits apocalyptic spiritual power against material power. The contest anticipates that of the history in Books XI and XII, along with that of Christ's purifying conclusion of history. The violence of the Battle in Heaven, the Crucifixion, and the Last Days are "justified" by Milton as the self-destruction of violence.

(VI, 732–733). The anarchs will feel the power of Christ, the Judge who sends chaff into the fire which it chose and in which it is cathartically consumed, while he, like the phoenix, goes through flame to renewed life. Easter is thoroughly manifest, even though it must shine through the paradox that Christ's "rising" from his Father's right hand involves his "fall" into sacrificial incarnation:

> . . . he o'er his Sceptre bowing, rose
> From the right hand of Glory where he sat,
> And the third sacred Morn began to shine [VI, 746–748].

Now, as the Battle in Heaven reaches its Easter climax, the smoke and combustion that seemed to be manufactured by Hell are revealed instead to be the projection of divine wrath: in one sense, projections of God himself, in his will, design, and judgment, appearing here as they will at the end of Eden and of the world. All the conflict of choice, all the threat of disorder, retreats; hills, once more creatively used, return to their place "obsequious" (VI, 783), much as the chaos preceding Genesis and prevailing on the Galilean lake ended at a word.[46] The Satanic hosts choose finally and fatally: they must prevail in "aspiring to his highth," or "fall / In universal ruin last" (VI, 793, 796–797). The Son sacrificially assumes the burden of total spiritual battle against such obstinacy. His face toward them is that of the final Judge in Book XII—"too severe to be beheld" (VI, 825). Typic images of the floods and plagues that accompanied the "historical" triumph of God's elect nation over the Satanic Pharaoh cluster around the onslaught. Divine chariot wheels already bruise the head of the Serpent.[47] With them rush images of chaotic falling; the diabolic hosts now apocalyptically wish that those cascading mountains might supply "shelter from his ire" (VI, 843). The overwhelming

[46] Frye, in *The Return of Eden*, p. 53, likens the purgative victory in Heaven to the purgation of the earth in the Flood.

[47] James H. Sims, in *The Bible in Milton's Epics*, p. 97, notes that the Greek version of the Bible suggests not so much that the Son will bruise the serpent's head as that "in majestic dignity [he walks] over a prostrate and utterly defeated Satan."

Son then ironically "raises" (VI, 856) the rebels, now (in place of the entombed Christ) cadaverously "drain'd, / Exhausted, spirit-less, afflicted, fall'n" (VI, 851–852), only to impel them like Gada-rene swine or the refuse of Hinnom over the wall of Heaven. With that, the reader is reminded of Book I and the yawning, deathlike mouth of Hell which then gaped to engorge the fallen host. Now the audience has thoroughly known the primordial disobedience and its fruit. The experience of sharing Satan's delu-sive fall and the events that produced it should have removed any film from its eyes. By this time it should also have realized fully that the events are in part typic; if it has not, it will not quite understand that Christ's victorious return from the Battle in Heaven, "Shaded with branching Palm" (VI, 885), forecasts the later "historical" entry into Jerusalem in a victory that leads to his mysterious trial and triumph over death. His present victory must predict full "assay" as well as triumph and final judgment.

Raphael's first narrative ends with a driving insistence upon its purpose: preventive mythic instruction. The interior epic has been prepared by Raphael and the narrator in order that Adam (and his participative sons) "may . . . beware / By what is past" (VI, 894–895) and in turn warn others:

> . . . list'n not to . . . Temptations, warn
> Thy weaker; let it profit thee to have heard
> By terrible Example the reward
> Of disobedience; firm they might have stood,
> Yet fell; remember, and fear to transgress [VI, 908–912].

Although the ending bears the severe accents of the Pantocrator, complementing the climactic judgment of the Son in the narra-tive, its mood should not be mistaken. It does not wish merely to threaten Adam with baleful punishment, for the interior epic had closed also upon the glorious obedience of the Son. Instead it seeks to add another form of prevenient aid so that Adam, created sufficient to stand, will maintain his stance—even though he still must remain free to fall. The intention is not to create fear of God but fear of a choice against self, future man, nature, and the God whom Adam had worshiped that same morning.

"WHAT NEARER MIGHT CONCERN HIM": CREATION OF MAN INTO COSMIC
CONCORD (BOOK VII)

Milton marks the halfway point [48] of the entire epic with an
invocation that is demanded partly by the new setting, partly by
his agon as author. Like Bellerophon, perhaps dangerously like
Satan, he has "presum'd" (VII, 13) to stretch his mind and craft
into the empyrean. Now he must "fall," safely sustained by God's
design, into his central "Native Element" (VII, 16) where earthly
choice is to be tested. With Raphael, as with Urania earlier,
Milton together with Adam and his sons takes the more bearable
stance upon earth, there to hear of the forms of being they can
better understand—their planet, themselves. But the setting of
course continues to be mythic. The inspired "singer" Raphael,
endangered when Lucifer in Heaven chose to become Satan, is, in
type, identifiable with the inspired singer Orpheus, threatened
with the "savage clamor" of Rhodope, and with the inspired poet
Milton, threatened by the "barbarous dissonance / Of *Bacchus*
and his Revellers" (VII, 32–33) : all one, whether in the court of
Charles or of Comus. The heavy "falling" pull back to "Lycidas"
and its doubts about the poet and his art is quickly transcended by
a prayerful imperative much like that which opened Book I,
imploring the renovative heavenly inspiration to fail neither in
supply nor in power to protect. Our stance descends, then, only to
encounter the original question: "say first what cause / Mov'd our
Grand Parents . . . to fall off / From thir Creator . . . ?" Adam
having now been "forewarn'd . . . by dire example to
beware / Apostasy . . . lest the like befall / In Paradise"
(VII, 41–45) , prevenient aid moves from Satan's fall to the Son's
renewal. Book VII is the epic's great *benedicite,* its celebration of

[48] Among critics who have called attention to Milton's narrative and structural emphasis upon this medial position are: Anne Ferry, in *Milton's Epic
Voice,* pp. 151–152, who places the narrator and audience at a center of time
and space and historical setting in the epic; Arthur E. Barker, in "Structural
Pattern in *Paradise Lost*" (*PQ,* XXVIII [1949], 17–30) , who indicates that the
shift from ten to twelve books made this center to indicate a divine comedy;
and John T. Shawcross, in "The Balanced Structure of *Paradise Lost*" (*SP,*
LXII [1965], 696–718) , who in great detail considers these and other effects
created by this center.

God-given creation—palpably present both in the earth and in
Adam's own "heav'nly born" body. As divine creativeness is about
to be joined in the narrative, it is directly invoked in the epic.
The invocation to the Book that recounts earthly creation asks the
continued guidance not of an earthly Calliope but of the divine
voice, "Heav'nly born, / Before the Hills appear'd, or Fountain
flow'd" (VII, 7–8).

Adam and Eve had heard "preveniently" of Heaven and Hell
but had found it hard to imagine evil in the realms of goodness.
They "believed" only when recoil took place. Nevertheless, Adam
understands the logic of Miltonic definition: evil did not originate
from Heaven, although it appeared within it; instead, evil appeared as choice within given beings. It is visible mainly in its
self-destructive "recoiling" effects, which "redounded as a flood on
those / From whom it sprung, impossible to mix / With Blessed-
ness" (VII, 57–59). Such definition and judgment of evil, which
also anticipate those "historically" demonstrated by Noah's flood
at the end of Book XI, quiet Adam's doubts. He strives toward
still greater knowledge, none of which is in itself forbidden. His
present danger arises not from knowledge but from forgetting
that earth is the shadow of Heaven. He finds Heaven strange, "far
differing from this World" (VII, 71); but as recently as the end of
Book VI, Raphael had explicitly warned him that earth in its
grosser way was very like Heaven. Adam has almost succeeded in
pushing the lesson, too, into the distant empyrean. Although he
recognizes Raphael's aid as like that of the Attendant Spirit of
Comus ("by favor sent / Down from the Empyrean" [VII, 72–73])
and is aware that the story of Heaven "concern'd / Our knowing"
(VII, 82–83), he has not really come to know it, nor is there sure
indication that he (or perhaps Milton) can determine how much
he ought to know. The problem resident in Adam's consideration
of "Things above Earthly thought, which yet concern'd / Our
knowing" is never absolutely resolved. His question might produce great human aspiration or, at the least, perseverance upright; it might also produce a sinful attack upon knowledge, of
which Eve and Satan are guilty. The subjective motive of the
quest—the reason within the choice—is the only final determi-
nant of rectitude.

Adam asks that the narrative, like Milton's setting, the heavenly inspiration, and the general stance of the poem, "descend" (VII, 84) to earth; ironically, however, the descent instead must involve God and a more pressing demand for ultimate reasons than even that which in Book I had initiated the entire epic. In a restatement of that demand, the second half of the work begins with Adam's request, which reflects the invocations of Milton, that his angelic muse relate

> How first began this Heav'n which we behold
>
> .   .   .   .   .
>
> . . . what cause
> Mov'd the Creator in his holy Rest
> Through all Eternity so late to build
> In *Chaos* [VII, 86–93].

His request is underscored with the assurance that, Joshua-like, he may command the sun to await the account of its and his creation or, if not, Jacob-like he may commune all night with an angel and "dismiss [him] ere the Morning shine" (VII, 108). Although our general human stance within Raphael's narrative has descended from Heaven to earth, it will continue to encounter in this lesser site all the soaring questions concerning God's reasons and man's use of them, including the promise of a long day's aspiration to Heaven as opposed to a mortal long day's dying.

The divine account of creation is haunted by the earlier, fall-portending description of human appetite as wandering ("amid the choice / Of all tastes else to please thir appetite, / Though wand'ring" [VII, 48–50]). There is always danger that men will worship not the divine giver but the palpable gift, or that they will Hellishly "wander" into intellectual as well as appetitive insatiety. On the edge of joy Raphael again explicitly warns all men against such craving for forbidden fruit, such intemperance in knowledge, the type of which has been Satan. Because Satan did not know "what the mind may well contain" (VII, 128), his ambitious head had conceived Sin. The reported voice of God supplies much the same judgment as does Raphael in person by saying that Heaven had not so much lost the angels as they had lost themselves: they are "self-lost" (VII, 154) in their attempted "self-creation," exactly as man with his wandering appetite may be. God offers men the opposite—"by degrees of merit rais'd . . . the way / Up hither" (VII, 157–159)—if instead of wandering, they will fare forward spiritually in "long obedience." The way lies open to evolutionary "Union without end" (VII, 161) of Adam with man and God, without the long struggle toward the Last Judgment.

Creation, one example of which develops even before man appears, is a joyous demonstration of the uniting of God with man. The first-begotten Son supplies the Word by which the world takes form from the seeming infinitude of matter that is also one aspect of God. This chosen renewal that opposes Satan's chosen fall constitutes, in a sense, the original entrance of the Son into the world. The world itself, the shadow of Heaven, answers God's "great Idea" (VII, 557) and begins to dance to the measure of his great design. A regenerative first "Christmas" hymn joins Heaven and earth in almost equal praise: "Glory they sung to the most High, good will / To future men, and in thir dwellings peace" (VII, 182–183). The total design of God also is celebrated, for in the fall of Satan (as in the sadly approaching fall of Adam) God will "Good out of evil . . . create" (VII, 188), even as the universe has been formed from chaos. One such specific reach of good will be the literal incarnation of the second Adam. Creative Cause, Substance, and agent move against the chaotic abyss, which in many ways resembles the wild wood of *Comus* or the appetites in representative Adam. Peace and generative order replace tempests like those on Galilee.

The divine geometer, whose golden compasses act as the creative extension of his golden scales of critical justice, then binds the created universe, partly by forcing it (in an image of both the "present" Hell and the future apocalyptic purgation) to expel downward "the black tartareous cold Infernal dregs / Adverse to life" (VII, 238–239). After that "fall," light, "first of things" (VII, 244–245), strides as if from Jerusalem ("her Native East"), but with it comes darkness, as rest and a kind of signification by opposites; when they are used so, light and darkness are not opposites but members joined in union. This Creation is attended with divine songs like those of the Nativity Ode and with angelic morning and evening praises like those already attributed to men—all celebrating life and union.

Similarly, on the second day water and land and air become one globe, now that the "loud misrule / Of *Chaos* [is] far remov'd" (VII, 271–272). Earth is born from the great waters like a child from the placental waters of a mother or like physical beings from Spenser's Chrysogenee. The land rises into its proper place for cooperative union rather than subservience, sun and moon take their different but cooperative roles (resembling those of Adam and Eve, greater and lesser in form but not in worth, she "borrowing her Light / From him" [VII, 377–378]), and all the varieties of other than human "living Soul" (VII, 388) find ordered places. All those latter creations are born from a mothering earth, a type of Eve—the animate, inanimate, and human all joining in receptive creation. These "births" contrast openly with that of Sin, for all these are perfect forms. Even the serpent moves impressively but without disharmony in that great fold. With grammatical daring, Milton demonstrates that the Creation was at this time essentially one: "Air, Water, Earth, / By Fowl, Fish, Beast, was flown, was swum, was walkt" (VII, 502–503).

Although nature, in a demonstratively "ascending" scale, is now complete in itself, creation "wants" a crowning touch, its completion, in man. His entrance is heralded with thematic words expressing his essence: *reason, erect, upright, govern, self-knowing* (VII, 508–510). He is expressly told that he is like the inhabitants of Heaven, "begotten" in their image: "Magnanimous to correspond with Heav'n" (VII, 511), he will "correspond" in the double sense of imitation and communication. Formed from chaotic dust like gunpowder or Jesus, he is creatively one both with the earth and with the Creator. (He of course can choose to reduce his being back into dusty chaff; we are reminded again that fealty to life and self is also fealty to God). Life itself is breathed into the human nostrils, then is breathed by them: but the human creature can reject that breath. Around this representative man, God places alluring gifts, the fullness of extra-human creation.[49] They perhaps are dangerously alluring, for they are "delectable

---

[49] Joseph H. Summers, in *The Muse's Method*, p. 113, describes the center as revealing "the divine image of God's ways at their most providential." Creation advises man of his happy state, much as the Battle in Heaven showed him his cause of woe.

both to behold and taste" (VII, 539), and wandering appetite seems so far to be offered no check. Sense is so endlessly gratified in this realization of Comus' fond dream that the proceeding narrative is shocked when a prohibition suddenly appears: one tree, bearing knowledge of good and evil, will allure like the rest but must not be tasted. With that division almost as much as with the "division" introduced into Eden by Satan, man's essential choosing begins.

A general stance within this choice and within earthly bounty, the two uniting in the human choice whether or not to continue the glory of being, is constant for most of the last two sections of *Paradise Lost*. It is the necessary point of human definition for Adam, Milton, and the audience. Because it exists before the Fall and endures beyond it, and because it provides the "original" definition for man and his moral world, it recapitulates or anticipates most of the major themes of *Paradise Lost*. Re-emphasized is man's creation upright, sufficient to have stood. Unlike the beasts', his mind marks him as "erect," choice-determined—for he must choose whether or not to retain that moral and physical posture. His reason will find employment in the naming of things, in the continuing praise of God, in the nearly perfect love of Adam for Eve, and in the questions directed to Raphael. However, although Raphael has warned that knowledge must be temperate, there had at first appeared to be almost nothing to urge appetitive temperance. Although it is likely that temperate reason could not coexist with unbridled appetite, the prohibition upon appetite, as Satan and Eve and perhaps all men will complain, at first seems "suspicious, reasonless." Not only does all other allurement in the Garden ask indulgence (and why should the one be different?) but also appetite in man seems to be more dominant and continuous than reason. However, until the prohibition appeared, reason, supposedly the essential characteristic of man, had seemed to be only an automatic assent to established divine conditions. Man might have been almost the same without as with it. To be operative, human reason needed provision for its own acts. Reason, far from being mere assent to sensual pleasure or a mere accompaniment, suddenly becomes definitive and dynamic, the power by which men can choose their characters and destinies as

well as those of their children. In affirming and maintaining
creativeness, the creative energy of reason will resemble that
power of creation just witnessed, in which "to create / Is greater
than created to destroy" (VII, 606–607). Like God's creativeness,
man's can directly battle Satanic destructiveness. The same penalty applies to the adversary of either God or man:

> Who seeks
> To lessen thee, against his purpose serves
> To manifest the more thy might: his evil
> Thou usest . . . [VII, 613–616].

If God gave man reasonable being, it is nevertheless man who
decides its character, history, and eternal disposition.

It is not really knowledge, then, that God has tried to "pro-
hibit"; it is the Fall. The coming of reason to the "knowledge" of
good and evil has even been furthered in the present by Raphael's
narratives, and Raphael's warnings continually indicate the deceptive ease, not the prohibition, of all choices. Both in the prohibition and Raphael's narratives, "Heav'n itself" is stooping to try
to spare Adam and his world the fatal experiential knowledge of
evil, from which, as Satan shows, there may be no turning back. If
Adam gives birth to Sin, to the chosen fatal act, he will replace
infinite "variety without end" (VII, 542) with finitude and death.
He is therefore stringently warned:

> . . . in the day thou eat'st, thou di'st;
> Death is the penalty impos'd, beware,
> And govern well thy appetite, lest sin
> Surprise thee, and her black attendant Death [VII, 544–547].

The warning might have prevented Eve's appetitive gorging of
death at the Fall. Even the penalty is not directly imposed by God
but by the nature of turning to what may be an attractive poison.
Reason has need of all its best effects, for under some circumstances the same attractive object may not be poisonous or sinful;
the definition and danger come in human turning away from
being. Without knowledge, Adam might not realize when he so
altered course. The narratives and warning have brought to

Adam, and to the audience, knowledge sufficient to tell when love becomes enslaved uxoriousness, and decent appetite gluttony. Within the epic, God's ways to men have now been justified, for the "senseless" prohibition is revealed to be a seasonable attempt to help men persevere upright.

God warns of the Fall in order that men, by knowing, may instead persevere within his original creation, that for which Heaven raises still another version of its eternal nativity hymn. To that praise man had brought his undiscording voice:

> . . . the Earth, the Air
> Resounded, (thou remember'st, for thou heard'st)
> The Heav'ns and all the Constellations rung,
>
> . . . . .
>
> While the bright Pomp ascended jubilant [VII, 560–564].

The gates of Heaven had been opened to man even as for him Sin and Death have opened the gates of Hell. Man is promised that if he maintains his being Paradise will be "lost" only in being transcended. His own being can evolve continually into greater and greater spirituality and approach God himself:

> Thrice happy men,
> And sons of men, whom God hath thus advanc't,
> Created in his Image, there to dwell
> And worship him, and in reward to rule
> Over his Works, on Earth, in Sea, or Air,
> And multiply a Race of Worshippers
> Holy and just: thrice happy if they know
> Thir happiness, and persevere upright [VII, 625–632].

Man was created a son of God: not "the" Son, of course, but the description of the one is startlingly like that for the other. Man, too, is "advanc't," a king over some forms of creation. He, too, can produce a "church" in his posterity. Most tellingly, he, too, is an "image" of God. As Raphael has stooped to inform Adam, so Adam, as rabbi, apostle, and "savior," will instructively aid his children, "that posterity / Inform'd by thee might know" (VII, 638–639) . Far from being God's automaton, Adam is his son, acting in original innocent glory rather than in the Fall's humiliated agony. The promise to man is immense, virtually infinite, so long as reason rather than unreason is chosen. *Mutatis mutandis,* the promise to Adam is held out to all men, both through God and through the Raphael-like offices of the epic. Its narrator accepts the burden of the Fall but also the exalted privileges extended by God to Adam and the "sons of men" (VII, 626).

Book VII closes the revelation of man's "happy State, / Favor'd of Heav'n so highly." Man is told by Raphael, an aspect of the creative Word, "Thy request think now fulfill'd" (VII, 635). It remains for men to justify their ways to God. To do so, Adam will now become first narrator of man's origin and original choices. Benevolent Raphael will act as reasonable judge.

"SOMETHING YET OF DOUBT REMAINS": TUTELARY DIVINE ASSAY OF HUMAN REASON (BOOK VIII)

Although the tutelary narratives with their methektic demonstration to Adam of the paradigms of choice have ended, Heaven's prevenient assistance continues when action returns to Adam direct. Eve's dream, the preliminary frame for the narratives, is balanced by Adam's colloquium with Raphael. Adam's account of man's choices will be judged in the light of the great paradigms. Complexities swiftly increase as somewhat removed mythic example is replaced by direct dialectical assay of human experience. Although Raphael accepts with brotherly interest Adam's "correspondent" narrative of his birth and his questions concerning the universe, as an aspect of divine Word the angel is brought to a worried frown. He tries and considers whether or not Adam can stand. The tutelary judgment is useful for precisely the same reason that the narratives were useful: if Adam heeds, his knowledge of his own possible fall may bring him to the renewal of right judgment.[50] This final harmonious colloquium may offer to the audience a saddening participation in innocence, but far more

---

[50] In opposition to those who would have Adam gain knowledge and morality within the crucible of direct experience, David Daiches, in *Milton,* p. 118, indicates that it is the weighing before experience that is choice; later may be too late. Virtue is to be known by "trial against the temptations of the world," not by embrace of them.

importantly it can supply fully relevant tutelage to Adam's sons. Although they can never inhabit Paradise, they can nevertheless gain and hold a postlapsarian inward Paradise by the same means that would have preserved the original Eden.

As the colloquium begins, Adam's human reason, recapitulating the Cartesian formula, moves out in "something yet of doubt" about our Shakespearean "goodly Frame" (VIII, 13, 15) of earth. Man seems to suspect that infinity itself may be mere waste, omnipotence the sprawl of useless energy. Adam's representative human question is not reproved, for Raphael finds it to be almost a praise of the Creator through interest in his creation. However, the quest is "prohibited" as wandering when it begins to try to comprehend causes. (Eve meanwhile, in an ominously opposite wandering that reflects her earlier narcissism and partly predicts the Fall, has left the colloquium's "studious thoughts abstruse" to move alone into the garden [VIII, 40]). It is not the bounty of God but the wandering of man that is immediately important. Man is shown that he has misjudged the relative importance of earth and sun, and of himself: the universe does not exist for him but for God, who in one sense fills it. What is more, doubt itself can possess danger. Although when wisely used it may lead up to knowledge, if unwisely directed to hidden causes, it can bring men into Hellish sterile speculation or fruitless atheism. The danger is not heresy but futility. Adam and the audience are asked to turn their minds from self-defeating fret about human systems of description (Ptolemaic, Copernican), which must always leave some "matters hid" (VIII, 167). Man should rather utilize the knowledge that has been fulfilled or may yet be: "Joy thou / In what he gives to thee . . . / Think only what concerns thee and thy being" (VIII, 170–171, 174).

We can too readily misunderstand Heaven's tutelary judgment of human reason. Raphael is not making straight the way for Alexander Pope, despite his advice to "be lowly wise" (VIII, 173). All of the most profound questions, any knowledge of man and the earth and of God's ways as visible therein, all of "what concerns thee and thy being" are freely available to man. He is warned against only the questions of the philosophers in Hell, those which man has no natural way of answering and about which he therefore always must remain in doubt. Specifically, Raphael warns against Eve's fanciful dream:

> Dream not of other Worlds, what Creatures there
> Live, in what state, condition or degree,
> Contented that thus far hath been reveal'd
> Not of Earth only but of highest Heav'n [VIII, 175–178].

A wisdom operating in those great spheres is not mean or worthless. It is "lowly" only in that it has taken the stance of "low" earth and what it can comprehend of "highest Heav'n," and in that it refuses Satan's impossible demands to know and be that which one cannot know or be without being the Creator he questions. Otherwise, it can be lofty and catholic.

The first man listens, understanding that the offered expanse of knowledge is sweet but that any other might produce "anxious cares" VIII, 185), acting as hellish will-o'-the-wisps that would lead unpersevering man into "wand'ring thoughts, and notions vain" (VIII, 187). Like the devils and the Stoic thought of Athens in *Paradise Regained,* they are negatives—"fume, / Or emptiness, or fond impertinence" (VIII, 194–195). Adam takes Raphael's and his own advice to turn to himself and earth, though not in fideistic retrenchment. His mind still soaringly entertains divine philosophy, and discourse with Raphael makes him "seem in Heav'n" (VIII, 210). Raphael assures Adam that human discourse is pleasing to Heaven—that, indeed, heavenly mind is like the human, as if of one creatural intelligence all. The first Adam, like the second, is so far a "fellow servant" (VIII, 225) with the angels.

As we have seen, when fiction presents a speaker and a listener, the audience automatically accepts its stance with the listener. As Adam assumes the narrative voice, the audience therefore shifts its stance, for Raphael becomes listener. One cost to us is that we now methektically listen to mankind with the cautious ear of Raphael and for a time share his frown.

Like Raphael and Milton before him, Adam becomes the historian and celebrant of human matters, not really "lowly," that concern him and his being. His physical "birth" intimates our individual human moral births, even as his narrative of that divine creation employs human words, words that constitute another "Divine Similitude" of the creative Logos. His account will place man's reason and action in divine "assay." Wisely, he now himself prohibits the completely insoluble and prideful questions Satan had dared: "For Man to tell how human Life began / Is hard; for who himself beginning knew?" (VIII, 250–251). He knows only that he was "born" from balmy sweat like later men, and, like the sea from the sun and the earth from the sea, within the unity of human and extrahuman earthly creation. His first, typic, God-given motion is ascent to upright stance. The great questions of man's interior relationship to himself and of his external relationship with other creatures are not yet answered: like Eve in Book IV, "who [he] was, or where, or from what cause, / Knew not" (VIII, 270–271). Recreating that formative time, his account enacts each man's history. Like his stance in Eden, his story is ultimately ours; like the story of Raphael, it too can be a revelation.

In man's beginning, then, a "lowly" human knowledge also appears. As Adam rehearses our history, he remembers first and essentially his human reason and its contact with divine Word; like a growing child, he had named whatever he had seen, himself not least. Although with that knowledge he then argued from sign that a greater single Being, a Father, must have caused him and creation, he found in nature "answer none" (VIII, 285) when he demanded intelligence of his own being. He therefore drifted to contemplative sleep almost as if he were drifting from his physical being. In that visionary state, which contrasts with that of Eve in Book IV by showing him his Paradise rather than a flight from it, the metaphysical answer he had fruitlessly demanded from nature was freely given to him. If his audience takes simple joy with him in the vision's identification of Adam as "First Man . . . , First Father" established in a "Garden of bliss" (VIII, 297–299), it takes prophetic pain in his being also the source of first disobedience, for which his sons must suffer in other gardens. He is led up into a high place, as his sons later will be led, to see the world. It is all exciting, "Tempting . . . [to] sudden appetite" (VIII, 308). Both Adam's dream mountain and Eve's dream pool reveal a Narcissus, one masculine, one feminine. New "wand'ring"

(VIII, 312) toward both knowledge and appetite tempts Adam, inducing in him a kind of Fall. As his earlier dreaming desire for God had been answered with the reality of the Presence Divine, so his present dreaming "sudden appetite" for fruit (VIII, 308) is answered by fruit "all real." There is an obvious threat that Adam will now choose a silly apple over God. God's agent or Word therefore gives him timely warning: God made all and prohibits the knowledge of good and evil. Like the audience, Adam does not understand God's mercy. He merely fears and resents the "rigid interdiction" (VIII, 334). His random detour toward unbeing, mere universal appetite, and wandering questions having nevertheless been halted, the waking Adam returns to the naming of things and understanding "thir Nature" (VIII, 353), using the knowledge God had supplied. He remains incomplete in his own eyes, however, and in that sense continues his "wandering."

So far, the myth of mankind's nascence has been amazingly rich. Born as all men are into the world all men share, the first man has inquired almost indifferently of his being. With no fear of death, he can casually contemplate even a drift out of self, out of existence. Into that "innocence" which closely resembles death come presences and forces that either are not historical and material or are not only such, insisting that Adam himself have a name, a progenital racial function, and a sense of God. This stipulated human being within that stipulated human destiny is moved to see the world which he inhabits but for a moment wants only to use it to please his appetite. At once, the greater presence he has felt before returns upon him in Raphael-like instructive judgment. Wandering in appetite or thought can lead him into "temptation"; the alluring trees and the whetted appetite must be "interdicted" at some point, or like Noah's contemporaries Adam will perhaps become only appetite or be destroyed poisonously by appetite—in either case, fading into the nonbeing or death that is the desired "prohibition" of the protective deity. Adam obeys, and returns to the use of reason in his world.

However, both appetite and an unfulfilled premise lead him into renewed question. Such wrestling can indicate the discontent that is also a divine dynamism leading him toward creative fulfillment. On the other hand, it may lead to nothing other than more fruitless wandering. In his first great choice, capable of either intimating fall or renewal after loneliness, Adam desires someone like himself to share his being and his world. Divinity answers that all the great world's creatures have souls and are "company." Adam holds to his plea, his reason wrestling with God, freely seeking and trying. He asks for an equal. His request is reasonable politically and religiously (in a Protestant sense) but of course carries within itself some seeds of Satanic temptation to "equality" with God. Divinity answers, amused but not angry, that if God is alone, why may not Adam be? Man then argues that his limitation, unlike God's infinitude, creates a need born of that limitation:

> Thou in thyself art perfet, and in thee
> Is no deficience found; not so is Man,
> But in degree, the cause of his desire
> By conversation with his like to help,
> Or solace his defects. No need that thou
> Shouldst propagate, already infinite;
> And through all numbers absolute, though One;
> But Man by number is to manifest
> His single imperfection, and beget
> Like of his like, his Image multipli'd,
> In unity defective [VIII, 415–425].

The speech displays both fit argument and irony, even error. In his claims of loneliness man has rather carefully ignored his communion with the divine presence, claiming that unequals cannot consort with each other. He moves to firm ground only when he says that he cannot beget an "equal," like of his like. He is neither the creatively begetting Father nor the destructively fathering Satan. Even as God will ask creation from his agent, the Son, so Adam needs a creative agent in order to fulfill the divine command of creation.[51] Given the paradigmatic choice between

51 Louis L. Martz, in *The Paradise Within*, p. 127, holds that Milton's account of the Creation answers "those who contend that Milton's God is wicked, [acting] to the sad exclusion of Faith, Hope, and Charity—especially Charity." In Milton, man participates in the Gloria for creation as well as in creation itself, for he is in his turn an "emanation" from Adam and Eve. See

unbeing and being, Adam brilliantly chooses creation. What is more, he asks that his reason serve another creature through "social communication" (VII, 429), even as divine reason has served him. The image of God has elected an *imitatio Dei*.

In its further implications, however, the speech discloses danger. It defines man in fractions and "needs" and "defects"; far from conceding that man cannot be perfect because only God is, it has sophistically turned the point into a claim that man is essentially imperfect. With a terrible irony wrung from a pun, it even insists that the need to beget is man's "single imperfection." Uxorious Adam will have cause later to assent grimly to this diagnosis, at times like Marvell rueing the "singleness" he had so easily condemned as imperfect. Man's reason was made individually sufficient and in its ultimate exercises must be independent of all save divine reason. The argument for union therefore threatens to be an argument for appetite and therefore a prophecy of surrender to the will of Eve at the Fall.

Nevertheless, the center of man's argument, which proceeds from "freedom . . . / Permissive," is unhesitatingly accepted. It shows that man promises to know himself, rather than only the beasts. God welcomes the reason that has now asked that which God has already designed. (Raphael's narrative had revealed God's prevenient gift of Eve.) Having judged well of "fit and meet," man will be given his "other self" (VIII, 448, 450). With hindsight the reader will perceive some grim truth in Eve's being promised as Adam's other self, for at times she will exactly represent his appetitive, wandering "antiself." But of course neither the gift itself nor Eve herself demanded such recoiling contrariety rather than completion.

The myth again becomes many-faceted as Adam, dazzled by his conversation with Providence, sinks down to the original position of his creation in a second, physical encounter with creation. Although the birth taking place in Adam directly recalls the birth

---

in addition Charles M. Coffin, "Creation and the Self in *Paradise Lost*," *ELH*, XXIX (1962), 13: Adam comes to God's design in desiring an Eve and collaborates with him in the creation. In much the same way, of course, the Son eventually recognizes God's design in Heaven and collaborates with it in both a physical creation and a spiritual recreation.

of Sin from Satan, Eve's creation through Adam ultimately derives from God, whereas Sin's derives only from Satan's anticreative self. Unlike that of Satan, Adam's present laboring dazzlement and "lowliness" can be put to divine use. The wound of Adam also looks for an instant like the wound of absence caused by Satan in Heaven, but like that wound Adam's wounded side closes at once and is in any case offset by creation; the wounded side of the second Adam also is intimated in this birth of Eve, but it too will give promise more of divine rebirth than of death. In these nuptial rites that anticipate the secondary creation of the human race, its "original" bent, Eve can be either a fulfillment of human love or a dangerous new delight, like Sin—"so lovely fair, / That what seem'd fair in all the World, seem'd now / Mean, or in her summ'd up" (VIII, 471–473) . The peril to man is clear: because idolatry is the reverse side of the coin of love, Eve may become his god. It approaches when he says that her absence left him dark: "I wak'd / To find her, or for ever to deplore / Her loss, and other pleasures all abjure" (VIII, 478–480) . It is upon him when he praises God for having "made amends" (VIII, 491) to man in this gift (as if God were somehow guilty) and thanks Heaven mainly for having given him this "fairest . . . / Of all thy gifts" (VIII, 493–494) . Man's choice and judgment grow increasingly "suspicious."

Forecasting Eve's separation from both human and divine love at the Fall, Adam confirms an increasing rush to solitary appetite in his intimate confessions to Raphael. Listening with Raphael, the audience also comes to frown in fear and judgment. Unlike his unaffecting honoring of other appetites, Adam admits, love of Eve can work a change, a "swerve," in the mind. Touch transports him, passion alters him; he is "here only weak / Against the charm of Beauty's powerful glance" (VIII, 532–533) . Possible Satanic parallels continue to rise threateningly upon him. If Adam permits it, concupiscence can lead him and Eve into their own direct birth of Sin. As it is, he is much too agile in blaming creation for his weakness, as he was before in pleading his need from weakness: nature left him deficient after Eve was removed from his side, or nature erred in making Eve fairer outwardly than she may be inwardly. (The end will see a total change, for

Eve then will most clearly present humanity's "inner Paradise.")
All the familiar complaints against the "wasteful" economy of
God and his creation lie waiting. They subside only because the
greater threat of Eve-worship sweeps to the fore, displacing not
only worship of God but also Adam's proper esteem of his own
rational powers (which should govern even his passion for Eve).
In framing the danger, Adam lavishly embraces it. Eve is to him
as the dazzling, but inferior, serpent later will be to Eve. She too
seems to assume God's absoluteness, including supreme wisdom,
virtue, and even original being. Although Adam realizes the
error, sensing that it involves a "fall" and degradation, he cannot
ward off the conviction that Eve is a goddess and that such beauty
as hers creates an awe as if a "guard Angelic" (VIII, 559) stood
about her. She must then be invulnerable. The irony is severe,
indeed, for her beauty is no guard for either herself or Adam.

Like Eve in her dream, Adam now has encountered all the
elements of a fall before the Fall. Such thoughts may freely come
and are themselves "free" unless they are unwisely chosen. Raphael, expressing audience anxiety because Adam not only worships Eve but accuses God of supplying his bent to that worship,
now acts with "prevenient" sharpness to combat "swerve" with instruction. He recalls Adam to his reasonable function, rebuking
him for doubting nature or surrendering his role. He demands that
Adam reawaken both magnanimity and respect for himself as
more reasonable than Eve:

> . . . weigh with her thyself;
> Then value: Oft-times nothing profits more
> Than self-esteem, grounded on just and right [VIII, 570–572].

The instructor reminds Adam that his essence is reason. Touch
alone he shares with beasts, but touch that follows the direction of
reason can supply creative love in place of self-seeking appetite.
The combination might provide a quasi-Platonic scale by which
men could ascend easily from human to divine love. Love is
judicious (VIII, 591), having his seat in reason rather than in a
physical site recently assigned it by Yeats. However, because man
has already in part chosen to sever his prior contact with divine
love because of his imperfect need for human love, the likelihood

is that human love will lead not to ascent but to Circean descent, threatening to remove man from the Platonic scale entirely. There would remain only the Satanic scale of "love," that which is measured by the affections of Satan, Sin, and Death and which leads to bestiality—and dust.

"Half abash't" (VIII, 595), Adam tries to retreat from the beast but falls into another possiblity of error. It is of long standing. When he argued with God for a mate, he had asked for an equal, but in one sense his essence demands that like God he instead remain alone. If he does not, his role as the more reasonable of the two may falter. Despite his earlier wish to lead a creature in reason, he is now sure that his love of Eve can stand as a "Union of Mind" that will "subject not" (VIII, 604, 607). It need not, but his wish for a marriage of true minds must be in part delusion. Eve may perhaps rise to his reason, but he can only fall to her appetite. Adam concludes that fortunately he has not yet made absolute choices and is "still free [to] / Approve the best, and follow what I approve" ([VIII, 610–611] even though his uxoriousness is already hardening into fate). He therefore turns the question to the heavenly love Raphael had spoken of, and is reassured that some form of "touch" is present even in divine love, for in Heaven distinctions between matter and spirit end, permitting the total "transunion" that earthly love seeks.[52] It is another version of the promises given to Adam over and over: if he aspires by due steps, he may ascend like the images that conclude *Comus* to higher and still higher forms of being, greater and greater realizations of himself and of human love.

Pursuing that promise, the great central dialogue of instruction comes to a close by voicing a revised form of the New Testament commandment:

> Be strong, live happy, and love, but first of all
> Him whom to love is to obey, and keep
> His great command; take heed lest Passion sway
> Thy Judgment to do aught, which else free Will

[52] William Empson (*Milton's God* [London, 1961], p. 107), among others, assumes a prurient blush from Raphael. It seems rather to represent ardor, the color of love. Raphael does not so much "change the subject" as complete it.

Would not admit; thine and of all thy Sons
The weal or woe in thee is plac't; beware.

.   .   .   .   .

. . . to stand or fall
Free in thine own Arbitrement it lies.
Perfet within, no outward aid require [VIII, 633–642].

To love God first, then Eve, though not in degradation of himself:
to this point, love makes swift union. The remainder of the
commandment separates representative Adam from definition
with either of those unions. Like each man, he is isolated once
again into liberty and warned that free will can end if passion
becomes a tyrant. His choices are far more dangerous than he
knows—he who confidently asserts that he is free to "approve the
best." He has revealed dangerous swerving from that best. He has
not really attended when told that the consequences can be far-
reaching. A choice freely made for evil will bind not only Adam
but his sons unfreely to the consequences of that evil. Whereas
passion's easy assent is surrender to determinism or a chain of
determinisms, the sometimes difficult refusal of degenerative passion, delivered by reasonable free will, is demonstration of liberty.
Most crucially, perhaps, Raphael's statement that Adam is perfect
within, as yet needing no redeemer, is not understood by Adam.
Not only has the man protested earlier that perhaps he is *not*
perfect, that nature (that is, Creation) left him weak before
passion, but also that he is not bound to perfection in his choices.
He can easily fall into fault, for his perfect capacity for proper
judgment does not insure that he will even honor proper judgment, and far less that he will necessarily act in accordance with
it.

But waiting humanity must be fully released into that field of
necessary freedom. As Heaven has chosen to stoop to man, so man
now must choose whether or not to maintain the upright contact
with Heaven. Although the direct divine presence is removed,
revelatory Providence will remain as guiding Word so long as it is
remembered or heeded. Furthermore, man has been promised
that he may in time become spirit, ascend to Heaven, and return
to the divine presence (V, 499–500) . Adam vows to honor divinity
in grateful memory. Unhappily, however, he does not indicate

that he will remember the lengthy instruction. Eden now lies entirely open to man's disposition of it, the divine protection having done all that liberty could allow. Adam and Eve do not wait until Book XII, then, to depart one aspect of Eden: the "Eden" of automatic benevolence, of direct goodness guaranteed not wholly by their will but partly by God's, now ends. They must come into the "wild Wood" of human choice—although still in Eden. Only there can Eden be maintained, for Eden demands the possibility of its own loss.

"One World Begin and End": Choice of human fall and of renewal within time (Books IX–XII)

At the entrance into the final third of *Paradise Lost*, Milton makes his circle just. The chosen fall introduced in the first invocation and typified in Satan, which the central part of the epic had seen divine instruction try to help man to avert, will now be realized in Adam and all his sons. The final invocation, like the first, and like that Johannine drum roll of fear in Book IV, insists that the action of Adam and Eve is also the agon of the author and the audience. As Paradise progressively is lost to human vision, so much the greater becomes the search for an inner paradise.

Again Milton confidently lays claim to the work as epic and asks that primary judgment of it be literary. Still transcending the Aonian mount, in the first and second Adams he will have introduced a new and superior kind of epic hero, one who excels Achilles, Odysseus, and even Aeneas—if only in leaving behind the Satanic, worldly, combative lust that in part inspired them. He has aspired restoratively to truth instead of "fabl'd Knights / In Battles feign'd" (IX, 30–31). Not inappropriately, former epic, when dealing in part with such less worthy heroes in such untruthful tales, had drawn and quartered ("dissected" [IX, 29]) many of its heroes in their bloody heroism. By contrast, *Paradise Lost* concerns "higher Argument," ultimate unifying truth, eternally living heroes. Its new hero, triumphant over his own sin and death by means of "Patience and Heroic Martyrdom" (IX, 32), will achieve and convey the paschalian joy of Easter.

The mood of the final invocation, although stressing change and "loss of Eden," is therefore not really a descent to different style; it is instead the highest reach the author can imagine. If his notes must change to "tragic" (IX, 6), they will find in the temporarily fallen heroes Adam and Christ, as in Samson, subject for magnificent tragedy; if he can in some measure wed Greek tragedy with epic, he will have soared above their hemispheric distinction toward a new literary kind. The fall and catharsis of Adam can be considered high tragedy, if in the definition of the genre we admit not only defeat but also consequent exaltation—the "begetting" in enlightenment of the tragic hero. Even more interestingly, if the new kind of hero enacted by Adam, "unsung" (IX, 33) by previous poets, is to demonstrate purgative "Patience and Heroic Martyrdom" (IX, 32), Milton will have added to Aristotelian fear, pity, and purgation the Christian elements humility, penitence, and salvation. The self-recognition and exaltation of such a hero will affect not merely a man or a nation. Like Milton as author, he will instead champion eternal reason and "justify" God's unerring design. Author and hero, like audience and subject, unite in monadic enactment of divine wisdom. Although honoring and imitating classical epic, Milton has radically recast its subjects and form. The range of epic action and the number of methektic actors and "authors" are expanded almost to the infinite. Fear of such daring invention causes him to ask if he can "raise" such a heroic poem, surmounting Olympus. Heroic faith and patience, mirroring those of the epic itself, answer that however much he alone may falter, his celestial patroness is beyond change. In token thereof, his unpremeditated verse will directly continue the similarly "unmeditated" praise by Adam and Eve (V, 149), for in the creative voice there will be no Fall. Consequently, his "intended wing" strongly surmounts Olympus still, still led on to "higher Argument" (IX, 42).

As audience, we should not mistake our stance nor the matter of this unfolding "tragedy." In witnessing man's "First Disobedience," we have not come to see mean events and the degradation of man, even though for a time we must watch as Paradise becomes Circe's pigsty, and man's birthplace, his future grave. We instead enter into the enactment of a great, typic human action, the model both of the human fall and of resurrection. Such a tragedy extends beyond the chosen limits of Sophocles or Aeschylus. The matter, too, must involve the most glorious as well as the most terrible realization of the humanity (indeed, of the virtual divinity) that we share with our "Grand Parents." It often is said that at the close of the poem Milton descended into the human and domestic, and he is awarded praise or blame accordingly. The basic premise, however, is ill-founded. Although it is true that we almost abandon direct attention to the mounts of Heaven or the pit of Hell, as even our vision of Paradise slowly dims out, their effect never ceases. We entertain in their place an explanation of their full earthly images in Eden and the world. In a strict exclusion of any other subject, we witness through Adam and Eve man's choice of God or Satan, life or death, as they involve his human choice and will. The proposed matter and our stance before it must offer a prospect of incomparable grandeur; and Milton is nearly always found equal to its expression.

At the edge of the Fall, it may seem that the epic must speed at once to the catastrophe demanded by drama, "history," and time itself. Insofar as man is concerned, all that is now past in *Paradise Lost* seems to serve as commanding prelude. Indeed, the final invocation stresses the irresistible impulse of man's chosen "fate" and the consequent alienation of creature and Creator:

> I now must change
> Those Notes to Tragic; foul distrust, and breach
> Disloyal on the part of Man, revolt,
> And disobedience: On the part of Heav'n
> Now alienated, distance and distaste,
> Anger and just rebuke, and judgment giv'n,
> That brought into this World a world of woe,
> Sin and her shadow Death, and Misery
> Death's Harbinger: Sad task [IX, 5–13].

Nevertheless, parallels between this final section and those that precede it become so numerous and insistent that we come to recognize recurrence, not departure, and the design of God that masters time, not the meaningless whirl of time on its lateral spindle. In Books IX and X, the Books of the Fall, Satan will once again maliciously command the stage before surrendering it to forces of renewal. As she earlier all but fell in dream, Eve now will fall in deed but for a moment will still be opposed by the renovative reason of Adam. Reflective councils in Heaven and Hell will be occasioned again by the Fall, but now Heaven will assert precedence in chronology as well as in judgment and salvation, thereby adjusting the initial "fallen" entrance of the epic into Hell. As in the first two Books the apostate son had tried to thwart God's design, the Son now increasingly brings that design to realization even within the Fall. When in Books XI and XII the epic moves from the Fall to its effects in time and eternity, the constant pattern of fall, renewal is repeated conclusively. The prospect of human history will see gracious counterpressure bring men up from the Fall, first to a partial, then to a total, restoration of man's loss. Eternity will offer the immense cosmic restoration within which Satan's choices, confirmed in self-destructive and purgative fire, disappear before the light of the Son's upright choices. The action of these seemingly tragic and historic Books becomes the eternal Act into which time and event are transfigured and resolved.

"WITHIN HIMSELF THE DANGER LIES": SATANIC FALL FROM EDEN (BOOK IX)

As the final section of *Paradise Lost* begins, Satan, the false counselor who now displaces the redemptive Raphael of the second part, once again commands the epic action and the shadowed stage of Eden. Although, significantly, this is to be our last direct experience of Satan in the epic, the audience again is asked to receive him as primary type or cause of Fall, even as it will shortly experience in the Son the primary type or cause of renewal. Within man's approaching typic trial, however, it is most instructive that we know first the primal choice against life and reason.

When Satan stealthily reappears in Eden, he represents for man hamartia become irremediable and perhaps "original"; as Satan infects men, so men will infect their children with sin. After nine days of spying "fall," he rises in Eden as an insubstantial, hellish exhalation or plague miasma until he chooses—as he now almost always chooses—to sink once more, as ironic "final sentence" (IX, 88), into the form of a serpent and the mentality of brutal unreason. Like man, he worships the earth for its resemblance to Heaven but like man may contrive fatal conversions of those beings and values. He too professes to believe earth a place worthier of gods than is Heaven (and has tried to become a rival to God); he is sure that earth represents the reformation and purgation of Heaven (as he sometimes considers Hell to be a condition better than that of Heaven); and he tellingly alters Adam's vague doubts concerning God's abundance of light into the conviction that earth commands all light. To such prophetic pride, earth has displaced God as center, all light being "for [him] alone . . . , / In [him] concentring" (IX, 105–106). Satan's momentary honest affection for either Heaven or earth must therefore sink first into serpentine election of "Rocks, Dens, and Caves" (IX, 118), and then into greed and blasphemy.

As always, Satan is harried by a continuous chaotic "siege / Of contraries" (IX, 121–122). He cannot free himself from the self-destructive attempt to destroy God's creatures, even though the recoil of "worse to [him] redound" (IX, 128). He hopes to find ease from "relentless thoughts" (IX, 130) in destruction, tearing down in a night what God through the Son had built in six days. Unable to comprehend how the loving God could bring angels—or devils—to serve tiny mankind, he nevertheless wants to bend all his force into destructive "service" to men. He mourns his fall into imbrutement as a serpent—"O foul descent" (IX, 163), an almost comic parody of the incarnate descent of Christ [53]—but cannot recognize its continuing cause, asking, "But what will not Ambition and Revenge / Descend to? who aspires must down as low / As high he soar'd" (IX, 168–170). His image will permit no sense of Christian ascent through humility, but only of sullen fall through pride. Even the knowledge that sin is self-destruction is dimly available to him, for his reason cannot be altogether un-

[53] Mother M. Christopher Pecheux, in " 'O Foul Descent!': Satan and the Serpent Form" (SP, LXII [1965], 190), indicates that Satan's supposed disguise rapidly becomes his chosen destiny.

made despite his having willed that it dim almost to blindness. He is half-aware that his punishment is his own doing when he admits that "Revenge, at first though sweet, / Bitter ere long back on itself recoils" (IX, 171–172). Such knowledge does not enlighten him, however, for he cannot perceive the recoil in his saying further that, "since higher I fall short" (IX, 174), he will attack man, not God—even though divine ministers have already hunted him into mist. To attack Adam is virtually to restage the futile Battle in Heaven, for Adam, like the Son, was also "exalted," if from a much more "base original" (IX, 150). Nor, of course, will he foresee the "recoil" to be dealt him by the second Adam, the Son he already grimly knows, who with significant anticipation of the Resurrection can receive his description of the first Adam:

> . . . this new Favorite
> Of Heav'n, this Man of Clay, Son of despite,
> Whom us the more to spite his Maker rais'd
> From dust: spite then with spite is best repaid
> [IX, 175–178].

So obdurate a course to such certain recoil (spite repaying itself in its own coin) could almost create pity for Satan, if as a resolute serpent he did not so confidently lead himself into temptation, there to coil himself into the labyrinth of unreason—awaiting us as audience, as well as Eve. Unwittingly, he has managed to show us the way of a true Son, the way of his own defeat: incarnation (but not imbrutement), lowliness (but not the lowering plunge of ambition), acceptance of the form of death (but not its end).

The pattern of fall and of audience stance within it having been re-established, we once more are significantly returned to the opposite choice of vital creativity and of our human sufficiency to stand within it, persevering upright. Into the place vacated by Satan come beneficent sacred and Homeric light, celebrative song, and the sacred human beings Satan is determined to destroy. The current of renewal is pathetically brief, however. In keeping with Satan's control of stance and with her two initiating "dreams," Eve again is first to speak. Following the law that audience stance will face rather than participate with the speaker, she is at once sharply set apart in alienation from audience, Adam, and Milton. She who is first to speak should, according to a hierarchy of proximity to the Word, be second. She has reversed the established order of male and female essence, first by complaining of God's masculine and Edenic abundance (for which she might have heard Raphael's explanation had she not prophetically removed herself from so much reason) ; then by commanding that Adam follow "what to [her] mind first thoughts present" (IX, 213), dividing their labors (along with their union) ; [54] finally by directing that he maintain by "choice" the symbolic union of woodbine with ivy while she moves alone to a spring of roses, pitifully seeking "what to redress till Noon" (IX, 219), away from him and the symbolic garland of roses he will weave. In her defiance of Adam's counsel and her own dream, she duplicates Satan's first act of isolation in Heaven, as she soon will duplicate his attention to a new voice (Sin's) and his implicative seduction of his peers.

Adam's answer for the time grants her freedom for such dangerous ambition. Forgetting God and Raphael, he addresses her as "Sole *Eve,* Associate sole, to me beyond / Compare above all living Creatures dear" (IX, 227–228). Literally true and unexceptionable, his statement nevertheless resigns her to her own presently dangerous nature, permitting no second. He further relinquishes even reason to her wandering motions: "Well hast thou motion'd, well thy thoughts imploy'd" (IX, 229). He knows that his delight in her properly should be adjoined to reason but supposes without a twinge of fear that she may have become "satiated" with his (or any) reason, seeking instead her own temporary "best society" (IX, 248, 249) in Satanic solitude. He leans toward her so selfishly that he cannot realize that her leaning away from him may be equally selfish. Only at the end of the exchange, having already yielded the day, does he recall Raphael's warning of a tempter. The wish to leave "Conjugal Love" (IX, 263) is also a wish to abandon God and her progeny. He attempts to recall them both to their proper functioning with one another and with *their* Maker: "Leave not the faithful side / That gave

[54] Mary Ann N. Radzinowicz, "Eve and Dalila: Renovation and the Hardening of the Heart," in *Reason and the Imagination,* ed. J. A. Mazzeo (New York and London, 1962), p. 163: In attacking the marriage of Adam and Eve, Satan attacked all human polity.

thee being, still shades thee and protects" (IX, 265–266). She is begged to remain vine to the stronger elm, avoiding the unshielded blaze of noon. A long reach of danger is visible to us when Adam virtually promises to save her or to endure "with her the worst" (IX, 269) rather than a redemptive "best," but with relief the audience, like Adam, observes the immediate danger seem to pass.

Because obdurate Eve will almost surely lead the readers into her own temptation, at the moment of fatal choice she receives the judgment of the Choric author. Lest he be unjustly charged with complete misogyny, it should be made clear that Adam and Eve here embody, not only masculine and feminine attributes, but also qualities almost allegorical. He possesses more of reason, she more of passion—including of course the highly honorable compassion of wife and mother; Mary will be "second Eve" for reasons other than those of mere time and succession.[55] The drama is not really a domestic Chaucerian or Shavian tale inquiring whether a woman shall be sovereign. It asks if reason-and-appetite in Adam-with-Eve, as it might in an individual man or in a state, shall fall from unity into civil war or civil indifference, the weaker assuming control of the stronger. If it does, not only Adam and Eve's domestic union but most divine and natural laws as well will have been revoked.

At the risk of overliteralness and bathos (which Milton avoids by avoiding a direct statement of the parallel), we may also note that Eve is "subordinate" because she is begotten from Adam. In a limited sense, he is her creator; he asks that she "leave not the faithful side / That gave thee being, still shades thee and protects." Her relationship to him, if taken in a figurative sense, reflects the relationship of man or angel to creative agents or the ultimate Creator. The rebellion is not necessary, for she today could act against Satan as the Son will in *Paradise Regained* and the Lady in *Comus*, especially after Adam's tutelary aid. For Eve as for Satan, the rebellious will does not seek true independence, for freedom of will is already complete. It instead seeks to undo

---

[55] For a discussion of Eve's compassion, see Dorothy D. Miller, "Eve," *JEGP*, LXI (1962), 544–545. Mrs. Miller stresses the incompleteness of Adam without Eve.

ontology, making the prideful rebel autogenerative, defying the text, "It is He who has made us, and not we ourselves." Ultimately, it is an attempt to equal or displace God—the only being who is his own cause. In a second figurative sense, Adam's rib has tried to assert ingrate autonomy from the parent body. As Michael says at the close, Eden was Adam's soil. In turn, Adam is her origin as God is his, and she now moves toward separation. Paradise is abandoned long before it is "lost."

When like a Dalila Eve answers Adam's warning with the pursed lips of a woman wronged, she may seem to act merely on the domestic level, but her looks have taken on "sweet austere composure" (IX, 272) in token of her usurpation of Adam's role as reason; originally he had been "less winning soft, less amiably mild" than she. Although Eve assures us that she overheard tutorial Raphael and knows all she should know, she convinces us she knows nothing, for she imagines that humans are changeless, "not capable of death or pain" (IX, 283) : evil could therefore exist only in Adam's loss of love for her. Although he attempts only a salving (not a purgative) response, Adam soon writhes in domestic coils familiar to postlapsarian men. He first addresses her in the chilly formality she has chosen, then falls headlong into her new error as well as his own old one, saying that she is immortal and free "from sin and blame entire" (IX, 292) . He belatedly tries to induce caution and union by warning that the tempter was crafty enough to have seduced angels. His reason having given ground before unreason, however, Eve presses the advantage sharply. Satanically, her reason increasingly deceives itself. Men are not free, she says, if they are fearful; and they need not be fearful, for a tempter can hurt only himself. She argues truly concerning God's gift of sufficiency but terribly ignores two great dependent truths: first, it will ultimately not be Satan who will hurt them, in the encounter with choice, but they themselves; second, the freedom she has argued includes the dreadful option of choosing slavery rather than freedom. She has all the easy confidence of untutored small reason.

Too late, the Fall already having progressed too far in Eve, Adam attempts to renew them in reason. He would properly act as a preventive Raphael to the ambitious Eve, instructing her in all that she has ignored. In his way, he justifies God's ways to men. Man, he says, is "secure from outward force" (IX, 348) :

> . . . within himself
> The danger lies, yet lies within his power:
> Against his will he can receive no harm.
> But God left free the Will, for what obeys
> Reason, is free, and Reason he made right,
> But bid her well beware, and still erect,
> Lest by some fair appearing good surpris'd
> She dictate false, and misinform the Will [IX, 348–355].

He does well to be on his guard; the audience recalls that even the angel Uriel can fail to detect Satan. It is significant that Adam personifies our possibly deceived reason as *she,* who may be misled by some "fair appearing good" (IX, 354) and then *dictate* falsely. Eve is rushing headlong toward just such a blind fault, such a certain "swerve." Out of mere curiosity or folly, albeit in a wandering motion, she is leading herself and, in a sense, her God, forward to the temptation. Adam knows that she should demonstrate her obedience and so maintain her fidelity in the familiar way, rather than that she should attempt to test her constancy by trial. Like the very question of fidelity, trial not only takes a leap into the unknown but can be "proved" only with the hazard of infidelity and the risk of disobedience. However, like the God who anxiously protected man across all the center of *Paradise Lost,* Adam must also grant Eve the freedom that is part of her essence. He can only remind her that "God towards thee hath done his part," and beg her, "Do thine" (IX, 375). Her seizure of his permission is comical in the domestic scene but terrible in its general implications: it assumes that freedom means license to do whatever one's fancy directs. Specious in her victory, she already confuses herself with sophistical, Satanic rhetoric:

> The willinger I go, nor much expect
> A Foe so proud will first the weaker seek;
> So bent, the more shall shame him his repulse
>   [IX, 382–384].

With that, she severs the human union by withdrawing the hand

she gave Adam at the outset [56] and will somewhat brokenly give
him again at the close of the epic. She who has now refused an ear
to Adam—and God—is ready to lend it once more to Satan.
Immediately, she suffers a terrible comparison with pagan deities
like those assigned to the devils in Hell. Specifically, she is like
Ceres just at the moment of her sorrowful conception of Proser-
pina, the human girl who after ravishment must be mate to
Hades. In them, a Christian audience infers Sin and Death.

So far, the two actors have seemed to be almost alone, the
audience merely standing by. Eve's fatal choice impels audience as
well as author into a half-bitter, half-elegiac apostrophe to our
"Mother" as she willingly leaves our Edenic stance within the
circle of divine and human safety and favor:

> O much deceiv'd, much failing, hapless *Eve*,
> Of thy presum'd return! event perverse!
> Thou never from that hour in Paradise
> Found'st either sweet repast, or sound repose;
> Such ambush hid among sweet Flow'rs and Shades
> Waited with hellish rancor imminent
> To intercept thy way, or send thee back
> Despoil'd of Innocence, of Faith, of Bliss [IX, 404–411].

Separated from her guardian by her own will, Eve has increased
her vulnerability over that of the Lady in *Comus* a hundredfold.
If it be said that she has none of the resources of the Lady, it
should be answered that she has had Adam, Raphael, and God.
Removed from the godlike elm, she is already in part Satanic;
humanly, however, she is also the pitiable "fairest unsupported
Flow'r, / From her best prop so far, and storm so nigh" (IX,
432–433). Her "best prop" had been her full humanity.

An abrupt shift of stance severs the methektic audience as well
as Eve from Adam. Divorce from Paradise [57] causes our agon to

---

[56] Among others who have commented upon the union or separation of
hands in *Paradise Lost*, Kester Svendsen, in *Milton and Science*, pp. 111–112,
associates the figure with the combination or severance of reason and emotion.
E. M. W. Tillyard, in *Studies in Milton* (London, 1951), p. 22, similarly
considers the "double hero," Adam and Eve, as uniting wit and will.

[57] The wealth of meaning in Eve's divorcement from Eden is noted by every
reader. Among them, Anne D. Ferry, in *Milton's Epic Voice*, p. 164, emphasizes the breaking of several circles in the poem; M. M. Mahood, in *Poetry*

become agony in the contemporary meaning. Adam's former control of epic stance is shockingly surrendered to Satan. Our second direct experience of a fall toward Hell is guided not by the rebellious archfiend of Book I, but by our general Mother. If terror for man is added to our wrenching pity for her, the effect may be a renewed catharsis of evil.

Her adversary awaits Eve like a greater Mephistopheles for Gretchen. Although it is noon in Eden, she has returned to the shadowy pool of self and to tempting fancy. In the coming assay, the softness she chose over Adamic austerity is the most dangerous human characteristic. It invites the destructive rape of innocence by evil because of the downward displacement of the hierarchy of being. Whereas in the past she and Adam had drawn inferences from themselves toward Heaven, she now permits the "serpent" to draw inferences from brutal nature to her. This downward revision permits her to see herself as the new apex, new ultimate; the audience sees, instead, only a wilfully unsupported flower. For a moment only, Satan is "stupidly good" in Adamic-Satanic love for her in whose "look sums all Delight" (IX, 465, 454), before rapacious hatred returns, pitching him upon his only pleasure—the destruction of pleasure, especially that which he fully loves but fully refuses. He would have feared reasonable Adam, "Foe not informidable" (IX, 486), because he fleetingly recognizes that his own capacity to be vanquished by man has painfully increased. It is instead appetitive Eve he will work upon, for although she is ambitiously "fit Love for Gods" (IX, 489), she is not herself terrible. Only the Son's love, as a token of the love possible from Adamic man as well as from God, is acknowledged by Satan to hold "terror . . . in Love" (IX, 490).

---

and Humanism, p. 185, would add the breaking of other circles, such as those of psychological wholeness; Joseph H. Summers, in *The Muse's Method,* pp. 61–63, identifies this Eve with Sin, especially in her bringing to birth the snuffing Death that will prey appetitively upon Eve; Frank Kermode, in "Adam Unparadised," in his edition of *The Living Milton* (London, 1960), p. 117, stresses that Eve's eating death permits the entry of death into the human body (and that death's terrible rape, the Dantesque cannibalism associated with Sin, and Satanic recoil are all implicit in Eve's act); and Svendsen, in *Milton and Science,* p. 128, notes that although Eve eats death, she will give birth to death's "devourer."

Brute sophistication and human credulousness now meet in the arena of human assay. Sin is about to be born in Eve. Like Sin, Eve too will bring forth Death, in herself and for the audience. The serpent that moves upon her, signifying Sin as well as Satan, coils and uncoils in a sensual maze of great beauty, but its beauty is as perverse as the forms to which seductive Zeus fell for the sake of lust. In this manner will history's false gods appear to other women. Another analogy clouds the scene even though noon blazes: Eve is to Eden's beasts like Circe to her herd, but Eve's role is about to be squarely reversed. She will fall below the beasts' level, brutalizing them all.

The course of the temptation now must be run, with Eve's tainted children standing as participating Chorus. The proper fame of the scene sometimes betrays an improper judgment. It is not a contest of two, so much as a realization by one. Although the serpent of course is present, even as the will to sin was present in Satan in Heaven, the real drama is played by representative Eve. In large measure, she here completes her self-temptation, that which now (but only now, when she chooses) can be said to have begun almost with her creation, when she narcissistically elected her own passional "softness." The addresses of the serpent, like those of Satan in *Paradise Regained,* give objective voice to what already has been thought. The objectification of the Tempter insists upon Satan's reality, of course, but it also represents that moment when choice plays seriously, willfully, with accepting evil. In a sense, man then creates Satan as well as sin. When man nears that fatal choice, Satan leaves his "mist" and dumbness. He becomes all too real and persuasive as a perverse "incarnate" Logos replacing the words of men and God.

Our secret human ambition and vanity, now fully revealed in typic Eve, are wrought upon masterfully. The serpent prods her isolative ambition first by nominating her "sovran Mistress" and "sole Wonder," he (like her) being "single" (IX, 532, 533, 536) . He helps her aspire above Adam by saying that she is "Fairest resemblance of thy Maker fair" (IX, 538), perhaps leading her also to hope that Jehovah really is Astarte. He then places her in God's very throne by directing a *benedicite, omnia opera,* recalling that of Book V, to her. Finally, he strikes at the center of her weakness by saying (IX, 545–546) that she should be promiscuously worshiped as a goddess among gods, not stoically reserved to "one man . . . (and what is one?) ." Solitude suddenly becomes the wish for multitudes, as Adam's wish for an adoring mate has been expanded toward infinity, in Eve's pride.

Eve is "not unamaz'd" (IX, 552) by the maze of his not unfamiliar words. She cannot see that with her own words she has openly pointed out the danger in any "Language of Man pronounc't," not by angel or man, but by "Tongue of Brute" (IX, 553, 554) ; knowing that beasts cannot speak to men, she might guess that a brute voice can speak only to the brute in man. Like a Grand Inquisitor, however, she relishes the miracle, refusing the marvels of the natural order in favor of Hellish deviations from it. She wants to know why the serpent is so fond of her—she who has all but severed, for the time, her union with man. The scene becomes a grotesque parody of Raphael's angelic communion with Adam, as does the ensuing exchange of human questions and demonic instruction. Now, of course, the human receives only brutal or diabolical "knowledge." Were it not for its importance as the final act of will, the apple would be not only a mere token but, literally, an afterthought.

Satanic knowledge involves equal measures of degradation of reason and increase of ambition. Temptation addresses Eve as "Empress of this fair World" (IX, 568) and promises obedience to her (the newly disobedient) . The compact of faith by Hell's faithless is shamelessly extended. The fallen angel truly tells the upright human being of his own self-seduction, in yet another narrative in *Paradise Lost* of the "first things" of creation. He expresses to his human audience the attraction of the tree of knowledge: it was generally appetitive, leading to "sharp desire" as well as "hunger and thirst" which should be satisfied "at once" (IX, 584, 586), lest reason intervene. The more telling human temptation, that of pride in mind and will, now dominates, even though appetite continues to lurk in the background. Eve thinks that as she is less than Adam, so the fallen serpent (more aspiring than other beasts) had been less than she. Her whetted hope is that the forbidden fruit can elevate (although in truth it can only imbrute) her, too, by so many degrees. Had not the enlightened serpent been able to consider "all things visible in Heav'n, / Or Earth, or Middle, all things fair and good" (IX, 604–605) — seemingly, all those things that Adam had discussed with Raphael? And does not the sapient being near her say, not altogether like Adam but without Adam's occasional attention to God and the invisible, that *she* is the crown of creation? After such seeming knowledge, what resistance?

Even though the Serpent of ambition seems to have prepared the way sacrificially because "the virtue of that Fruit [was in him] first prov'd" (IX, 616), Eve hesitates, in some remaining human coldness to the summons of bestiality. The witnessing audience can wish for her and for themselves that she might recognize the "virtue" of the tree not as reason but as cormorant Sin and Death, and that Satan's "first" proof would not lead her so readily to a second proving. But in imitation of Adam with Raphael, she questions not self or Satan but God, almost repeating the complaint of God's superabundance. Such complaint all but asks that she be led to the forbidden tree that will "disburden" (IX, 624) death to the children she fleetingly considers. Appetite quickly leads her beyond the saving doubt that certifies choice. Unlike the frowning Raphael, Satan is "blithe and glad" (IX, 625) as a Comus in his reply: the way to the tree, like that to Hell, is now "ready, and not long" (IX, 626). In a human surrender as dangerous as that of Adam to her, Eve accepts the guidance of the serpent. In clear noon, she has none of the reservations of the Lady in *Comus'* darkness. When he whispers, making the "intricate" seem straight, "If thou accept / My conduct, I can bring thee thither soon" (IX, 629–630), she doubly accepts his "conduct," saying, "Lead then" (IX, 631). The audience again may wish for a warning voice in order to identify Satan's "thither" for Eve. Although she confusedly thinks that it is a route of aspiration leading to a (grimly ironic) disburdening excessive "Nature of her Birth" (IX, 624), it will instead be Hell. He leads her as brightly as an illusory will-o'-the-wisp that also plunges men into hellish "Bogs and Mires . . . / There swallow'd up and lost" (IX, 641–642).

"Humane" Eve again resists for an instant when she sees the tree that is prohibited. Nevertheless, she with her reasoning question of God yearns toward it, wandering into terrible irony when she states that the tree is "Fruitless to mee, though Fruit be here to excess" (IX, 648). The "fruit" for herself and for the fruit of her womb will be great, indeed: full as the teeming womb of Sin. A brief, failing association of gender unites her with God's law, "Sole Daughter of his voice" (IX, 653). She instead vaunts that merely human "Reason is our Law" (IX, 654). Because she has in actuality revoked that law, the gates of Hell yawn open. Satan feeds her with another self-tempting question: how can a fruit be denied men, if they (pridefully, diabolically) are "Lords . . . in Earth or Air" (IX, 658)? Parodying Christ's zeal for men, he "raises" man by specious sophistries, insisting that towering human reason can comprehend "highest Agents, deem'd however wise" (IX, 683); by reducing God to agent, he has vacated the position of the First Cause—but only to assign the office to Eve, now "Queen of this Universe" (IX, 684). The self-temptation that had worked for him obviously should work for her, who also is "vent'ring higher than [her] Lot" (IX, 690). It should lead her similarly to applaud her "dauntless virtue" (IX, 694) in trespass, as Satan has applauded his own and expected God to endorse it. But his words now tumble on each other in a chaos of falling premises and abortive conclusions, recapitulating the whole temptation and fall: "if what is evil / Be real, why not known, since easier shunn'd?" (IX, 698–699). In the eternal framework his question recoils upon himself, but in fallen time all the easy dismissal of angelic warning, all the curiosity to know evil, and all the failure to realize that choice can in one way be final and fatal, coil in his words. He concludes with the absurd but doubly seductive apostrophe, "Goddess humane" (IX, 732), tempting both her superhuman ambition and her human pride.

The degrading rape of human essence by a diabolical Zeus has all but succeeded. His words, seductively "impregn'd / With Reason, to her seeming, and with Truth" (IX, 737–738), join natural human appetite and "desire" (IX, 741) to taste the fruit. Eve only seems to waver, for she has already called this fruit "best" and its taste "too long forborne" (IX, 745, 747). She is convinced that because God is privative, his prohibitions upon man's ambition to be good and wise must "bind not" (IX, 760). So sure is she that the death-devoted Serpent lives absolutely that she takes him as God and law, as "Author unsuspect, / Friendly to man" (IX, 771–772). With that, unsuspecting indeed, she is undone, accepting the role of Sin from "Author" Satan. The words that rush from her are Sin's children, cursed with condemnations, ironies, horrors:

> What fear I then, rather what know to fear
> Under this ignorance of Good and Evil,
> Of God or Death, of Law or Penalty?
> Here grows the Cure of all, this Fruit Divine,
> Fair to the Eye, inviting to the Taste,
> Of virtue to make wise [IX, 773–778].

The terrible "cure" will of course work purgatively against good, God, and law, insuring an all-too-successful cure from ignorance of evil, death, and penalty. She and Adam had been blessed with direct and tutorial knowledge of good. The account of the Battle in Heaven had also supplied a vicarious knowledge of evil sufficient to have prevented their agonized plunge into its direct knowledge and consequent direct effects. She now strains toward that knowledge which loving pity had "prohibited" them, having tried to spare them, to help them persevere upright against imbrutement and the grave.

The hand that had refused Adam does not refuse the hellish Dead Sea fruit. At once, nature shudders as it had at the birth of Sin and will again at the death of Christ, for Eve—now lacking the knowledge that she abandoned as she thought to gain it—does not realize that she is "eating Death" as monstrously as Death tries to devour Sin, and that she has gluttonously "ingorg'd" that bitter fruit "without restraint" (IX, 792, 791). Hoping to be a god, she—like a greater Caliban—has instead plunged downward gluttonously, drunkenly, to the beast. Her praise, earlier denied to God, is prophetically lavished instead upon the terrible, idolistic tree of death, upon which she has elected to crucify herself[58]

---

[58] Ann Gossman, in "The Use of the Tree of Life in *Paradise Lost*" (*JEGP*, LXV [1966], 684), records the association of the tree of life with the cross, with the phoenix of resurrection and with the genealogical "tree" of the house of Jesse.

and some of her sons. It now will receive her morning song.[59] She will reach up with it to frightful maturity "in knowledge" (IX, 804) of death. She abandons the preventive guidance of divine or human reason in favor of direct experience without reason, praising it as highly (and from some of the same motives) as did Chaucer's Wife. In that instant, she has lost Eden. The audience realizes that her experience is also human history, and that by her human choice all doomed lateral human time, stretching from Cain to the Second Advent, suddenly has displaced blessed eternity. She resolutely divorces herself also from immutable love and life. If Heaven therefore resents her, she can hope—as Hell has hoped—that God, that "great Forbidder" (IX, 815), is far away and uncaring. As for forsaken Adam, she rather pities him, wondering (as he never had) if perhaps she should not remain alone in her new superiority. "Inferior," she now agrees with Satan, is not "free" (IX, 825). On the other hand, if God is to punish, then Adam and all future men should go down with her in company. She has assumed Satan's determination that men share in his destruction rather than in the love of men and God. If her specious words recapitulate some of the comic folly of Hell, she nevertheless terribly transforms love into death, baring her teeth in a Satanic election of time, change, and ending:

> Confirm'd then I resolve,
> *Adam* shall share with me in bliss or woe:
> So dear I love him, that with him all deaths
> I could endure, without him live no life [IX, 830–833].

Because her ensuing idolatry of the tree has involved the worship of Death, Eve returns to Adam as Sin, the agent of his death.

It is necessary for the general audience, which must be judge as well as participant in the Fall, to see Eve within the general "tragedy." Because she was first presented to us so handsomely and because at the end of the epic she offers the final word of sacrifice and compassion, we wish to forgive her, even to say that she is to be pitied more than censured. We grant a kind of

---

[59] Marjorie Nicolson, in *John Milton: A Reader's Guide to His Poetry* (New York, 1963), p. 288, emphasizes the typic idolatry in Eve's repeating the reverence of Hell to Satan.

admiration to her softness and gullibility, and are appalled by the grim severity of Milton's judgment upon Adam and Eve in *Of Christian Doctrine*. However, if she is taken at the moment of her fall as dramatic character alone, she is fit to stand with the grandly terrible women of literature—Medea, Clytemnestra, Lady Macbeth—in all save the circumstances of direct bloody-mindedness and murder. For that matter, she involves and nearly traps Adam and all his sons in spiritual as well as physical death, thereby outdoing any of her dubious sisters. Although her ambition will be graciously thwarted in other ways so that natural compassion and properly used "softness" will come to align her more nearly with Mary than Medea, for the moment she is superior in evil even to Milton's Dalila. That is no mean fame. A modern audience almost has to rub its eyes until the mists formed by disbelief, by its amused superiority to Genesis, and by all its comic stories about Adam and Eve, clear away. It then may accept Eve not only as a tragic personage, magnificently gifted but now greatly fallen; it also may understand why generations of Christians hated her in her fault exactly as they hated Judas.

The serpent's blithe evil becomes hers as she implicates Adam. She recapitulates Satan's seduction of the angels in Heaven. Death hovers behind her loving words: "never more / Mean I to try, what rash untri'd I sought, / The pain of absence" (IX, 859–861). Milton's puns assault her present self-knowledge and past disobedience, for if she was once "rash untri'd," all that followed should also be judged rash. The primary assault, however, is upon her will not that she die for Adam but that he die with her. She wildly parodies his wish for a mate by claiming that it was not for herself that she wanted the godhead she trusts she gained but for him, and without him "can despise" it (IX, 878). It is a Satanic lie. She has moved upon Adam in mazing sophistries, but at the final moment an imperious command much like that of Satan in *Paradise Regained*—"Thou therefore also taste" (IX, 881) — discloses her tyrannical pride more surely even than do her final words:

> Lest thou not tasting, different degree
> Disjoin us, and I then too late renounce
> Deity for thee, when Fate will not permit [IX, 883–885].

Eve having enacted Sin and eaten Death, Adam will now follow the steps of uxorious Satan to such a bride and such progeny.

The original morning stance with Adam has been released into Eve's command. The unwilling audience must stand with her to witness the second general human fall. Because death of a sort has returned with Eve, Death precedes Adam in response. The uniting nuptial circlet of roses that Adam had woven for Eve falls, its morning flowers withered, "wedded Love" having already collapsed toward death or isolative lust. His garland image of nuptial love has been replaced by her isolative severed bough; and it is he who now is to be harvested. As sin flames in Eve's distempered cheeks, death prophetically seizes upon Adam even as it had once warningly visited Eve in her dream: "horror chill / Ran through his veins, and all his joints relax'd" (IX, 890–891). When Adam speaks, horror having only momentarily sped through him as through nature, his self-temptation towers in turn. It causes him to second Eve's displacement of God by ambition and sexual vanity:

> O fairest of Creation . . . ,
> . . . Creature in whom excell'd
> Whatever can to sight or thought be form'd,
> Holy, divine, good, amiable, or sweet! [IX, 896–899].

Although he grieves that she has been ravished from obedience, "Defac't, deflow'r'd, and now to Death devote" (IX, 901), there is not yet much conviction in his outcry. It instead suggests an odd, perverse kind of stimulation. In the past, he had opposed his reasonable "renewals" to her potential falls. This time it is he who breaks the circle. If sin has been only a possibility in his mind before, it is now peremptorily born. Not only does Adam fashion Eve into a semblance of forbidden tree and fruit; he also exalts her into "Goddess of Nature"—exactly as Satan had addressed her. Adam imitatively abdicates reason in himself and ignores the reason of Raphael's tutelage. Most tellingly, his sudden decline into lecherous effeminacy is registered in the progressive fall of the epithets he assigns Eve. The sublime "holy and divine" decline anticlimactically to the bathetic "amiable, or sweet." A moment later, in imitation of Eve with the serpent, Adam begins to have a grudging respect for her daring. Suddenly then to him it is not Eve who had been ravished, but Eve who is ravisher, she who could "violate / The sacred Fruit forbidd'n" (IX, 903–904). The blasphemy is staggering. As she had granted direction to Satan earlier, so now Adam grants her the lead, "for with thee / Certain my resolution is to Die"—rather than to remain "in these wild Woods forlorn" (IX, 906–907, 910). Eden has become for him more repulsive than the Wood of *Comus*, even though it lately had been the fit habitation of Raphael. Unlike the romanticists of later generations who applaud Adam as an Orpheus before the fact of Eurydice's death, Milton judged that Adam should have resisted the unalterable claims of appetite, uxoriousness, and death in order to assert those of reason, redemptive love, and life. This was the moment to have redeemed Eurydice. Instead, the descending Satanic "link of Nature" (IX, 914) draws him to her now deathly embrace. In a grim parody of the marriage sacrament, he vows that her now diseased flesh is his, that "from thy State / Mine never shall be parted, bliss or woe" (IX, 915–916). The bond must now disseminate the contamination of disease. The audience briefly recognizes the transverse application of his vow to themselves, the grand sons of these parents, as Adam surrenders the human creature into Eve's and Satan's examples.

It all passes so quickly. We have barely time enough to see that Adam has not only deceived himself in words almost as giddily as Eve had but also that he too recapitulates Satan's Fall. From considering Eve within God's creation, he rapidly comes to think only of her outside that creation, and then only of her "sweetness." Love has been excluded, somewhat fittingly, making Eve only an "apple" of appetitive gratification. If she has erred, he will share the error rather than correct it or part from her. For a moment he looks with direct eyes at the death she has chosen, but in the end he cannot concentrate upon either God or death, but only upon her.[60] He much too easily chooses sin and death if they must be the "wages" of his appetite. To do so, he parrots the

---

[60] The case for Adam as heroically selfless in following Eve into the Fall is developed with feeling in A. J. A. Waldock's *Paradise Lost and Its Critics*, p. 54. His case is weakened not only by the suspicion that Adam follows his own selfish interest but also by our wistful wish that Adam had tried, like the Son, to redeem the human being from her fall: see C. S. Lewis, *A Preface to Paradise Lost* (London, 1942), p. 123.

specious arguments of Hell. He believes human appetite has triumphed over death and God. Man has speciously "risen" from "sad dismay / Recomforted," and now submits happily to Satanic fate, to "what seem'd remediless" (IX, 917–919). Adam's is not a stoic gesture. In his present chaotic confusion he instead may well believe that the fatal Fall is remediless by Adam's God—that is, in a parody of the Son's protest over the seemingly Draconian judgment against humanity, that God cannot act against their disobedience, either in punition or correction.

Despair, the unwitting reverse of the coin stamped with defiance of God, now enters Paradise. Adam has attended Raphael poorly, for the angel had insisted upon both self-recoiling justice and continual freedom of choice. Baffling himself with the ludicrous contradictions of Satan, Adam vainly hopes that the Serpent, now the "first" cause, will receive death, but on the other hand is convinced that the Serpent must exist in a higher degree of life (IX, 930, 934). If Satan and Eve had come to speak as the one language of temptation when she moved to her fall, Adam and Satan now speak with the one voice of damnation. Adam aspires to godhead, or at least to being as "Angels Demi-Gods" (IX, 937), but by means of sin rather than by the ladder of aspiration and attainment pointed out by Raphael. Like Satan, and in parody of the Son in Book III, he is sure that God "cannot" bring man to death, for then all creation would be "Not well conceiv'd of God" (IX, 945). In the now familiar Satanic way, Adam strives to displace to God the cause for straying and the blame for any consequent punition. On one occasion, our representative man even shockingly speaks directly for Satan, voicing as Satan's words the charge, "Mee first / He ruin'd, now Mankind; whom will he next?" (IX, 949–950). Finally, in a terrible compact with the death that already stains the lips of Eve, he says, identifying her (or himself) with Death, "If Death / Consort with thee, Death is to mee as Life" (IX, 953–954). So degenerate has his reason become that he can scarcely differentiate life from death, or his union with Eve from a disgusting repetition of the incestuous *ménage à trois* of Satan, Sin, and Death. He stakes his whole choice not with the freedom of reason but with the passional, imprisoning hellish "bond" of nature in its fallen condition.

Eve's gratified praise of Adam's fall mocks Christ's union with man in sacrificial love: "O glorious trial of exceeding Love, / Illustrious evidence, example high!" (IX, 961–962). This love reaches only to "one Guilt, one Crime" (IX, 971) in Adam, however. These human participations in Hellish parodies are grim enough in having elected the degenerate association, but they are even worse in having created the need for the love and death of the Son. Such love as Adam's does not deliver from death but surrenders men to it, whether in condemnation for sin or in gracious sacrifice for redemption. With parodic hypocrisy, Eve offers her own single death but waives the offer at once, announcing that her fall in reality will open the way to greater and still greater life. She does not aspire to the increase of spirituality offered by Raphael, however, but only to more and more rarefied sensual satisfaction:

> Taste so Divine, that what of sweet before
> Hath toucht my sense, flat seems to this, and harsh.
> On my experience, *Adam*, freely taste,
> And fear of Death deliver to the Winds [IX, 986–989].

Perhaps, like Adam, the audience may not listen closely enough to the coiling betrayals in Eve's speech. For the moment, she enacts Sin. Her ambition for divinity rages unabated. She lives now for Faustian escalations of sensuality, having made her senses—rather than communion with God—"Divine," experience a dogma, and human pleasure the one scale for judgment. She urges that Adam "freely taste," although they themselves have warningly claimed that fate has replaced any freedom. Her words are terrible in their final implication that the fear of Death will be disseminated universally—borne, like spore on the winds and genes in the blood, to all her children and to waiting Nature. Her avowals of love hold no contrition. Apart from that, they suggest, not sincerity, but Sinlike chivalric affectation: she "Tenderly wept, much won that he his Love / Had so ennobl'd" (IX, 991–992).

At once, death and sin begin to range the entire world. Nature, now acting with the audience as Chorus and participant, groans (as she will again at the "second" death of Adam-in-Christ) when deadly "mortal Sin / Original" (IX, 1003–1004) is consummated by Adam, who although undeceived "took no thought" (IX, 1004), and by Eve, as intent now upon cementing the union in sin as she had been intent earlier upon forsaking its virtue. As Satan had sunk down in the intoxicated birth of Sin in Heaven, so Adam and Eve fall drunkenly to its birth in the dust of Eden. Their proud spirits tumble first into Circean intoxication, which they still imagine to be "divinity" (IX, 1010), and then into the flaming lust that intimates Hell, the selfish, forgetful coupling of Satan with Sin, the future idolatry of Israel,[61] and a swift degeneration into bestiality.[62] Although Adam toys with Eve's attractiveness, he is reduced now to the coarse, damning irony of Cavalier *double-entendres,* as when he says Eve "well this day . . . *purvey'd*" (IX, 1021—italics added). His words slur in intoxication and sexual excitation. As he says, Eve now inflames his sense. Hellish implication haunts that Augustinian burning, which is shared by the "contagious Fire" (IX, 1036) of Eve. Although men in lust imagine that they grow wings of divinity, their bodies instead are altered from being the pleasing instruments of creative love into serpentine devices of sin. No longer aspiring, lustful men "swim" toward Chaos and Hell. From this fallen lust, not from Edenic love, will our human generation begin. The illusory union of Adam and Eve in sin is brief solace for all they have lost but have not yet missed. It is no solace at all for the audience, which knows that its second father, Cain, together with all his children, descends from this partial love: if Eve gorged upon death, Adam breeds with Sin. The sleep that follows is gross and restless, like Eve's after her ambitious dreams. It prefigures their Death-like antagonism and revulsion from one another when they arise. They now possess the knowledge that they so eagerly had sought and that God had so ardently tried to prevent their choosing:

[61] James H. Sims, in *The Bible in Milton's Epics,* pp. 207–208, draws the connection with Israel's idolatry and harlotry.

[62] Mahood, in *Poetry and Humanism,* p. 221, remarks that as Eve aspired above man, Adam wished to descend beneath his essence. John M. Steadman, in "Heroic Virtue and the Divine Image in *Paradise Lost*" (*JWCI,* XXII [1959], 89), might add that Adam's movement away from Aristotle's "heroic and divine" virtue must bring him toward *theriotes,* brutishness.

> . . . thir minds
> [Were] dark'n'd; innocence, that as a veil
> Had shadow'd them from knowing ill, was gone,
> Just confidence, and native righteousness,
> And honor from about them, naked left
> To guilty shame [IX, 1053–1058].

It is as if a Samson *agonistes* had chosen to couple once again with a guilty Dalila.

After their "blithe" and sophistical babble has ebbed, they are dumb and constrained with one another, now as isolated and antagonistic as Satan with Sin and Death. The former eternal ave tendered Eve because of her name has collapsed. She now signifies timely evil. She has been instructed not by an angel but by a Worm of death whose only truth was his description of fall. The grim knowledge gained, as our parents now see, is only that foretold to the audience in the invocation to Book I:

> Good lost, and Evil got,
> Bad Fruit . . . if this be to know,
> Which leaves us naked thus, of Honor void,
> Of innocence, of Faith, of Purity [IX, 1072–1075].

(In Book X, the Son will "reclothe" men in these virtues [l. 222].) Sensual stains appear on those ornaments of virtue and on their faces, which have begun a metamorphosis toward imbrutement. Man's shame and self-judgment are such that he asks for concealment—in effect, for a mountain to hide him, as the devils will ask at the Last Day. Somewhat Oedipally, Adam also wants to hide his and Eve's creative organs of generation, which by sin have become as ugly to him as the nether parts of Sin. Their orgy has produced at least one child—shame. Through God's design, however, this child, grim and ugly though he now seems, is the beginning of their salvation. Their winning native innocence has been lost, but they have not been able to lodge in the obstinate shamelessness of Satan. They do not merely regret the external pain of their sin; they will judge it themselves, gradually, as shameful. They perform a recognition, then a reversal. In terms of the new heroism and new tragedy, they now can approach penitence.

The good fortune of this shamefacedness is at first lost upon them, of course, as it is all but lost upon the audience and Milton. We grieve for their fall from "that first naked Glory" (IX, 1115). Nor can the fortune of their Babylonian exile from the Eden they had known (figuratively, they have already departed from the paradise of their innocence) ever seem wholly good, even though it too moves them toward self-judgment and repentance. They "sat them down to weep" (IX, 1121), but thus far they bring forth only hot Satanic tears for foolish loss.

Appetite already having been set free to rage, gusts of passion and fires of excitation sweep them into the second stage of their loss, convulsing them with the double shudders nature had felt. The knowledge of evil increases, permitting men "union" only in warfare and hatred. As Raphael had earnestly warned them, such a consequence was inevitable:

> For Understanding rul'd not, and the Will
> Heard not her lore, both in subjection now
> To sensual Appetite, who from beneath
> Usurping over sovran Reason claim'd
> Superior sway [IX, 1127–1131].

Eve has replaced Adam, the serpent has replaced Raphael, and Adam's appetite has replaced his reason: rebellion and disorder have already seared Eden, defeating the double gifts of created wisdom and tutorial grace. Unlike the Fall in heaven, the Fall on earth found none who remained true. Freedom has fallen, its place usurped by a hell "beneath" (IX, 1129). Adam bitterly complains that he does not know why Eve desired to wander, what or "whence" the desire "possess'd" her (IX, 1137). Because Adam in effect dispossessed her of his reason and let her wander, Satan or ambition quickly possessed her, exactly as devils in the Bible possessed men. Adam rightly sees, however, that the Eve-like wish to prove one's constancy is already to have questioned it and probably to have abandoned it. Whereas God may safely "assay" his creatures, men who try to test their faith are in all likelihood instead trying their doubts. Raphael's frown could have told Adam as much.

Eve in response becomes possessed by a second infidelity. The human union is further broken by ingratitude and hatred. To

Adam's reproof, she answers merely, Dalila-like, that he that morning would have been as vulnerable, as alone, as she. It is yet one more Satanic effort to make men equal only in sin or blame-worthiness. She is right, of course, in insisting that she exists within freedom and in retorting that his reasonable instruction that morning had been so faint that it eventually did no more than "permit, approve, and fair dismiss" (IX, 1159) her to what-ever new energy, whatever wandering options, might fill the va-cuum. Adam's answer swells with anger, the type of that which the son Cain will justify against the son Abel. Reversing her implica-tion of him into her God-aspiring sin, he selfishly protests that, but for her, he might have been a god. The charge is as ungrateful to God as it is to her.

Despite his immediate unjustness, however, he is being led to re-establish the whole foundation of divine freedom and of human responsibility within that freedom. That morning he had enacted God's Word, much as Raphael had spoken it earlier:

> . . . what could I more?
> I warn'd thee, I admonish'd thee, foretold
> The danger . . . ; beyond this had been force,
> And force upon free Will hath here no place
> [IX, 1170–1174].

He is wrong in only one thing. Free will having given way to bondage, force of passion or history will find a human site immediately. "Free will" is in part a contradiction of terms, for only when will chooses freedom can it remain free; even the wavering toward foolish choice imposes a bondage upon the will, suggesting that reason has already relinquished the control by which human will can remain free. Fate commences simulta-neously with folly, unless divine aid somehow "restore" the Eden of wise consideration. Adam now realizes that his choice of Eve—entirely proper, if held as one among the total field of wise considerations—had displaced his choice of God and therefore assumed the character of fate. He has reached the new, sad wis-dom that sin had initiated. In that sense, he has very surely attained the knowledge of good and evil:

> I also err'd in overmuch admiring
> What seem'd in thee so perfet, that I thought

No evil durst attempt thee, but I rue
That error now, which is become my crime,
And thou th' accuser [IX, 1178–1182].

In this way, Adam has neared cathartic self-knowledge, but veers back instead into ironically "fruitless" hours of "mutual accusation" (IX, 1188, 1187) not unlike those of Satan with Sin and Death. Fruitless the fruit, and men can foresee only an apparent stasis like that in the Battle of Heaven, the world of human history (XII, 537), or the mazes of Hell—until Heaven manages to stoop to them.

So far, the participating audience has been forced to watch human beings as beautiful as the Apollo and Nike of Olympia cast away the advice of a divine "Attendant Spirit" and, with the pressure of a malevolent will, tumble headlong, first into nonsensical folly, then into brutish Circean appetite, and finally into union only within the mutual hatred which Satan had not really even hoped for. He had thought only to make God hate his creatures, not his creatures hate God and themselves. The dim hope that self-hatred will create human self-deliverance seems to have died. Men have left the sanctuary of free choice and the instruction in good and evil for a dungeon of self-imprisoning "fate" and the direct experience of evil heaped on evil. It is now, not in prelapsarian Eden, that they are threatened with iron determinism, with being the mere puppets of a mechanical destiny. The fall has been terrible. Except for a dim confidence that a key (no longer in their power) still turns within their prison door, there would be no hope that Adam and Eve could bring our human steps a little onward. At this moment, they in themselves are hopelessly bound by their self-performed and self-condemning act, eyeless and enslaved in Paradise.

"REPAIRING WHERE HE JUDG'D US": FIRST VICTORY OVER ABSOLUTE
CONSEQUENCE (BOOK X)

Book X relieves the stunned Hellish inertia into which Adam and Eve, together perhaps with the methektic audience, had sunk after the delirium of the Fall. It insists that the Fall be opposed by renovative reason, in the form of divine judgment. Although such judgment conceivably might produce its own kind of error, it nevertheless reinstitutes reason and choice, both of which must exist before mercy can safely aid man. Mercy too must be "choice"—not merely an indiscriminate permission for error. In Book III, God had promised to "uphold" man. Judgment, although it seems harsh, is not content that man lie dully adrift in the fires of Hell or the chaos of lost Eden. It insists that the suspense of man's "fruitless hours, but neither self-condemning" (IX, 1188) be snapped. If men can consider themselves within the vertical judgment of God, they may be renewed, even as God wishes their renewal. With the Son, mankind must be its own judge if it is in any way to know or be a savior.

The Book is a chain of judgments, fulfilling those of the proem and Book III. God verifies as eternal judgment what in Book III had seemed to be only lateral prophecy. The Son assumes his projected human role of judge and savior. Adam pronounces judgment upon Eve, Eve upon the serpent, and the Son upon the three of them—and upon himself, as suffering Servant. The unholy trinity also reappears in order to receive the absolute judgment of recoil, under which serpentine Satan will eat the dust-determining fruits of temptation forever. Finally, the court of all humanity stands in judgment upon all men through their "Grand Parents," assuming the initial question of the epic assay: "what cause / Mov'd our Grand Parents . . . to fall off / From thir Creator, and transgress his Will?" (I, 28–31). Men are no longer selfishly merciful to themselves, for they now refuse to be comforted by any assurance that Satan was the total cause of fall. As men come into the second arena of trial in Book X, they may either be totally lost or in some measure restored. The tears of Adam and Eve for mankind offer the judgment upon themselves that can become mercy for another, anticipating the typic burden Christ will carry. The entire Book, then, witnesses how fall can become renewal, how judgment can proceed to redemption, and how assurance of sin can be transformed into active mercy, pity, and charity. If Paradise is lost in Book IX, much of its territory "within" is recovered in Book X. Most importantly, reason—that essential human characteristic which is divinely and humanly "choice"—is victoriously reasserted.

For the first time since action descended into Eden, the epic revisits the great poles of choice as it takes the stands of judgment. "Lycidas" is recalled as the all-seeing eye of God observes the mingled grief and pity with which the angelic guards judge men. The epic assumes that the pathetic jury of their progeny anticipated by Adam and Eve will be represented by the author and audience. It also tacitly assumes that this first judgment is an instructive type of the Last. The Apocalyptic-Sinaic voice of God confirms the Son's earlier chosen bond with man and charges him to be both judgment and mercy: Judge and Savior. He is the confirming "fate" of those who chose unbeing. That is his face of justice. He is also the prevenient servant of those who elect goodness, in a role that predicts his later function as incarnate man, descended into human flesh. That is his face of mercy and sacrifice. Man in the Son must redeem man in Adam. In final judicial redemption, the Son asks, "Whoever judg'd, the worst on mee must light" (X, 73). He puns in vigorous judgment of the missing third party to the trial, he who is essentially absent: "Conviction to the Serpent none belongs" (X, 84). But Satan's own unreason, not Christ's reason, offers the proper recoiling condemnation for Satan.

This creative judge, recapitulating some of his role in Book III and in creation as well as forecasting his role as final judge, descends to Adam and Eve in their "discompos'd," fruitless shame, asking why they have alienated themselves from life and the source of life. Their solitude is now as wrong and dangerous as that of Eve in Book IX. Although Adam makes routine chivalrous gestures, he selfishly blames Eve's beauty for his fall. Less loquacious, "with shame nigh overwhelm'd" (X, 159), Eve quickly blames the serpent. Accounted both man and judge, the Son first figurally judges and triumphs with us over typic Satan, "Whom he shall tread at last under our feet" (X, 190) —there to eat the dust of temptation and death. The first cause of man's disobedience, as assigned at the beginning of the epic, has been mastered. Suddenly the act of human judgment and victory becomes absolute and eternal, yet the time-established audience knows itself a participant: "our" is not a regal singular pronoun only. Our sense of time within and without the epic becomes so compressed that we all but escape time, for this judgment involves not only the initial episode of the epic, when in Book I "Satan [fell] like Lightning down from Heav'n" (X, 184), but also all of Christ's prelapsarian, historical, and apocalyptic victories over Satan. Almost like a son to his mother, Christ tells Eve, now again typically and heraldically addressed as "Woman," that she must bring forth children in her sorrow and to their sorrow, but the audience later will see that maternal sorrow for the suffering Christ is also maternal joy for the Savior Pantocrator. Similarly, Adam, now judged as Raphael had warned him he would be judged ("Was shee thy God, . . . thy guide, / Superior? [X, 145–147]), is consigned to an inhospitable earth and to dust; death must end, in pain, the life that begins in pain. However, the Creator can again cause the dust of the earth to be creative, resurrective. Although both our "Grand Parents" must "labor" in both birth and death, the Son, acting now for the greater Father of the human family, assuming the role of servant in the fullness of mercy, clothes their inner nakedness. The robe of righteousness does not shield them from God's sight. Instead, it returns them to the reasonable moral freedom they had discarded, and prepares even now for their future inner paradise. The judgment of man in Eden all but becomes one with the judgment of all creation at the end of time. As such, this judicial stance is filled with triumph even though it originates in defeat.

A prior verdict condemning men has already been announced in Hell, the counterstand to which we now return, where half-jealous Sin and Death determine to join their "Author" on earth. Satan has parodied Christ in preparing a place for his own. Like wandering, adventurous Eve, Sin believes that she feels intoxicating wings growing inside her, in a "secret amity [of] things of like kind" (X, 248), but they are to be only the dismal promise of a still vaster crowd of hellhounds. Death and Chaos are not so euphemistic or delicate. They "snuff" human and material carrion as our world shifts into its receptive, deadly postlapsarian imbalance, already suffering from Satanic eclipse. The Persian ramp with which Sin and Death link Hell and earth, using all the explosive stuff of the volcanic Hell now erupting toward earth, permits Milton to form his remarkably graphic narrative center, general setting, and cosmography:

> . . . and now in little space
> The confines met of Empyrean Heav'n
> And of this World, and on the left hand Hell
> With long reach interpos'd; three sev'ral ways
> In sight, to each of these three places led [X, 320–324].

Sin greets the returning Satan with parodies of the relationships of potent God to manifesting Son, scarcely realizing that the manifestation of zero is zero. As he had left Hell in cowardly haste before, he returns to it partly in murmuring cowardice now, characteristically letting his progeny think they receive their glut, while leaving them to face their champion. Even at best, he might have told them with knowledge that Hell would be wherever they go. But none is permitted to relish his disastrous triumph. Satan now falls, even as Christ, for man, ascends. Although Satan hopes that he has parodically made the world into a revised perfection (X, 483) and although he still tries to oppose God with rival principalities and purposes, his return to Hell is a certain renewal of his fall. When he explosively "rises" only in the midst of the abysmal Pandemonium, he joins his host to him in condemning ironies ("successful beyond hope" [X, 463]) but reports what he believes to be God's judgment of man:

> [Man] by fraud I have seduc'd
> From his Creator, and the more to increase
> Your wonder, with an Apple; he thereat
> Offended, worth your laughter, hath giv'n up
> Both his beloved Man and all his World [X, 485–489].

His assurance and Homeric laughter collapse when he reports the judgment upon himself. This is to be no potent Odysseus returned to Ithaca, but only a tawdry magician. He writhes in words:

> True is, mee also he hath judg'd, or rather
> Mee not, but the brute Serpent in whose shape
> Man I deceiv'd: that which to mee belongs,
> Is enmity, which he will put between
> Mee and Mankind; I am to bruise his heel;

His Seed, when is not set, shall bruise my head:
A World who would not purchase with a bruise . . . ?

[X, 494–500].

But he is not a Redeemer. When he tries to laugh at men's designs as Heaven has laughed at his, he receives immediate judgment; only Christ's wounds will purchase the world. Hell, instead, immediately imbrutes. The shout he expects as he tells devils to rise, like the risen Christ, "into full bliss" (X, 503), turns to hisses. His humiliation is a magnified vision of his seeming victories.[63] "Recoil" as an operative image even accepts the internal serpentine pun when judgment rolls back upon him: "a greater power / Now rul'd him, punisht in the shape he sinn'd, / According to his doom" (X, 515–517). What is more, his chosen Son and enemy, Death, now all but triumphs over his father, as Satan feels his "Visage drawn . . . sharp and spare, / His Arms clung to his Ribs" (X, 511–512); he nearly becomes both serpent and cadaver, the images of what he himself has brought to birth. Far from rising from dragon's teeth, all the soldiers of Hell sink downward to Hell's soil as they had once been driven into the floor of Heaven and as they had appeared at the outset of the epic. All Hell vainly gnaws the dusty fruit of temptation and rebellion, now decayed into its true form—the ashes of sin and death. Meanwhile, Death has made his Hell in Paradise, forcing all natural things, including human rosy cheeks and lips, into his "vast unhide-bound Corpse" (X, 601).[64] Man, however, is reserved for the terrible further seasonings of Sin. The universe itself now is prey to returning chaos.

The stance of the poem now "repairs" to the center of judgment in order to assess this foray. The apocalyptic judgment of the Creator, of Being, stands out against the seeming ability of Sin and Death "to destroy, or unimmortal make / All kinds" (X, 611–612). In sharp scorn for their pretensions, God designates

---

[63] John M. Steadman, in "Tantalus and the Dead Sea Apples (*Paradise Lost*, X, 547–573)" (*JEGP*, LXIV [1965], 35–40), notes the suggestion of recoiling temptation in Tantalus.

[64] John M. Steadman, in "'Bitter Ashes': Protestant Exegesis and the Serpent's Doom" (*SP*, LIX [1962], 210), identifies Hell's diet with the "draff and filth" of sin that will be purged at the Last Judgment.

them to be his jackals, unwitting renovative scavengers who will purify the world from "man's polluting Sin" (X, 631) until such time as "Heav'n and Earth renew'd shall be made pure" (X, 638). These drudges do his bidding in the world, and, although impure themselves, create purity. Milton begins now to suggest that the tomb of Calvary contained not the Son but Sin and Death. As at the Creation and Incarnation, Heaven's hymns again break forth, for in God's eternal design this renewal becomes identical with creation.

That glorious song can be of comfort to the audience as the stance returns to this world, having merely touched it in company with rising Sin and Death earlier, for it has now become not Eden but our fallen world. Hellish and chaotic confusions of temperature and elements assault it. Even the planet itself has "swerved" from its axis. Among creatures, the former harmony has been broken. While hallelujahs mark the unity of Heaven, here there is only fearful outcry as "Beast now with Beast gan war, and Fowl with Fowl, / . . . to graze the Herb all leaving, / Devour'd each other" (X, 710–712). Carnal food has appeared in answer to the carnal appetites of men—and of Death. A correlative storm of inner passions afflicts Adam, who senses that the jury of his sons will curse their father for death, his only gift to them. However, his increasing conviction of sin, rather than obdurate insistence upon continuing it, marks his difference from Satan together with the faint beginning of his paradise regained. By associating himself as maker with God, he sees the folly of his Samson-like judgment against God and his gifts, including the supposed penalty of death. Having polluted the clear river of Eden, Adam must recognize that all its currents have become diseased. He now hopes only that death is an end both for him and for mankind in him, in which case the supposed punishment would be a blessing. Although it is impossible for him to continue in that despairing assurance, Adam significantly has detected that man's self-chosen punishment can become God's gracious blessing. He ruefully realizes that life is too great for easy eradication. Life demands life, even if it is that of eternal damnation or punition. His stubborn questions now discover (and "justify" for all men) the answers God had supplied in Book III:

> . . . all my evasions vain . . . lead me still
> But to my own conviction: first and last
> On mee, mee only, as the source and spring
> Of all corruption, all the blame lights due;
> So might the wrath [X, 829–834].

He is too fond in both cases, but the struggles of this mariner to move beyond his shallows of pride, "from deep to deeper plung'd" (X, 844), increase the hope that he can thereafter attain light beyond light. He can come to be a form of Christ to himself, although he cannot redeem his children. He first must cross that judgment which is despair, wishing beyond Job in his self-condemnation that he had never been or that death might now obliterate him. In terrible irony, he is aware that the human hymn has changed from celebration of life to the invocation of death.

Gradually, the sinful Adam is led to his own judgment, after which he can become the type of human salvation in the second Adam. Although he cannot see it, his readers are aware that he has removed the "stony" from his heart. He lies down once more in the position of his creation, thinking still only to ask for death. All signs point instead toward his spiritual resurrection. When Eve approaches, Adam does not at first see that he cruelly flings his invocation to death upon the penitent Eve by his overly severe and selfish judgment. As he imagines his sons will reject him, so Adam rejects Eve. He castigates her as "Serpentine . . . , all but a rib / Crooked by nature . . . sinister . . . this fair defect / Of Nature" (X, 870, 884–85, 886, 891–892), thereby rebelling against both the creative gift he had implored and the Creator who had granted it. But as Adam's grief for his sons has led him to compassionate right reason, so Eve's compassion and lonely agony now bring her to him. Resembling Mary Magdalene as well as the maternal Mary, Eve falls to his feet, insisting that he is her life.[65] Much of her selfishness and weakness has been purged, leaving selfless, sorrowing love for Adam and their children—or, if need be, a fierce Roman willingness to end the race. Adam reminds her that their seed, though tainted, will vanquish Sin, Death, and

[65] See Joseph H. Summers, "The Voice of the Redeemer in *Paradise Lost*," *PMLA*, LXX (1955), 1082–1089, for additional discussion of the role of Eve.

Satan. Both commiseration and respect temper the force of Adam's judgment, much as mercy will leaven the judgment of God upon man. The earthly reconciliation of man with woman promises the greater reunion of God with man. The final stance of the Book regains the place of judgment, for Adam and Eve make it now a place of prayer. Their selfish outcry against a self-elected destiny is replaced by a redemptive wish to save one another and mankind. In token of the eventual manifestation of divine love for erring man, Adam releases his anger, forgiving Eve. They arise from their falls—Adam's toward Death, Eve's toward Sin. They also seek from fallen nature the beneficent form of fire, thereby themselves finding out good from evil. If men can no longer be immortal and superabundantly blessed in their Edenic home, they can nevertheless "cultivate" the debased Paradise of their souls and build a house of God, in order to accept his renewed sheltering amidst the tempests they have chosen.

"CITY OF OLD OR MODERN FAME": THE CITIES OF THE PLAIN, AND THE FIRST PURGATION (BOOK XI)

After such knowledge in Book X, Adam and Eve reach toward such forgiveness as is possible under judgment, and the audience to whatever tutelage is possible under four thousand years of the Fall—the Fall itself, within history, being a judgment of God upon history. Although Milton intended to oppose the two Books of Fall with two final Books that promise regeneration and renewal, the difficulty he met in Book X in reconciling judgment with both punishment and salvation would appear to have been compounded in Books XI and XII, wherein lateral fallen history must be reconciled with eternity. Many past readers despaired of this history even more feelingly than Adam does, but from reasons ostensibly literary. If both final Books are appendices and if Book XI in particular is a depressing vision of meaningless deaths, conveyed in flat, prosy verse, did not Milton nod into disaster in contriving them? For example, the divine instruction and reproof by Michael seem to be wasted on Adam. After Adam has been punished and has repented, why show him so much of history? From an author's viewpoint, why present Adam with so much that is repetitious and therefore of decreasing interest to readers? Among other objections, have not all the sins and the salvation of men in history already been enacted in the sins and contrition of Adam and Eve? Recent studies have supplied many historical answers to such queries, but two other answers often have been overlooked.

In the first place, Adam must repent "originally," not only for himself but for all his sons, and together with them (for he now rejoins us as audience to this historical revelation) be brought up from suicidal and genocidal despair to tragic patience and endurance.[66] We must move from a despair like that of Hamlet in Act III to his tragic patience in the final act. If Adam does not parallel that tragic ascent, the human race will alter its original definition so radically that all racial continuity must be lost. Original compassion must accompany original sin, or no "sonship" in human love and sorrow will be possible. Man's first disobedience created tidal waves of consequence; therefore, part of the hard knowledge Adam bought with his Fall is of its further pain and proliferation. He cannot be Christ, but as a human father he must at least be as redemptively compassionate as he is guilty. Although he must descend to the physical matter from which he had been raised, by means of regeneration he can nevertheless be raised from the spiritual dust of sin and death. Similarly, Eve must bear some of the agony of her sons that Mary will feel for her son. The "first" Eve has abandoned the purity and proper softness that characterize the "second" Eve and has lent necessity to the suffering of all women and their sons: all the more reason that she will share the agony and redemptive pity of every "second" Eve, particularly that mother of the sacrificial second Adam.

In the second place, Books XI and XII as a unit stand in very close relationship with the first four Books of *Paradise Lost*. In both, the audience must methektically witness Satanism, Sin, and Death, but in both it must also be made aware of God's design,

---

[66] Irene Samuel, in *Dante and Milton* (Ithaca, N. Y., 1966), p. 228, considers that Michael acts to cure man. D. C. Allen, in *The Harmonious Vision*, pp. xvii-xviii, notes that as Michael is to Adam, so Milton stands to us as auditors. Summers, in *The Muse's Method*, ch. 8, is generally instructive upon Michael's function.

which can circumvent and in large measure transform the unholy three into their opposites. As in Book I (l. 5) the audience received first the promise of restoration by "one greater Man" and then the guidance of a divine muse showing the way to both Hell and Heaven, so now we first witness the promised regeneration of men and then are given a priestly guide, in Michael,[67] both to the hell in human choice and the salvation inherent in reasonable divine judgment. Book XII increasingly intimates Books III and IV. Whereas Books I and XI fall deeper than the mind of Hell into its eternal vanity and self-destructiveness, Books III and XII look persistently upward to renewals (physical purgations, as well as new covenants) that promise absolute regeneration. The revelations of history in Books XI and XII, like the great archetypal actions of Books I–IV, are not primarily "for" Adam, who either does not receive them directly or has already been instructed and judged. In much the same way, the progress of future kings in *Macbeth* is intended primarily for an English audience rather than for Macbeth. Partly for that reason, the historical incidents in the last two books, despite a popular impression to the contrary, are really surprisingly few. Milton is not intent upon a patristic survey of history but upon our seeing the design of God within human time. We are given God's confirmatory judgment upon men's recoiling sins in a few sharply relevant enactments. Promised grace is seen both in individual lives and in a quickly ascending scale of new covenants, reaching from law and the election of Israel to love and general redemption.

Such instructive revelation of the weak choice of men and the strong grace of God may bring Adam to tragic peace and Christian regeneration, but its literary intention surely must aspire to both instruction and catharsis for the audience. If the two can be united, methektic purgation can be made preventive. As such, Books XI and XII are relevant more to Milton and his audience, the "mutes and audience to this act," than to Adam; we move within the process of history as visionary Adam could not. If the fields of choice and fall for Adam or for Satan have seemed too distant from us, lost in time or story, or on the other hand, if they

[67] See Frances A. Yates, *Giordano Bruno and the Hermetic Tradition* (Chicago, 1964), p. 103: To Pico della Mirandola, Michael is high priest.

have seemed too necessitarian, suggesting that the choosing sublu-
nar creature must swerve, then his present sons, as well as Adam,
will see sin and its wages (for those who choose such rewards).
The whole majestic tapestry of typic choice and typic consequence
embraces "future" history as well as "past" myth. Following the
consistent pattern of *Paradise Lost,* Book XI like Books I and II
tends to dwell demonstratively upon the wages of sin, but somewhat like Book III, Book XII moves discursively to its close with a
triumphant account of men who choose well. If the harsh judgment of Book XI resembles that of God in Book III, it also looks
to the Last Judgment, when by divine choice like that of Christ in
Book III, man is happily saved while the world's dross, self-consumed, flames away. Like choice, judgment can open on eternity
gained, as well as on Paradise lost.

Book XI significantly opens upon God's "Prevenient Grace"
(XI, 3), which acts to deliver Adam and Eve from stony hatred of
each other and of God—Eden already having become wilderness
or tomb, unless from man a "second stock proceed" (XII, 6–7).
Their humbled hearts become "fertile," and in that sense are
already resurrected, regenerate, Christ-promising. The vinicul-
tural metaphor promises the second "stocks" of Christ and Noah
and the regeneration available to every man. Sighs and "inspir'd"
prayers (XI, 7) replace rage and curses. As Raphael had earlier
welcomed his colloquy with Adam, Heaven again finds human
conversation "important" (XI, 9). Although by sin Adam and
Eve produced an obliterating flood, dovelike human sorrow and
pity cause it to abate. Milton does not risk drawing the analogy of
Noah "achronologically" from the end of Book IX to its beginning, but he forcefully enters the analogy of regenerate Adam and
Eve with restorative Pyrrha and Deucalion. Metaphorically,
within the fallen Adam and Eve were all the originating wicked
of the earth; penitent, they are the two regenerating parents,
grace having implanted the possibility of renewal in mankind
(XI, 23).

Prayers lift men's thoughts once more to Heaven, and with
them the human stance for the author and the audience of *Paradise Lost.* The Son yet again acts as medial servant, judicial and
redemptive "Advocate," and "Priest" (XI, 33, 25) to both God

and man, insisting that the fruits of men's prayers are better than material fruits of Eden. In that sense, Adam and Eve already are acting within an inner Paradise, "happier far." The Son again offers himself as regenerative surrogate for man, accepting "good or not good ingraft" (XI, 35) into himself—man's second stock, paying for all man's knowledge of death with His human death. In death, too, man in either his own infrequent goodness or through the Son's universal goodness may be led to a heavenly Eden. God can make even death an agent of creativity and love, so that every mortal fall may become in some measure fortunate:

> . . . let him live
> Before thee reconcil'd, at least his days
> Number'd, though sad, till Death, his doom (which I
> To mitigate thus plead, not to reverse)
> To better life shall yield him . . .
>
> . . . . .
>
> Made one with me as I with thee am one [XI, 38–44].

As before, the Son pleads in part to understand God's design. His prayer seeks the production of greater good out of temporary evil, life "more abundant" after the evil of death, a "life" (XI, 42) made one with God as all in all. The "serene" (XI, 45) Father replies, as before, that the prayer already is granted because it, too, has always been within the eternal design. Much as Satan had to leave Heaven, however, man must leave the Eden he undervalued. A pure habitation necessarily has to purge that which is alien from itself. Man also has in part imbruted himself and by his altered nature now can receive only the food and air coarse enough for him. In this strange way, the expulsion from Eden is a Popean service to man: if he remained in Eden, he would have died of a rose in aromatic pain. A more important image is the purging of whatever is "gross" (XI, 53) by fire. The vision is prophetic not only of flaming Paradise but of the Last Judgment. For that matter, death serves man in much the same way as does the expulsion from Eden. If death did not terminate his life of trial, man might have to endure earthly temptation and sorrow forever. As it is, death is man's punition but also "his final remedy," permitting him access to "second Life, / Wak't in the renovation of the just"; death ironically becomes in part re-deemer (XI, 62, 64–65). God has made death the avenue to Heaven for all men who choose Heaven. Are both the expulsion and death, then, added versions of Fortunate Fall? In a limited sense they are, for God's design has made both serve goodness, even (in an immediate "better life" after death) seeming to accelerate man's attainment of completion in goodness. In the purely mortal sense, of course, they are not, for man suffers terrible agonies of shame and death that were never necessary until he chose them. They are of man's ill choice but God's counterbalancing design.

A trumpet like that which will announce the law to Moses and the divine judgment at the end of time sounds for a heavenly consult upon that portion of being that is called human. Man now knows evil, and God's reviving motions in him cause him to sorrow for that knowledge. God must act mercifully to save man from a "dream at least to live / For ever" (XI, 95–96) —the temptation of the Tree of Life. Like the other prohibition, this is revealed to be gracious rather than niggling. Both "trees" are in part metaphors for appetitive rebelliousness. Without eating of the Tree of Life, man had already possessed immortality in Eden, just as without the Tree of Knowledge he had been given all useful knowledge of good and evil. As in the one case he gained only grim experience of evil, so now he could gain only the false dream, the delusion, of an immortality of evil. Physically imbruted now, redeemable only by purgative death, man would find his immortality within sin and sorrow a curse far greater than placid immortality was to Tithonus—as God had foreseen:

> . . . I at first with two fair gifts
> Created him endow'd, with Happiness
> And Immortality: that fondly lost,
> This other serv'd but to eternize woe;
> Till I provided Death [XI, 57–61].

As by God's grace Satan's bad son will become man's excellent gift when death is used for consummate redemption by the true Son, so divine countereffort appears in God's order of expulsion from Paradise. Adam and Eve are to be banished from the Paradise they wantonly rejected, yet harshness is to be mitigated by a divine covenant like that which will appear with Noah: God will renew his "Cov'nant in the woman's seed" (XI, 116). At the end of the stance in Heaven, God again indicates that, given the conditions of the Fall, physical immortality could only "delude" (XI, 125) man. He must instead discover his salvation in what God creatively refashions from the grim death men chose.

The stance is now returned to Adam and Eve, revisiting them within both the judgment and the "reviving" grace of God. The great perspective from Heaven is not abandoned, however, for the Son judges them apocalyptically yet resurrectively, causing "new hope to spring / Out of despair, joy, but with fear yet linkt" (XI, 138–139). Some of the hope may be illusory, but the general typic ascent possible to God-aided man has begun. In one way, Adam is already reconciled to God, and to that extent has aspired beyond fallen Eden. He now prays not in order to alter God's design but to confirm it. He misjudges the design, however, by thinking that death was only an easy metaphor for shame and by believing it to be past. Trying too innocently to trammel up the consequence, he assumes that penalties are done, that Eve is regenerate, that she (rather than Mary) can be the blessed "Mother of all Mankind," and that by her "Man is to live" (XI, 159, 161) rather than die. Both have surrendered their audacious Satanic interest in Eve as goddess and empress, but in defining her as "Matron" (XI, 136), they continue to assume that she is immortal, an untainted fountain. The misunderstood new role is expressed as such by Eve, who ventures even into a Magnificat: "I who first brought Death on all, am grac't / The source of life" (XI, 168–169).[68] She has supposed the Fall to be only a slight interlude. Like Satan in Hell, men cannot believe that they have altered *themselves* by their choice. Nor can they yet see, any more than Belial can see in Hell, that the Fall now "is" wherever they are. Eve pathetically assumes that the penalty of labor (including all human childbearing) can be discharged in Eden, even though nothing can "be toilsome in these pleasant Walks" (XI, 179). But the Fall proceeds. The lights go down in Eden. Prophetically, a divine eagle, "the Bird of

[68] Kermode, in "Adam Unparadised," p. 120, emphasizes that Eve, the bringer of death, is also (by means of her repentance) the bringer of life.

Jove," drives "Two Birds of gayest plume" out into our world, even as a Satanic hunting beast intent on prey again (as in Book IV) leaps after "a gentle brace" (XI, 185–188), racing toward the eastern gate. Seeing man in all the creatures now hunted and judged, Adam begins to realize that agony and death define man's new state, that which he chose when he became to "Death devote." Into the dark pinfold of earth Michael descends to confirm that knowledge, but also to bring renewed instruction, if Adam, who is afraid because he sees the actions of Heaven with a carnally dimmed eye, can receive it.

Fearful Adam, his attention still fastened upon Eve, calls upon her to expect (with him, of course) an annunciation, "great tidings" (XI, 226), like those to be given Sarah and Mary. Man's naive excitement wanes as he sees the angel approach, not in gracious sociable mildness, but in an eschatological and Sinaic "blazing Cloud," appearing "solemn and sublime" (XI, 229, 236). Michael continues so. Even though he, like the Son later, has appeared incarnate as "Man / Clad to meet Man" (XI, 239–240), his character is that of king and judge—in order that it may become also that of redeemer, for his service to man begins to restore the inward blissful seat even while the outer paradise is fading. He enforces the reason man had possessed before the Fall. With Adam, the audience accepts the stance of human witness, wondering on its side what God will make of a diminished thing. Michael kindly (if misleadingly) tells us that man will not die utterly, even though he must leave Eden. However, he obscurely indicates the mortal necessity that man go forth as dust to dust, returning to "The ground whence [he] was . . . tak'n, fitter Soil" (XI, 262).

As horror had stricken nature at the Fall, so it falls on man as he understands these consequences. Bearing still some of her old ambitious pride, Eve cries out that expulsion is "worse than . . . Death." Eden, she says, has been "Fit haunt of Gods." "Accustom'd to immortal Fruits," she cannot "wander down / Into a lower World" (XI, 268, 271, 285, 282–283). She has not understood, nor has Adam, that because they have degenerated, they already inhabit the lower world. They chose against the immortal fruits, instead "eating" death. Her Edenic "flow'rs" (XI, 273) had faded at the same instant as Adam's garland of roses. Eden has already been lost; it merely has not yet been left. By instruction, however, Eve need not again "wander" in the great world nor again foolishly seek immortal fruits among the shadows of death.

Michael divorces her from Eden, the physical site that she had made idolatrous, requiring that she cleave instead to Adam (as she lately had not done). In a reverse reflection of the choice by which Satan had made himself and his every habitation Hell, Michael asserts that Eden now rests in her duty and love to Adam: "Where he abides, think there thy native soil" (XI, 292). (At the close of *Paradise Lost,* she accepts this duty and phrases it as love: "with thee to go, / Is to stay here" [XII, 615–616]; in that, she accomplishes part of her "paradise within.") Although in sadly altered literal place, she can nevertheless choose to regain her original role with God and man in Eden. Adam too recovers from his death-prophesying "cold sudden damp" and his Samson-like "scatter'd spirits" (XI, 293, 294). He still has not discovered the depths of his choice, for like Eve he resists his chosen change to places "inhospitable . . . and desolate, / Nor knowing us nor known" (XI, 306–307). The bitter knowledge that he must become a type for Cain, the wanderer upon earth, was also "tasted" in the forbidden fruit. He seeks one way of appealing the judgment: Is not to leave Eden to leave God—an "idolic" God of place and "fit" soil? Should not God's worship be materialized here with altars and a "monument to Ages" (XI, 326)? It is of course one last way of clinging to the physical Eden that man has physically forsworn, rather than of accepting the spiritual Eden that he may continue to choose.

The reply is another demonstration of God's favor even within the Fall. The loss of Eden is the gaining of "all the Earth"—"No despicable gift" (XI, 335, 340); in earth, God's presence is universal. Man learns with joy what Satan had learned to his misery: that although God's creatures may abandon their contact with him and his gifts, he never leaves them, and that he may attempt even to increase the creative gifts they neglect. Eden would have had to be lost in one sense anyway, for it could not have contained all the generations of men. Within the purely human perspective, Adam has had only to come down from his patriarchal pre-emi-

nence "to dwell on even ground now with [his] Sons" (XI, 348) ,
but the parallel of the incarnate second Adam lends radiance
even to that "descent." Representative man, knowing now that
God's protection and "steps" (XI, 354) are around him always, is
taken to a high place for instruction in history as a moment's
glimpse into the eternal "foresight" (XI, 368) of God.

This is the final stance of *Paradise Lost*. During the vision, both
Adam's and Michael's historical presences give way to those of the
readers and Milton. Something like the reality of Hell, its "dolorous mansions" open to "peering day," will now appear, utterly
stripped of the rhetoric permitted to Satan. What Adam is shown
we must receive—partly as human agony to be suffered, partly as
human ethic and religious stance to be learned. The ethical position is stated first and reappears as the final word both for this
section and the entire poem. Michael speaks for God:

> I am sent
> To show thee what shall come in future days
> To thee and to thy Offspring; good with bad
> Expect to hear, supernal Grace contending
> With sinfulness of Men; thereby to learn
> True patience, and to temper joy with fear
> And pious sorrow, equally inur'd
> By moderation either state to bear,
> Prosperous or adverse [XI, 356–364].

The historical vision intends moral instruction of a highly
specific kind. It hopes to produce that new kind of epic hero
Milton has promised, possessing "the better fortitude / Of Patience and Heroic Martyrdom / Unsung" (IX, 31–33) . Patience
will trust God and reason rather than seek "heroic" self; human
"martyrdom" in death will resist selfish despair. Although such a
hero will be fully realized only in Christ, he must be partially
realized in Adam and in every elective "Son" of God. As Adam in
Books XI and XII becomes a type of Christ, so Christ's agony and
resurrection constitute a type within general human spiritual
biography. At a slightly lower level, Adam is to produce a combination of Aristotelian, Stoic, and specifically Christian philosophical attitudes. Moderation and imperturbability, although

classically derived, will now maintain not only personal ethics and serenity but also penitential trust in God.

The mount looks down upon the theater of mankind, that which the Son will also see in *Paradise Regained*. Adam will be asked to view even more of "Earth's Kingdoms" (XI, 384), stretching geographically from Cathay to Egypt and temporally from Xerxes to Montezuma. He, as father, must receive all that each postlapsarian son will assume to be his own particular world and condition. To do so, while Eve sleeps and is given a fitting foresight in dreams, Adam must tend again toward the trance of nonbeing into which he had nearly entered before the creation of Eve. From the prostrate position of his creation, but now within a first phase of regeneration, Adam is virtually resurrected by Michael. His eyes are purged with rue, the bitter herb of grace that is akin to the purgative lesson of Book XI, and with euphrasy, the "eyebright" herb that promises delight or enhancement of heart or mind and that suggests the increasing redemptive joy of Book XII. Adam's "mental sight" (XI, 418) is renewed, even as his carnal eyes are "healed" with three baptismal drops from the Well of Life (XI, 416). Now partly a tragic hero, partly a prophet, partly our all-seeing "Grand Parent," and partly the representative man indicated by his very name, Adam must "see" for mankind, not for himself alone. With his falling asleep to the moment in order to gain entry into all history and even into eternity, Adam for a time surrenders his presence into that of the author or of ourselves.

The author's tragic notes are accompanied by assurance that his Muse is buoyantly eternal, even as his mortal blindness is opposed by immortal euphrasy, Siloa's healing stream, and the truth that shines inward and there plants eyes. The readers in turn as typic men take up the watch as man's fallen "swerve" is opposed by God's gracious counterpressure within sharply significant human choices. In the tragic "recognition" of Book XI, we first must see the full wages of sin among men and know the full measure of human death. In the tragic "reversal" of Book XII, we, like Adam, will ascend from that terrible knowledge to the welcome realization that many men—especially the second Adam—will choose against that extinction. We are repeating the experience of

Books I and III, of course, but now we know that the flame or the light involves us directly. It matters little whether we view history as a road forward from Adam or as a road backward from ourselves, for in this lesson historical alpha and omega are one.

Our first (because typic) encounter of opposing human choices is that between Cain, the destructive "sweaty Reaper," and Abel, the Christlike "Shepherd . . . / More meek" (XI, 434, 436–437).[69] Divine favor recognizes Abel's sacrifice as better, electing or "begetting" him much as God had once elected Christ. Cain, like Satan before him, is possessed by envy, and similarly produces death. Each witnessing Adam is made to suffer the whole fall of man again, including now a portion of the agony felt by both of Adam's choosing sons. The assurance that justice will be done to Cain and that Abel's death, like that of Lycidas, will "lose no reward" (XI, 459) cannot wholly relieve our human terror at seeing death. Nor, for that matter, can it allay our terror over Adam's ignorant complicity in that death, for he says too readily, "Alas, both for the deed and for the cause" (XI, 461) —which is himself. The cause within himself will soon be shown to him again, but first he must wrestle with the full knowledge of the death he so easily elected. Because Eve could not abstain from death and even in a sense has, like Sin, given birth to Death, it now spawns universally among men in every hideous form.

That intolerable sight of that absolute Cain among Adam's human children brings representative Adam to compassionate tears. They purge from him the hatred he felt in Paradise and thereby ally him with the greater second Adam. His tears, it is true, spring at first from self-pity alone. He demands as of old (like Samson) to know: Why should men be given life, especially that of a divine similitude, if only to lose both life and beauty so foully? The ancient question again blames God's abundance and justice, not man, "once / So goodly and erect, though faulty since" (XI, 508–509). The answer is sharp. The Fall came not from a

[69] See H. R. MacCallum, "Milton and Sacred History: Books XI and XII of *Paradise Lost*," in *Essays in English Literature from the Renaissance to the Victorian Age*, p. 154: "The opening tableau of Cain and Abel is itself a kind of dumb show which reveals through mime . . . the essentials of the drama to come."

withdrawal of either God's image in man or God's gift of immortality. Man threw both away, desiring instead brutish "ungovern'd appetite" and the rival "Image whom they served" (XI, 517, 518). Adam and Eve recreated themselves, that is, in the type or image of Satan. There can be no escape from some form of the death inevitable to the Satanic type. It need not always be frightful; if life has been temperate, it may come like the harvest of ripe fruit. However, even such a death has already involved the loss, the virtual "death," of "youth, . . . strength, . . . beauty" (XI, 539). The crestfallen Adam no longer fears, but rather too eagerly welcomes, the death that will end his "cumbrous" life (XI, 549). Michael reprovingly indicates that man must instead concentrate upon neither mortal life nor death, upon neither his coming hither nor his going hence, but only upon the eternal quality of his living.

If man has veered toward welcoming his son Death-as-deliverer too fondly, because of the example of Cain, he now sees Cain once more—and the threat in Cain's passional nature becomes reversed. We now must witness the parent of Death—Sin. The illusion of human progress begins. The lost Abel's shepherding comes to be attended not by Pan's pipes but by artful music, intending not to temper but to move human passions; men also learn to forge destructive metals. Enlightened, God-fearing mountain dwellers like Abel come down into these "progressive" cities of the plain. Seductive Eve-like women sway before them, weaving a net of love to which the Adamic men at last respond with "heat" (XI, 589). Adam heatedly reverts to his original weakness, disdaining Michael's projected human "end," the "ripe Fruit" of peaceful age, for this apple in which, again, "Nature seems fulfill'd in all her ends" (XI, 535, 602). He has to be shown a second corrosive truth about himself and Cain, almost as harsh as the first. Passions of the Fall fill the tents of Cain. It is these that Adam has chosen as his essence, in place of his "nobler end / Holy and pure, conformity divine" (XI, 605–606). The holy men who, like Satan or Samson, also had been sons of God surrender themselves to the pleasurable embrace of Sin. Soon the recoiling, purgative flood must follow: seductive Sin still spawns hideous death, "for which / The world erelong a world of tears must weep" (XI,

626–627). As he had at the original Fall, Adam sullenly tries to blame woman for all man's loss, but Michael will permit no such false judgment. Man must acknowledge his own guilt, much as even Satan had to acknowledge his son, Death:

> From Man's effeminate slackness it begins,
> . . . who should better hold his place
> By wisdom, and superior gifts receiv'd [XI, 634–636].

Like a death rattle, the pace of death choices increases among history's men. Giants war in a replica of the typic Battle in Heaven. Men give themselves up to almost endless civil war, increasing and magnifying the war of Abel with Cain (for there too a sweating giant fought with a shepherd). When Enoch chose against such bestiality, making the Abdiel-like choice "of Right . . . , / . . . Justice, . . . Religion, Truth and Peace, / And Judgment from above," a Cain-like nation would have killed him had he not with divine aid "ascended" (XI, 666–668). Adam now must confess that men have almost ceased being men; they have become the ministers of death. Military combat, the highest pitch of human glory in the past, had supplied the typical hero of past epics. The contrast provided by Enoch, typical of Milton's new hero of patience, shows the good man's opposite reward, "real" as well as literary.

However, Enoch was one against historical multitudes. Adam must see in contrast the death-devoted life he himself has chosen, which history now correlatively confirms. Evil choice is seen to multiply among men demoniacally until hellish vapors and exhalations gather and tempestuous chaos returns. Those who had already drowned their humanity are drowned in all but apocalyptic purgation. Our stance asks that we apostrophize Adam direct in viewing his beneficial sorrow: "thee another Flood, / Of tears and sorrow a Flood thee also drown'd" (XI, 756–757). In part, it is man's bent "of Nature" toward Cain that has been purged, baptismally "drowned," by Adam's penitential tears. Milton hazards a rash conceit in order to show that regenerate man, like God, can reverse the apparent physical meaning of death. Adam's "flood" of tears, counteracting the chosen punitive flood for men, is a kind of fortunate fall. From it man can be raised. However,

Adam's first weak effort as redeemer instead laments with Tiresias
the necessity for bearing any guilt but his own. Unlike Oedipus
and the Son, he wants no Godlike "foreknowledge" (XI, 768) nor
the consequent bearing of another's grief. He must nevertheless
accept the hard truth that in history either war or human peace
produces almost identical corruption: Cain-like men continue to
choose Sin or Death separately or in league. There is no hope for
men in typic progressions from valor to luxury to civil war, or
from vassalage to servile luxury. In both routes, great provender,
political as well as economic, had again created an Eden in which
men could live "that temperance [might] be tri'd" (XI, 805), but
in both cases men had again fallen. If in this dark night of Hell
and history one man—Enoch, or Noah, or the Son—continues
typically to choose aright, the image of the Flood can concentrate
not only right and evil choice by men, but also consequent destruction, chaos, re-creation, and reconciliation of God with man.
After careening again between despair and hope, Adam begins to
rest more solidly in the recurrent, typic, central appearance of

> . . . one Man found so perfet and so just,
> That God voutsafes to raise another World
> From him, and all his anger to forget [XI, 876–878].

Resurrection and "second stock" (XII, 7) are offered not only to
men but to humankind, and to the physical world as well. Adam
errs only in the assumption that one man can absolutely eradicate
the choice and consequence of many. To such a foreshortening of
human time, wisest fate must still say no. For such absolute purgation, men must await the resurrective end of time, when "fire
[will] purge all things new" (XI, 900). In the meantime, the
world has been brought to a new, resurrective physical covenant,
signaled after purgation by the rainbow. As man never entirely
abandoned God, even in the attitudes and tents of Cain, so God
will not even there abandon men. The purgation prepares the
way for "another World."

Most of Book XI continues to find Adam in despair and man in
tempestuous sin, and to leave the audience in shocked receipt of
its historical form of fall. Intimations of ascent arose with Abel,
Enoch, and Noah. From this low point onward, right choice in-

creases in history and (presumably) in Michael's human auditors. In Adam, the visions have entered into his innermost meditations, becoming the very process of his regeneration. Having purged himself of the sin and death represented by Cain, he can now become increasingly like his other Son.

"AND MAN AS FROM A SECOND STOCK PROCEED": LATERAL AND VERTICAL ASCENT, TO CHRIST AND THE PARADISE WITHIN (BOOK XII)

In Book XII, Michael's instruction takes narrative form,[70] with our human witness fixed at our post-Edenic stance between a world destroyed and a world restored. Man has been given the renovative hope that he can act within either a material or spiritual "second stock" (XII, 7). Adam has reached at least the halfway point of his own spiritual progress to such an inner paradise. Yet the scales for humanity in general remain unbalanced. Although the Flood produced for a time the awed piety that the Fall once had evoked in Adam, it did not hold; in surrendering to Satanic choice, men had lost both individual and communal liberty. Satanic man instead constructs in the world a second Pandemonium and babbles in it like the devils in Hell. Now standing with God, Son, and Michael in judgment of men,[71] human reason in Adam having been restored to Edenic similitude with the divine, the first man curses the perverted human choice, as perverse to the definition of man as Satan was to that of "angel." He sees in fabricating man a wretched tyrant, a vainly ascending builder who would be lord of both man and God. Adamic man in the audience at first may not recognize himself in the error, so, Hamlet-like, Michael again reveals him to himself:

> Justly thou abhorr'st
> That Son, who on the quiet state of men

[70] H. R. MacCallum, in "Milton and Sacred History," pp. 165–166, discusses the shift to narrative as reflecting a movement from nature to grace. Barbara K. Lewalski, in "Structure and the Symbolism of Vision in Michael's Prophecy, *Paradise Lost*, Books XI–XII" (*PQ*, XLII [1963], 29), notes that, Oedipally, man's insight increases as visionary "sight" declines. Frye, in *The Return of Eden*, p. 110, indicates the shift to scriptural revelation.

[71] Louis L. Martz, *The Paradise Within*, p. 148: The audience must see history through the eyes of both Adams.

> Such trouble brought, affecting to subdue
> Rational Liberty; yet know withal,
> Since thy original lapse, true Liberty
> Is lost, which always with right Reason dwells [XII, 79–84].

Poor Adam, and poor audience; each time Adam (for them) affects horror with his future sons and their generations, he finds the horror original with himself, the type of human prodigal son who relinquishes his birthright of liberty and reason. In a concomitant curse, he who discards personal liberty loses political liberty. Even during redemptive Noah's time, men again fall. However, the promise of a second stock increases. Rather than surrender errant men again to their own Flood, God "elects" one better nation, much as he had exalted the Son in Heaven. From Israel, "all Nations shall be blest" (XII, 126), the twelve tribes in part predicting the Twelve Apostles. Within Israel, Abraham duly appears as the first major historical type of Christ, the "Seed / [In whom] All Nations shall be blest" (XII, 125–126). The line of anticipatory, redemptive types among the elect people rises through Isaac, Jacob, Moses, and Joseph. In the descriptions of Joseph and Moses, for instance, the former is a "younger Son / In time of dearth," in a land where his people's "infant Males" (XII, 160–161, 168) are slaughtered, and the latter leads his people up from enthrallment to a "promis'd Land" past hellish locusts, "Palpable darkness," and a Pharaonic "River-dragon" whose heart is like ice doubly hardened after a thaw (XII, 172, 188, 191). God triumphs over the enemy here as he did over Satan in Heaven. After catastrophe, he calms the Red Sea as the Son will calm Galilee. The elect nation receives laws in the wilderness much as the Son will there confirm such laws. Increasingly, however, Israel feels the need of a present man rather than the demanding "types and shadows" of religious suggestion, a man to be "Mediator" (XII, 232–233, 240). Moses supplies the function "in figure" (XII, 241), awaiting the time when the Son will inhabit human flesh, even as the Father spiritually inhabits the Mosaic tabernacle.

Man rightly sees the election of Israel as a type of the forgiveness of mankind and a mighty favor from God, his sin-dimmed eyes having received the redemptive euphrasy that clears his vi-

sion and eases his heart (XII, 274), but even yet cannot understand why punitive laws, new "prohibitions," are needed. The
Christian answer is that Mosaic laws are an aid from God to
buttress God-supplied reason, although in the long run they will
be insufficient. Man will need instead something more originally
Edenic within his fallen world—a newer convenant of love and
worship of being by which he can ascend from

> . . . shadowy Types to Truth, from Flesh to Spirit,
> From imposition of strict Laws, to free
> Acceptance of large Grace, from servile fear
> To filial, works of Law to works of Faith [XII, 303–306].

Moses, the giver of law, cannot offer the new dispensation. Instead, that office will descend to *"Joshua* whom the Gentiles *Jesus*
call, / His Name and Office bearing" (XII, 310–311). In type, he
is Jesus. He will "quell / The adversary Serpent, and bring
back / Through the world's wilderness long wander'd man / Safe
to eternal Paradise" (XII, 311–314).[72] The progress to compassionate incarnation impels the historical account swiftly past
David to the second Adam, noting by the way the typic preliminary fall of Israel to Babylon. A "Nativity Ode" carries Adam
into the rejoicing that Milton and the reader had once before
shared. Adam is to be fulfilled in the purity of Mary and Christ,
who are as much his children as is Cain. What is more, they
choose to be children of God, and are in that fashion "elected."
Adam is fondly sure that with the birth of Jesus the Serpent will
be destroyed, but Michael must warn him that post-Edenic conditions permit no such heady heroism (wisest fate still says no). In a
second Creation, in some ways holier than the first, the Son will
work to purge evil from man, even though in that purgation he
himself must move through "a reproachful life and cursed death"
(XII, 406).[73] The elect will then be not Abraham's seed alone but

[72] John T. Shawcross, in his edition of *The Complete English Poetry of
John Milton* (New York, 1963), p. 481, notes that both *Joshua* and *Jesus*
mean "savior." See also C. A. Patrides, "Adam's 'Happy Fault' and XVIIth-
Century Apologetics," *Franciscan Studies*, XXIII (1963), 238–243, for discussion of sacrificial divine redemption, "more wonderful" than the original
creation by fiat.

[73] Harry F. Robins, *If This Be Heresy: A Study of Milton and Origen*
(Urbana, Ill., 1963), p. 22: Irenaeus believed that Christ recapitulated the
entire history of man.

the "Sons / Of *Abraham's* Faith wherever through the world" (XII, 448–449). He will reveal death to be a shadow, mortally necessary but in no wise the death of the soul that Satan had wished. Far from it:

> But to the Cross he nails thy Enemies,
> The Law that is against thee, and the sins
> Of all mankind, with him there crucifi'd [XII, 415–417].

Mortal failures having been "crucified," restored man may choose his peace. Now for all men death may be "like sleep, / A gentle wafting to immortal Life" (XII, 434–435). When death comes to believers, it will be "like that which the redeemer di'd" (XII, 445), and dies every Easter, into resurrection. Eventually he will judge the dying world. He will then waft the blessed finally to immortal life, but the others, self-chosen dross, will fall into utter nonbeing.

Man is overwhelmed in seeing the simple total design of God's power and goodness. He lauds God with the cry that has been taken to read, *O felix culpa!* It does not quite do so. Man is amazed to see the spiritual "creation" (XII, 472) of such good from such evil, an act that seems more wonderful even than the material creation from chaos. However, his evil is never in doubt. He is only astounded that so much continuing glory can be wrought from conditions that in Book XI looked so terrible. However, as Adam's question about the fate of the apostles indicates, there remains a danger that he will force the question of salvation back to materiality. Michael therefore stresses the reality which all the types shadow forth—the spiritual Comforter and divine "inward consolations" (XII, 495), understandable only through and by "the Spirit" (who has produced understanding by Milton according to his great argument), rather than the materialistic forms Milton associated with Roman Catholicism.

Meanwhile, the world labors still, not only with the teeming birth of Sin, but also toward the gracious entrance of the Son. The true and creative Son will eradicate the monstrous, abortive Sin. With Adam, men at last understand what Christian heroism means. Adam's tragedy has led him to enlightenment very closely paralleling that of the later mutes and audience to *Samson Agonistes*. He has attained calm of mind:

> Greatly instructed I shall hence depart,
> Greatly in peace of thought, and have my fill
> Of knowledge, what this Vessel can contain;
> Beyond which was my folly to aspire [XII, 557–560].

He sees with the reader that the new heroism, to be enacted partly by himself and by other types of Christ, will culminate in Christ and every son who chooses to be like Him (for Christ in turn is a type,[74] of sorts, for his apostles and ministers) :

> . . . to obey is best,
> And love with fear the only God, . . .
>   . . . with good
> Still overcoming evil, and by small
> Accomplishing great things, by things deem'd weak
> Subverting worldly strong, and worldly wise
> By simply meek, . . .
> Taught this by his example whom I now
> Acknowledge my Redeemer ever blest [XII, 561–573].

Michael congratulates Adam upon his paradoxical (Christian) ascent to humility and his "heroic" reliance upon a second Adam. He even shows Adam and all mankind with him the justifications of man by which Paradise in one sense can be regained:

> . . . add
> Deeds to thy knowledge answerable, add Faith,
> Add Virtue, Patience, Temperance, add Love,
> . . . : then wilt thou not be loath
> To leave this Paradise, but shalt possess
> A paradise within thee, happier far [XII, 581–587].

Not that it is now instantly attained. The descent from the mount of speculation leads us back to "our first Mother," Eve. She is now properly receptive to instruction by Adam "in one Faith unanimous though sad," concerning not only the evils men have produced but also mankind's "happy end" (XII, 603, 605) . Trag-

[74] Robins, in *If This Be Heresy*, p. 160, records that prophetic revelations in the Old Testament were often associated directly with Christ. C. A. Patrides, in "Milton and the Protestant Theory of the Atonement" (*PMLA*, LXXIV [1959], 7) , notes that Christ is in another sense the "perfect man": in all except his first being, he is self-creating. See also Patrides' more recent *Milton and the Christian Tradition*, pp. 7–25.

edy surrenders to Dantean comedy only in the immense perspectives of eternity, however. Men will be happy insofar as they understand and utilize God's design, which now includes their own deaths. Their immediate character is tragic as they enter the fallen world, that which Adam and the chorus of poet and readers have already witnessed.

The last "renewing" words of man in the epic are given to Eve, balancing well her swerving dreams and chosen fall. This time she has remained constant. God has filled her dreams with vision, which replaces her own vanity. She all but enacts Mary, to whom will come the annunciation of the Word made flesh; if the pain of childbirth rehearses the Fall, the fruit of her womb doubly indicates resurrection. With pure consent she now asks Adam to lead her into the lower world and her "place," as she had once fatally asked his enemy, Satan, to lead her into absence. Her immediate paradise is found with him in her complementary role. Her elective exaltation into being the first Mary nears when she realizes that, unworthy though she may be as a handmaiden, "By mee the Promis'd Seed shall all restore" (XII, 623).

Eden begins to sink, even as the larger world will sink under the flood that Adam has foreseen. By choice, Paradise has become for man a Hell of "torrid heat" and "fiery Arms" (XII, 634, 644). Its flames are punitive and Hellish but also purgative and Heavenly, suggesting the tragically heroic phoenix image that closes *Samson Agonistes*. The descending cherubim half suggest those of the restorative Nativity.[75] For God, the destruction of Eden is a form of resurrection, in which dross and chaff burn away so that a new world may be born.

The powerfully affecting conclusion pulses with double meanings that continue to convert seeming disaster into unlimited promise. Our parents go out to choose—all over again, but in a setting that they have elected—their lateral, historical place of (restless) rest. They also choose, continuously, their "vertical" eternal rest. With their hands again joined as they had been

[75] William G. Madsen, in "The Idea of Nature in Milton's Poetry," in *Three Studies in the Renaissance: Sidney, Jonson, Milton* (New Haven, 1958), p. 268, sees a visible regeneration in the restorations of union—Eve to Adam, man to God.

before sin and death brought isolation into human lives, Adam and Eve "wander" safely beyond Eden.[76] Although their way is "solitary" (XII, 649), the pathos of the final lines should not mislead us. The world is no mean gift. Providence moves before them as it will for the Israelites in Exodus and for Milton and his readers in the epic. The swerve Satan has effected, and will effect again, is nevertheless as "near" behind Adam and Eve as God is near ahead.[77] Their sons Cain and Christ [78] beckon to them within and without history. Their enlightened way will lead Adam and Eve themselves to a heavenly Paradise, we may suppose, judging from Michael's promise of happiness at their mortal end.

For us as audience and inheritors of our "Grand Parents'" choice, however, their way leads outward from the altar of judgment and praise, through the great theater of mankind, into our midst.[79] They enact humanity. God's design within history is their and our great general action, stretching from a beginning in time, through this middle, to an end only with time itself. Beyond time, individual human choices must elect union with timeless, dynamic Idea. Because phylogeny also recapitulates ontogeny, author and audience assume the "Grand Parents'" roles. "Answering his great Idea" (VII, 557), we continue to move in an action, yet are defined in eternity: So God with man unites.[80]

[76] Sims, in *The Bible in Milton's Epics*, pp. 138 and 236, indicates that divine aid awaits those in need—even, perhaps, in the expulsion from Eden, in which there is as much deliverance as damnation (because of association with the story of Lot and Sodom).

[77] Sims, in *The Bible in Milton's Epics*, p. 130, sees in the laborer's return an allusion of dust to dust. It can also indicate a direction "homeward" to Heaven.

[78] Robert A. Bryan, in "Adam's Tragic Vision in *Paradise Lost*" (*SP*, LXII [1965], 197–214), traces the movement of sin westward in history; but it is of course pursued and diverted by the parallel movement of the gospel.

[79] J. B. Broadbent, in *Some Graver Subject*, p. 287, charges that Milton walks away from his poems at their conclusion. It seems to me that they are instead given to the instructed audience for further enactments.

[80] Barbara K. Lewalski, in "Structure and the Symbolism of Vision," p. 35, sees that the way from Eden for Adam and Eve leads to the Promised Land. Michael Fixler, in *Milton and the Kingdoms of God* (Evanston, Ill., 1964), p. 228, makes much the same analysis of the conclusion: in losing Eden, men gained Heaven.

[5] "Since No Man Comes"
God's Ways with His Son
in *Paradise Regained*

Although much had been promised Adam at the close of *Paradise Lost* that might bring him to his inward Paradise, Eden itself had disappeared in flames. The Flood later must obliterate even its last traces. Only the waste wilderness of hellish and human history will remain. The Garden of Eden must become a Wasteland or a garden at Gethsemane, even as human praise of God for life must alter into human prayer that the divine will somehow may be done even within death. Although the nearby river Jordan and holy cities may mark the memory or imitation of the setting in Paradise and although heavenly voices again may return to men at those places, the desert must nevertheless now stand as the visible sign of the original sin and isolation of man. With the ending of *Paradise Lost* came the ending of the former conditions of Paradise. The matter is no longer that of a perfect man falling but instead of the Son's becoming perfected in knowledge and will within the fallen world. Similarly, *Paradise Regained* must deal not with immense bounty and one simple choice but with a shifting, uncertain, but still more necessary flow of choices. As death is now the only avenue to renewal, so only in this desert can each man hope to attain that "paradise within . . . , happier far." Even the patriarchs and prophets and the holiest Son of God, along with the reflective author and audience, now must experience some form of its forty days of trial.[1] The

[1] Arthur E. Barker ("Structural and Doctrinal Pattern in Milton's Later Poems," in *Essays in English Literature from the Renaissance to the Victorian Age, Presented to A. S. P. Woodhouse*, ed. Millar MacLure and F. W. Watt

desert has replaced plenteous Eden as the original setting and experience for every man. Divine aid itself is now given not through an angel and a garden but through a devil and a desert, in which the human will is *to be* "regained."

In a sense, the Quaker Thomas Ellwood was correct in thinking *Paradise Lost* an incomplete statement. It does not quite indicate the altered physical and religious condition of mankind—the seeming withdrawal of God, the seeming deterioration of nature into tormented wilderness, the seeming collapse of human life toward death, both physical and spiritual. *Paradise Regained* takes up that cross. In its mainly desolate, unpromising, and necessary setting, Milton places the two major stances of the brief epic: in the first, men wait in a desert of suspense at Jordan; in the second, unaccompanied even by the usual audience involvement, the Son of God waits in the negative, desert site of Eden.

Although Milton's central use of this postlapsarian site and condition was a daring literary stroke, it has produced two reflective retreats into uneasiness or refusal by several generations of readers, including—to Milton's displeasure—those of his own lifetime.[2] The first objection held that the Son could not lose nor Satan win, historically or theologically, even though the desert threatens the Son in much the same way that death and sin successfully threatened Adam (who also was a son of God). The more serious reaction conceded the action to be literarily acceptable but deplored the practicing quietism, negativity, and inaction of the Son's agon, to say nothing of the answerable plainness of style—all of which must alienate Milton's audience.

The first, simpler reaction is answered by the desert stance itself. It insists that for the Son or any lesser man the inward Paradise cannot be "given" or conferred; it must be gained. As Michael had told Adam, it can come only after the choice and

---

[Toronto, 1964], p. 179) notes how frequently Jewish history had encountered this desert; Jewish law, however, must now be transcended. Northrop Frye, in *The Return of Eden* (Toronto, 1965), pp. 123–124, adduces many parallels between Israel and the Son.

[2] Ants Oras, in *Milton's Editors and Commentators from Patrick Hume to Henry John Todd (1695–1801): A Study in Critical Views and Methods* (New York, 1964), p. 146, remarks Milton's displeasure, as recorded in early *Lives*.

achievement of "Deeds . . . Faith . . . Virtue, Patience, Temperance, . . . Love" (*Paradise Lost*, XII, 582–583). *Paradise Regained* will dramatize not a theophany but the achievement of moral certitude—somewhat the same justification by faith that the first Adam had experienced in the original Eden. If such "justifying" virtues have been divinely announced for a man such as Jesus or Samson, so much the worse for him, laterally; such unfallen virtues can grow only within the fallen desert sands of doubt and incomprehension. Like the first Paradise, the second can be lost. Unlike the first, it is even initiated within loss. If in *Paradise Lost* evil might come and go in the minds of men, in the fallen world of *Areopagitica* and *Paradise Regained*, awareness of evil must come into the mind in order that evil may be rejected. Furthermore, the apparent deprivations of the desert sometimes must be deliberately maintained when to seek another way would be to lose the way. It is not essentially negative to refuse imbrutement, the seven deadly sins, delusion, and self-deceit. They must be discarded in favor of positive action and creative time. For that reason, when Satan most urges relief from the desert, the true Son the more devoutly rests within its contradictions and vacancy. There could hardly be more absolute demonstration that the choice characteristic of Milton's fiction remains fully, terribly open in *Paradise Regained*. Consider the two major antagonists within that stance: they are two sons of God, one holy, the other diabolic. Somewhat like God and Satan when considering the man Job, they initially share almost identical premises but then freely make diametrically opposed choices. At the outset, each can perceive and sometimes even seriously consider the other's position.[3] The holy Son entertains all the doubts that become "temptations" long before Satan gives them the extreme statement of final choice. Within his admittedly "fallen" lights, Satan in his worldly wisdom is quite serious, even sincere, in recommending his heroic choices to the human Son. His "temptations" often seem to Satan himself to be no more than helpful proposals, for if he were in a situation like that of the Son, his own recommenda-

---

[3] Barbara K. Lewalski, in *Milton's Brief Epic* (Providence, 1966), p. 159, emphasizes the "genuine dramatic encounter" of the poem.

tions are exactly what he would choose: Are they not what he in his apostasy always *has* chosen? And are they not what the first human representative, Adam, once chose?

If our concentration is narrowed to the soteriological Son himself, we find not a predetermined answer but the open assault of question. Whereas the weak Satan can be helpfully or arrogantly assured, the strong Son must be in doubt: it is the nature of the desert, which is the concealed "beginning" of his mission. Many of the seeming errors "obtruded" (II, 387) by Satan will in due time be not diabolically wrong but divinely right and just, the proper fulfillment of the Son's holy mission. Soon the Son *will* turn stones of a sort into bread, prepare a Last Supper, save Israel and the Gentiles, and in some measure command the Temple.[4] To him as to all of God's sons, the temptation does not inhere in the object or the act but only in the will to command the announced mission of savior (in one form or another) as one's own, carried forth in one's own way and in one's own time. Even here, it is not easy to differentiate ardor from error. "What from within" (I, 198) the Son himself feels may create a dilemma at the least or an unpardonable sin at the worst: can he, or any lesser man, know when urging comes from God's will rather than his own, and can he be sure on the other hand that his patience has not become a Hamlet-haunting failure to act? Because author and audience become thoroughly involved in these questions reflectively, it is difficult to see how the field of choices within and without the direct action could be more perplexingly open.

It is therefore the second objection that is more injurious to the reputation of *Paradise Regained*. Our preliminary discussion will move directly against that adversary of Milton. Those who dislike *Paradise Regained* on the grounds of its seemingly flat and dispassionate style and action (even while approving these effects in twentieth-century poetry) [5] are put off much as they are by the

---

[4] Howard Schultz, in "A Fairer Paradise? Some Recent Studies of *Paradise Regained*" (*ELH*, XXXII [1965], 287), points out that Christ has title to a natural kingdom, his by right as Son.

[5] For defenses of the style of *Paradise Regained*, see David Daiches, *Milton* (London, 1957), p. 219; William G. Madsen, "The Idea of Nature in Milton's Poetry," in *Three Studies in the Renaissance: Sidney, Jonson, Milton* (New Haven, 1958), p. 265; and Louis L. Martz, *The Paradise Within* (New Haven and London, 1964), pp. 171–176.

Lady in *Comus,* for the height of the Son's doing seems to them only the refusal to do. The objection will be met very briefly from grounds of theology and literary theory, but, as was also the case with the first objection, it will be answered principally from a discussion of stance. The two stances can best demonstrate why Milton's advocates find the poem active and meaningful not for the characters alone but for the methektic audience as well. A preliminary sketch of the structure will also proceed directly from a description of the stances.

Even without considering the powerful effect of the stances upon *Paradise Regained,* it is possible to reply to the objection of inertia by holding that God's implicit design is dramatic beyond any immediate nay-saying, involving as it does the heavenly begetting of the Son and his coming double victory, temporal and apocalyptic, over sin and death. During the time that a protective nay-saying in the present maintains the dynamic eternal design, a counter choice for Being is firmly, if not so overtly, in process.[6] The implied outcome of this theological contest, whether "dramatized" or merely intimated, is the salvation or helplessness of mankind. Finally, because of the Son's exemplary action and meaning for the individual Christian and for the Christian church,[7] the action should possess lively implications for an audience. The apparently undramatic conference in the desert reveals the type of Christian victory over Satan, Sin, and Death. However, although the Son is near the theological still point of all this moving world, that very stillness and remoteness may seem to sustain the opponents of *Paradise Regained.*

The answer from literary theory and tradition is as much a reminder as a defense. It notes that Job, who is partially the model for the hero, even as the Book of Job is partially the model for the form of *Paradise Regained,*[8] acted out the same "negative"

---

[6] See Frank Kermode, "Milton's Hero," *RES,* n.s. IV (1953), 322–323, for the Son's necessary foray out into "trouble." Northrop Frye, in "The Typology of *Paradise Regained*" (*MP,* LIII [1956], 227–238), defines this encounter of Christ with Satan as the second in a triad (the Battle in Heaven, the temptation, the Last Judgment).

[7] Howard Schultz ("Christ and Antichrist in *Paradise Regained,*" *PMLA,* XLVII [1952], 790–808) reads *Paradise Regained* as a "parable for the church."

[8] Barbara Lewalski, in *Milton's Brief Epic,* pp. 18–25, makes the vital comparison with the Book of Job; see also pp. 93–103 for other literary models.

rejection of temptation and was led to a similar reward. Hercules and Virgilian heroes, the somewhat more remote models for the Son in *Paradise Regained,* also acted by rejecting appealing error. Plato's Socrates, who supplies still another example of such a hero and a model of dialectical literary form, necessarily rejects most alternatives during the course of a dialogue on ethics.[9] Milton's physical model for Jesus may have been the early-Christian Apollo figure—beardless, alert, questioning. Although we must avoid seeing in him the Arian Son, we are to remain aware that he is the greater *Man* promised as hero by *Paradise Regained.* Spenser's Guyon presents a full parallel for such a hero. In a modern example, Henry James is likely to ask his characters for "inactive" moral decisions rather than for heroic activity. Unlike some authors, Milton sought an answerable style. The style that answers the matter of *Paradise Regained* is strikingly demonstrated by the almost doggedly commonplace entrance into the epic and by the quiet, seemingly anticlimactic close. He assigns heroics and florid rhetoric to the father of lies. Following principles of literary decorum as well as imitation of the often gnomic utterances of Jesus in the Bible, Milton reserves spare, oracular diction for the Son and for his advocate, the narrator of the poem. Literature, then, can answer the objection by pointing to a traditional form and style, by asking that the work be understood within its own prescribed expectations rather than those alien to it—a request now largely answered, in a noteworthy example, for the pastoral form of "Lycidas."

As is true for all works of art, the ultimate defense must be that of *Paradise Regained* itself. Following the regular avenue of these essays, I suggest therefore that the intensity to be sought and found in *Paradise Regained* rests partly in the two opposed stances themselves, in the "situation," somewhat as it does in Frost's "The Road Not Taken." They legislate the matter and its reception. They are reminiscent of two of the stances in "Lyci-

---

[9] Irene Samuel, *Plato and Milton* (Ithaca, N.Y., 1947), p. 21: "Even if the very dialectical method by which Jesus wins his victory did not point to the Dialogues as a model, the themes and arguments show how much Milton had assimilated from Plato."

das"—that of remembered Edenic promise and that of present weltering oceanic loss. Although the third, eternal stance of "Lycidas" is strongly suggested in *Paradise Regained* as the result of choice between the two stances and indeed appears briefly during the rescue and celebration of the Son, it is not put to so direct a use. Promise is associated with annunciative Jordan, although even that stance grows strangely suspenseful and doubtful. Loss is associated with the desert, but that stance gradually witnesses a regained paradise.

The two characters of the agon, along with the participative audience, are caught not so much in physical action as in intellectual and volitional comprehension of the stances. *Paradise Regained* takes its first stance with the high creative promise of consecrative Jordan. There all the persons of the drama gather and witness a seeming union of God with man. Even when the stance is shifted to the desert, Jordan's promise to all the participants continues to vibrate. To enter the desert, however, the Son must leave the stance at Jordan as vacant as death, apparently abandoning his mission, his flock, and even his God. He must wander alone in the sterile desert—which, however, in a major recoil, Satan's storm will cause to blossom. The baffling reversal of the Son's own early stances teases both him and his followers (who are Chorus for his more distant followers, the audience) beyond human thought. The exchange of stances delights but also mystifies his adversary. Satan cannot comprehend the reversal but brings ready heroic answers for righting its "wrong." Each Satanic temptation will suggest a return of some sort to Jordan and the heralded mission. The two mentalities then strive in different ways to reconcile vital Jordan with the deathlike mount of temptation where man's Eden once before had collapsed forever—and those two mentalities are legion among men. What seems to be life and fidelity to the one is death and faithlessness to the other. Satan would have the Son demand his promised Kingdom at Jordan, thereby assuring its fall, whereas the Son, by accepting the desert, guarantees that all of Jordan's promises will be fulfilled.

Satan is inwardly sure that he understands the meaning of Jordan: the Son is to be a literal king of a literal nation or nations. He believes that the Son shares as "divinity" only the transcendent pride of his God (I, 87–88). To Satan he is largely a material threat—perhaps, in a literalizing of the Lord's Prayer attribution to Him of the power, the kingdom, and the glory, the means for routing Hell from its "worldly" possession of earth and history. He envisions Jesus as a rival Satan more than as an opposite. He therefore pledges to act before "in the head of Nations he appear / Their King, their Leader, and Supreme on Earth" (I, 98–99). He will of course try to direct the Son into worldly consummation of some of those very powers.[10] If Satan succeeds, Christ will be of the devil's and the world's party, and there will be no contest. By his nature, Satan intends evil, but he also sincerely believes that he, also a son of God (who, although he may choose to be a devil, cannot choose *not* to be a son of God), can guide a misled new hero back to the old diabolic and human heroism. Sinfully conservative Satan remains sure that he understands all the announced terms of Jordan: to be master of nature must mean to gluttonize; to be kingly means to exact public service; to be wise means to vaunt in "superior" sophistries; and to be godly means to challenge God's laws. In a sense, it is himself as much as the Son that he "tempts" in the assumed roles of prophet, priest, and king,[11] and again he falls almost automatically.

Although Satan is never truly opposite or even parallel to the Son, becoming nearly allegorical or unnecessary during those times when the Son revolves doubts in his breast, descends into himself, or is vacant, and although as master illusionist and prince of the air he cannot command the sense of being that the historical Christ possesses, he is sufficiently real as the type and voice of worldly wisdom. Like the knowledge illustrated in *Paradise Lost*, Book XI, such lore is founded only on the lateral chaos of experi-

[10] The temptation for Christ to "become" the expected Jewish Messiah is very strong. See Michael Fixler, *Milton and the Kingdoms of God* (Evanston, Ill., 1964), p. 234, and A. S. P. Woodhouse, "Theme and Pattern in *Paradise Regained*," *UTQ*, XXV (1956), 174. Woodhouse holds that the Son has already outgrown that form of ambition, however.

[11] The Son revolves "exegetical comments on the Scriptures" in his breast, however, and is always several paces ahead of a question by the time Satan has posed it (Barker, "Structural and Doctrinal Pattern," p. 182).

ence. To it the Son must oppose vertical faith and constancy. For the Son, Satan's consideration of the stances defines the drama with alarming "activity": he represents the choice of sickness over health, madness over sanity, death over life.

The Son, who differs from Satan in moving from doubt to certainty whereas Satan moves from brassy assurance to wracking fear, revolves the same dangerous questions that Satan had asked in Heaven and that Adam had answered wrongly in Paradise. Even the setting in lost Eden insists that he, like them, may fall. In a way, he has much more cause. If they were tried for temperance in the midst of abundance, he is tried in terrible privation, threatened not with disobedience but with "distrust" (I, 355), despair. Like Eve, he may want to hazard desperate action—not to save himself, however, but to fulfill the ordered service to God. An innocent Samson, he finds the desert, his Wasteland, "ill sorting" (I, 200) with the annunciation at Jordan. His wish to do present "public good" is thwarted by solitude, his hope some day to "rescue *Israel* from the *Roman* yoke" mocked by his being "led / Into this Wilderness" (I, 204, 217, 290–291). Until that instant during the temptations when patience prevents the murmur of worldly impatience, there is every chance that the dry lips of the Son will demand, "My God, my God, why hast thou forsaken me?"—and choose in God's place the rival god who stands by, sympathetic, brisk, and available for service. The apparently deserted "positive" of God's annunciation and will is threatened by the apparently full "negative" of the Satanic worldly will.

Lest the desert stance become the denial of Jordan, however, the Son in even his first, preparatory soliloquy readies his strength for fighting the good fight. He already understands how spiritual contradictions may be resolved and points the way to the new, post-Arthurian heroism such understanding has prepared:

> . . . victorious deeds
> Flam'd in my heart, heroic acts; one while
> To rescue *Israel* from the *Roman* yoke,
> Then to subdue and quell o'er all the earth
> Brute violence and proud Tyrannic pow'r,
> Till truth were freed, and equity restor'd:
> Yet held it more humane, more heavenly, first

By winning words to conquer willing hearts,
And make persuasion do the work of fear [I, 215–223].

He is to be *both* more humane and more heavenly, in a new dispensation of love; befitting his dual functions, his persuasion must triumph over worldly violence both in men and typic Satan. Although it will defeat Satan's old heroism, Christ's response to the tempter is directed well beyond him. It is intended to be charitable persuasion of the methektic audience, too.[12] Within his humanity as well as his divinity, Jesus as new oracle is to instruct mankind generally, vastly enlarging upon the limited instruction that had been given in Eden and on Sinai.

But is the doctrinal and exemplary also moving to an audience? Is the action still so "heavenly" that ordinary "humane" interest in the Son is impossible? Again, the stances help to indicate the nature of audience *methexis* in *Paradise Regained*. We are to share the action of one stance, the pressure of questions in the other. Our physical place is fixed at Jordan and with the waiting disciples. Milton took some risks in establishing the audience there with the Chorus of followers who watch and wait. We may wholly identify with their principal action, which is mere suspenseful waiting. Their discovery of patience, a clear preparation for the time when the Son, if considered in the body, will permanently leave them, is a paradigmatic subplot, self-consistent and self-containing. However, if it seems beneficial in permitting us entry into the general agon by means of a purely human parallel to the principal contest, it also can harmfully seem to complete in itself our general human *methexis*. Having known such Gloucesters, why should we, and how can we, enter into the "undramatic," transcendent, inner world of a new kind of Lear? The

[12] John M. Steadman, "*Paradise Regained:* Moral Dialectic and the Pattern of Rejection," *UTQ*, XXXI (1962), 426: Christ's temptation in the desert is exemplary for the Christian's trial "in the field of this world"; George Williamson, "Plot in *Paradise Regained*," in *Milton and Others* (Chicago, 1965), p. 82: "The poem centres on Christ as teacher of mankind, a role parallel to that of Job." Such comments create no basic disagreement with Martz (*The Paradise Within*, p. 187), for even if the Son's is an "inward combat," it remains judicial and exemplary, like the meditation of Adam upon Cain in *Paradise Lost*.

demands of the other stance again supply much of the answer, indicating as well a demand upon the audience somewhat like that of *Paradise Lost:* if in the earlier work we had to acknowledge some love of Satan and distaste for God, in *Paradise Regained* we must acknowledge our taste for "fallen" literary and intellectual heroics like those of Satan rather than like those of the Son's choice and Milton's brief epic.

For the audience as for the Son, it is the desert stance that draws men from obscure home to glorious annunciation, through a series of challenging definitions enforced by the suspense of Jordan and the questioning of the desert, to a second annunciation and return to a quiet, fulfilling human role in the everyday world. The "drama" of most of *Paradise Regained* resides in the resultant peculiar "new acquist / Of true experience" (*Samson Agonistes*, 1755–1756), but it concentrates radically within the word "acquist." The desert requires our gaining or regaining definitions and decisions rather than our "doing" in a physical sense. The question is not so much, What shall a man do? as its greater progenitor, What shall a man be? The large demand of *Paradise Regained* is that we share a largely solitary, internal procedure of dialectic. It is a "drama" intending to prevent or oppose, rather than to enact, the Fall. We must strive to will and understand. If our effort must take us through some fire of literary disbelief in the Son and Satan and, perhaps more importantly, confront us with our own literary inexperience of this sort of "epic," our involvement, oddly enough, may be enhanced rather than discouraged. In small measure, it can supply the literary parallel for the doubts and temptations of the Son. The literary temptation for the audience, rather like the theological temptation for the Son, is to fill a necessary vacuum by means of some decisive, traditional, fallen action. Milton's identification of the Muse of *Paradise Regained* may point to such a possibility. The same Spirit that leads the Son "into the Desert, his Victorious Field / Against the Spiritual Foe" (I, 9–10) leads the author in his work, and may therefore "lead" the audience into its own literary form of wilderness. Experienced deeply, our doubts may lead us away from the old heroism of violent, unredemptive action. For both the Son and the audience, human error would allow the glamorous Satanic desire called impatience (and "Neaera's hair") to best Christian patience in the desert "Field."

Just at this juncture, then, where intersecting lines of belief, doubt, temptation, will, patience, and action meet, the principal agon of the brief epic takes place. As Michael had warned Adam, men must resist the old heroic idea that Satan and the Son will fight a duel. Only in the fancy of Satan or fallen man can such a physical combat even be imagined. The agon of the new heroism instead involves the attempt of the Son and the reflective audience—and, for that matter, of Satan—to "wrestle" with the seemingly contradictory intentions of God.[13] Each must attempt to bridge the abyss between God's annunciations to his sons and the ways in which those sons are led, or bring themselves, to spiritual choices. Following the fall of the first Adam, it is certain that human choices will have to be made in a form of wilderness, for wilderness now occupies the site of Eden. It is no dispraise of Milton, then, but instead high praise for the new form of expressiveness that he may have intended here, to say that the audience themselves must experience a somewhat bewildering new form as they come to literary terms with *Paradise Regained*.

These advocacies of the brief epic retain a share of its exploratory character. A more demonstrable claim, together with another way of seeing audience involvement, has to do with the structure of *Paradise Regained*. If considered from the vantage point of its stances, the brief epic is more symmetrical than has sometimes been realized. The invocation, though remaining apart from the direct action, nevertheless insists upon eventual victory by the Son over that wilderness through which the poem (led by the same Spirit as the Son) must necessarily move. Both the design of God and the design of the poem insist that the wilderness is the path of victory. The action proper begins with the assemblage at Jordan and the great annunciation, to which the Son has come from obscurity. Apart from Satan's illusions, only this annunciation and the balancing scene at the Temple are supernormal; their dramatization insists that we receive the divine annunciation of

---

[13] Woodhouse, in "Theme and Pattern in *Paradise Regained*," p. 168, shows the pattern of rejection to be a Passion, if passion is implied in the root *pass*.

the Son as the condition or impulse for all the dialectic in the wilderness. The consults of Heaven and Hell take due note of the Son within that proclamation, and for different reasons are pleased with his removal to the desert. Audience and followers begin the watchful waiting and the attempt to come to patience. The audience, supplied, as the followers are not, with awareness of the desert and the process of the trials, must strive for understanding within its patience.

In the desert, as the two sons with two different mentalities consider the one mission in which both have immense stakes, the tests themselves proceed somewhat Ramistically in four stages of decreasingly general questions. The Son wishes to be both humane and heavenly, whereas Satan wishes him to be more "human" and worldly. The trial (a "trying-out" as well as a test) involves the complementary questions of the personal and public meanings of the announced mission. As he encounters each question, the Son considers but rejects the worldly meaning and fulfillment (for the time being) by opposing to them a transcendent spiritual equivalent. In Book I, Satan recommends the extremely broad personal service of bread and the equally broad public gift of Greek rhetoric, only to be answered with definitions of spiritual "Bread" and spiritual "Word." This encounter sets the pattern for the rest. In Book II, Satan offers the private services of nature and the public services of wealth toward assertion of kingship, and is refused in terms of the "Bread" of self-control and a "Word" disdaining popular, material kingship. The Satanic offer in Book III, of personal glory and public power for the salvation of Israel, is rejected for glory in God's eyes and a self-elective spiritual power for Israel. Book IV, unfolding the final test, sees Satan offer the usurpatory sonship of the Roman emperor as personal "bread" and the great public wisdom of Athens as public word. The Son rejects them both by choosing divine Sonship and the wisdom of Heaven. Although the last stage is in a sense highly concrete, its implications of sonship and wisdom recall the initial great paradigmatic meanings of "Bread" and "Word." [14]

[14] Mason Tung ("The Patterns of Temptation in *Paradise Regained*," *Seventeenth-Century News*, XXIV [1966], 58–59) accepts as the pattern of temptation that indicated by the Chorus (I, 178–179): *temptation* to bread,

Finally, after the desert tests are completed, the work as a whole moves in full circle back to a setting of annunciation. Because God had produced the first annunciation, Satan attempts to manage the second, placing the Son upon a spire of the Temple. Unwittingly, Satan has thrust the mission forward all the way from Jordan to Jerusalem. This time the annunciation proceeds from the mouth of the "undoubted" Son himself, reinforced by the heavenly hosts and their celebration. The exit of Jesus from the annunciation of Jerusalem is also of a kind with his "obscure" entrance at Jordan, for he "to his Mother's house private return'd." The audience perhaps may wander by the way within the dialectic, but Milton attempts to be very sure that in the action the audience will receive a comely, quasi-Aristotelian whole.

This description of the structure of the poem suggests the last of our prefatory considerations. Tradition makes it inevitable that in *Paradise Regained,* Christ will be expected in his functions as prophet, priest, and king. However, Milton's text does not altogether warrant identifying these specific functions with specific temptations. The four-Book structure and Milton's alterations of the Biblical accounts make it difficult to fix even the textual limits of each temptation. (The banquet scene illustrates both the fascination and the frustration awaiting all critical matching of roles with temptations.) Nevertheless, we remain almost instinctively sure that three temptations took place. That number seems to be required by Biblical suggestion, by the vaguely intimated analogy with the three days' battle of the Son with Satan at Easter, and by the parallel temptations of Eve to appetite, sovereignty, and a demonstrative action asserting divinity.

Although not without grateful awareness of such studies of roles, this essay will circumvent the problem of the Son's trimorphous function in order to concentrate upon that which is common to them all: a question not of whether or not Jesus is the Son, for even Satan concedes that title, but of what it means that he is to "save" himself and mankind. All scenes and dialectic in the poem radiate from that center. An unobtrusive vertical pattern insists

---

seduction to the banquet, *allurement* to the kingdom, *fear* in the storm, *undermining* at the pinnacle. See also Williamson, "Plot in *Paradise Regained,*" p. 83: "The symbolism of 'bread' is related to Christ's fasting, and that of 'kingdoms' to his destiny."

that in each unwilled physical ascent in the poem (from Jordan, to the plateau, to the mount, to the Temple) the Son regains or reaffirms his exaltation to the saving "blissful seat" of reunion with God, and that by contrast each willful ascent by Satan leads him to his own renewed fall. At the close of the poem the witnessing reader, too, is caught up in the ascent. The Son's triumph there permits him to "begin to save mankind": to raise the fallen sons of Adam toward an eternal Paradise, now "regained" for men (IV, 635). However, that vertical pattern is not so important structurally and processively as the lateral dialectical pattern. In it, the antagonists meet the single question as if it were not trimorphous but, at most, triune.

They test the central question in three (or four) closely related forms: [15] What does it mean to the Son to save himself and his "wretched" (I, 345) public? What does it mean to be king or leader, both generally (in definition) and specifically (in history, serving Israel and the Gentile nations)? What does it mean to be the Word? The questions are met in characteristic ways by the opposed mentalities. The Son hesitates, awaiting still another kind of annunciation within his reason and will; Satan leaps. Their initial reception of the questions seems to differ sharply in no other way, except perhaps in Satan's assumption that his worldly wisdom with its worldly gifts can ironically "save" the misguided Savior. Only in the desert trials do these polar differences appear:

I. Christ knows that at some time he must be "Bread" or "Word" of life, saving himself and also supplying his body and wisdom to needy men.

I. Satan disguises himself as a worldly shepherd eager to lead the lost sheep, Christ, into physical life (which may be spiritual death).

II. Christ at some time will command nature to his service, if only to purify it, and will seek at least the "glory" of God's kingdom.

II. Satan offers himself as the economic giver of the world's gifts for both life and glory, providing instruction for the lost shepherd boy.

[15] Fixler, in *Milton and the Kingdoms of God*, p. 267, indicates that Satan's testing of the Son tried him as son of Man, son of David, and son of God.

III. Christ at some time will be king—the ruler, in action or in wisdom, or in both, over Israel.	III. Satan, as king of the world's kings, offers the throne of David to the lost Messiah.
IV. Christ at some time will be the principle of purification for Gentiles and of wisdom to all peoples.	IV. Satan, as emperor of Pandemonium and its academy, offers the empire of all the world and all its wisdom to the lost sage.

These stages of "assay" [16] lead the two sons out into the final encounter, wherein the magician Satan, to his amazement, precipitates a renewed real annunciation. The Son suddenly appears eschatologically as the Judge of all creatures and as victor over Satan, sin, and death. The divergence of the two sons that had begun in the stances at Jordan and the desert becomes absolute, marking the one as the true Son of God, the other as the enemy to all truth and Being.

"Save Thyself and Us Relieve with Food": The tests of "Bread" and of "Word" (Book I)

Generations of readers have contrasted the quiet, almost perfunctory movement of Paradise Regained through invocation, setting, and consults in Heaven and among Hell's hosts with the swelling power and amplitude of similar effects in Paradise Lost, usually to the discredit of the later work. They may be less than just. Milton probably intended not contrast but continuity of a sort compatible with literary and theological decorum and saw no need to supply the equivalent of a second Genesis and Isaiah for Paradise Regained. In one way, however, our entrance into Paradise Regained is vastly different, virtually discontinuous, from that of Paradise Lost. Instead of receiving first an instructive excursion into old-heroic Satanic punishment and mentality, we are introduced immediately to the somewhat spare, "truthful" look and sound of the new heroism. Because the invocation now fully endorses that heroism, the language of the poem at once

[16] See a detailed scheme for the structure in Woodhouse, "Theme and Pattern in Paradise Regained," pp. 170–171.

reflects the attitude of the hero. The style is the man while he is under temptation. It is also the way of our literary experience of the temptation with him. This seeming quietness is the new, "true" creative heat, replacing the earlier noise and bravado. But spare and truthful are not necessarily small and dry, nor does understatement prevent emotional power. It is worthwhile stopping for a moment at this seemingly characterless entrance.

It insists upon continuity with *Paradise Lost* by marking the successful retrial of man in the second Adam. Within this act is implicated total human experience and meaning. As the first trial had brought mankind "all our woe" (*Paradise Lost,* I, 3), so the retrial recovers Paradise "to all mankind" (I, 3) after trial "through all temptation" (I, 5). The Son's general trial itself is both anticipatory and final. He is tried in the testimony of his life by an eternal court and "tried" for strength at the outset of his mission; he also is himself involved as eternal and apocalyptic Judge, the spiritual victor over forces of nonbeing and anarchy. Both "humane [and] heavenly" (I, 221), then, the Son can raise temporal Eden by the obedience that will carry him through the desert and through death, but in doing so he will also "create" or maintain the final New Jerusalem, the greater Eden and final Paradise. The Promised Land in any Christian sense must always lie beyond a material wasteland, a Sinaic desert. It is odd that T. S. Eliot failed to see how closely his vision of this world's wasteland approximated that of Milton.

The limits of the work for both the protagonist and the methektic author are set almost casually, first by the invocation to the guiding spirit and then by the epithet, "glorious Eremite" (I, 8). Milton almost parenthetically asks guidance from the same spirit that leads Jesus into the desert. By this time, confident obedience needs no insistence upon that inspiration nor long prayer that it be conferred. Milton's agon, like that of the hero, will not be physically painful, so there need be no personal pathos; as author, he here will attempt to achieve full understanding of heroic election rather than of temptation and sin. The "prosperous" (I, 14) acts of the author *here* and of the Son *there* are in effect one, raising Eden in a waste wilderness either morally or creatively. There is now little need for the poet to assert that his subject and his inspiration will bear him above the literary Aonian mount. The quiet confidence of the invocation is crystallized in its internal epithet for the Son—"this glorious Eremite." The strange glory of a superhuman understanding achieved within almost total deprivation will be the subject of this brief epic. Both author and protagonist must "fulfill" and create this worthy new heroism by means precisely of this straitened setting and stance. Much as Satan will soon assert that the situation "admits no long debate" (I, 95), so the invocation and its epithet limit the place and function of the trial: the Son is to be here *only* that glorious eremite, both desert-blessed and desert-abandoned. However, the oxymoronic adjective "glorious" should serve to remind us that the universe may be found in this narrow room, for here "all" temptation (I, 5) will be encountered and defeated.

The first physical stance of the epic further establishes the nature of the coming agon. All participants—God, still-wandering Satan, Christ's immediate followers, author, audience—are placed at the Jordan because a prophetic desert baptist and the voice for God, far more awful than mere fallen Roman trumpets, have "now" proclaimed that the kingdom is "nigh at hand" (I, 18, 20). The annunciation is ambiguous, offering opposed interpretations of both "kingdom" and "nigh." The agency of this salvation has not as yet been named. In a character that foreshadows the nature of the coming temptations as well as the quiet conclusion of the work, the new-heroic son of Joseph—"obscure, / Unmarkt, unknown" (I, 24–25)—comes last to the Jordan. Both the human voice of the prophet and the divine voice of God exalt him, even as the Son had been exalted in Heaven. (The roles are essentially one: in Heaven or on earth, the Son is to create form from chaos, suffer death for men, and triumph finally over error.) For an instant, the original Eden seems to have been restored on the banks of the Jordan. The assurance shared by Jesus and his followers at Jordan dies, however, with the echoing words, leaving only a desert of suspense. Although the Son has received double "identification" as the Son of God, absolutely nothing happens. There is not even anticlimax. The Son faces only incomprehensible inertia and solitude, after having been proclaimed the active savior of mankind.

For the moment, however, the continuing stance at Jordan does not permit us to see that doubly "desert" stance to which the epic will retire. Instead, still at Jordan, we witness Satan's mentality as he tries to understand, in terms of the old heroism, what the exaltation of the Son can mean. The audience stance never really shifts to Satan in *Paradise Regained*, largely because he enters and leaves the scene magically and because in each instance the Son has already entertained his questions before he arrives. It now only shifts slightly as the audience, in distant dismay, watches envy and rage seize Satan and observes his tyrannical consult in midair turn to nothing, even as it recognizes in his assumption that he had won the battles of Eden and history (for his present devils are gods in the world) an inability to see and hear the annunciations at Jordan. The audience is sufficiently fallen, however, almost to tempt itself with his worldly questions: Is the Son to be a king in the world? Was the descent of the dove meaningful? Is this man the Son of God who was exalted in Heaven? If in *Paradise Lost* Satan was ignorant of his own son, Death, so in the silence that now shrouds Jordan are all creatures uncertain of the Son and the mission. We may be drearily aware of Satan's self-entrapment as he thinks to trap the second Adam, but we give unthinking consent to his description of the Son as claimant to heroic sovereignty: "King . . . Leader . . . Supreme *on Earth*" (I, 99—italics added). His familiar unreason lets him think that he ruined Adam but causes him, again "nigh Thunderstruck," to shudder under the threat that Adam's seed will now inflict the "long threat'n'd wound" (I, 36, 59). However, we as yet know too little to know in which assessment he errs. I do not believe that Milton tried to avoid the Arian issue in this or in later scenes. It is Satan, not Milton, who confuses himself with a divorce of the divine from the human. Milton quietly identifies the two as one, all men being in some measure sons of God; Christ, both by talent (God's election) and by his own choice, is, however, more fully so than most men can choose to be. Yet the audience, like Satan at Jordan and the Son in the desert, cannot absorb this sense of unity nor understand in what way the mission of such a Son is to define his being king and leader, supreme—on earth.

Still in the stance of Jordan, we as audience receive from God what is virtually another annunciation, one that partially dispels the airy fog of diabolic ignorance. Satan must "unweeting [fulfill] / The purpos'd Counsel pre-ordain'd" (I, 126–127). His testing of himself and the worldly argument he has projected upon the audience have initiated the desired human trial, including the Son's discovery of the truth about his mission. With that assurance, poised in the stance of Jordan (where Satan had expected to stage all the trial, there "likeliest [to] find this new-declar'd / This man of men, attested Son of God" [I, 121–122]), we turn from God's unwitting "servant" Satan to His "begotten" Son. In him, God's creative will had moved upon human matter as it once through him had moved upon the material universe. Significantly, we are reminded of the similar trial of Job, from which Satan had learned nothing. With satisfaction, we hang upon the reported words of God—only to realize that we have really heard only puzzling voices, intimations, signs, hints, and doubts. God no longer walks on earth. Beyond the annunciation, then, we must gradually sense Jesus in the second stance. He stands alone in a desert of vast space and silence. God's puzzling way continues to be announced, moving in strange lights and shadows around the solitary figure: this is to be a new Job and new Adam, who paradoxically must conquer by "humiliation" (I, 160); he cannot yet confer salvation upon men, for now he must save himself in merit, through doubt becoming "perfect" (I, 166); Adamic appetite and fallacy must be offset by superior reason in a second Adam. The jubilant response of the angelic chorus, although reassuring, is as little enlightening as the jubilation of the hellish host. Heavenly conviction that the Son will "vanquish by wisdom" (I, 175) sounds strangely like that of the Elder Brother in *Comus,* especially when it believes the Son to be "secure / . . . though untried, / Against whate'er may tempt, whate'er seduce, / Allure, or terrify, or undermine" (I, 176–179). Although the Son is secure against direct hellish blandishments, neither he nor the attendant reader is secure against human doubts and fears. The drama will see the Son's doubts persistently rout Satanic assurance, in humanistic more than theological victories. Satan is to be the agency for the Son's assertion of strength in the "trial" of wisdom.

The stance now shifts firmly from creative Jordan and its questionable, though true, promises. Although, like that of the disciples, our "dramatic" physical stance remains behind, our penetrative mental attempt to understand Christian bereavement must follow. The figure of the exalted Son fades continuingly from the great moment of Jordan and the promises given the audience in the second annunciation; he is drawn away from the mission he was to "begin" (I, 186), from the sheep he is designed to serve, and from life itself. He first recedes into the renewed obscurity of Bethabara, where he is fixed for a moment with his followers,

> Musing and much revolving in his breast,
> How best the mighty work he might begin
> Of Savior to mankind, and which way first
> Publish his Godlike office [I, 185–188].

Then he all but disappears into the desert. The Word that Jordan promised he should make public seems to fall mute. Not only has he entered what may be a private desert of doubt, led on "thought following thought" (I, 192), but he also has been led to a site "deserted" of the men he is assigned to save, for he is "far from [the] track of men" (I, 191). The audience is mentally drawn to enter the dark absence with him. Thoughts like angels—or locusts—swarm in him. Inward prompting as well as outward annunciation has told him that he is elect in Milton's sense, but all such signs are distressingly "ill sorting with [his] present state" (I, 200).

The pain increases with each memory of an annunciation or of an inward prompting to save mankind. The seeming permission for him to feel himself divinely inspired, to command power and wisdom, and to defy death had anticipated each of the present temptations. Even as a child he had fixed his mind on truth and public good, convinced that he would "promote all truth, / All righteous things" (I, 205–206). He had then gained all knowledge requisite to the mission, much as Adam had gained like knowledge from Raphael and Michael; he had no need of the Athenian rhetoric offered by Satan. He had at times "aspir'd" also to directly "heroic" deeds against Rome and all "brute violence and proud Tyrannic pow'r" (I, 215, 216, 219); at other times, he had wished to persuade the unwary soul from error, in a higher-than-Attic rhetoric. (That is, he had wavered between the services to men typified by Michael and by Raphael.) He now recalls that his mother had encouraged such "aspiration," much as in other circumstances Satan had encouraged Eve:

> High are thy thoughts
> O Son, but nourish them and let them soar
> To what height sacred virtue and true worth
> Can raise them, though above example high;
>
> .   .   .   .   .
>
> For know, thou art no Son of mortal man [I, 229–234].

Like the voice at Jordan, Mary had indicated to him not only the glory of heavenly adoration but also the seeming promise that Jesus should possess the earthly throne of David. The Magi too had believed her child would be "king of *Israel*" (I, 254) . His own memory records still more overt gifts. His "aspiring" experience in the Temple not only brought him more affirmations of glory; it convinced him, too, that he was the Messiah of whom the Law and the Prophets spoke. (It also makes him vulnerable to temptations of priesthood and sagacity.) Although he has been told that his way lies through death, he as little realizes death's meaning as Eve did before the Fall. He fondly reconstructs the opening scene at Jordan, which had brought him to the time that he "no more should live obscure, / But openly begin" (I, 287–288) —but not until the final line of the poem is that promise of "beginning" echoed and fulfilled. In the present, the gentle statement that follows suddenly grows tense with the stir and clash of questions: "And now by some strong motion I am led / Into this Wilderness" (I, 290–291) . He awaits God's time and God's revelation of purpose, but carries a heavy burden of impatience and bewilderment.

He has considered three questions which, if they were increased in pressure, would become self-temptations: he has nearly exalted himself into God, assigning proof of his being and mission, not to God but, like Eve, to "What from within I feel myself"; he has aspired to all power and worldly wisdom ("public good . . ./ . . . all truth, / All righteous things") , in order to pit them against temporal dictatorships or corrigible error; finally, he has almost hoped that his Godlike formulation, "I am" (I, 263) , obviated death, carrying him instead "Through many a hard assay even *to* the death" (I, 264—italics added). He has not swerved to improper aspiration, but the audience is suddenly aware of the hair-thin line separating his legitimate hopes of service from the illegitimate ambitions of Eve. Like him, we are men whom the Chorus of *Samson Agonistes* will find entangled in the ambiguities of the divine will, "various [and] contrarious" (*Samson Agonistes*, ll. 668–669). Doubled doubts about both the initial aspiration and the subsequent degradation of the Son assail both protagonist and audience.

The setting both metaphorically and directly magnifies all his doubts. The once exalted "Morning Star" (I, 294) now moves toward fallen Lucifer and seeming oblivion—"a pathless Desert, dusk with horrid shades" (I, 296) that resemble those of Israel's typic wilderness and those of Hell. Audience stance becomes increasingly distant from the Son, who seems bent upon death in places "by human steps untrod" (I, 298). Neither he nor the audience can yet realize the soaring promise couched in the ambiguity of that phrase; for the time being, it can mean only that he is separated both from his followers and sympathetic drama. The reader must now remove from the narrative and dramatic conditions of epic to those of recorded dialogue, although he will briefly resume the initial dramatic stance at the beginning of Book II and at the end of the work.

The long period of superhuman meditation passes quickly by. Like Israel after its forty years' sojourn, the Son now ironically enters the Promised Land—the desert—of his mission. For one prelapsarian instant, the second Adam seems to renew the first as he existed prior to Eve. A form of human Eden is created when he, like Adam, awakens to human appetite. Unlike the first Adam, however, this Son can endure solitude. Around him, the wild beasts of the desert are as mild as they had been before Adam brought carnivorous death into the world. Like that other Eden, however, this soon discovers its Satan, disguised now, like Comus, as a holy pastor and "Shepherd" and hoping to be such a guide.[17]

[17] Elizabeth M. Pope, in *Paradise Regained: The Tradition and the Poem* (Baltimore, 1947), pp. 44–48, details the tradition for Satan's disguises. Unlike Uriel in *Paradise Lost,* the Son penetrates all disguises. However, Satan, despite himself, does act as a "guide," of sorts, moved by the purposes of God to lead the Son through necessary assay.

If he had once dazzled Eve's senses, he now hopes like Archimago to bewilder the Son's reason. What appear to be puns upon *Eve* nevertheless both guide Satan back to the first Eden and bring him near comedy as, in "quest of some stray Ewe," he returns "from field at Eve" (I, 315–318). Yet the thrust of doubt into this Eden, even if the Son has prepared himself by contemplation of the questions doubt will raise, is by no means comic. The Son had challenged the ways of God in leading him, not to the "open" salvation of men, but to his own isolation in the desert. In two stages, Satan, the false shepherd, enacts the doubt. The first stage of the trial, which ends in Satan's self-betrayal, probes Christ's human doubts, asking what "ill chance" (not divine will) brought him, "single" (I, 321, 323), into this desert, a Chapel Perilous from which no man has ever returned alive. If implication must insist that the speaker himself is then Death, the threat from physical "hunger and . . . drought" (I, 325) is thereby only increased. Although the question of the Son's saving himself for his own sake in order that the mission may be honored is primary, the second, and far more important, question of his mission to others swiftly gains full power. Satan inquires woundingly of his public service, "admiring" (I, 326) at the stance in the wilderness. Both of them all too clearly recall the stance of Jordan. At the end of Satan's speech, he lets slip his vainglory by saying that, even in the hellish desert, "Fame also finds us out" (I, 334). The plural number speaks volumes. Dialectically this self-betrayal is of great importance, for it openly demonstrates to the Son the essence of such mentality and of its choices. If such a revelation does not resolve the Son's questions, it nevertheless clearly shows the result of one deadly response. The Son therefore answers the charge of "ill chance" by saying that he, like the composing author in *Paradise Lost,* is guided by whoever "brought me hither" (I, 335). The obtrusive Satan and his concern about divine solicitude are shrugged aside with the quick rebuff, "No other Guide I seek" (I, 336). There is an altogether serious anticipation of the injunction *Get thee behind me, Satan,* directed both to Satan and the insistent self. If this were a comedy of manners, however, we would say that in his first stage of trial, that of the Son's personal fear of loss, Satan's affectation had been discovered and that he had been roundly snubbed.

The test is not finished. In a lightning-swift, deceptive shift from the role of supposed leader to that of supposed follower, Satan turns wholly to the second stage, in which the structural pattern of *Paradise Regained* is permanently established in the general appeals of "Bread" and "Word." [18] Although the materialistic and personal initial attack seems always to drive toward the Son's survival, it always broadens to include the question of his material service to his flock. Similarly, the ensuing attack upon spirit and meaning, if directed frontally to the public side of the Son's mission, nevertheless carries with one wing the question of the Son's mere survival to perform that service.

The two questions always diverge from a common point and return to it. When Satan begins the second stage by inviting the miracle of turning stones into bread, he is not such a fool as to tempt Jesus only with the food, even though it is true that the Son has "hunger'd then at last" (I, 309). The temptation is not so much to be Eve as to be the Eucharist:

> So shalt thou save thyself and us relieve
> With Food, whereof we wretched seldom taste [I, 344–345].

The taunting, allusive play upon fear of death should remind us that Milton does not dissociate this test of the Son from the crucifixion, but the immediate effect is to give extreme, objective form to the Son's present fear that God's way in the desert leads him only to death. If so, he should therefore take the collapsed mission into his own hands, for the duty of "salvation" would demand first his own human salvation. To this fear is added the seeming appeal from the public need of the "wretched" (if in that word Satan slyly embraces the Son as damned, he much more affectingly enacts all those whom Christ came to save). Reinforced by images both of the historical gift of manna to the Israelites and of the present godlike gift of Messianic bread in place of a desert stone, it seems to ask both compassion for others and fulfillment of the Son. For that matter, if this "food" were considered to be his own body, sacrificed as Host, even the first

[18] Fixler, in *Milton and the Kingdoms of God*, pp. 257–258, identifies the temptation of the banquet with "the Eucharistic sacrifice of Christ himself." Lee S. Cox, in "Food-Word Imagery in *Paradise Regained*" (*ELH*, XXVIII [1961], 225–243), associates "Bread" with "Word" as opposing the lies of Satan.

condition—loss of the material body—would become proper. The danger in both "salvations" is that merely human fear or compassion will seduce the Son's will from that of the Father.

The answer of the Son to the first assault predicts the pattern of his response throughout the tests. Although even the objection of passivity can be removed if one agrees that his consignment of his will into that of the Father exalts him into Being and Creativeness whereas choice of his own will would dissolve him into Satanic chaos, we need not seek that somewhat external defense of his action. We need only see that he rejects a prideful, materialistic simulacrum of being or action in order to insist upon its true, spiritual, form. That form is not enacted visibly save in himself, just as he is, however: hence the feeling of inaction reported by some readers. The Son's answer to the test of physical hunger in either himself or his flock is that one should lift his attention to the greater hungering after righteousness and the greater provender of a spiritual "Bread":"each Word / Proceeding from the mouth of God" (I, 349–350). The Son draws not Satan's so much as our attention to the manna God provided Israel in almost this same "barren waste" (I, 354). If men sought first the manna of God's kingdom, allusion all but utters, they then received manna for the body. If they sought the food of lies that Satan now offers, the desert would truly offer them only his stone, never God's bread. If they seek life, the desert stone may become Moses' life-giving rock.

The pattern here established—spiritual rather than material choice, which then happily guarantees that the material need will be supplied—guides the next, closely related step of the assay. If there ever was any serious question of identity, it now is answered; the Tempter is detected through his disguise. Yet Satan nevertheless requests "each Word" from the Son, promising "to hear attent / Thy wisdom" (I, 385–386). He is not wholly insincere, for he has some claim to knowing God's ways; occasionally, as with Job, he is an agent of those ways. However, it is clear that his notion of the "Word" supplied by him to men in their dreams and fantasies is as empty as his materialistic notion of the "Bread." He had deceived the Gentiles with lying oracles that were materialistically confined to place and person. Anticipating his rejection of

Greek philosophy in Book IV, the Son quickly both defeats the incomplete Satanic form and triumphantly presents the new (that is, the renewed) one:

> . . . henceforth Oracles are ceast,
> And thou no more with Pomp and Sacrifice
> Shalt be inquir'd at *Delphos* or elsewhere,
> At least in vain, for they shall find thee mute.
> God hath now sent his living Oracle [I, 456–460].

This Word, recapitulating the promise of the Nativity Ode, will not be limited even to the physical person of this Son, for it is to be spiritual, an "inward Oracle" (I, 463). Having elevated the conception of mere word into divine Word, the Son returns to the question of bread. Scorning the manna of God, Satan has lived on lies, "never more in Hell than when in Heaven" (I, 420). He is therefore, like a cadaver, "ejected, emptied, gaz'd, unpitied, shunn'd" (I, 414). "Lying," the Son tells him, "is thy sustenance, thy food" (I, 429) —like the ashes in *Paradise Lost*, Book X. Lies bait his self-entrapment and are the recoil of all his wisdom. He has foisted off his "delusions," lies, and destructive emptiness upon the Gentiles, those "wretched" whom he dared to represent as he opened the temptation. He had served them as the false ministers of "Lycidas" had served their own flocks. Now this deception is ended: "no more shalt thou by oracling abuse / The Gentiles" (I, 455–456). As for the Son, the inward Oracle is the living Bread and Word of God as long as the chain of Being indicated in the phrase "of God" is maintained. Far from retiring into passivity in all his choices, then, the Son actively chooses and even creates reality and substance. He has appeared within history as a living Oracle (I, 460) in order to redeem it. By contrast, the seemingly materialistic Satan can (with one exception) offer only banquets that vanish, kingdoms that disappear, and his own illusionistic entrances and exits. The exception to these pompous frauds is his material and spiritual fall toward the fiery purgation of chaff in the Last Judgment.

The Son's past and future victories are implicated in the present quick triumph, which causes Satan to be "inly stung with anger" (I, 466), the first of several progressive wounds he will feel in the course of the work (resembling his wound and fall from Heaven in *Paradise Lost*). However, the test is returned into his hands as Book I comes to a close. He softly brings the Word into doubt by suggesting that it is the sounding brass of mere preachment, quite unlike the difficult deed:

> Hard are the ways of truth, and rough to walk,
> Smooth on the tongue discourst, pleasing to th' ear,
> And tunable as Silvan Pipe or Song [I, 478–480].

Not only does he again cast the deeds of the mission in doubt and again anticipate the later temptation to the sophistries of Athens, but also he asks the Son to continue, for him alone, these winsome (and unperforming, and therefore meaningless) melodies claimed to be the Word, the living Oracle. The screw is excruciatingly tightened by the understated parenthesis: " (since no man comes) " (I, 484). Much of the original field of doubt—doubt of self, of public mission, of God—seems reopened. The Son's Olympian reply, however, in which he separates himself from further immediate dialogue, shows how far the argument has moved:

> Thy coming hither, though I know thy scope,
> I bid not or forbid; do as thou find'st
> Permission from above; thou canst not more [I, 494–496].

This speech allusively gives assent to the coming "permitted" crucifixion, but it also insists upon a central truth for both these sons of God: it is always only God's will that shall be done, for there is "no other Guide," the only question for them being their own assent or defiance. Satan indicates his own insubstantiality in the face of the question by disappearing, like most of the objects of his temptation.

The Son, although he declares he is of God, is again left absolutely alone with no place to lay his head, while brute "Fowls in thir clay nests [are] couch't" (I, 501). The conditions for doubt and assay have not changed, and for a swift moment the audience once more feels them in their full intensity. The brief epic nevertheless insists that all the while God's champion has been firmly but quietly raising a new Eden (and new epic) in this waste wilderness.

"More Show of Worth": The tests of nature and of wealth (Book II)

Book II, opening the second day of tests in the wilderness, descends slightly from the great abstract questions of divine Bread and Word to entertain their less general equivalents: the private appetite of the announced King and the wealth, the Son's by right, which according to Satan's worldly wisdom is the one way to public power and service. The Book swiftly reminds the audience of its methektic, "dramatic" involvement in the action by returning us to the stance of Jordan, there to renew in active, human terms the effect of the Son's inexplicable disappearance into the desert. For a brief time, the desert trial that constitutes *Paradise Regained* is made to exist not only for us, but of us, as we share with two apostles and with Mary the temptation of privation that Christ himself has been undergoing.

The doubts of the Son—and the temptations of Satan—are intensified when seen through the eyes of his followers, who must lack the Son's higher portion of divinity and who have as yet received none of his strength from trial. If he is uncertain of God's ways with him, Andrew and Simon are even more doubtful. They enact in anticipation the doubt that will make Thomas a proverb, Peter the traitor of a morning, and the audience men for whom faith in things unseen will be instinct with doubt and difficulty:

> Now missing him thir joy so lately found,
> So lately found, and so abruptly gone,
> Began to doubt, and doubted many days [II, 9–11].

The private and public definitions of mission, which Satan and the Son had considered so generally in Book I, are to dominate all the doing and saying of this second day, filling both Books II and III. Their central importance to the Son and needy mankind is therefore vigorously established in advance of the second day's testing. Men now helplessly return to Jordan, the place of their encounter with God, much as Eve and Adam had wished to repair where God had judged them and much as Christ's followers later will seek out the empty grave. The yawning emptiness of Jordan suggests that all men, like Andrew, Simon, and Mary, must learn that God is not confined to place, nor "gone" if the place no longer contains the confrontation. Unlike Satan, they will learn that an "inward Oracle" (I, 463) supposes an inward Paradise, even as they will learn from the Beatitudes an inward way to inherit the earth. For the moment, however, blankness suggests the total failure of Jordan's annunciation not only to the Son but also to his attendants at Jordan, making Jordan a desert for them. Because this test tries human patience to its utmost, it is useful to God as well as to Satan. It outdoes any of the lesser trials stage-managed by Satan alone.

Beneath this test, the "high hope" of those who await the Son has sunk into "relapse" (II, 30). Such human fears, whether in his followers or in himself, must tempt the Son toward precipitating his mission as leader of his despairing people. Not only his follow-ers but also his entire elect nation pray that "the Kingdom shall to *Israel* be restor'd" (II, 36). Under the stress of this anxiety, the fearful human flock alters prayer into imperative: "God of *Israel*, / Send thy Messiah forth" (II, 42–43). Although Andrew and Simon come into temporary peace with God's will at the close of their speech, and thereby indicate what must fill any spiritual vacancy, their doubts measure the severity of the coming tests of spiritual against worldly rule. Mary also falls to "Motherly cares and fears" (II, 64), casting some doubt not only on the recent annunciation but also even on that in which she was told of God's gift to her. Like the Son, she cannot understand how God's prom-ises to her and her Son could have come only to this. Although she reaches exemplary tragic patience like that of Manoa in *Samson Agonistes,* it is contingent upon the experience of the Son. Unlike *Paradise Regained* in its total action, she has not fully realized the implication of her memory that "he could not lose himself" (II, 98). Instead, his mission seems to her as blank as the Jordan is empty.

Such emptiness, such absence of any means that can resolve the annunciation or the doubts its delay has caused, extends from the human stance at the Jordan into the desert that is in part the direct metaphor of absence. There, the two Sons of God are equally vacant and blank, partly because the test is the only present activity possible but also partly because both the end of the trial and the operating energies within it are ambiguous, double-faced, ironic.

The renewed stance at Jordan with Christ's human followers had prepared us to receive the Son's preparatory musings in the desert stance as human. As if in reflection of the sifting fall of uncertainties around those closest to him, who are also heavily committed to the suspended mission, Jesus "into himself descended" (II, 111). If the phrase hints at a mysterious parallel of the Incarnation, it is also strongly suggestive of the full human descent into the human self, of psychological penetration to the innermost consciousness, of the continuation of the revolving doubts (and assurances) of Book I, of the dangerous full discovery of selfishness, and of the harrowing of an individual Hell. The Son may choose either to purge any threatening personal Hell and enter into his full mission or to make still further descent into the hell of Satanic selfishness. His possible pull to the latter is not disguised:

> All his great work to come before him set;
> How to begin, how to accomplish best
> His end of being on Earth, and mission high:
> For Satan with sly preface to return
> Had left him *vacant* [II, 112–116—italics added].

"How to begin": to that question, Satan, as a thing-driven alter ego or devil's advocate, will supply a multitude of worldly answers.

Although Satan will appear before his hosts in similar blankness and great doubt, the Son is in the more perilous position. Those who believe that in *Paradise Regained* Satan has no power should note the effect here. Because Jesus knows that the tempter is to return, his mind is held by the assay, much as the Lady was immobilized by Comus until the advent of Sabrina. He seems "vacant" of the "holiest Meditations" (II, 110) with which his spirit had been fed, and of the God whom those meditations had concerned. Even the promised return of temptation constitutes a kind of disabling preoccupation. The difficulty is not quite the same as that which Eve allowed herself, she who by "wandering" into the trial of temptation insured temptation's success, but it nevertheless creates a temporary mental desert. The waiting disciples have reason to fear.

While that vacancy holds, the stances of the poem fully accept the negativity which seems to possess both Jordan and the desert. For a short time we must rest with the blank Satan and know his truly fruitless meditations. He acknowledges that on this second day the Son has "ris'n" (II, 127), threatening to return the demonic spirits to Hell, but of course Satan cannot realize that he all but voices Christian mysteries. For that matter, he cannot act upon the knowledge he does possess—that the Son is no Adam, since he manifests "more than human gifts . . . / Perfections absolute, Graces divine" and an immediately threatening "amplitude of mind" (II, 137–138, 139) —for he returns to the temptation with dogged self-compulsion. However, he can recognize materialistic folly in others if not in himself. When Belial suggests tempting Christ with the lure for the first Adam—"women . . . more like to Goddesses / Than Mortal Creatures" (II, 153–157), as Eve had once seemed to both Satan and Adam—Satan believes that he pays proper tribute to the second Adam by rejecting in his place any attraction to Cain's tents. Instead, he proposes to fill the blankness of the lapsed mission with the delusive "substance" he himself would choose:

> . . . worth, . . . honor, glory, and popular praise;
> Rocks whereon greatest men have oftest wreck'd;
> Or that which only seems to satisfy
> Lawful desires of Nature, not beyond [II, 227–230].

His reservations indicating that he hopes to "wreck" the Son should not mislead us, nor should our sense of Christ as "counter-rock" encourage us. Satan knows that these desires have often enough misled men from God, and may at times realize that they will somehow "wreck" even him; nevertheless, they also represent his serious sense of the proper "Word" and "Bread" for the mission. He characteristically confuses the Son of God with the son of Philip, the former type of the hero; with Solomon, the earlier type of the governing sage; and with the Stoic misogynist, who refused beauty merely from fear of being "led captive" (II, 222) by it. Although it is amusing to see Satan assume the negative role of the Son when Belial assumes his own role of tempter, it is terrible to watch his shrewd but clumsy baiting of a trap with his self-delights, hoping to reduce the announced beloved Son into a mere Alexander the Great. Facing the questions of nature and wealth, both vacant sons will "descend" into themselves definitively.

Our knowledge of the Son's vacancy and of the Satanic plot to fill it with seemingly acceptable forms of glory and a respectably moderate use of nature increases the force of the test a hundredfold. More than ever, the line separating fulfillment from defilement of the mission becomes blurred. The things of the world are not open to categorical judgment as being either material *or* spiritual, as bearing the aspect of either Satan *or* Christ. They waver in the field of definition, composing a great *tertium quid,* much of which later will properly be employed by its distant Creator. Temptation therefore finds the field of action almost irrelevant, moving instead to motive—the reason for action that is one definition of will. Only their motives can reveal the radical differences between Satan's and the Son's estimation of how the world is to give service and be served.

When the Son first speaks in Book II, he almost recapitulates the apostles' cry of need as he considers the hunger which now assails him. Although nature formerly had held its demands in abeyance, it now asks his attention much as the apostles ask his presence. In both requests, "Nature hath need of what she asks" (II, 253). He attempts to fill the need with reliance upon Providence, whose power and will are stronger than its creature, Nature, and which can satisfy her seeming imperatives "some other way" (II, 254). The lesser hunger and need are bravely replaced with the greater, the hunger "to do my Father's will" (II, 259).

No matter how courageously his reason meets the question, however, there is doubt about that portion of his will that is unconscious, fantastic, appetitive. Dream allows him to "descend" to this more distant level of mentality. The dream is of course a test, as was the earlier dream for Eve. Into it, evil—or merely the id—can freely come. At the very least, the subject of the dream ("meats and drinks" [II, 265], if only those served Elijah by ravens or ministering angels) can offer a false comparison with Elijah, leading the Son to demand service to his natural needs. At the worst, it can indicate that he remembers all too well his reference to Elijah in Book I. There, he noted that after forty days Elijah had been fed. (He does not note another instructive forty-day period: after forty days in the wilderness of waters that removed Eden, Noah entered into a new covenant.) "The same I now" (I, 354) can therefore either express a demand for divine relief or a doubt of divine Providence. These "presages and signs, / And answers, oracles, portents and dreams" (I, 394–395) could easily be Satanic. Instead, they are no more than visionary "revolvings" of questions, again developing the grounds for belief in advance of the explicit test by Satan. "Fasting he went to sleep, and fasting wak'd" (II, 284), in allegiance to his own former words about the "Bread" of God and in example to all men of government by the inner man rather than by the senses.

Only now can the otherwise objectionable pun upon *raven* and *ravenously* exert its full Augustan force. The ravens that fed Elijah ("Though ravenous, taught to abstain from what they brought" [II, 269]) supply the Son a lesson in restraint of will and trust in God; if the ravenous nature can be controlled in the service of a higher nature, so much more should be the human. The Son's temperance makes the dream as little disquieting as night had been for Adam in Eden; it thereby institutes another restoration of mankind. He can say, with the morning light, that although "appetite is wont to dream" (II, 264), its illusions need not command the servants of God. This particular illusion, which did not illusorily "fill" the Son's vacancy, now gives way to the far more perilous, because apparently far more "real," dream that flies at noon. The nature of its illusion is hinted when the Son mounts a high place, thinking to seek out a cottage, herd, or sheepcote, perhaps to find out if divine will will now permit his hunger to be appeased in the natural way. He encounters instead an illusory Arcadia that composes a powerfully real temptation.

The first day of temptation had stressed wilderness privation and offered erroneous relief. The second day, although beginning in the confines of desert and natural hunger, will instead offer illusions of overflowing Canaanite abundance—first, as Satan had promised, of provident nature, and then of present wealth, the means to public power. The desert sands are magically replaced by a shady grove, seemingly nature's best rural work—the proper haunt for (suspiciously) Greek "Wood Gods and Wood Nymphs" (II, 297). Like Trianon or the Bower of Bliss, it is self-consciously Arcadian. It also resembled the groves of Peor-Baal. Its master, no longer the expressive eremite of Book I, is now a man of the fallen world and its powers, that arena announced for the Son's mission; he was bred in "City, or Court, or Palace" (II, 300). An earthly Eden in false restoration rises "like an Exhalation" (*Paradise Lost*, I, 711). If it resembles Pandemonium, not only the worldly history of *Paradise Lost*, Book XI, but also the metaphor of insubstantiality welcomes the sense that earthly capitals and their powers are illusions. (Historical Jerusalem, Athens, and Rome were themselves more nearly forlorn wildernesses than tempting capitals when Milton wrote; from his perspective, the objects of physical power were as insubstantial as those illusory objects of appetite.) Nevertheless, the "vacancy" in the Son's thoughts, and perhaps of his will, has suddenly been filled to overflowing. By giving Satan ironic leave to return, much as Eve had been given human leave to go from Adam, the Son will doubly relieve the vacuum—first, by receiving Satan's renewed temptation; second, by introducing true substance that will overcome temptation and overwhelm the Tempter.

At just this point, when the two sons again will become absorbed by dialectic, they once more remove from any sense of "dramatic" stance with the audience. Like the followers at Jordan, readers must now wait. The dialogue of course permits us to "know" more than the contemporary Simon and Andrew, but the vacancy of all those who wait in this action can be filled only with the confirmed self of the Son, which is still in process of proof. The dialogue resumes the preliminary conditioning of the Son's will. Although this process is distantly instructive to Christians and enormously interesting in itself, it is precedent to ritual. Our stance remains caught in the methektic suspense and patience of the disciples at Jordan (or by analogy, of Christ's followers during the night of prayer at Gethsemane); waiting and watching are commanded so that methektic action can resume, once the interior "descent" of the Son is ended.

The dialectic begins with renewed suggestions that the Son has been doubly abandoned by God. Not only is he more utterly cast off than the "fugitive" Ishmael (II, 308), the wandering Israelites, and the fasting Elijah, all of whom at one time seemed abandoned or accursed of God, but also God by such a time as this had always come to their aid. Woundingly revoicing the Son's earlier cry, "Where will all this end?" Satan notes, "Of thee these forty days none hath regard, / Forty and more deserted here indeed" (II, 315–316). The desert is a correlative of God's desertion of the Son and the Son's desertion of his mission to men. Time is made to seem a flood that quietly bears away God's present Noah.

The prior test of the dream has largely filled the vacancy in which the Son began this Book, providing him with a ready reply when Satan, who all too well knows that appetite is wont to dream, tries to reopen the temptation of hunger. Through this temptation, he leaps ahead to the first stage of a temptation to worldly kingship. Much as in Book I the question of bread and word had opened first upon private survival and then upon public dissemination of truth, so in the second Book the test of kingship first considers nature's private service to the Son before involving him in his public concerns. Although deceit infests Satan's words, his first statement is nevertheless true: all creation should serve the Son. Not only is he by general definition the Creator of all things (in his distant heavenly function) and lord of all things (in the original human definition that he, as second Adam, must in some way restore), but also, by the annunciation of Jordan, he is their present king. Even as a magnanimous ruler or saint, he need not relinquish command of nature, for command of a sort can "save" fallen nature much as its materials can save him; the pacification of the desert animals is just such an indication. Satan therefore presents Nature as pathetically eager to serve its Lord:

> . . . behold
> Nature asham'd, or better to express,
> Troubl'd that thou shouldst hunger, hath purvey'd
> From all the Elements her choicest store
> To treat thee as beseems, and as her Lord
> With honor; only deign to sit and eat [II, 331–336].

The alluring notion is discolored, even before Satan's miraculously insubstantial dinner appears, by a word associated with

Adam and Eve at the Fall—"purvey'd" (*Paradise Lost,* IX, 1021) . Even if the word did not raise the question of the propriety of serving appetite, along with related questions of its being the right season to assuage hunger, experience alone would lead the Son to reject any material offering from Satan. In every sense, it is unreal—like the apples of Hell. He has been offered not God-permitted material sustenance and beauty but only mirage, "dissimulation" (I, 498) , the waking form of his night's dream. Satan's command, "Deign to sit and eat" (III, 336) , is a dangerous parody of Christ's request at the Last Supper. Whereas the Son will present both the divine act and the material symbol of a higher "partaking," Satan presents not even the matter—only absolute illusion. Even the apparent human beauty and grace of the servants are really only the less-than-Greek emptiness of "Spirits of Air, and Woods, and Springs"—harpies, in the upshot—to whom the Son quietly opposes "Angels ministrant" (II, 374, 385) .

The artificiality of the banquet reduces Satan's argument that the Son should command such creations of nature to solecism. When Satan assures the Son that the food is not interdicted like the apple in Eden, he tries to cast the Son, rather than himself, as Doubter: "What doubt'st thou Son of God? sit down and eat" (II, 377) . The lack of punctuation after *thou* indicates, not hesitation about food, but doubt of the divine character, which all creation should of course serve. The temperate answer of the Son returns doubt doubly upon the Tempter and his "guiles," for the insubstantial provender disappears to the Hellish "sound of Harpies' wings" (II, 391, 403) . Both the giver and the gift always were disgusting as well as barren.

The Satanic mind quickly concedes that the Son's command of the question of natural service, that more limited application of the question of "Bread," has withstood bodily hunger and its illusions. The next stage of the trial sees Satan again shift roles, now assuming that of the cosmopolitan kingmaker to the simple young Nazarite who would be the Word. The doubts the Son had already revolved in his soliloquy are intuitively probed by Satan:

> Great acts require great means of enterprise;
> Thou art unknown, unfriended, low of birth,
> A Carpenter thy Father known, thyself
> Bred up in poverty and straits at home;

>Lost in a Desert here and hunger-bit:
>Which way or from what hope dost thou aspire
>To greatness? [II, 412–418].

This public stage of trial is closely related to the private one, offering as the "means" to kingship material gold, without which Satan assumes political and social virtue to be helpless. In the world he knows, all high public virtue makes its way only over the practical pavement of money. The stage of temptation associable with the Belial of *Paradise Lost* has given way to that of Mammon. The answer is unexpectedly humanistic. The Son "patiently" (II, 432) opposes both the means to kingship and the kind of sovereignty proposed by Satan. Poor, virtuous rebels—he as simple Nazarite tells the arrogant dictator, Satan—have often toppled materialistic autocrats. Such men are the true shepherds, opposing the false leaders offered by Satan in Book II and enacted by him in Book I. Not only are all of Satan's democratic presumptions in *Paradise Lost* overturned, but also the discussion of two types of kingship proclaims the final victory of the Son:

>But men endu'd with these have oft attain'd
>In lowest poverty to highest deeds:
>. . . and the Shepherd lad,
>Whose offspring on the Throne of *Judah* sat
>So many Ages, and shall yet regain
>That seat, and reign in *Israel* without end [II, 437–442].

But he turns from the apocalyptic to the exemplary. Not only will the form of kingship he chooses be that of suffering servant, its crown "but a wreath of thorns" and the mantle on his shoulders "each man's burden," but also each wise and virtuous man, by mastering his "Passions, Desires, and Fears" (II, 459, 462, 467) will be superior to any literal king. The microcosmic but spiritual soul is thereby elevated to far greater importance than the greatest macrocosmic but literal kingdom. The only other kingdom that "attracts the Soul" (II, 476) of the Son (an attraction Satan later will exploit) is the kingdom attained by guiding nations to truth, not mastering them by gold. Even in Satan's chosen arena of human history, the new heroism has achieved more glory than could either wealth or pride. Repeating the intimated sacrifice that closed Book I, the Son's human magnanimity considers the surrender of a kingdom more noble than its assumption; divinity considers it better to sacrifice a life than to withhold it.

The end of the trial is heavy with rebukes to all Satanic theory and practice of sovereignty, and to any ambition that asks rather than offers service. The entire Book has as radically redefined kingship as *Paradise Lost* redefined heroism, leading it away from the control of Cain and Satan to that of David, the virtuous Romans, and beyond, for Christian definition gradually will transcend even that of humanism. To the question, What does it mean that the Son has been announced as King? both sons have received answers that in large measure fill the vacancies with which the Book began. The Son can affirm that leading nations to right worship is "more Kingly" (II, 476) than any example of political kingship, thereby spiritualizing the word entirely. Satan, too, has perhaps learned from this "instruction." When he next tries to define kingship, it is within what he assumes to be the high reach of wisdom. Offering the knowledge of Athens in Book IV, he will add:

> These rules will render thee a King complete
> Within thyself, much more with Empire join'd
>
> [IV, 283–284].

If the immediate question of the Son's being King of Israel has not yet been met, that which is in some ways more important has been encountered and dispatched: he already knows how to be king over the wish to be a Satanic, worldly king.

"Witness Whence I Am": The tests of glory and of Israel (Book III)

The tests of the second day come in waves, still apparently emanating from the evil will of Satan though all the while operating within the announced "exercise" (I, 156) of God. However, in the center of the action both word and deed increasingly shift from the control of Satan to that of the Son, even as his exercise in patience and endurance continues. If his words when the brief epic opened were gnomic and laconic, in Book II his long defense of the magnanimous rule over self demonstrates not only the proper tempering of his own will but also the substance and authority of the new public "Word" that he will both embody and profess. The complementary wounds of Satan now increase. They will point him to the great folly of another battle with Heaven. The mounting triumph of the Son's Word over Satan's rhetoric has wrongly led some readers to infer that Satan and his words are therefore weak. Not so, but in Hell's perpetually rash hour, he risked hellish sophistry in combat with holy wisdom, the same holy wisdom that soon will reject as incomplete even the highest reaches of Athenian wisdom. A reversal (peripeteia) for both sons, implicit from the moment the Son willingly entered the desert, from this time forward reveals its measure and force.

Satan's sense of the waves of temptation is curious. Although the matter of each temptation becomes increasingly concrete, Satan nevertheless thinks that with each he has raised the stakes. To him, at least, there is no contradiction. He believes that to offer more things means to offer more of the world. To the Son, this hellish mentality becomes ever more gritty and offensive. When Satan as father of lies pitted fallacy against a "living Oracle," he had accepted this hazard; the more he offers trivial stuffs of illusory importance, the more easily the Son rejects them, even though they increase in value to Satan. Were it not that the Son's Word in refusal is important for victory within the epic and for instruction without, the dialogue would now come to an end. There is decreasing warranty for any external refutation of Satan's proposals.

This third assay will consider first the "Bread" of personal glory, tempting the Son either to demand it or to deny that he is an image of God. It then will challenge him as the Word, the Messiah, the promised leader of lost Israel. It is perhaps the most nearly dramatic of the temptations, if from drama we would ask the anger and judicial rebuke of the Son. He is no Samson *agonistes*, yet it is a highly significant moment when he moves from proper doubts of himself and implied doubts of God's way with him to an ardent defense of God. He then also "publishes" (I, 188) the grounds of most of his argument in *Paradise Re-*

gained. Whereas God made all and is to be worshiped for his creative manifestation—even of the present desert—Satan would only unmake and mar. The Satanic definition of glory and his prospect for the salvation of Israel necessarily must share in his nonbeing. The distance between the values and definitions of the two sons has become so great that the contestants seem almost to have abandoned dialogue in favor of absolute definition of their two attitudes towards the poem's stances. The audience is increasingly pressed, not only to understand the exemplary choice by the Son, but also to consider as ultimate two different statements of being:

> . . . his word all things produc'd,
> Though chiefly not for glory as prime end,
> But to show forth his goodness, and impart
> His good communicable to every soul [III, 122–125].

This is how the Son considers himself and the abundance of creation; Satan, on the other hand, presses a definition of nothing,

> For where no hope is left, is left no fear;
> If there be worse, the expectation more
> Of worse torments me than the feeling can.
> I would be at the worst; worst is my Port [III, 206–209].

For a time, the two sons compose a great paradigm for being and unbeing, and for correspondent human choices, resembling that of Heaven and Hell in *Paradise Lost*. In *Paradise Regained,* however, the audience more nearly awaits the conclusive proof than shares the test.

The Book opens upon the "peripeteiac" victory for the Son and a correspondent descent of Satan further into himself as he blankly admits that the second Adam has come splendidly through the test of "what is of use to know" (III, 7) . Although this admission must cast in doubt those things useless to know which Satan will now offer, it nevertheless permits Satan to open the familiar wound of the Son: if Jesus has such knowledge, why must he and it be hidden, "Affecting private life, or more obscure / In savage Wilderness" (III, 22–23) ? Should not virtue and wisdom be nature's brag, and is not fit fame as much due one's magnanimous self (so capably defended by the Son in Book II) as due the needy world? Again the worldly Satan flaunts the example of Alexander, who at the present age of the Son held all Asia, while the Son's desert spring seems to show no bud nor blossom.

Such a temptation Milton had felt strongly as a young man, but at his present age he is almost impatient with it; the Son easily condemns all report of fame that rolls illusorily in the world's mouth, whereas the speaker in "Lycidas" had found that condemnation difficult. If the author has suffered some loss of confidence in man, he has gained assurance of divine judgment: true glory can grow only in the City of God, for Circean throngs of the city of men are "a herd confus'd . . . / Of whom to be disprais'd were no small praise" (III, 49, 56). As a part of his judgment against politically fallen man, the Son's prophetic soul may ruefully judge the human constancy that will be shown himself on Palm Sunday and at Gethsemane. If this judgment seems harsh past all compassion or mercy, it proceeds not only from the Son's persistent removal of questions of value from matter to spirit but also from his demonstration to the Tempter that the essence of Alexandrian glory, the height of the old heroism, is to "rob and spoil, burn, slaughter, and enslave" (III, 75). The second Adam increasingly speaks in the victorious and judicial tones of the final Judge, for Gethsemane prepares an apocalypse. He condemns the imperial slaves of glory. They may think themselves gods, but like *Comus'* swine or devils, they roll "in brutish vices" (III, 86), already members of Satan's hosts. Satan and his worldlings are abandoned to their own delusive senses of glory; the Son's, like that of Lycidas, must derive from Heaven. Glory and fame "more humane and heavenly " must be sought in the new heroism—that of peace, patience, temperance. Its models are Job and Socrates, but even for them human glory is beside the point. The only possible true glory is that of God, for in him alone is there sufficient Being to possess, and judgment to know, glory.

"Murmuring" (III, 108) as he had at a similar intellectual defeat by Gabriel in *Paradise Lost,* Book IV, Satan suggests that such a Son is unlike the glorious Father, who (in Satan's comic extravagance) demands "Glory from men, from all men good or bad, / Wise or unwise, no difference, no exemption; / . . . Glory he requires, and glory he receives" (III, 114–117). The Son all but blushes like the angry angels in *Paradise Lost,* so fervent is his rebuttal: goodness and being have flowed out from God infinitely; if his creatures do not offer thanks, they then surely will offer—as Satan well knows—"Contempt instead, dishonor, obloquy" (III, 131) . Contempt for God therefore must involve contempt of oneself. The Son judges Satan with the extremely hard truth of *Paradise Regained*—that God gives his glory only to those who eschew human glory, because if they act as rivals and seek their own fame, they cannot avoid contempt, dishonor, and obloquy to both themselves and God. Satan, with increasing suffering, absolutely demonstrates this truth: "he himself / Insatiable of glory had lost all" (III, 147–148) . The economy of glory has its obvious counterpart and proof in this very desert setting. Increasingly, the fallen world is revealed to be the final desert.

So Satan finds that he must once again turn away from temptation of the self, to which the Son shows himself invulnerable, toward temptation for the sake of others. If not king of Israel for his own glory, will not the Son be king of Israel for bleeding Israel's sake? Is not that a duty? The Son answers that it is indeed, but that the enactment rests in the Father's time. In any case, it is not likely to be the material kingship that Satan or even his own human questions might envision. Although Jesus seems about to reiterate the defense of magnanimity from Book II, he instead moves steadily beyond it. Now comprehending most of his mission, he almost points the way to the Cross, where Satan will be finally defeated and through which each man can find his own "reign":

> Be tried in humble state, and things adverse,
> By tribulations, injuries, insults,
> Contempts, and scorns, and snares, and violence,
> Suffering, abstaining, quietly expecting
> Without distrust or doubt. . . .
> . . . who best
> Can suffer, best can do; best reign, who first
> Well hath obey'd [III, 189–196].

Although the Son states his service to man and God humbly, toward Satan, who occasions the suffering of men, he springs like a tiger: "Know'st thou not that my rising is thy fall, / And my promotion will be thy destruction?" (III, 201–202). All Satan's doctrines of glory and triumph are reversed, recoiling upon him derisively yet in final severe judgment.

For a moment, the "rising" and fallen sons of God, once almost brothers and even now ultimately concerned in one another, speak in utter frankness. This exchange can scarcely be said to be dialogue or even mutual self-revelation. It is instead their ultimate choice of identity. Satan, who is never without pathos when he realizes his fall, grimly wraps himself in his decision for destruction. He sometimes could wish for love from the Son's annunciative "gentle brow" (III, 215) rather than the sure confirmation of self-chosen destruction. It is desperation as much as continuing temptation that leads him to urge Christ to his apocalypse; Christ's absolute reign will hasten His own (apparent) destruction. But any sense of mutual sonship is rent sharply as Satan again attempts to bring obloquy upon God and man. He tells the Son, who has barely seen Jerusalem but wants to rule the world, that He, like Eve, must consult the "best school of best experience" (III, 238) if He is to know the world. Should that lure fail, Satan baits the opposite hook: the Son must know the world, if only to "withstand" (III, 250) its power with equal power. Satan cannot force himself to learn wherein power truly consists, for in that knowledge must rest his own destruction.

The Tempter therefore takes the second Adam up higher into a specular mountain, as Michael had taken the first. Time and space, history and geography, unroll as earthly powers pass in swift historical array, set amidst rich fallen lands pointedly unlike the barren but Edenic desert. Most of the kingdoms are Oriental despotisms, but sultanic Satan could not be expected to consider them distasteful. Nor could he adversely judge the chivalric kings of Europe. It is with such examples of kingship, then, that he urges Christ to assume his announced salvation of Israel, entering the historical world as king of the Jews, perhaps—realistically—in political alliance with Parthia. Satan, who can have as little affection for elect Israel as for the elect Son, seems to envision a combination of the historical kingdoms of David and the Eastern Alexander. Surely, he says, in still another judgment proceeding from the lateral flow of history, that is the way to be a savior of one's people. From this suggestive wilderness Christ can emerge as the new Moses, but unlike his predecessor he can "reign," possessing the East from *"Egypt* to *Euphrates* and beyond" (III, 385, 384).

Much as he had refused earthly wealth, the Son refuses again all the accoutrements of nationalistic power—"fleshly arm / And fragile arms" (III, 387–388), which are as foolish and inadequate in spiritual warfare as was cannon in Heaven. Like popular praise, this "cumbersome / Luggage of war" (III, 400–401), so dear to the old heroism, is cast aside. As for Israel and his supposed duty to it, he refuses to recreate the material and political welfare it threw away. In a renewed emphasis upon individual, microcosmic responsibility for one's own liberty, he insists that if Israel is captive, it has "wrought [its] own captivity" (III, 415) and in the political sphere must deliver itself. God will yet save it "by some wond'rous call" (III, 434), but not by means of a political champion. Although Satan's mentality will not permit him to recognize the apocalyptic implications of the promise that one day God will bring his spiritual Israelites to their "native land" (III, 437) past the cleft Jordan by means of a second Joshua, the narrative voice closes Book III in affirmation that the vow has come from Israel's *true* King.

The Son has vanquished most doubts of his mission by finding the full spiritual meaning of the annunciation, elevating the conception of fame from that of mob popularity to that of eternal glory, the definition of kingship from that of the throne of Israel to that of the self-rule which is an "everlasting Kingdom" (III, 199), and Israel itself from a corporation of bodies to a metaphor of the immaterial church, the self-elect: "So fares it when with truth falsehood contends" (III, 443). Wisdom both "humane" and heavenly has carried the day and predicted the final Judgment.

"Worth Naming Son of God": The tests of Sonship and of wisdom (Book IV)

The waves of testing on the second day break finally upon issues that seem to Satan both concrete and ultimate—the most lavish fruits his world can offer the Son with which to fulfill the mission. Succession to the empire of the world or to the mantle of "super-imperial" Greek philosophy are to him the supreme material gifts, carefully reserved until the end. Oddly enough, however, the issues for the Son return to those abstract concerns of Book I: the meaning of the "Bread" of his personal and material service, and the meaning of the "Word" of his public redemptive doctrine. The increase of matter proffered by Satan will demand not only the accustomed proclamation by the Son of a spiritual equivalent but also the opposing simplicity and spareness of those two symbols, or ikons.

The issues are of course in part historical, for history alone can supply Satan with his sense of the mission and of the heroism proclaimed for the Son. Satan is sure that if the Son is to be savior of the Gentiles he must become emperor of Rome, and that if he is to be Rabbi to the world, he must succeed to the academies of Athens. By refusing these historical definitions of his mission, the Son elevates the issues above all the patterns of history. Ironically, only Satan believes in his own suggestion for the proposed Christian path of salvation—first for Israel, then for the world. The Son as resolutely as ever has looked through the material illusions of even Christian history.

Perhaps for that reason, at the end of Book IV, Satan abandons the series of temptations that comprise the principal substance of *Paradise Regained,* moving to an entirely different kind of test. If judged from the Bible or tradition, it must be considered the final temptation of three, but Milton altered tradition so significantly that the scene at the Temple becomes distinct from the temptations of the desert. Although it has connections with them, it differs radically in place, character, and result. I am not convinced that the difference proceeds from a theophany. The annunciation at Jordan has already supplied as much revelation as Milton feels necessary to *Paradise Regained.* Nor am I altogether persuaded that the difference arises from a mysterious identification of the Son with, or as, God. The Son has intimated the part of his nature that is divine throughout, and Satan has recognized it insofar as his mind can receive intimations of spirituality. Although effects of theophany and claims of divinity are present in the final scene, it seems to me that its primary function is artistic. If the ending is considered in terms of stance and symmetry, it re-establishes a stance of annunciation but increases its applications, balancing the first scenes in the epic with the last.

As the final Book opens, it is Satan rather than the Son who now is found paralyzed within doubt, the test of kingship having routed his definition. He had hoped to sleek his tongue with persuasive rhetoric, thereby supplanting (or absorbing) that spare persuasion of Book I which the Son has elected to express the Word. Instead, doubt appropriately recoils upon the father of lies. What is more, image after image of pointless or nasty futility now assaults him—of the losing gambler, of flies defiling (sacramental) wine, and of waves beating against solid Christian rock. They all end apocalyptically in "froth or bubbles" (IV, 20) .

He still has a concrete gift to trade for a soul, however. He shows the Son Rome in its awful glory. Milton no doubt wishes his audience to remember that this historical grandeur has long since collapsed into nothing, reinforcing his assurance that history and its cities of men are thoroughly illusory. In that "desert," Christ could be "Son" (IV, 90) to an aging, corrupt emperor, replacing a sty [19] with piety and returning enslaved Rome to freedom. The Son elects to act, not with or against the historical human tyrant, but against the spiritual cause and type of tyranny: "What if I withal / Expel a Devil who first made him such?" (IV, 128–129) . If Satan wished to impel a miracle, he is at the verge of receiving in a new form the recurrent miracle of the Gadarene swine, the Battle in Heaven, and the Apocalypse. The general reversal is nearly complete. Not only does the Son translate all issues into those of the true Bread and true Word, but also he increasingly forces Satan beneath his foot, bruising the head of the Tempter, reversing the initial current of doubt and fear. As for the people of Rome, representing all the Gentiles, they, like the Israelites, have discarded their conferred liberty. No material aid can free "These thus degenerate, by themselves enslav'd" (IV, 144) . Sonship in such an inheritance cannot exercise even passing appeal to the Son of God. Political or pontifical Rome is dismissed as easily

[19] Woodhouse, in "Theme and Pattern in *Paradise Regained*," p. 177, notes Milton's skill in recalling Eve's apple in Rome's banquet.

as was the heroism of Alexander earlier, the two at best being only barbaric simulacra of the body of the church and of the new hero.

Satan's total materialistic defeat is signaled by his desperate offer of the entire unwanted fallen material world, really at the price only of the Son's agreement. The end of the Book and the end of all the long battle of the Son with Satan are made manifest in the Son's response. He becomes much more—or divinely less— than merely patient. He rises finally as judge of Satan's presumptuous ingratitude, which would give away the whole world he presumes to be his for the sake of pride, parodying the Creator's gifts to men and revealing the abysmal follies of materialistic intemperance. In essential decision Jesus banishes the foe "behind him," having now seen him "plain" (IV, 193). If evidence were needed, the question of the Son's identity has been firmly answered in a virtual theophany. The issue of personal service, of the "Bread" of life, is therefore closed.

The last illusory offer of the remaining worldly form of public service is preceded by Satan's fearful plea that he, too, is a son of God; that such trial (as Eve had confidently claimed just before the Fall) can hurt no one; and most importantly, that the kingdoms of the world were all fantastic anyway. Thus offhandedly does he again validate the Son's judgment against illusion. Eventually, Satan has to disbelieve the very objects he has offered for worldly belief. Instead, his mentality repeatedly tries to comprehend the Son's mentality, if only in order to sway it. Having tried, as with Belial, to work from within an understanding of the Son's virtues, he now tries to understand, and even to advocate, human wisdom. Having failed to find an Eve, Satan must now hope to find a Faust. To do so, he even accommodates himself to the Son's own annunciative experience in the Temple. Desperation as well as hope guides him, for this is the last ground remaining to him. (The audience recalls that the narrative gave force to his feeling of desperation by insisting that the victory of the Son will be "not of arms, / But to vanquish by wisdom hellish wiles" [I, 174–175]).

Even in the province of wisdom Satan still argues from history, however. He tries to meet the Son's refusal of humanist learning by arguing that one must know it, if only to counter it or, like Paul, to preach to it in Greece and Rome. He still has not realized that Eve's surrender to the fallacious argument of knowledge-from-experience will not recur, nor that his appeal from fame ("Be famous then / By wisdom" [IV, 221–222]) has long since been refuted, nor that the implied image of mental dictatorship ("as thy Empire must extend, / So let extend thy mind o'er all the world" [IV, 222–223]) will be disgusting to the libertarian Son. The Son does not disdain Greek art and philosophy, despite some of the alarmed outcries of anti-Miltonian criticism. Satan has forgotten that Jesus showed mastery of similar knowledge long ago, in the Temple; the Tempter is caught out again in obtruded diligence. The Son grants that although much Greek thought may be true, because of its limitations it still must be classified as speculative or fanciful, of no more intrinsic worth (though surely of less intrinsic harm) than that of the devils in Pandemonium. Acting himself as a Socrates,[20] he finds it merely incomplete or irrelevant. Greece groped darkly for ontological and teleological knowledge which he sees face to face; not finding it, the Greeks cast obloquy upon God by considering deity to be deterministic "Fortune and Fate" (IV, 317). The Son by no means abandons humanistic thought but insists that the end of education is the self-ordering that may exist without such thought. His own words and choices throughout have demonstrated his independent abilities. If the Gentiles have some light from the truth of God, it is because the original light still shines dimly in nature, but far better are the open and direct revelations of the Bible.

Surely our fondness for Greece need not blind us to the historical and literary premises that guided Milton here, especially when Satan attaches the hope of a dead empire to Greek thought.[21] If Milton is to be Christian at all, he must assume that the various and contradictory—if beautiful—speculations of Greek philosophy were at best only partly true; not only Christian apologetics but also Pyrrhonism had amply documented the charge. The true philosopher, soaring above the Aonian mount, is the true Chris-

---

[20] Barbara Lewalski, in *Milton's Brief Epic,* pp. 300–301, terms Christ "in some respects . . . a second Socrates living over again the experience of Socrates."

[21] Williamson, in "Plot in *Paradise Regained,*" p. 78, notes Satan's "stress on empire."

tian.[22] If Milton is to be Protestant, he must declare even that each man with his Bible is his own measure of truth, never the servant of the doctrines of any tongue. And if he is to persevere in premises that embrace both theology and history, then Christ must partly revoke but also partly fulfill and thereby enlarge the promises of Greece and Rome, as Paul significantly did in his sermon at Athens.[23] The Renaissance would find nothing contradictory in that premise, nor would it find in it reason to charge Milton with apostasy. His loving descriptions of Greece indicate no betrayal; they give way only because the greater Pan had come. Finally, if he as an English author is to soar above the Aonian mount, he must assert the claims of both Hebrew [24] and English poetry, carrying out his charge to himself in the "Vacation Exercise." Being divinely led, even as the Son is, he should exceed at least the *matter* of Homer. But all these explanations in the end are beside the literary point. In the action of *Paradise Regained,* Satan has attempted to establish one particular efflorescence of creatural grace and wisdom as somehow needful to God or as superior to divine wisdom. By such presumption he, along with Adam and Eve, had fallen. Being gifted with divine wisdom, the Son must not so fail, either as man or as more exalted agent of God. Surely it is not that Milton loves Greece less, but that he exalts Jesus more.

With his triumph in wisdom, the major tests of the Son are concluded, for Satan *now* is "quite at a loss, . . . all his darts . . . spent" (IV, 366). His defeat is so final that all his remaining efforts will be little more than swinges of the scaly horror of his

[22] Nesca A. Robb, in *Neoplatonism of the Italian Renaissance* (London, 1935), pp. 28–29, defines the Petrarchan philosopher as "the true Christian, but the Christian who has known how to use all culture as a means of moral growth."

[23] James H. Sims, in *The Bible in Milton's Epics* (Gainesville, Fla., 1962), p. 183, finds likenesses between Satan and the Athenian Sophists who heard Paul. See also Edna Newmeyer, "Beza and Milton: New Light on the Temptation of Learning," *Bulletin of the New York Public Library,* LXVI (1962), 493, for Beza's conviction that Greek learning leads to pride. Greece allegedly believed (as Satan in *Paradise Lost* tries to believe of his creation) that man's knowledge is of his own manufacture.

[24] Cox, in "Food-Word Imagery," p. 235, intimates that praise of Hebrew literature is praise of the Heavenly city.

folded tail. *Paradise Regained* here shifts stances and matter from dialectic and desert back toward the originating annunciation and the entrance of the Son from obscurity. By means of symmetrical balancing of terminal with initiating materials, a great literary resolution takes place. The action ends reminiscently upon a dream of the Son, his encounter with the mentality of loss, his annunciation, and the framework of divine care. The audience stance is relieved from its long patience at the edge of Jordan. It is caught up first in the threat at the Temple that evolves into greater exaltation of the Son, and then, through him and with the angelic chorus, into the Paradise that he has regained:

> A fairer Paradise *is* founded *now*
> For Adam and his chosen Sons, whom thou
> A Savior *art* come down to reinstall,
> Where they shall dwell secure, . . .
>
> . . . . .
>
> Hail Son of the most High, heir of both worlds,
> Queller of Satan, on thy glorious work
> *Now* enter, and *begin* to save mankind.
> Thus they the Son of God *our* Savior meek
> Sung Victor [IV, 613–637—italics added].

But before achieving that sense of a spiritually continuing Easter, the chronology of the epic must insist upon the second night and a signal image of the final victory over Satan, Sin, and Death. Even though the official tests have ended, the way toward Easter morning is necessarily attended still by Satan, for he is the type of threat or fear of death. In both desperate parody and contemptuous worldly wisdom, he presumes to judge his Judge, consigning him forever to the desert, agony, and death. Shaking his materialistic head, asking the perilous question that had once been so harrowing to Christ ("What dost thou in this World?"), he sneers that the kingdom announced at Jordan must be only allegorical, more completely illusory than the fantastic kingdoms of the world, as unreal as he believes eternity to be—a kingdom "as without end, / Without beginning" (IV, 372, 391–392). So timeless and spiritual a kingdom may quite escape from all realizable, redeemable time, including that of the Son's mission on earth. All spiritual equivalents to Satan's material (but self-admittedly unreal) objects exceed the grasp of Satan's mentality. It is a mark of the unreality of both him and his material world that, despite his claims for the reality of the objects of history, he threatens the Son with only a night of dreams and the spurious dangers of natural tempests.

The dream might once have been terrible, for it intimates a fall into chaos. Together with the correlative "dehortatory" tempests,[25] it forms a Chapel Perilous, beset with images of death and Hell, "Infernal Ghosts, and Hellish Furies" (IV, 422). The patient, untroubled Christ, now resolute because of the very tests with which Satan had hoped to destroy his resolution, is as little shaken by these natural yet inconsequential fears as he was after the dream of Elijah. In the similar morning that follows, nature merely uses the dampness to restore an Eden, as Christlike flowers revive and birds soar in Easter carolings.

Into this renewed Eden, Satan for the last time comes to attack a vulnerable man, threatening the Son with the death that the night had portended and urging precipitate selfish relief—"not when it must, but when it may be best" (IV, 476). He is dismissed as easily as the storm, the two being as "false" as the heroism Satan had earlier purveyed. Satan, not the Son, suffers the fury of the passional storm. He rages that he, too, like man, is a son of God, and that either man or Satan may be more substantial than a (Gulliverian) *lusus naturae,* "Virgin-born" (IV, 500). He pushes toward supernatural knowledge of the metaphysical worst, always his port, by bearing the Son miraculously to the Temple.[26] He scornfully (but self-analytically) says that this which they have placed beneath their feet is the Father's house, and that "highest is best" (IV, 553). He perhaps thinks to anticipate or reflect the Crucifixion by thrusting the Son aloft into what ap-

[25] John M. Steadman, in " 'Like Turbulencies': The Tempest of *Paradise Regain'd* as Adversity Symbol" (*MP,* LIX [1961], 82), identifies Satan's argument from apparent evils as "dehortatory," opposing the exhortatory argument that anticipates good fortune.

[26] For a full discussion of the complexities of temptation in the Temple scene, see Elizabeth M. Pope, *Paradise Regained: The Tradition and the Poem,* pp. 99–102. Frye, in *The Return of Eden,* p. 141, shows that the Temple becomes the temple of Christ (which of course is also the inward Paradise, the upright heart and pure, of Adam and the narrator in *Paradise Lost*).

pears to be certain death; like Comus with the Lady, Satan meets rhetorical defeat with attempted violence. Certainly he hopes to "begin," as with the stone of the first day, by finding out "what more thou art than man" (IV, 538), and by again demanding, with the thief on Golgotha, that the Son save himself from physical fear (and thereby "save" himself from God's will and the salvation of men). He dares finally, in a last reflection of the tests of "Bread" and "Word," to move from that threat of fear to the question of the Word, by quoting Scripture.

The recoil that he engenders provides a triumphant victory for the Son, of course, as he "perseveres upright" within the spiritual reality he has championed throughout, while Satan falls again in the material world he has represented. Far from having been brought to despair of God, the Son has always distrusted Satan, and the present recoil fastens absolute self-distrust upon the Adversary. If the Temple is a spiritual image of Heaven to the Son in his victory over Satan, it is also an image of all the material glory he has put beneath his feet and an image of similar redemption for all men. The Son ironically has fulfilled for men Satan's request of Book I—"save thyself and us." Epic similes at once reinforce the literary point: God's Son has triumphed over "Earth's Son" (IV, 563), the new oracle supplanting the bestial sphinx, which to its own cost had badly defined men. The sometimes local test in the desert is thereby led into both universal literary application and almost infinite theological significance, stressed by the ironic internal return to an annunciation impelled by Satan and by external analogies with the original exaltation of the Son in Heaven; with the Battle in Heaven; with the temptation, judgment, and restoration of Adam, together with the corresponding alteration of physical Eden into a physical desert that nevertheless can offer spiritual Paradise; and with the Crucifixion, which for Milton "means" that the Son nails his enemies to the Cross; and with the final Judgment and purification of the earth.

The recoil that is Satan's eternal punishment is seen not only in the repeated annunciation of the Son as being of God—this time, in an immense step forward, not at Jordan but at the Temple of Jerusalem to which the boy Jesus had prophetically come and which the Savior will both cleanse and in a sense inherit, in place of an Israelite or Roman throne—but also in the true gift to the Son of a Lycidian banquet shaming all those illusory cates contrived by Satan. Like the lesser Job, the greater has found his possessions restored. The victory of the Son in Heaven, in the flesh, and in the typic wilderness has countered the falling-away of the first Adam. The sons of men now can anticipate a still "fairer Paradise" (IV, 613), when eternity will have eradicated all temptation. There is every indication, that is, that the Son redeems men only for the possibility of Heaven, not from earth, for here each man still must choose his own Paradise or Hell. The long and inexplicable sojourn in the desert has ended with its eternal blossoming, the token of both the Resurrection and the New Jerusalem, which is the reborn form of the entire earth.

However, like the Nativity Ode, *Paradise Regained* holds that both the resurrection of the Son's body out of time and the purification of the world from history into eternity must await the full process of human time, even if the models of both appear recurrently within time and beyond it: "wisest Fate says no, / This must not yet be so." Instead of impelling his mission at once by confronting Jerusalem, Rome, or Athens, the Son departs the epic almost as he had entered it, still in human terms "obscure, / Unmarkt, unknown." This disposition guarantees artistic symmetry. It also announces Christ's victory far more signally than did the scene on the Temple. His doubt has been purged and his vacancy filled. Whereas he initially doubted because the annunciation proclaiming that he "no more should live obscure, / But openly begin" had seemed denied by the desert, he now knows that the desert and obscurity have instead supplied the beginning. God had also said that the Son's great victory was to be one of "Humiliation and strong Sufferance," which would overcome "Satanic strength / And all the world, and mass of sinful flesh" (I, 160, 161–162). The desert has provided the full form and action of that contest. Artistically, the quiet return will reassert the annunciative Jordanian stance for the audience, demonstrate his comforting presence to the waiting apostles, and convey a blessing to Mary. It will also continue the Son's triumphant humility and substantiality as contrasted with the pompous illusions and vacuity of Satan. In a sense, the entire mission, as well as the brief epic, is here concluded, despite the charge of the angelic choir, "Now enter, and begin to save mankind" (IV, 635). The form of the Son's victory and of the consequent spiritual redemption of mankind has been realized; there remain only assured predications. Those deeds, even the Crucifixion itself, will be almost anticlimactic, because for the Son it is the motive (the choice, the will), not the consequent deed, that most matters. The will and new heroism of the Son, as "exercised" in the agonistic obedience of *Paradise Regained,* have fully countered the wills and old heroism of Adam and Satan that led to massive disobedience and fall.

But, it may be objected, if the strife is over, the battle done, in what sense is this hero of patience and triumphant wisdom a "savior" of men? Is the question still as baffling as it was when the Son and Satan first entertained it in the desert? I am not certain that within the brief epic Milton abides the direct question, for he is concerned primarily with spiritual resolution for the mission. It is perhaps for this reason that the heavenly hosts speak of his "beginning" to save mankind. The idea of a total redemption by the Son is flawed at the outset; there can be no neat symmetry—first a fall in Adam, then a redemption in Jesus—because Adam fortunately repented and in some measure "redeemed" himself. His first disobedience was followed by his own recaptured obedience. Furthermore, in *Paradise Lost,* types of Christ prior to the Son had encountered all the forms of salvation, including salvation from physical as well as from spiritual death. It is difficult to avoid the conclusion that for Milton "th' exalted man" (I, 36) of *Paradise Regained* is in part exactly that: an exemplary man holding true the image of God in man, but not otherwise directly effecting the salvation of other men, any more than in the poem he would effect the literal salvation of Israel and Rome. Divinely, the Son always manifests the creative counterpressure of compassionate, creative grace against man's swerve toward sin and death. Humanly, he supplies as well the consummate model of absolutely creative human choice. Beyond that, men continue in that freedom which Satan somehow dimly understood but perverted when he told the Son, "Save thyself." As God had supplied the

Son, so the Son supplies man, with the "beginning" of his salvation; but the choice and accomplishment must be man's own.

To some readers, such a doctrine involves blasphemy, reducing the Son to man and suggesting that he is not wholly necessary in the scheme of salvation. To others, it involves another form of blasphemy by elevating each man into a "Son of God" (IV, 520). These opposite objections unreasonably contest Milton's position. For the purposes of *Paradise Regained,* he merely takes seriously the general epithets "son of man" and "Son of God." As the sin of the first Adam marks the sons of men but does not damn them if they choose to be sons of God, so the "redemption" of the second Adam marks men both by grace and by example but does not save them if they elect damnation. For man, there are no impassable gulfs or Great Walls of definition set between his being son of man, son of God, and adoptive son of chaos or Satan. The choices for men constitute an extremely broad and active field. In *Paradise Regained,* the Son again chooses ultimate aspiration toward God. Satan again chooses ultimate alienation. Both sons partly manifest and partly symbolize those ultimate choices or commitments. In a fully exemplary sense, then, they thereby can be said to "save" or "damn" those men who consciously or unconsciously enact those choices. In almost every other sense, men themselves damn or save themselves.

Yet there remains one final distinction. Milton does not abandon his belief in the transcendent reality of Jesus and Satan. Great examples for mortal men though they are, they also exist supernally and infernally. The very power of their commitments seems to confer upon them potency and atemporality on a level far above that of merely human sons of God. They have been designated as objects, or examples, or types of human choice. Although emphasis usually rests overwhelmingly upon *human,* it must nevertheless permit Milton his full sense that Satan and the Son are also objects, not merely poles, of human ethics or mentality. This firm, if sometimes shadowed, belief of Milton's can direct us to a final sense in which his Christ may be said to be savior. Of the great objects or symbols in *Paradise Lost* and *Paradise Regained,* only Adam and the Son are "made flesh" along with historical men. However, whereas Adam selfishly discards his promised godliness, the Savior freely surrenders his exaltation. Perhaps his divinity, like the magnanimity championed by the Son in *Paradise Regained,* is most fully realized in the seeming surrender and extinction of divinity. Incarnation may best "prove" divine compassion. If Christ chooses the human struggle alongside man, it becomes in a sense his struggle *for* man. If he shows man by truly upright human example what patience and wisdom can achieve, the demonstration may very nearly save man. I believe Milton does not intend to show that redemption has been inhumanly conferred, but instead that it is achieved in the height of the human choice for God. It is then that man is restored into the sonship of God.

[6] "A Person Rais'd"
Election and Redemption
in *Samson Agonistes*

If *Samson Agonistes* were no more than a magnificent but perhaps unsuccessful imitation of a Greek tragedy, there would be little reason for considering the effects of stance or even of matter in the drama. Classic tragedy in its very form and setting tends to determine physical place and action, the nature and general judgment of the Chorus, and the transforming effect of reversal or recognition. Because *Samson Agonistes* also soars somewhat above the Aonian mount of classical models,[1] however, becoming—in T. S. Eliot's sense—almost more a "poem"[2] than a play, even Milton's tragedy can find such considerations relevant. The major addition to classic drama is of course the Christian involvement of both the hero (as a type of Christ or of a Christian) and the audience.[3] Furthermore, the fable is again considered to be "true," so that song and substance again are one—a present action within Chris-

---

[1] D. C. Allen, *The Harmonious Vision* (Baltimore, 1954), p. 94: Samson moves beyond formal tragedy into God's greater *"fabula."*

[2] A more recent restatement: *"Samson Agonistes* is a dramatic poem. It is not a play. . . . Words replace stage action" (Roger B. Wilkenfeld, "Act and Emblem: The Conclusion of *Samson Agonistes" ELH*, XXXII [1965], 161).

[3] For a major modern statement against the play as tragedy, see Martin E. Mueller, *"Pathos* and *Katharsis* in *Samson Agonistes," ELH*, XXXI (1964), 156–174. For a similar statement against the play as Christian, see William G. Madsen, "From Shadowy Types to Truth," in *The Lyric and Dramatic Milton*, ed. Joseph H. Summers (New York and London, 1965), pp. 95–114.

tianity, not an imitation of such an action. Christian doctrine thereafter complicates the classic form by significantly reducing some elements even as it significantly increases concentration upon the agonists: Samson, Manoa, and—by Christian implication—the methektic audience.

In enlarging the scope of action for the hero, *Samson Agonistes* notably decreases the directly participative roles of the Chorus and most of the other characters. Samson and Manoa become more confident in both doctrine and poetry than is the Chorus. Because these two are their own best Chorus, the Chorus usually learns and receives judgment from *them*. Perhaps for that reason as well as the nature of the fable, the Chorus often functions as a number of specific Danites heavily involved in Israel's fortunes; it is in that sense more directly concerned in the play than is the usual Greek Chorus, but in another sense it has surrendered its unitary function and become individuated—members of an Israelite group, rather than collectively a Chorus. Similarly, although the remaining characters are by no means reduced to allegorical roles any more than is Satan in *Paradise Regained,* like him they seem somewhat less than necessary for the meditative agon of the hero: the early Manoa becomes in part the empty wish of Samson for easy release, Dalila the renewed question concerning God's will for Samson both in his original strength and in his present impotence, Harapha and the Officer projections of Samson's reviving championship of God [4] against Philistia and Dagon. For the very reasons that produced such reductions, however, the action of the hero himself seems vastly increased over that in most classic models.

The tragedy threatens to burst its chosen unity of place by indicating the offstage temple of Dagon as the final and most true (if unseen) setting for Samson's phoenix-like action. The stance there, toward which most of the play impels us, is eventually far more "real" than the given stance in Gaza. The tragedy threatens also to burst the unity of time, for God's will reaches not merely to a house (like the house of Atreus or of Cadmus) or to the elect

---

[4] Roy Daniells, in *Milton, Mannerism and Baroque* (Toronto, 1963), pp. 213–216, shows that Samson both witnesses deity like a Greek tragic hero and avenges God like a Hebraic champion.

nation Israel, but to all the generations and even to the end of the race of men.

Inevitably, it is Samson himself, the tragic personage in a Christian drama, who most causes the play to expand significantly beyond even the classical unity of hero. Milton has reductively divested him of almost all traces of the barbarous folk hero or the solar figure. Little remains of his association with Israel except his comment upon a self-enslaving nation, a comment almost as appropriate to Lycidas or Adam or Milton himself as to Samson. Instead, his association with Christian audience and Christian meaning becomes paramount. In the two major stances of the action, he, as representative for the audience, conducts us first into the hell of physical-spiritual enslavement, then leads us to a place of deliverance. In that exemplary action, he also enacts the natures of the first and second Adams.[5] Their singular elections are united in his beauty and strength. Their single temptations concerning the use of God's elective gifts and human freedom of will are combined in him. In a sense, their temptations are expanded, doubled: the line at which God's leading leaves off and his own begins is for Samson always more dim, causing him to be guiltless in a first marriage but guilty in a second, guilty in desiring his own death but guiltless in following God's mysterious pathway through death and agony into general redemption.

More than anything else, perhaps, the death and reward of the tragic personage in *Samson Agonistes* mark the play's movement beyond most classic models of tragedy. As Samson reflects Milton's definition of a new hero, so his tragic agon and death receive new interpretation and significance. As agonist, Samson is both a heroic athlete in God's cause and a man enduring moral agony. In the one character, he struggles against Dagon; in the other, he opposes his own weakness, guilt, pride, and despair. The audience, too, should discover in the Christian agon both a grueling victory in its Olympiad and an exalting defeat in its Theater. The

---

[5] For the interpretation that Samson enacts both Adams, see A. S. P. Woodhouse, "*Samson Agonistes* and Milton's Experience," *Proceedings and Transactions Royal Society of Canada*, sec. 2, ser. 3, XLIII (1949), 165. See also Ernest S. Gohn, "The Christian Ethic of *Paradise Lost* and *Samson Agonistes*," *Studia neophilologica*, XXXIV (1962), 243–267.

strange death that looms ahead for Adam and the Son in their agons rests almost at the heart of *Samson Agonistes,* in which a death both for guilt and for God's service becomes a victory of sorts. Death and sin are transfigured in the symbol of the phoenix:

> . . . erewhile a Holocaust . . . ,
> Revives, reflourishes, then vigorous most
> When most unactive deem'd,
> And though her body die, her fame survives
>   [ll. 1702–1706].

In *Samson Agonistes,* this figure is no mere pious but vague promise of an afterlife. In the same semichorus, Milton pointedly invests the life of Samson (and Adam, and Christ) with its full significance:

> But he though blind of sight,
> Despis'd and thought extinguish't quite,
> With inward eyes illuminated
> His fiery virtue rous'd
> From under ashes into sudden flame [ll. 1687–1691].

Such strange glory of singular election, such purgative flames of trial, and such redemptive purgation in sacrifice variously light the ways of all Milton's heroes. Each becomes a human burning bush in which God is revealed.

Somewhat more generally, the phoenix image also associates the tragic experience, Eden, and the entire created world with the action of Samson. His life prepares a progress of reflective stances: glorious creation, chaos or dissolution, rousing motions, exalted service ("This day will be remarkable in my life / By some great act, or of my days the last" [ll. 1388–1389]) , purgative fire, resurrection. From such action comes the "new acquist / Of true experience" (ll. 1755–1756) that concludes the tragedy, which is also a justification of God's ways to men in both the most general and the most personal of applications. It clearly bears both sorts of meaning for the author. Milton at the close may justly insist with Manoa, "Come, come, no time for lamentation now, / Nor much more cause: *Samson* hath quit himself / Like *Samson*" (ll. 1708–1710) . If Prospero is a projection of Shakespeare's mortal farewell to his fancy, Samson serves for that of Milton. The revived hero of Israel is a fitting last creation (in assigned position, if not in chronology) for the blinded poet, who with it could "quit himself" in comparable strength.

The phoenix image, together with the implied design of God, extends *Samson Agonistes* beyond the classic model in yet one more way, threatening to move the play beyond tragedy entirely. Although one might suggest the term "elegiac tragedy" [6] as a description for the play, the question still stands: Can a tragedy be Christian? As Dante saw, Christianity may present a divine comedy of ends that is nevertheless a particular human tragedy within the process of living. In such a work, we may feel excruciating immediate pain for suffering man even as we realize the most exalted joy in a general reconciliative triumph. Milton had written exactly such a poem in "Lycidas." The morality plays and some of the drama of T. S. Eliot provide other Christian parallels. It is as if a "harmonizing" double vision is empowered to witness lateral human agony and at the same time to see its meaning and "meed" within divine ("vertical") peace and light. Quite generally, *pathos* (as in the Passion) and *drama* (a creative doing) have always been closely interconnected in Christianity. Because the Fall and the Crucifixion are necessary within the Christian sense of human meaning and experience, the *pathos* will be inescapable. Because such suffering is always seen within the context of God's will, however, in which the causes of suffering may be purged and the sufferers redeemed, the *drama* is almost certain to demonstrate renewal. The fortunate conclusion by no means lodges the work in either a Popean evasion of particular suffering or in a retreat from tragic form. Milton never argues that partial evil is universal good. Yet if the agent comes to despise that evil and to redeem his time by choosing that goodness shall correctively operate in and through him, the resultant energy can be spiritually creative, redeeming not only himself but also those who witness.

[6] Joseph H. Summers, in "The Movements of the Drama," in *The Lyric and Dramatic Milton,* ed. Joseph H. Summers (New York and London, 1965) , p. 154, notes that we may invent a new term for Miltonic tragedy but adds that "it seems unlikely that a new word will help us much with the realities of the drama."

The redemptive, more than Aristotelian, purgation which Samson undergoes leads him to a great regenerative action for God and for himself. Milton's references to Paraeus and Gregory Nazianzenus probably permit us to expand classic pity and terror to include the conviction of sin and repentance. If so, the tragedy will see Samson proceed from the infernal sin in which he was "The glory late of *Israel,* now the grief" (l. 179) to the purgative repentance in which he finally becomes God's "faithful Champion" (l. 1751). Unlike the earlier works, *Samson Agonistes* begins long after the typic Fall. On this occasion, the clock reads 11:00 P.M. during the great darkness before the Easter dawn. Tragic attention rests now upon the regeneration of the will; it must be roused from the wish for mere easeful death, which could be given by defeat or victory indifferently, rather than for strenuous, agonic death that would be the gate to life. In enacting the tragic role of his peculiar election, Samson also reveals the form of the general believer moving from "fallen" and blinded Adamic sinfulness into upright faith and sight.[7] Catharsis or lustration, too, has become strongly Christianized, intimating the Christian form of redemption.

Although involving the action and the hero as they embody the cause, the theory of catharsis was always intended to apply primarily to an audience, much as the Roman Catholic Mass in part dramatizes Christ but intends the action to be "for" the worshiper. Three applicable effects of such purgation for an audience—homeopathic, "ethical," and Christian[8]—are joined in *Samson Agonistes.* An ulcer or ulcerous passion is cleansed; inward light is granted to the soul of the blinded, Oedipal sinnersaint; and the "vertical" phoenix, opposing the lateral images of

[7] M. M. Mahood (*Poetry and Humanism* [London, 1950], p. 211) considers that Milton found his best "pattern-hero" in Samson. George Williamson, in "Tension in *Samson Agonistes,*" in his *Milton and Others* (Chicago, 1965), p. 101, notes that Samson's insight is contrasted with the Philistians' internal blindness. See also John Huntley, "A Revaluation of the Chorus' Role in Milton's *Samson Agonistes,*" *MP*, LXIV (1966), 144.

[8] Paul R. Sellin, in "Sources of Milton's Catharsis: A Reconsideration" (*JEGP*, LX [1961], 714), and T. S. K. Scott-Craig, in "Concerning Milton's Samson," (*Renaissance News*, V [1952], 47–48), discuss the implications of lustration in *Samson's* catharsis. The concluding holocaust also supplements Scott-Craig's discussion of the "loosing" implicit in the catastrophe.

oceanic loss, figures the union of self-knowledge with divine knowledge in a repentant sacrifice, which in turn leads to renewed or increased life. The audience is asked to "stand" within the drama beside the hero and his interlocutors. Tragedy will methektically purge the audience, not so much of abstract pity and terror, as from crucial errors of choice and judgment. In *Samson Agonistes*, Milton has provided an epitome of his practice: ritualistic participation in the divine act of creation by the author, by the subject and style of the work, and by the audience. In stating that he never meant the drama for the stage, Milton may in part have intended that we envision it as being "for" and of a vaster stage—that on which a part of the great poem of God's design is enacted, well or badly, by all humankind.

Milton always took enormous risks in handling Christian subjects, as criticism of the last half-century has often pointed out. However, as was suggested in the Introduction, it has not always shown comparable awareness of the prizes he stood to gain if the risks were met. In *Samson Agonistes*, the possible prize is a unity of artist with art, audience, and a supposed reality long since lost, remembered dimly only in some Greek works and perhaps the medieval church play. The risks and opportunities are met almost flawlessly. The play mutually involves three great illuminative or redemptive patterns: (1) the dynamic wayfaring of every Christian from despair, through an apathetic "vindication" of God, to a participative celebration in divinely ordained regenerative action; (2) the progress of Christ (and partly of Adam) from election, through debasement, to restoration, in a mysterious victory over death; and (3) the "doing" of the classic tragic hero, often similar to that of the Christian martyr, who because of weakness falls from an extraordinary height of service but who, by means of suffering, recovers to ennobled understanding and renewed service. (A tragedy somewhat like that of *Samson Agonistes* could have been written about the Apostle Peter). Structurally, the drama's five central episodes symmetrically assign the two initial segments of interview with Samson to the "fallen" Israelites, the central one to Dalila (a Philistian who should have been an Israelite wife), and the last two to the falling Philistians. The stinging thoughts that assault Samson before the middle are transformed to stinging assaults upon the Philistians thereafter. The ending, although still somberly meditative, is nevertheless also militantly triumphant. Both the poet and the Creator may claim from the great demonstration a *nunc dimittis:* "his servants he with new acquist / Of true experience from this great event / With peace and consolation hath dismist" (ll. 1755–1757).

"The Rarer Thy Example": The trial of election and of diffuse despair (lines 1–325)

The first words in *Samson Agonistes,* developed as prologue by the agonist alone in his "wild Wood," contain the moving energy of the entire tragedy:

> A little onward lend thy guiding hand
> To these dark steps [ll. 1–2].

To whom does he speak? To a literal Greek *kophon prosopon,* a technical "mute person," perhaps, but also to the approaching chorus; to his "guide" in the temple of Dagon; to his tempters, who lead him through and beyond his original doubts; to his own restless mind; to God; and to the audience "to this act" (*Hamlet,* V, ii, 346). The imagery of *Samson Agonistes* is so penetrative and commanding, after the relatively mean language of *Paradise Regained,* as almost to constitute one definition of drama, of *doing.* As the action begins, we are asked to see ourselves as well as Samson in the imagery of creative light *and* restlessness as opposed to imprisoning shade *and* "rest" (l. 14). No longer may audience or approaching Chorus walk the futile circle of questions that is also a mill at Gaza, for the play demands a phoenix-like rousing of all persons. By means of such imagery, the hero is at once "led" into the universal demand for choice—here, the choice of sun or shade, unease or rest.

Such a human choice, as the conditions of imagery at once demonstrate, is beset with irony. In an implied accusation of God, Samson welcomes the "amends" (l. 9) made him by a day of rest in the "breath of Heav'n fresh-blowing . . . / With day-spring

born" (ll. 10–11), which relieves him from the "common" darkness (l. 6) of his prison. This light and that shadow are equivalents for God's creativeness and the sterile despair of Dagon (and
of Samson also, when he abets Dagon). However, Samson's choice
of light on this day serves not God but Dagon, for a Philistian
parody of the Sabbath had contemptuously lent God's fallen hero
"this rest" (l. 14). What is more, he wants only to "respire" (l.
11)—in reality, to die—in this "dark" light. Rest is the last wish
that may be granted him if he truly is to be led "onward." God
must be his divine Taskmaster, recapitulating the pattern *fall,
renewal*. He must be brought to a God-granted wilderness of trial
and recovery. Even the semblance of rest frees restless thoughts [9]
that swarm upon him like hornets, much like the thoughts that
swarm for the Son in *Paradise Regained* when he, too, considers
the Champion he might have been, "Ill sorting with my present
state compar'd" (*Paradise Regained*, I, 200). The unaccountable
route of physical and spiritual suffering leads Samson "onward"
to compare his glorious election, in which he was chosen of God,
with his chosen fall: his unresting thoughts resolve "times past,
what once I was, and what am now" (l. 22). As yet, they can
foresee no future, since neither he nor God seems to have that will
which shapes events. (All that is to come has been predicted,
however, in the prayer to be led onward.) In the midst of stinging ironies—annunciation that has become degradation, life that
is like death, sunlight that confers only darkness upon him,
strength that has become weakness, restless thoughts that will
somehow lead him to reconciliative rest, and the relief from Dagon's prison that will nevertheless move him back victoriously into
Dagon's temple—he is brought upward from the sepulcher of self.
There he had weltered, "diffus'd" (l. 118) and apathetic. The
punishment of his thoughts now raises him from that grave and
produces a future. The thought which now leads him onward will
receive the character of the "eager thought" of Lycidas, the revolving considerations of the Son, and the creativity of the Spirit
that once before "Dove-like sat . . . brooding" upon a similar

[9] F. Michael Krouse, in *Milton's Samson and the Christian Tradition*
(Princeton, 1949), p. 111, notes that *agonia* came to suggest not only an
athletic contest but also agony of mind.

chaos (*Paradise Lost*, I, 21). The hope of that creative resurrection is intimated in the phoenix image: even now, Samson lies in the "diffuse" ashes from which revelation and new life can come. If the audience, unlike the author, cannot be directly associated with that creative Spirit, it will nevertheless share the spirit of creative awareness providently supplied in the imagery and doing of *Samson Agonistes*.

Significantly, Samson in turn leads his Christian audience into uneasy recollection of their own spiritual biographies when he restlessly recalls, while seeking explanations of his being and of God's ways to him, the annunciation of his birth by angels, his summons to priestcraft and to the redemption of his people, and his fall. The Christian reader, even if he knew nothing of exegetical tradition, might well see in Samson a figure of his own condition: had not God similarly announced to all men that they were of "the Image of God / Express" and given them "rule" of the earth (*Paradise Lost*, VII, 527–528, 520), and had not man, like Samson, fallen? Although the image of the phoenix predicts sacrificial purgation even within the annunciation, because "an Angel . . . all in flames ascended / From off the Altar, where an Off'ring burn'd, / As in a fiery column charioting" (ll. 24–27), neither Samson nor the audience can yet perceive the way of Elijah or of sacrificial holocaust in these willed steps onward, even though this great action is exactly that foretold by which Samson would benefit *"Abraham's* race" (l. 29). So much the less might human eye see the revealing parallel with the Son of *Paradise Regained*, who shares the annunciation, the ordination to priestcraft, a seeming debasement "lower than bondslave" (l. 38), and the purgative triumph of will. For the present, all persons, because of both the memory and the seeming defeat of divine annunciation, are instead plunged to a conviction of defiling imbrutement in the present fall (ll. 36–38) —"O glorious strength / Put to the labor of a Beast, debas't / Lower than bondslave!" With a great serpentine involution of labials and liquids and sibilants, the verse coils around Samson's self-condemnation, which becomes our own. From this time forward, he is virtually leader to our Chorus.

Self-contempt, which is an aspect (albeit dangerous and suicidal) of repentance and restoration, seems to explain his rage as he terribly demands that we "ask for this great Deliverer now, and find him / Eyeless in *Gaza* at the Mill with slaves" (ll. 40–41). The verse knows more of his Good Friday thought than he does, however. It almost voices the cry, "My God, my God, why hast thou forsaken me?" for Samson suddenly finds that his charges against himself have been diverted toward the God who blessed but apparently punishes him. He had not thought to charge God openly with anything except the contradictory annunciation, but to his surprise he finds that he has thrust God's will into the center of accusation: "Yet stay, let me not rashly call in doubt / Divine Prediction" (ll. 43–44). The paradoxically "staying" restlessness is his suspicion that only he, not God, should be blamed for the fall. Such hesitation may increase his despair of self but will at least lead him from the absolute, fatal hopelessness of the Christian—despair of God. From this sepulchral depth, even within it, God's "divine prediction" is most in operation when Samson most despairingly questions himself. The typic "great Deliverer" is now, far more than before, being readied for his great action.

Yet now the human cry of protest is shattering. Samson fiercely castigates first his Eve-like "impotence" (l. 52) of mind, that mind which should have commanded his body. In his past temptation, the freezing winds of absolute liberty had swept over him; like Eve first and then Adam, he had sought rest in the warm "prison" of his senses. That rest, "hung . . . in my Hair" (l. 59), had destroyed itself. He is again seized with hatred for the very gift God gave him, that dubious strength that had become hybristic ("to mee strength is my bane" [l. 63]). Paradoxes chafe restlessly within his self-condemning judgment. The verse presses toward revealing to him that he must return to that hated elective strength in order to serve God. What is more, the verse will ask that his wisdom come to accept and rejoice in that strength rather than condemn it (God's gift) as weakness. Finally, however, his rejection of pride in his "own" self-willed power is a sign of true penitential strength. He knows that he was not of himself "sufficient to have stood, though free to fall," but rather, "Proudly secure, yet liable to fall" (l. 55).

The Oedipal energy in his protest therefore reaches forward, increasing both its pathos and its steely questioning of himself and

God. As Samson in part speaks for the audience, so Milton feelingly speaks with Samson now, and it must be a cold reader indeed who would reject the author's voice as a species of "fallacy"; if universality can be claimed for literature, surely the author in a work such as this can inhabit the province of his own fiction. The seeming loss of human strength, the plunge into impotency, could scarcely be more strikingly shown than in the agonizing but symbolically deceptive affliction common to tragic heroes and poets: blindness. In this, as well as in the restlessness of thought, the clear, sweet light of day is savagely denied to Samson, preventing the wished-for (but despair-ridden) day of rest. The physical torment is great as Samson recognizes that God's light, the light he had this day sought out, like God's gift of strength is limited "to such a tender ball as th' eye" (l. 94) or, even more slightly, to his hair. The body of this onetime hero, like the slender life and tender physical eye of every man, is "so obvious and so easy to be quench't" (l. 95) that we are invited to discredit all human strength—but only during this immediate stage of the agon, while it is good that purely human strength be questioned and rejected. Infinitely worse is his metaphysical torment. It brings the irony implicit in his day of rest in the sun to swift maturity. His real sepulcher is not the prison but deprivation of God, "dark, dark, dark, amid the blaze of noon" (l. 80). Light, both in nature and in the "great Word" (l. 83), has seemed to die. Although the hand that led him on, making unnecessary "amends," has brought him into the open air, it has also increased his whipping spiritual discomfort, for there he is only "dark in light expos'd" (l. 75). Open revelation and judgment are more painful than the dark prison.

Samson's inferno seems complete. He tries to seal himself up in his despair: "Myself my Sepulcher, a moving Grave, / Buried, yet not exempt / By privilege of death and burial" (ll. 102–104). It is as if we could witness the Holy Sepulcher just before the time when agony would become the potency that similarly could put down stone walls. Samson's sepulcher, however, is stained and blighted, his potency suspect even to himself. Although some "rousing" (l. 1382) motions have sprung from restless thoughts and have moved Samson through rejection of pride in either his champion's body or his vanquished mind, and although he has progressed beyond accusation of God (except for God's baffling economy in placing great gifts in slight material vessels), his life is mockery to him and, so he believes, to God. If it was well that he remove from apathy, he has done so—but only to descend into life-resigning despair.

As the Israelite Chorus enters, replacing solitary defeated *prologos* with what is for a time a solitary despairing *parodos,* Samson at first believes that it signals the resumption of his circle of punishment, his enemies having returned to mock him. There is to be no such ironic ease for either the Nazarite or the Israelites. Each "personage" must make his way toward God in agons that are separate in realization yet one in origin, process, and purpose. Samson does not realize that with God he has already transformed the circle at the mill into the trajectory of tragedy, and that all Israel and Philistia must now act within that "doing."

The Israelites had suffered in his fall. Now they must experience with him, slightly after his "leading," the enactment of human despair and revival. The choric general audience of Christian believers, too, no doubt recognizes distantly its part in the tragic enactment—the typic fall of the one Adam, the typic sacrificial death of the other, and the reflective double trial of each man. The Chorus will help move the drama forward by contributing its own restless thoughts upon the agon it shares with Samson. Dialectic will seek not difference but unity. As for the audience, its immediate contribution must be a withdrawal of immediate sympathy for Samson.[10] The cause of Samson and God must be forced upward from sepulchral rest. It is now time that "restless thoughts" (l. 19) lead all participating human consciousness onward in order that the phoenix may sometime rise.

Solitary at first, the Chorus increases the agony for Samson even as it begins its own agon by duplicating his progress in self-awareness. As Samson had begun the play alone, so when at first the Chorus speaks of him but not to him, the effect is to initiate its own solitary agon. To this somewhat imperceptive "Hebraic"

---

[10] Emile Saillens (*John Milton* [Oxford, 1964], p. 327) notices that however much friends and enemies may try to divert Samson from his goal, they only bring him that much more surely toward it.

Chorus, Samson seems, at best, exactly as enslaved, chaotic, and "dead" as he had thought himself:

> See how he lies at random, carelessly diffus'd,
> With languish't head unpropt,
> As one past hope, abandon'd,
> And by himself given over;
> In slavish habit, ill-fitted weeds
> O'erworn and soil'd [ll. 118–123].

At worst, he appears to the Chorus as the fallen Beelzebub appeared to Satan: "O change beyond report, thought, or belief!" (l. 117). Its members, too, painfully recall the heroism that had been, contrasting it with the shame to which he and Israel have come. They cannot yet see that he will again be "That Heroic, that Renown'd, / Irresistible *Samson*" (ll. 125–126); for the present, each question and recollection is only another weight upon their mutual prison door. Samson mourns their loss almost more than his own. His pain increases as it is relived in them, much as Adam's pain was magnified by seeing the effects of his sin upon his children. In turn, the Chorus must mourn the loss of that strength which had championed Israel, Samson's loss of eyesight (which also suggests a spiritual disintegration back into "gloomy night" [l. 161]), and his loss of freedom. Nevertheless, they impel the action forward by replacing his hopeless term "Sepulcher" (l. 102) with their word "Dungeon" (l. 156), and by suggesting that he is self-imprisoning. Though only at a great spiritual cost, inward light and freedom are available to him—and them. If he chooses, he can be like the imprisoned Paul at Philippi, for although "inward light . . . / Puts forth no visual beam" (ll. 162–163), it cannot be quenched like the light in the tender eye.

Still within its first reaction to Samson, the Chorus is given an additional function. If we as audience have forgotten the magnitude of the action we are to witness, the Chorus reminds us that this drama will indeed soar above the Aonian mount:

> O mirror of our fickle state,
> Since man on earth unparallel'd!
> The rarer thy example stands,
> By how much from the top of wondrous glory,

Strongest of mortal men,
To lowest pitch of abject fortune thou art fall'n
[ll. 164–169].

For a second, we hover near the medieval conception of tragedy. Milton's Chorus avoids full allegiance to Fortune and the older tragic mirror that his words inevitably conjure up, however, by indicating that Samson's power and wealth had been spiritual, translatable into virtue and strength. With them he, like the Son of *Paradise Regained,* might have "subdu'd the Earth" (l. 174). Even at the outset, the Chorus had recognized that Samson's past unarmed exploits had "made Arms ridiculous" (l. 131). His fall has not been from material high estate but from esteem of self and God. Similarly, his greatest pain and bondage strike inward, despite his outward shame. He experiences his greatest agony in the clear free air after the Philistians leave him alone. With him, the Chorus half realizes that human "high estate" (l. 170) always has to do with virtue, not with outward glory or martial heroism. However, it is not yet fully aware of its own agonic recapitulation of Samson's experience, nor does it yet accept the hope that Samson can still subdue the enemies of God. Although his "unarm'd" (l. 126) victory over Philistia with the gates of Azza forecasts his triumph in the temple of Dagon, it cannot imagine his revival. In a despair that now reflects that of Samson, it believes that his and Israel's virtue and power lie in ruins.

Far less does Samson understand the first agonic words of the members of the Chorus. To him, their speech is as diffuse and chaotic as his random sprawl has made him seem to them: "I hear the sound of words, thir sense the air / Dissolves unjointed ere it reach my ear" (ll. 176–177). Both he and the Chorus must build from the ruins of pride and hope.

The Chorus therefore offers a catharsis by which he (and later they) can be roused, for "apt words have power to swage / The tumors of a troubl'd mind" (ll. 184–185). Their immediate hope to ease the "old man" rather than to impel the new is no doubt too slight, almost Manoan. Facile comfort is not the need of Samson, "The glory late of *Israel,* now the grief" (l. 179), especially if words would merely salve over his fruitful suffering, leading him back instead into the apathy he often craves. The larger intention of the Chorus, however, is that of tragedy itself. Tragedy demands purgation of the malignancy rather than specious comfort for it.

Now in the first episode, the two agonists, Samson and the Chorus, begin to speak together, ending the despairing isolation with which each had entered the play. Samson reacts to the offer of catharsis with strength. For the first time, he notices that he "revives" (l. 187), even though only into the somewhat grim knowledge of true friendship. When the wheel of fortune is high, he now sees, friends "swarm" (l. 192) like flies, but in trouble only this Chorus and his "swarming" (l. 19) thoughts remain with him. He dimly perceives that favor may appear in affliction, when with irony that is almost divine humor, he blesses the blindness that conceals him from the Chorus' pity and shame. Although confessing that he steered his divinely conferred (and presently refitting) vessel to shipwreck, he cannot further increase his "revival." He instead stumbles into the reverse of his former pride, fearing mostly that his treasonable surrender of the "secret gift of God" (l. 201) to a woman has made him a public fool in Israel. This reborn concern for old heroism more than for his offense to God permits him to displace to God the question of guilt (recalled upon himself, however, by the accusing epithet, "Fool" [l. 201]). Samson again judges the Deity for having failed him through yoking his "immeasurable strength" with "wisdom nothing more than mean" (ll. 206–207). It is that disparity, not his bad piloting, that he now blames for shipwreck; it "drove [him] transverse" (l. 209). The pun in "mean" turns the charge back upon himself, of course. His renewed complaint, as old as that of Eve or Satan, is empty. Even a merely "mean" wisdom must contradict it; of wisdom, he, like every man, possessed sufficient to have stood.

Although the Chorus in response thinks to rebuke him, it too in a sense stands up still for human folly. Although asking him not to rebuke God, it nevertheless concedes that even wisest men, physically weak because of their conception in lust, have been deceived by women. This familiar judgment shifts the guilt over to a Dalila or to necessity, making the fall inevitable in all men, "pretend they ne'er so wise" (l. 212). In such a case, how could a poor Falstaffian Samson stand? Such judgment offers Samson, not strength, but salve for his weakness, pleading sanely but from doubtful premises, "Deject not then so overmuch thyself" (l. 213).

Still following Samson in his progress, the Chorus also then shifts the question of responsibility—or of its tarnished reverse side, folly—to their God. They ponder Samson's responsible first marriage, in which he had come to a Philistian woman, "motion'd . . . of God" (l. 222). Was not the foolish second marriage prompted by the same cause? Not yet God's champion, Samson somewhat lamely says that precedent had led him to think "it lawful" (l. 231) by his own volition to come to Philistian Dalila. His Hebraic metaphor penitentially notes the surrender of his polity, his Jericho, to her "peal of words" (l. 235) which seductively concealed the attack by woman. Although he begins to blame himself for the immediate error, he leaves the question of ultimate responsibility very much open. The Chorus thoughtfully accepts his metaphor of surrender, intimating that he then must be the cause that *"Israel* still serves with all his Sons" (l. 240). As Samson was unjust to God, so the Chorus is unjust to him. Dialectic must now seek true judgment.

The episode generally has moved in a series of swift dialectical probes of responsibility for human spiritual bondage. Each time Samson or the Chorus attempts either to "swage" (l. 184) guilt or to divert blame to God, a further question leads the search back to the human will. Reversing Samson's sometime removal of guilt to God, the Chorus has attempted to remove all of Israel's responsibility upon him. Accused unjustly, Samson is forced to consider the justice of his accusation of God.[11] Much as Adam in *Paradise Lost* is made to see history from a divine perspective, so Samson must view the landscape of human responsibility from a divine stance that will deny him all comfort for himself. In causing the

[11] Bernard Knox, in "Sophocles' *Oedipus,*" in *Tragic Themes in Western Literature,* ed. Cleanth Brooks (New Haven, 1955), pp. 8–14, indicates that the tragic figure becomes a paradigm, not a measurer (as he had thought) but that which is measured. However, Samson for that reason can come to act as judge.

human mental stance to proceed from the mill at Gaza toward the holocaust in the temple of Dagon, *Samson Agonistes* initiates the great ascent to tragic victory.

Samson takes the forward-looking stance in order to answer the Chorus. The dialectical probe having revealed that Israel's case and its claim are essentially like his own, he sees that to embrace or reject the one he must do the same with the other. Like the Son of *Paradise Regained,* he severely decides that Israel is self-imprisoning. The deliverance that had been offered Israel by God's "great acts" (through Samson) —acts which always "spoke loud the doer" (originally and ultimately, God) —had been ignored (ll. 243, 248). Although he does not fully realize it, Samson's case against Israel is identical with God's case against him:

> . . . in Nations grown corrupt,
> And by their vices brought to servitude,
> Than to love Bondage more than Liberty,
> Bondage with ease than strenuous liberty;
> And to despise, or envy, or suspect
> Whom God hath of his special favor rais'd
> As thir Deliverer; if he aught begin,
> How frequent to desert him, and at last
> To heap ingratitude on worthiest deeds? [ll. 268–276].

Samson unknowingly charges Israel—and himself—with the sloth of Belial and with Satanic resentment of a person elect. Implicitly, he also indicts Adam and Eve in Eden and the Jews with redemptive Christ. Although Samson's personal pride sounds again in the final lines, which are objectively reminiscent of Michael's complaint in *Paradise Lost,* Book XI, he has been nevertheless led "onward" to clear perception that he must himself accept his judgment upon Israel. Both the hero and the nation appointed of God had failed both God and themselves: "Ask for this great Deliverer now, and find him / Eyeless in *Gaza.*" His next speech demonstrates that he has accomplished most of that immediate progress. The issue no longer is that of Israel's past neglect of Samson nor of his past failure to be its champion, but only of his present and future faith and will as he consents to act in "God's propos'd deliverance" (l. 292).

With that achievement, the Chorus breaks into its reflective stasimon, a hymn of praise. The hymn lifts upward from the action. Man must believe in God; but he must also experience the world of weakness and death. Because of the shock of such a realization, he may conclude that God is not just, and therefore wander in vain attempts to bind the great God to a precedent. As Samson had done in the case of his marriage to the woman of Timna, man would try to impose laws upon the infinitely dynamic lawgiver. On the other hand, if the Chorus rejects Samson's first marriage, it refuses a divine mystery, a holy contradiction resembling that of the incarnation of deity or of the virgin birth. The Chorus must pull down all its *"vain* reasonings" (l. 322— italics added), which mirror the Philistian mill circle. Both protagonist and Chorus have begun to purge their folly, trusting no longer in human strengths and "Laws" but in "God's propos'd deliverance" and the just ways of God, ways "justifiable to Men" (ll. 309, 292, 294).

Even the hymn must remain only prospective, however, for no acts have yet justified its words. God has perhaps been justified beyond human doubt, but men have not been confirmed in faith. As Samson had sunk to despair even in the midst of belief, so the Chorus again sinks to baffled concern over the incomprehensible election and suffering of every Nazarite:

> He would not else who never wanted means,
> Nor in respect of th'enemy just cause
> To set his people free,
> Have prompted this Heroic *Nazarite,*
> Against his vow of strictest purity,
> To seek in marriage that fallacious Bride,
> Unclean, unchaste [ll. 315–321].

The great meaning of the play has been introduced into our midst, but no voice within the play is yet quite prepared to proclaim it. However, the central hymn is even now being generated by the enactments of Samson with the Chorus:

> God of our Fathers, what is man!
> That thou towards him with hand so various,
>
> .   .   .   .   .
>
> Temper'st thy providence through his short course
> [ll. 667–670].

The hymn must proceed from man's greatest suffering, which is also his greatest hope: the knowledge of his own weakness. Despair of self is almost as disabling as despair of God. From that sepulcher, the representative hero Samson must now be raised.

"Sense of Heaven's Desertion": The trial of earthly and of heavenly redemption (lines 326–709)

The judgment of both Samson and the fallen Chorus in the first episode had explored restlessly from the base of spiritual chaos. God had seemed far away, baffling both in his annunciation and in his seeming withdrawal. The effort to fix responsibility for the falls of Samson and Israel had sought after deity, only to be turned back by the realization that man had wrought his own enslavement. Although Samson had spoken briefly for himself and God against false charges in a faint, bitter stirring of revival, and although the Chorus had come to expect dynamic divine freedom rather than fate and to follow restless human thought rather than vain dogma, despair had returned like a somber cloud at the close. At best, Samson and Israel still seem condemned to an external dungeon; at worst, to both an inner and external sepulcher. Not until Samson—and with him, the methektic Chorus and audience—returns to the championship of God will their blank despair be ended. God, and the will of man for God, must be manifested against the images of darkness and death. It became apparent earlier that the characters themselves might constitute or present stinging thoughts to Samson, even as he may provide redemptive "onward steps" to them. Manoa will therefore bring additional impetus to Samson's thoughts even as the father, in turn, will enter into his own awareness of fall and renewal. The lines of force in the play thus work dynamically against each other: Samson's "reviving" insight into the ways of God casts him into a deeper sense of his human futility, yet at the same time he is becoming the valorous champion of God. The choice for God rises from the midst of negations, including an increasingly passionate wish for death.

The way to such a championship is of course attended with ironies. Much as Satan unwittingly informed the Son of God in

Paradise Regained, Manoa, the disapproving earthly father, reveals to Samson the character of a sacrificial but approving heavenly father. Manoa's efforts to secure earthly ransom for his son
are offset by the restlessness accompanying God's punition—
which is also the sure testimony of God's continuing interest in his
champion. Even Samson's despair and punishment therefore become signs of God's potency and presence. Most importantly, the
well-meaning materialistic errors of Manoa serve to reveal the
baffling spiritual truths of God.

In a final driving irony, Manoa, who had hoped to bring his son
from error into redemption, is instead led by his son. Although it
has been argued that Manoa must be the tragic hero of *Samson
Agonistes* because only he describes the full tragic arc of action
from error through access of knowledge to catharsis, while avoiding both the suicide and the Christian transcendence of Samson,
that is surely an overliteral interpretation. Like the audience, but
somewhat more tardily, Manoa in his turn joins in the action
begun by Samson and assumed by the Chorus. On the human and
tragic level, it is God's seemingly fallen champion who must
lead—first in original election, then in hornet-stinging thought,
then in reforged championship of God, finally in victory over
death. In all things except the will of God, he has already become
the "great Deliverer."

When his earthly father comes third upon the scene, the most
agonizing and Christlike part of Samson's struggle is initiated. It
begins with a cry *de profundis:*

> Ay me, another inward grief awak't,
> With mention of that name renews th' assault
> [ll. 330–331].

That this grief, resembling that occasioned by his earlier recollection of annunciation, is good in "awakening" Samson further
from apathy, or that the assault of this and previous restless,
stinging thoughts must lead him to dynamic action for God, is for
the moment cruelly beside the point. The chaotic despair of his
very being has been renewed. Even the initially pert yet rigid
Manoa must share the sense of dissolution. The Chorus relentlessly
points out to Manoa the fallen state of his son. However, in order

that the action may continue, it also adds intimations of Samson's redemptive role. The sonship of Samson is witnessed in three perspectives: first, that he is fallen, "diffus'd," chaotic; second—in almost a translation of *ecce homo* ("behold him where he lies" [l. 339]) —that he is the type of Christ, who like Samson will fall prisoner and go to an apparently humiliating death; and third, however, that he is as "signal" (l. 338) —significant—in his dejected as in his exalted station. Such identification of low with high is a paradox that both tragedy and Christianity will resolve.

This episode (and its quasi-dialectical stasimon) sees Samson sink through the remaining strata of egotism into a complete self-condemnation. He fully recognizes himself, not the Philistians, as his jailer. His despair is cathartic in that it restores his confidence in God's ways, God now having been freed of all blame and having received again the confidence that once had attended Samson's annunciation. His penitential remorse is also prophetic. He lashes himself for having become a tame wether in place of the announced ram of Judah, but in doing so, he not only assumes the burden of his "effeminate" (l. 410) guilt but also prepares himself for sacrifice. The related debate on temperance achieves a further anticipative catharsis. If in the past he failed in the one crucial test of temperance, he will not fail again in the approaching test with Dalila. If he can both govern and chasten his will, he may prepare a "tempered" act to refute the Chorus' outcry: "God of our Fathers, what is man! / That thou . . . / Temper'st thy providence through his short course, / Not evenly." Finally, he finds that his thoughts increase the seemingly immedicable tumor of self-lacerating despair—unaware that despair, if realized and active, can homeopathically purge his despairing apathy and diffuseness. When he prays for death as "the close of all my miseries, and the balm" (l. 651), he believes he asks only for "salve." In ways yet concealed from him, however, he is readying his will for salvation—for the triumph of God over Dagon, his own victory in a "death so noble" (l. 1724), and the catharsis of Manoa's folly as well as his grief.

Because Samson's death is not only the end that his pain and despair wrongly seek but also the rightful gateway both to his championship of God and to the tragic realizations of the drama, perhaps we should understand and judge it at just this point, when it is first asserted as Samson's desire. Our age has condemned any death wish as psychotic, suicidal, or—as Eliot framed our verdict in the Fourth Knight's speech in *Murder in the Cathedral*—both: "Suicide while of Unsound Mind" (Act II). It is natural that we should look at Samson with suspicion, not only because of his bloody, vengeful end, but also because of our doubt concerning its motivation. We look almost as shrewdly at Manoa and the Chorus when they claim exaltation and would design monuments for Samson. Surely, we think, Milton could not have been unambiguously serious about Samson's death and its reception by the personages of the drama. Although Milton's materials are perhaps alien to the modern temperament, his intentions seem to me unreservedly "sincere." Although we too sometimes ask what is worth dying for, we seldom stay for an answer; in *Samson Agonistes,* an answer is first implored and then celebrated. By permitting a "revived" will for God and God's uses of men to lead him to a human death that becomes a triumph for both himself and God, Samson recovers from wishing away a valueless life. If the literal bloodiness of his death offends us, we should recall that his is the way of martyrs, including Christ. If the vengefulness against Philistia seems savage, we should recall that Dagon and his worshippers partly enact and embody Satan and his hosts. No one would wish away our interesting and challenging contemporary readings of Samson's character and action. At the same time, however, one might wish that the critics took into account the Son's abstract prescription for most particular, *enacted* Christian "doing":

> I shall first
> Be tried in humble state, and things adverse,
> By tribulations, injuries, insults,
> Contempts, and scorns, and snares, and violence,
> Suffering, abstaining, quietly expecting
> Without distrust or doubt, that he may know
> What I can suffer, how obey [. Who] best
> Can suffer, best can do. . . .

. . . . .

> Know'st thou not that my rising is thy fall,
> And my promotion will be thy destruction?
> [*Paradise Regained,* III, 188–202].

These and related questions mount into dialectic play when Manoa takes a plaintiff's stance against God's champion, God's ways, and God himself. With each of his words, Samson, the Chorus, and the audience coldly perceive their own previous errors. The father calls all heavenly goodness and all human election into question by voicing again Samson's former fear that the elective gift "often proves our woe, our bane" (l. 351). Having prayed for a son, Manoa (somewhat like Mary in *Paradise Regained*) condemns the living gift, for like Dalila it draws a "Scorpion's tail behind" (l. 360). Also like the Mary of the Passion, he sees his son, "Select, and Sacred, Glorious for a while" (l. 363), now "Ensnar'd, assaulted, overcome, led bound" (l. 365).

Raising himself, Samson quietly undertakes the opposite case; he again champions God from the stance of God. In words almost repeating those of God in *Paradise Lost* ("They trespass, Authors to themselves in all / Both what they judge and what they choose . . . / . . . they themselves ordain'd thir fall" [III, 122–128]), Samson now, like the Chorus earlier and like our "Grand Parents" in *Paradise Lost,* asserts:

> Appoint not heavenly disposition, Father,
> Nothing of all these evils hath befall'n me
> But justly; I myself have brought them on,
> Sole Author I, sole cause [ll. 373–376].

Having restrained the earthly father from Satanically making himself God over God, and having refused to say any longer that it is God who has made sin and not he himself, Samson is able to judge his first marriage. Far from its having been a precedent binding upon God, that marriage, although sanctioned, should have warned him that a Philistian wife might commit treason. He recognizes his folly in refusing the tutelage of experience, including the triplicate temptation by Dalila. This exemplary man no longer questions God, but only the desperate folly of wrong choice. He knows that his dungeon and imprisonment began, not with his capture by the Philistians, but instead with his knowing surrender of right choice. His present humiliation "is not yet so base / As was [his] former servitude," nor his present blindness so terrible as that which "saw not how degenerately [he] serv'd" (ll. 415–416, 419). He was most the slave when he seemed most the hero and will soon learn that the reverse may also become true. His agony in acknowledging his own guilt is in some ways worse than that of Oedipus, for Oedipus could not recognize his guilt during its birth, and had even fled Corinth trying to escape it. Samson—as he now knows—had walked knowingly, if self-deceivingly, into his shame. Whereas Oedipus could not directly "see" the sin of his lusty eyesight, Samson would not.

Manoa cruelly exploits Samson's noble confession by making a merely prideful statement that he, the human father, had known best all the while. His son had erred in claiming that God moved him to the Timnan bride. He almost quotes Falstaff at his son: "Thou . . . Temptation found'st"; the Philistines, Manoa asserts, thereupon "found soon occasion thereby to make thee / Thir Captive" (ll. 426–427, 425–426). He thoroughly approves the justness of Samson's fall and wants him to continue paying "that rigid score" (l. 433). He sounds exactly like the Miltonic God of popular misconception, berating his son Adam in smug mercilessness. Manoa further acts like Job's comforter, telling Samson the very worst: far from his having received a parodic day of rest, the champion of Israel must this day hear his fall celebrated as God's defeat and Dagon's victory, in rites resembling those of Comus and Belial.

This father and son at first seem to present only a bitterly ironic contrast to their divine counterparts in *Paradise Lost*. However, even though they speak as "fallen" human father and son, Manoa can bring Samson onward into increasingly full response to the divine Father who had elected him. As the Father in *Paradise Lost* had encouraged the Son toward pity for men, the father in *Samson Agonistes* unwittingly encourages the son toward understanding of God. Samson immediately reassumes the divine stance. From Manoa's revelation, he sees what his full human guilt meant—not to himself or Israel alone, but to God. Such comprehension also produces increasing understanding of him-

self. Both attainments glow in his "confessions" that speak both to
the earthly father and to the divine Father:

> Father, I do acknowledge and confess
> That I this honor, I this pomp have brought
> To *Dagon*, . . .
> . . . to God have brought
> Dishonor, obloquy, and op't the mouths
> Of Idolists, and Atheists; . . .
> . . . and doubt
> In feeble hearts [ll. 448–455].

In grief, he now must know that he has betrayed God even as
Dalila had betrayed him, and that somewhat like Adam to his
sons, he causes the fall of faith in weak men.

Despite his increased understanding, however, Samson and Israel remain fallen, while Dagon and Philistia stand triumphantly
erect. At the moment when his awareness seems to have advanced
him to stand with God and his own responsibility, Samson again
slips back into his deathly inertia. Death might relieve him from
the stinging thought of this greatest treason. With an unwitting
pun, he says that God's direct contest with Dagon "relieves"
(rather than "revives") *him* (l. 460). He trusts God irresponsibly,
not yet aware that to be God's champion, either literally or figuratively, he must not only detest but also act against Satan. In this
retreat, he is once again only the lapsed champion of God; he is
not yet restored as God's champion.

All of Manoa's premature attempts at catharsis or false comfort
also buckle into increased despair. First Samson, then the Chorus,
disavows false hopes. Neither ransom nor refuge in the general
virtue of temperance is of any avail. The tumor seems "immedicable" (l. 620), God's ways contrarious, and the only solution a
quick, meaningless end of life.

In his specious, parodic catharsis, Manoa seeks to be "relieved"
himself by relieving Samson from his punishment. He would
deliver the "great Deliverer" by paltry ransom, agreeing with the
Philistians that God's elect "now no more can . . . do them harm"
(l. 486). The well-meaning earthly father, having taken a some-

what Philistian enjoyment in seeing the parodic humiliation of his headstrong son, would now utterly condemn him (and God) to defeat and humiliation. Manoa's brisk, bland despair is far worse than the seismic despair of Samson. The son rejects such a terrible comic ending, insisting that his guilt is at least as "signal" as that for which Gentiles imagine a fit "abyss and horrid pains" (l. 501). When Manoa retorts that Samson is composing his own affliction (as Samson is now aware that he made his own punishment), perhaps even choosing suicide, the old fear that man's choice may not be God's design returns in full. Samson meets it by praying for the relief of death: death that would avoid error as well as pain. In memory, he again judges and eradicates the pride and self-will that Manoa had blamed for his refusal of ransom:

> . . . like a petty God
> I walk'd about admir'd of all and dreaded
> On hostile ground, none daring my affront.
> Then swoll'n with pride into the snare I fell
> [ll. 529–532].

When God had prepared a table before him in the presence of his enemies, Samson had seen only a luxurious banquet. Unlike the great ram imaged for Judah, and as yet equally unlike the Agnus Dei, "like a tame Wether" (l. 538) he was shorn of his sacred hair. Having imaged the entire Fall, he realizes all too keenly that it has doubly unmanned him. What he cannot see is that his penitential despair has been readying him to be both the lamb *and* the champion of God.

Next, the Chorus tries to restore Samson by recalling that his God-given and human-directed will had been always firm against enslavement to wine, for he had preserved the "cool Crystálline stream" (l. 546) of the Twenty-third Psalm. The conditions of Paradise, or of the Attendant Spirit's first stance in *Comus,* are praised and thereby claimed for Samson:

> O madness, to think use of strongest wines
> And strongest drinks our chief support of health,
> When God with these forbidd'n made choice to rear
> His mighty Champion, strong above compare,
> Whose drink was only from the liquid brook [ll. 553–557].

Samson can take no comfort from the memory, however, not realizing that it shows how potent his mind and will can be. He knows only that his mind and body, his election and his will, had never been altogether tempered; temperance with wine was only a foil for intemperance with women. He takes no interest in the "rousing" information that his hair has been renewed. Having condemned both his strength and its weakness, he thinks the locks "redundant . . . / Robustious to no purpose" (ll. 568–569). If he in part temperately rejects riotous natural fecundity, like doubting Eve he is not sure that either God or he can use the abundance of man's strength.

Manoa, as yet unable to understand the soul's despair, continues to insist that Samson seek the catharsis of mere ransom. He even hopes for an equivalent material restoration of Samson's sight. He does not advise tragic patience—only stoic calm. Samson wearily replies that all his strength for shame as well as glory is exhausted. As Manoa leaves, he urges Samson to accept "healing words" (l. 605) from the Chorus. Tragic irony takes his words as an unwitting receipt for tragedy, which alone can produce redemption and "calm of mind, all passion spent" (l. 1758). Tragic *methexis* also will ironically take him at his word. From this time forward, the agon will be increasingly manifested in Manoa.

The specious offer of the earthly father serves to return the thoughts of the Chorus and Samson sorrowfully to the ways of the heavenly father. The agon plummets them both back to abysses of despair. Samson pictures himself as a new Job, beset hopelessly with "immedicable" outward and inward tumors of his own making. He no longer despairs of God, but of himself for God. His worst affliction is the sense that God has abandoned him. Like Job, or Christ in the Passion, he finds divine election followed by such alienation to be torment:

> I was his nursling once and choice delight,
> His destin'd from the womb,
>
> . . . . .
>
> But now [he] hath cast me off as never known
> [ll. 633–634, 641].

He abandons all hope of either catharsis or redemption: "Hopeless are all my evils, all remediless" (l. 648). He forgets that even as a tame wether he remains among the sheep of God's pasture. However, the same tragic irony that had moved in Manoa's last words moves in his, for cathartic death as God's champion will indeed offer him "the close of all [his] miseries, and the balm" (l. 651), even as it guarantees that the "race of shame" will become also the "race of glory" (l. 597).

The Chorus, in a great responsive stasimon, duplicates his agon. It tries to recommend patience, but is in turn dismayed by the conviction that God is gone. To avoid such despair, man must "feel within / Some source of consolation . . . ; / Secret refreshings, that repair his strength" (ll. 663–665). Although such hope for catharsis and "revival" has already been answered in the regrowth and "celestial vigor" (l. 1280) of Samson's hair, the Chorus as yet lacks eyes to see. It raises a great pathetic hymn that finds in Samson's physical lot the lot of God's Everyman. Men receive none of God's easy and routine gifts to angels or animals, but instead are brought high upon God's creative wheel only to be thrown proportionately low—"unseemly falls in human eye" (ll. 690). Fortune and her wheel might be bearable precisely because they are mechanical and blind; intolerably, God's wheel moves with knowledge. It is unbearable that his elect should be racked upon it. The Crucifixion and the deaths of all the martyrs impel the cry of the Chorus:

> Oft leav'st them to the hostile sword
> Of Heathen and profane, thir carcases
> To dogs and fowls a prey, or else captív'd:
> Or to th'unjust tribunals, under change of times,
> And condemnation of th' ingrateful multitude [ll. 692–696].

Worse still, the godly seem always to receive the treatment "justly" (l. 703) due only the unjust and dissolute. Man seems to have been abandoned by God to the caprices of Fortune. A baffled despair like Samson's increases upon the Chorus of Israelites. If these things are true, good men must in every case "come to evil end" (l. 704). Surely, if God exists, he has either left man or, "contrariously," given up his elect to evil. The prayer of the Chorus reveals itself to be contrarious, however—commencing in pious wish but plummeting to despairing complaint. Like the words of Samson and Manoa earlier, its final phrases vibrate with ironic receipts for a tragic catastrophe and catharsis:

> So deal not with this once thy glorious Champion,
> The Image of thy strength, and mighty minister.
> What do I beg? how hast thou dealt already?
> Behold him in this state calamitous, and turn
> His labors, for thou canst, to peaceful end [ll. 705–709].

"All Wickedness Is Weakness": The trial of flesh and of glory (lines 710–1060)

A Christian, "elegiac" tragedy will include in its catharsis the purgation of sin. If the purgation is devoutly wished, it involves, not only the removal of sin by means of the homeopathic, penitential awareness of sin, but also its replacement with a new and vital energy. The value of Dalila in the action of Samson is not so much to return him to the scene of his sin for retrial, for he has already been there in his restless thoughts; nor to offer him ransom [12] within the sufferance of Philistia, for that offer has already come from Manoa; nor to present to him his general Adamic weakness, for he knows all too well that he has become a tame wether. It is instead to try all of Samson's despairing defenses of his own weakness, thereby leading him "a little onward." If her appearance can properly "rouse" Samson, both the defenses and the despair will near their end. The Nazarite, now risen from his typic fall, will turn his renewed moral and physical strength against Satanic Philistia.

Although Dalila comes, ultimately, to renew the triumph of Dagon and Philistia, she as a woman is not to be opposed with physical strength; her purely verbal and intellectual attack can therefore put to the proof Samson's despairing claim that he possesses only "impotence of mind, in body strong" (l. 52). A victory will indicate strength in the one, recovery in the other. Although she is a woman, she can also present a case for national

---

[12] Ann Gossman, in "Milton's Samson as the Tragic Hero Purified by Trial" (*JEGP,* LXI [1962], 528–541), compares the insulting offer of ransom in *Samson Agonistes* with a similar offer to Socrates.

glory parallel to Samson's.[13] With the notable exception of her service to Philistia and Dagon rather than to Israel and God, the heroic ways she seeks resemble those he had once sought, and her arguments in their behalf are those he must have offered. If he now knows, strongly, that such heroism was selfish, suggesting not so much God's champion as the Philistian giants "swoll'n with pride" (l. 532), not only will he avoid the snare again (for the temptation itself is so weak as to be almost irrelevant), but also he will make ready instead the new heroism that is now to follow. The Chorus, too, will move from its early necessitarian belief that all men, like Samson, must err "and by bad Women [be] deceiv'd" (l. 211), into ethical belief that mankind can govern their sexuality (which women in some measure represent) even as they govern other passions. If in its Hebraicism it thinks mainly in legalistic modes, it nevertheless has come to think more liberally and hopefully. Rousing motions from defeat take place in both Samson and the Chorus during this episode and stasimon, and the audience cannot but be led onward by the rising confidence in the new heroic self and in God. A form of justification by faith here gives into complementary justification by deeds.

That increased activity brings up the central question of this central "act" of *Samson Agonistes:* ever since Dr. Johnson announced that the play has no Aristotelian middle, middle-hunting has been the peculiar avocation of many Miltonists. I believe that the action as well as artistic symmetry places the "middle" exactly in this episode. It is here that despair gives way to active contest. The two preceding episodes, in which despair embraces both Israel and its fallen champion, are hereby balanced against two following episodes, in which Samson contests the wills of Philistians but tempers his champion's will to that of God. Furthermore, Samson with Dalila rises strongly to the defense of himself, Israel, and God. In replaying the Adamic role, he rejects a fallible human companion for a form of union with God. His agon shifts from a wrestling with his doubt, sin, and terms of punishment to direct victorious struggle—first mental, then potentially

[13] As Brooks Otis, in *Virgil: A Study in Civilized Poetry* (Oxford, 1963), p. 265, considers Dido the *alter* of Aeneas, so Dalila is in almost all things the "other" that Samson must not become.

physical—with the enemies of himself and his God. Champion over himself, he can again be God's champion.

In all this, Dalila is of enormous importance. Readers sometimes considered her to be without motivation and therefore without character. I suspect that they tried to receive her only in her role as wife. Our delight in her, like Adam's in the women of Cain's tents, should never blind us to her function. She serves Dagon and Dagon's master, and is herself a "manifest Serpent" (l. 997). A rich trading vessel unlike Samson's wrecked ship, she will trade Satanically upon the kingdoms and ease of the world—if Samson will bend to her will. She appears not even as a lapsed conjugal partner but as Satan, the Adversary: she comes to the scene as a part of the triumph of Dagon over God's champion. Her wish to keep Samson in "safe custody" (l. 802) makes her accessory jailer in Gaza. Perhaps she arrives in secret response to those reviving locks she had so easily trimmed before, reducing Samson to a ridiculous "tame Wether." However, the recoil upon her of his energy and belief is prompt. He who had recently despaired of serving God now has his chance to try again, for Dalila represents the historic god-devil Dagon as surely as Sin represents Satan. Reviving motion from both God and Samson's own will arouses him to defeat her Satanic and Eve-like enticements. Sentimentalists may feel that his only enemy was romantic weakness, but Milton insists that Dalila is the primary opponent, virtually the hypostasis of Satanically seductive hatred. Samson surely all but judges her among other self-pardoning criminals: "Murderer, . . . Traitor, Parricide, / Incestuous, Sacrilegious" (ll. 832–833).

Unlike the serpent-dazzled Eve, the once-bitten Samson at first flinches from the encounter and its paradoxes ("My Wife, my Traitress" [l. 725]). As true tears had once helped Eve, false tears of parodic repentance introduce Dalila's merchandising effort.[14] Like the Chorus and Manoa, she has come to offer him catharsis of a sort, asking if she can appease his mind (the steady center of all

[14] Marjorie Nicolson, in *John Milton: A Reader's Guide to His Poetry* (New York, 1963), p. 361, notes the association of Tarsus ships with pride. Kester Svendsen, in *Milton and Science* (Cambridge, Mass., 1956), p. 165, notes that the hyena was at its most guileful when seeming most mournful. See also Robert A. van Kluyve, " 'Out, Out Hyaena!' " *American Notes and Queries,* I (1963), 99–101.

the action) into the easy surrender of his heroic mission. To choose against that appeal, he must once for all remove from "diffuse" chaos. To her easy trust in materialistic appeals and nationalistic expediency, he must oppose the sharp distrust he had formerly brought to God and his own gifts. To her image of a marital compact built upon distrust and reservation, he must oppose a divine compact built upon trust and commitment. He will thereby take firm control of his ship, whereas hers will move toward shipwreck—not entirely figuratively, for she probably is among those crushed with Dagon by the final strength of God's sacrificial champion.

Samson's choice against "appeasement" reflects the choice he has unconsciously made against despair. He charges that she is

> Not truly penitent, but chief to try
> Her husband, how far urg'd his patience bears,
> His virtue or weakness which way to assail [ll. 754–756].

The conditions of human existence are various and contrarious indeed when in the upshot "virtue" may be "weakness," and vice versa. Every virtue can be twisted into an accomplice to vice, for "wisest and best men . . . , / With goodness principl'd not to reject / The penitent" (ll. 759–761) may find themselves forevermore "Entangl'd with a pois'nous bosom snake" (l. 763). For a moment, Milton causes meaning to precede Samson's knowledge of it and the contest to lead Samson. Samson has said that men such as he must "wear out miserable days" unless they are "soon cut off / As I by thee, to Ages an example" (ll. 762, 764–765); although the way seems clear only to despair, the syntax has a way of reversing so that Samson very nearly says even now that he is an example to ages because of his having victoriously cut away the "bosom snake" of sin rather than because of his typic despair.

The arguments of Dalila, cresting in three waves, reinforce such convertibility. Partly offered in self-defense, they are also double attacks: they try to strike down Samson's present resistance by recalling to him the similar weakness of his past. First, she arranges falsely cathartic complicity between her curiosity and his surrender, asking that they be humanly (and totally) weak together. Her arguments are as old as Eve: that her curiosity then and now is natural to women (thereby giving great point to Samson's charge that she is a model, either way, for the ages); that Samson should have denied her plea (thereby blandly making an equation neither Adam nor Samson ever dared make, but which Eve in *Paradise Lost* and Satan in *Paradise Regained* framed casually: the "importunity" of temptation is nothing, a form of illusion); and that they are both one in human frailty, "weakness . . . with weakness come to parle" (l. 785). She next attacks beyond his weakness to his enslavement, intimating that because he was first false to himself in love, he had forced its redefinition; she had merely ratified the change. Her Orwellian argument that love is slavery contains the murderous intention borne by Eve at noon and the present condemnation of Samson to prison. Although she rather winningly suggests that her prison of love had existed only to prevent Samson from leaving her, her Satanic will glints through such verbiage like a serpent. She has always willed exactly his present condition—weakness, imprisonment, blindness both to day and night in Gaza:

> I knew that liberty
> Would draw thee forth to perilous enterprises,
> . . . . .
> *Here* I *should still enjoy* thee day and night
> Mine and Love's prisoner [ll. 803–808—italics added].

The grin of a death's head and the formula, love equals hatred, show through her words, especially when she argues that love is a *felix culpa* not to be despised: "Love hath oft, well meaning, wrought much woe, / Yet always pity or pardon hath obtain'd" (ll. 813–814). She leads the argument that love is slavery into a preposterous corollary: justice is total permissiveness. As if she were Eve in the dream rejecting Adam's strength, Dalila asks Samson again to release his own mistrusted, unpopular strength of mind: "Be not unlike all others, not austere / As thou art strong, inflexible as steel" (ll. 815–816). If preceding episodes had seemed to judge God's cleansing justice as too hard, Dalila offers a defiling Satanic catharsis in which "justice" would forgive all weakness and treachery. The serpent is sly indeed to attribute strength to the "tame Wether" but ask that it be only the strength of a "forgiveness" that is really surrender. Her speech is an open parody of liberal theology.

Like the obdurate Satan with Christ, however, she seems not to know that she actually creates in Samson the will to contest. By daring to assume as much weakness in his reason as he had earlier ("Though fond and reasonless to some perhaps: / And Love hath oft . . . wrought much woe" [ll. 812–813]), she brings him to abandon his refuge in "impotence of mind" and to gather form from his "dissolved" chaos. His judgment upon both his folly and her wickedness is "impartial, self-severe, inexorable" (l. 827). As Samson has already seen, his imprisonment had begun not in Gaza but in his enslavement to Dalila. She is now being defeated by the wisdom Samson believed he lacked. Her weakness had never included his romantic love of love but only a Mammon-esque love of gold. Her actions, weak because wicked, have sprung only from lust for gold and for war which, because it has been a "furious rage" (l. 836) in her, can only evoke a return of furious rage in him. The strongest simultaneous defense and counterattack for Samson is the self-involving statement, "All wickedness is weakness" (l. 834). His diffuse, withdrawing despair is now as impermissible as her deceitful attack.

Deceit having failed her, Dalila shifts to apparent candor. She no longer asserts equality and correspondence with Samson in weakness but in the old heroism, implicating Samson in the modern plea that international crime is excused by "bonds of civil Duty / And of Religion" (ll. 853–854). Public good, says this parodic champion, must outweigh the private (failing to see, or thinking that Samson will not see, that a supposed public good has led him to be this public spectacle). Finally, if his austerity and inflexibility are such virtues, she will match them: it is precisely her Philistian virtue, truth, and duty that caused her to betray him.

Samson will not for an instant release the serpent. She has "feign'd" (l. 872) her argument from religion, for, had it been of worth, she would have refused to marry an alien. Once married, she had accepted his polity; if Philistia entreated her to treason, she had the obligation to defy it. These skirmishes with a mere alien wife, however, are minor. The principal encounter is with

Dagon, whom Dalila serves. If Dagon once had sought her championship by "ungodly deeds" (l. 898), then he was no god and the service is not binding. The arguments for Philistia and Dagon topple together because of internal contradictions: as the wife was not a wife, so the professed god was in proof ungodly.

Her concession that he is victorious over her Satanic sophistry—"In argument with men a woman ever / Goes by the worse" (ll. 903–904)—really neither admits the feminine error into which Eve wandered nor concedes the victory. If Dalila's third attack had abandoned the past to move into a defense of her present service to Philistia, she now extends a last false comfort for the present to Samson. Like Manoa, she offers him "ransom" into an invalid's old age; he must forget all catharsis or consolation for what is "past cure." It is the reverse of her former plea for forgiveness. Having then asked that he tolerate her crime, she now asks that he tolerate the life of fearful defeat.

Her renewed assault operates under the changed condition of his reviving championship, however. At best, her vision of a rest home is not inviting. Samson recognizes it as a viper's den, no matter how much it is disguised behind the illusions of a Circe or Comus (Dalila's "fair enchanted cup, and warbling charms" [l. 934]). He has learned the "Adder's wisdom" (l. 936) that all such offers of ease and peace are ways to spiritual death. If, like Satan in Heaven, she could hate him whom "all men / Lov'd, honor'd, fear'd" (ll. 938–939), her hatred is in the grain. It was his majesty and goodness that she hated, not his championing of Israel. Like the Son when facing the choice of death or dishonor, Samson can say, as he will later say to the Officer, "This Gaol I count the house of Liberty / To thine whose doors my feet shall never enter" (ll. 949–950). Seeming bondage in Gaza is none, so long as he now freely refuses the true bondage.

Given her materialistic and seductive character, Dalila's last attempt is of course a contest of the flesh. She hopes that through touch he may return, like Adam "uxorious," to her will. She takes seriously his self-condemning, God-accusing charge that he is impotent of mind, believing him therefore also weak to fleshly "attacks" on his body. An unrepenting Eve has callously returned Adam to the tree, hoping that he can again burn to dross in lust.

Instead, the action threatens to speed directly to the catastrophe through typifying the contest between Samson and Dagon. In his sudden rage he is moved to "tear [her] joint by joint" (l. 953) as if she were the lion of his youth or the Harapha to come. Now all his championship is remembered—and forecast. He knows that he must die for this defiance, releasing Dalila into her "hast'n'd widowhood" (l. 958). Although he briefly attempts to act as minister rather than scourge to Dalila, like Hamlet to Gertrude, the attempt is foredoomed:

> Bewail thy falsehood, and the pious works
> It hath brought forth to make thee memorable
> Among illustrious women, faithful wives [ll. 955-957].

His knowledge that she is altogether an enemy turns the attempt into scorching irony and leads to the renewed indictment that for gold she sold God's champion into slavery and death. Those who sympathize with Dalila must seek a correlative sympathy for Judas.[15]

For a moment, Dalila, like Satan, looks fearfully into the final "anger, unappeasable . . . / Eternal tempest" (ll. 963-964), of divine fire that will purge hellish dross. But like Satan, she then resolutely embraces her worldly lot. If she is damned in Israel, fame will find her out in the fallen realm of Philistia; better to reign there than "serve" as Samson's wife. Her wish for vain Philistian monuments to her fame will be fulfilled ironically in the great wreck of the temple of Dagon, whereas Samson will receive a memorial altar.

The Chorus, involved at second hand in this contest of passion with reason, recognizes that in the episode just finished Dalila, like the tempting Satan of *Paradise Regained,* had finally "manifested" (l. 997) her evil will in total enmity. Not so easily is it freed from a sense that she is Eve, powerful by necessity whether in original love or later loss. Samson has to remind it that Dalila has been no pleasingly innocent or penitent Eve, but at best the Eve of the moment of temptation: woman resolved in "wedlock-treachery endangering life" (l. 1009), disrupting order within the center of the ordained human union.

---

[15] Krouse, in *Milton's Samson,* pp. 51-52, indicates much of the tradition that associates Samson with Christ as a direct figuration.

In its stasimon, the Chorus responds with what at first seems a statement of misogyny but surely is instead a reflection of its increasingly libertarian awareness that the self finally must decide what is fit and good—if necessary, in the face of all necessities, compacts, and unions. The traitress-wife had "shorn the fatal harvest of [the] head" of Samson (l. 1024)—or Christ, or Orpheus. If the Chorus had formerly believed that even the wisest men could not avoid the fatal fall to such an end, Samson has just demonstrated the heroic capability of reason. It is reason, then, more than misogyny, that leads the Chorus to its powerful awareness of Eve within the fall. Everyman-Adam, it sees, must "[break] through all opposition, / And all temptation . . . remove" (ll. 1050–1051). Each Adam if necessary must resist with "despotic power" (l. 1054) the wandering of self-love that is called Eve, whether it appear in his wife, his state, his church, or himself. The attitude need not seem ugly to modern readers. The metaphor of Eve or Dalila merely insists, somewhat tautologically, that the Eve in mankind is dangerous. Myth has long since demonstrated that the Adam in Samson was disastrous, and asks that a compact of union exclude disunion and distrust. (If militant feminists remain offended, they can read the mythos in *Comus;* there the positions of Samson and Dalila are reversed, the masculine Comus providing temptation for the governing Lady.) In the angry judicial Samson, the gullible Adam has been corrected. His example has drawn the participating Chorus a little onward. The audience, which at first might have resisted the contest of Samson with his wife, enters into the agon methektically, Samsons in their own right, when Dalila elevates the nation, first above love, and then, being a utilitarian Philistian, above all personal rights, standards, and judgment:

> . . . at length that grounded maxim
> So rife and celebrated in the mouths
> Of wisest men, that to the public good
> Private respects must yield, with grave authority
> Took full possession of me [ll. 865–869].

For once, Milton does not follow Protestant temptation into equating her stand with that of the Catholic church. In her perversion of Socrates, she represents much more: all tyranny, all legalism, all false compact, whether they appear in the family, the state, or the church. By scornfully refuting her, Samson acts not only as the champion of God but also of Milton and all the Thoreauvians and libertarians of his audience:

> . . . if aught against my life
> Thy country sought of thee, it sought unjustly,
> Against the law of nature, law of nations,
> No more thy country, but an impious crew
> Of men conspiring to uphold thir state
> By worse than hostile deeds, violating the ends
> For which our country is a name so dear;
> Not therefore to be obey'd [ll. 888–895].

General independence, except from God, has replaced baffled dependent despair, the contest having passed its mid-point. From now forward, Philistia, not Israel, will fear, despair, and fall to irredeemable chaos.

"This Strength, Diffus'd": Consent to the championing of God (lines 1061–1440)

The Chorus that had gladly seen Dalila as a gorgeous trading ship fears that her successor represents a storm directly threatening Samson's own "Vessel . . . , / Gloriously rigg'd" (ll. 198–199). The Israelites still lag somewhat behind Samson in the action, not yet fully aware of the meaning of the restoration of Samson's inward as well as his external strength. That this "storm" (l. 1061) is at once a welcome challenge from an enemy, a pentecostal, reviving wind in his Wasteland, and a sign of the physical agony to come is clear to Samson. The diffuse welter of ocean has given way to streaming vertical currents of the fiery altar. His once tormented rhetoric is now compressed severely into a gnomic insight far beyond the riddles he, like the young Oedipus, once had solved: "Fair days have oft contracted wind and rain" (l. 1062). So his election had become clouded; so within the blaze of noon have reviving, but painfully cathartic, storms sprung up. God's design will confront the recreated champion of God with a Goliath-like antagonist.[16] If he were only an Irus to Samson's Odysseus, he would be useful in leading the disguised champion onward to the great contest, but he is much more; eventually, the almost architectural "pile" (l. 1069) of his great body will join the god Dagon and his temple in ruins.

When in the fifth episode a Philistian officer replaces the crestfallen Harapha, Samson's great zeal for contest alters at first into obdurate refusal to serve. He who had begun the play as a slave now imperiously commands the enemy commander. However, the pentecostal wind of God's design entirely directs the ship that had once been shipwrecked by its too human pilot. He who at the beginning of the play had brought "Dishonor, obloquy" (l. 452) to God will conclude his agon in action that will serve God's "glory best, and spread his name / Great among the Heathen round" (ll. 1429–1430). The unwitting Philistian commander serves only to lead the blazing "Deliverer" to his triumph. The reversal (*peripeteia*) of the third episode having been enacted, all the somewhat misleading conditions of the beginning of the play now rush toward their opposites.

Those who deplore violence have questioned the return of Samson to physical heroism at the end. Whereas the Son's victory in Heaven—analogous to some myths of the harrowing of Hell—seems safely allegorical, Samson's victory in the temple of Dagon is all too real. Milton probably foresaw no such difficulty. If Samson's one talent which was death to hide, announced by angels to his parents, was his "glorious strength," and if his mind no longer runs impotently across that strength but instead confidently directs it, then his great triumphal (yet tragic) act will of course be physical. It will be in part the reification of a spiritual triumph for God over the typic enemies of God, but it also will stubbornly remain the bloody destruction of Philistia in a bloody sacrifice of Samson. Such violence may be an essential component of most tragedy and martyrdom. To wish it utterly away is to wish away the rare, ultimate trial of spirit with flesh, exemplary to lesser struggles of far less (or no) violence. Tragedy often suggests that the great triumphs of the spirit must be gained in company

[16] Northrop Frye, *The Return of Eden* (Toronto, 1965), p. 28: In Milton the tyrant, like the conventional hero generally, is almost always "demonic."

with great agony of the flesh. Perhaps the modern world has evolved beyond such ideas by holding that physical suffering is absurd and without meaning, but in literature and religion they remain current. To discard them from Milton would ask that we also discard the bloody deaths around Hamlet and the physical torments of Christ and Christian martyrs. Theology as well as literature and history led Milton to this end for this hero.

Samson meets the new contest already purged of vain excuses for despair. The entrance of a parodic Philistian hero may seem to rouse Samson only to his own old heroism, but his physical championing must not be confused with the spiritual agon in which his will unites with that of God. Nowhere, perhaps, is the spiritual progress more clear than in a change upon the early expression "diffus'd." Although divine energy was implicit even at the first, the Chorus, upon seeing Samson, had described him as "carelessly diffus'd . . . , past hope, abondon'd." Now a far different meaning swells in the word. Samson rejoices in the annunciation he had once doubted, saying that God gave him his strength, "diffus'd / No less through all my sinews, joints and bones, . . . while I preserv'd these locks unshorn" (ll. 1141–1143). Lest there be any doubt about the character of the championship to which he returns, Samson scandalizes Harapha by disparaging "glorious arms / Which greatest Heroes have in battle worn" (ll. 1130–1131). He instead releases his strength and will into those of "the living God" (l. 1140). It is never Harapha as such, but Dagon, whom he challenges. Although the following quotation is slightly out of context, it nevertheless speaks truth for Samson:

> . . . I to be the power of *Israel's* God
> Avow, and challenge *Dagon* to the test,
> Offering to combat thee his Champion bold,
> With th' utmost of his Godhead seconded [ll. 1150–1153].

In this last purgation of fear and despair, Samson guides both the Chorus and audience. A sure sign of his "onward" progress is the continued gnomic terseness of his language, resembling that of the Son in much of *Paradise Regained*. Indeed, the contest of Harapha and Samson is powerfully reminiscent of that other agon, for here, too, both God's enemy and God's champion rehearse the meaning of Samson's annunciation, fall, and present agon. If the exchanges approach the comic, it is only because the weakness of a *miles gloriosus* who swiftly proves to be a tame wether is made to look foolish next the buoyant, reviving strength of Samson. If Samson had earlier believed his "genial spirits" slack, his "hopes all flat" (ll. 594, 595), displaying in proof the description of the Chorus—a fallen hero "with languish't head unpropt, / . . . by himself given over" (ll. 119–121)—that role is now quickly shifted entirely to Harapha. When the Chorus reaches the stasimon, we see how far the action has progressed.

As the fourth episode begins, Harapha takes Satanic pride in proclaiming himself to Samson much as Satan had to Ithuriel: "Thou knowst me now / If thou at all art known" (ll. 1081–1082). His Philistian egotism is of a kind with Dalila's. Not only does it come from the will to oppose Dagon to God, but also it hopes that God's champion was never more than the mere equal of a given Philistian: "We might have tried / Each other's force in camp or listed field" (ll. 1086–1087). Samson is so thoroughly revived that his brief answers carry the calm wit of the Son's in *Paradise Regained*. If Harapha wants to learn of Samson, let him taste: "Boast not of what thou wouldst have done, but do" (l. 1104). God's champion recalls that he once had opposed, singly, the "whole united powers" (l. 1110) of Philistia; now, even though blind, the new tragic hero can best the old martial hero Harapha in spite of the giant's armor, even as in the catastrophe he will extend and complete the earlier victory. Harapha, attempting to champion arms against grace, reveals Dagon's weakness by considering such strength to be magical.

In the half-comic upshot, strongly suggestive of Homeric laughter, the reconciliation of Samson with his God is made complete. Samson returns to joyful "trust . . . in the living God who gave" his strength (l. 1140). No doubt remains about the nature of the gift. The champion sweeps toward its climactic use by challenging Harapha to Dagon's temple, where Samson will be pleased to have Dagon try his "magic." There the bully can "feel" whether Dagon or God is stronger (ll. 1149, 1155). Although Harapha

weakly tries to force Samson back into his old doubts of self and
God, despite the evidence of his "boist'rous locks" (l. 1164),
Samson now meets all thrusts confidently, almost buoyantly:

> . . . these evils I deserve and more,
> Acknowledge them from God inflicted on me
> Justly, yet despair not of his final pardon
> Whose ear is ever open; and his eye
> Gracious to re-admit the suppliant [ll. 1169–1173].

Harapha's attempt to convict Samson of his sins as "Murderer,
. . . Revolter, . . . Robber" (l. 1180) against Philistia works no
better than Dalila's companion argument from false duty. Looking above history to the Mover of history, Samson merely urges his
mission the more powerfully:

> I was no private but a person rais'd
> With strength sufficient and command from Heav'n
> To free my Country; if their servile minds
> Me their Deliverer sent would not receive,
>
> . . . . .
>
> I was to do my part from Heav'n assign'd,
> And had perform'd it if my known offense
> Had not disabl'd me [ll. 1211–1219].

His exaltation had been accompanied by the "strength sufficient"
to have stood to it. In contrast to his refusal to touch Dalila is his
invitation to Harapha to "survey" (l. 1227) that sufficient
strength. Harapha wilts—not merely comically, as readers have
sometimes believed, but Satanically, the giant having become as
aghast before God's champion as Satan comes to be in *Paradise
Regained*. The champion of Israel easily dismisses Harapha as a
gigantic father of Satanic giants, including the ectype, Goliath.
Perhaps more significantly, Samson calls Harapha an unsubstan-
tial "bulk without spirit vast" (l. 1238), reminding us of Death's
"vast unhide-bound Corpse" (*Paradise Lost*, X, 601).

Samson concludes the scene in the resolute determination that
has been mounting ever since the encounter with Dalila—indeed,
since that with Manoa, when he determined his stand in Gaza,
sure that it must involve death. The "Deliverer," "a Man con-

demn'd" (l. 1224), now looks forward to death's "deliverance" sturdily, militantly, like a type of Christ or of every Christian:

> . . . my deadliest foe will prove
> My speediest friend, by death to rid me hence,
> The worst that he can give, to me the best.
> Yet so it may fall out, because thir end
> Is hate, not help to me, it may with mine
> Draw thir own ruin who attempt the deed [ll. 1262–1267].

In its methektic stasimon, the Chorus celebrates the revival that it feels with Samson and the heroism and divine energy that it has come to share with him—"plain Heroic magnitude of mind / And celestial vigor" (ll. 1279–1280). Gone is all doubt of human wisdom and of divine potency. Physical heroism against tyranny will be possible because it has been produced from "patience . . . / Making . . . each his own Deliverer" (ll. 1287–1289). At first, action is separated from patience, but in Christian heroism they eventually become one. A major virtue of Samson as exemplary hero is his capacity to encompass both, for his "exercise" this day has moved from the trial of patience to the trial of action. Patience is godliness become enduring and therefore liberating; it outlasts "tyranny or fortune" (l. 1291) and so defeats both. It has restored Samson as "great Deliverer" and encouraged each man individually and the minority "elect" within human history to seek the inward freedom that will be either their own deliverance or its ultimate condition. Although the ode celebrates the virtual triumph of God's chosen but fallen people, having perceived the absolute deliverer God through the earthly deliverer Samson, it ruefully admits that Samson's day of restless thought has nevertheless remained "this Idol's day" (l. 1297). However, the heroic "Laboring" (l. 1298) of this day is now to produce ultimate decision and revelation.

And so the last episode brings on the idol's representative power, a Philistian public Officer, who unknowingly has accepted Samson's challenge to Harapha while thinking to return God's champion to the jeering contempt of heathen Philistia. Samson's first reaction, keyed to the Chorus' celebration of inward freedom, is to oppose his "conscience and internal peace" (l. 1334) to the command, much as Cleopatra preferred death to public shame. Although he still seems to threaten Philistia, telling the Officer, "Perhaps thou shalt have cause to sorrow indeed" (l. 1347), he takes delight in firmly refusing the enemy command [17] that had required him to use his "glorious strength" like a mountebank. He has also refused, typologically, to bow down and worship Dagon, no matter what the offer from a kingdom of the world.

The fearful Chorus follows slightly behind him in his progress. As the Israelites had dreaded the Officer at his approach, so they half argue that Samson, acting in fear or prudence, should go to the temple: does he not already serve Dagon at the mill? And, using the argument of *Comus*, is it not true that "where the heart joins not, outward acts defile not" (l. 1368)? Samson purges from himself and them such logic of fear: although to work as a slave is not to worship, outward acts of worship performed under the constraint of "outward force" (l. 1369) become acts of assent. Samson's hesitation, then, has been a form of patience: he must be certain that his inward promptings move from God's will rather than from his own fear or pride. For a last instant, he waits within the care of patience:

> If I obey them,
> I do it freely; venturing to displease
> God for the fear of Man, and Man prefer,
> Set God behind [ll. 1372–1375].

Then with the suddenness of absolute conviction, he reaches consent:

> Yet that he may dispense with me or thee
> Present in Temples at Idolatrous Rites
> For some important cause, thou needst not doubt
> [ll. 1377–1379].

The rousing motions he has felt in his thoughts lead him on with joy. His Gethsemane well past, he quietly states that "for a life" (the life of his soul) he has changed his purpose (l. 1406). For the last time, a promise of mere ransom is offered by the Philistian for

[17] Samson's heroism culminates in wisdom and general strength, *sapientia* and *fortitudo* (A. B. Chambers, "Wisdom and Fortitude in *Samson Agonistes*," PMLA, LXXVIII [1963], 320).

this "compliance," which may "free" (ll. 1411–1412) Samson. The painful oxymoron involved in the phrase "compliance: set . . . free" stamps such ransom as fraudulent.

All fear of servitude has vanished, along with all hope of an insulting ransom of the body back into a useless life. In this, his last scene, Samson quits himself like Samson. He knows that he goes to a death, for the Philistian lords, priests, and people are inflamed by wine, hatred, and religion. Much as there had been no question of continuing an empty life under Philistian sufferance, so there is now no question of "suicide." He is to be killed; he must die by the force of "prison" and popular noise in order to be freed from them. The only question is whether or not his death is to be that of hero as well as martyr. He no more commits suicide than he would have had he died in battle, for the pillars become his "weapons." The shift toward such aggressive use of Dagon's temple against itself is indicated when Samson, ironically answering the Officer's statement, "I am sorry what this stoutness will produce," retorts, "Perhaps thou shalt have cause to sorrow indeed" (ll. 1346–1347). Furthermore, because apocalyptically he destroys a pagan temple and its nation for all time, there is a distant Christian promise of his "destroying" his own "temple" in order to raise it. In the end, his will has moved into perfect temperance with God's. What is to come will be "Nothing dishonorable, impure, unworthy / Our God, our Law, my Nation, or myself" (ll. 1424–1425). If he still speaks of self, he properly places it in the last order of emphasis.

The leave-taking Chorus in its enactment of the action has also now arrived at such consent and blessing. It too knows that he must die, but considers such a death to be a "vertical" act that will renew Samson's annunciative communion with "the Angel of thy Birth" (l. 1431). It knows that his initial plea to be led a little onward has been answered: "Go, and the Holy One / Of *Israel* be thy guide" (ll. 1427–1428).

The glory of Samson's annunciation is fulfilled. The image of the phoenix appears like a palimpsest within that of the flaming angel of the Annunciation, indicating present death but future rebirth. The agon of Samson is over. The Chorus re-commends him to the spirit of Heaven. As for its members, they with Manoa

must take Samson as glorious example while they complete their
own agons in tragic understanding.

"Erewhile a Holocaust": Consent to tragedy and catharsis *(lines 1441–1758)*

A reader versed only in Shakespearean tragedy may find it
surprising that classical tragedy manifests among other differences
a long ending, seemingly anticlimatic. In *Samson Agonistes*, the
hero leaves the stage when the play is only four-fifths run. It is
true that reports of his death manage to keep his "action" current
on the stage, but the conclusion still may seem to dwindle undra-
matically. The mistake, of course, is to suppose that in a play
influenced by Aristotle the hero alone would compose the substance of the drama. He contributes only a part of its action. In
the methektic tragedy *Samson Agonistes*, other characters, the
Chorus, and the audience must complete it. Paraphrasing Lin-
coln's tragic words for Gettysburg, we might say that it is for the
living to complete that meaningful action which the dead has
advanced, were it not that death has so little, finally, to do with
the action of *Samson Agonistes* and that Samson's agon finds
death to be a spiritual irrelevancy. His death holds suggestions
instead of Christian "deliverance." Even the classic kommos becomes significantly changed from an ode of mourning to a resurrection carol. The final parts of the play, like the resolution of
Samson's individual agon, lead all its participants from doubt
within the chaos of death to cathartic "calm of mind, all passion
spent."

Samson's death and victory occur off stage. His place on stage in
the tragedy is assumed by Manoa, who now in turn must convey
the action. He brings back with him both the human despair and
the human hope that Samson and the Chorus have long since outgrown. Some of the Philistians, it seems, are ready to sell Samson
out of slavery for the same reason—gold—that had brought Dalila
to entice him into it. Manoa's bright wish receives a terrible reproof from the echoing last words of Samson: "Nothing dishonorable, impure, unworthy" (l. 1424) .

Manoa is spared further well-meant uncleanness by the great
dirge or hymn (a form of the paradox of Easter) arising from
Dagon's temple; like the terror of Good Friday, "it tore the Sky"
(l. 1472). Although Manoa had noticed the revival of Samson's
hair and was sure God would "use him further yet in some great
service, / Not to sit idle with so great a gift" (ll. 1499–1500), he
still does not understand that Samson seeks divine redemption,
not ransom nor the old heroism. Similarly, he cannot yet realize
that his wish for the renewal of Samson's eyesight will lead to the
tragic inward eyes of the second semichorus. Tragedy will also
reverse Manoa's hope and the hope of the Chorus for some bodily
deliverance upon themselves: "In both which we, as next, participate" (l. 1507). Having sworn itself to share in Samson's agon,
the Chorus must accept into itself the rending scream that follows.
Good Friday is again intimated in a "universal groan" (l. 1511).
The nexus of pathos and heroism that defines this tragedy is
reached as Manoa keens, "Oh it continues, they have slain my
Son," while the Chorus, in terrible triumph, corrects him: "Thy
Son is rather slaying them" (ll. 1516, 1517). However, even the
Chorus, faintly like Satan in *Paradise Regained* and Manoa in
this play, still hopes for the heroic, unreasonable and
miraculous—not the tragic. They hope that Samson has regained
his eyesight and that, like an Odysseus in Ithaca, he now walks
"over heaps of slaughter'd" (l. 1530). Manoa at last knows better;
God's holiest miracles are never of that unnatural or unreasonable kind.

The report of the event fells the last restless attack of false hope.
Before he had learned all, Manoa had ironically but prophetically
fixed the final tragic stance: "That still lessens / The sorrow, and
converts it nigh to joy" (ll. 1563–1564). First, however, he has to
feel the pain of death and confess death's necessity, which earlier
he was too fondly hopeful to admit:

> What windy joy this day had I conceiv'd
> Hopeful of his Delivery, which now proves
> Abortive as the first-born bloom of spring
> Nipt with the lagging rear of winter's frost
> [ll. 1574–1577].

It is especially painful that Manoa casts his grief in directly paternal images of conception, delivery, and first bloom, even if a counterironic "revival" eventually will revalidate them all in a transcendent spring borne by a pentecostal wind of renewal. And he must fear that the elective strength given of God was punishment even at the end: "O lastly over-strong against thyself" (l. 1590) . But he is told how Samson, clothed in Philistian garments and preceded by a parodic Palm Sunday shout, in the blaze of noon patiently revealed his heroic strength in all the tasks set him, then "pray'd" with his mind rapt on "some great matter" (ll. 1637, 1638) before revealing his (and God's) inward "greater strength" (l. 1644) in the climax. Not only were the lords of Gaza destroyed, but also the leaders of "each *Philistian* City round" (l. 1655) : in one stroke, God's champion, Samson, has destroyed the root and branch of all Satanic Philistia.

Even now, the grieving Chorus cannot quite understand that Samson consented to his tragic victory, for it at first assigns his death to old heroism and "dire necessity" (l. 1666) , believing him to be a suicide. Its kommos threatens to present only a renewed human despair. Because of that limited, materialistic interpretation, the first semichorus is therefore led "onward" to a far greater overview of time and to a stance of judgment looking far down upon the Philistians, seeing the irony of their having unknowingly commanded their destroyer to come upon them:

> So fond are mortal men
> Fall'n into wrath divine,
> As thir own ruin on themselves to invite
> [ll. 1682–1684].

As in God's design Samson ultimately was his own deliverer, so ultimately were the Philistians their own executioners. (Some of the technically and morally vexing questions of suicide and vengeance are thereby absorbed into "justifications" like those of *Paradise Lost;* furthermore, "wrath divine" is seen to be in part mere noninterference with the ends men choose.) This realization leads the second semichorus into a similar grand perspective and judgment upon Samson, developed through the controlling image of the phoenix. The two semichoruses have become like two inward eyes,[18] cleared gradually across the play from an original blindness like that of Samson. Their spiritual blindness—lack of knowledge, lack of trust, lack of self-deliverance—has been purged, partly through witnessing Samson's agon, partly through undertaking their own. They realize that the tomb of a Samson or a Christ is also an "ashy womb" (l. 1703) pulsing with vigorous life. When Samson had been "most unactive deem'd" (l. 1705) at the beginning of the play, he had then most surely been undergoing revitalization, in a second annunciative birth, within the "ashy womb" of Gaza. The cathartic effect of the general action is clear also in Manoa, who now comprehends the heroism and consent, a true second "birth," that had appeared in his son's death. As father, he, like God the Father, must find it glorious:

> To himself and Father's house eternal fame;
> And which is best and happiest yet, all this
> With God not parted from him, as was fear'd,
> But favoring and assisting to the end [ll. 1717–1720].

Easter and resurrection seem in the offing, but first the sacrificed body must be washed and the tomb [19] prepared with Lycidian "Laurel ever green" (l. 1735). Samson will be a monument, a kind of "vertical" example and genius of the shore, to "valiant youth," who "from his memory [will] inflame thir breasts / To matchless valor, and adventures high" (ll. 1738, 1739–1740). Not that his sensual error will be blotted out: virgins will also bewail "his lot unfortunate in nupital choice" (l. 1743), the pure weeping for the painfully purified. Although Manoa insists (perhaps self-righteously) that causative sin be remembered, this does not pull down the whole play into a mere protest against unfortunate marriage, any more than the gravestone in *The Scarlet Letter* signals a mere protest against unfortunate love affairs. Surely it is

[18] For a useful discussion of the relation of the evening dragon to the sight imagery of *Samson Agonistes,* see Lee S. Cox, "The 'Ev'ning Dragon' in *Samson Agonistes:* A Reappraisal," *MLN,* LXXVI (1961), 577–584.

[19] Knox, in "Sophocles' *Oedipus,*" p. 23, indicates that the grave for a tragic hero is a monument for a holy *hieros,* not a memorial to the conventional hero.

rather an intimation of resurrective services for both Adams, met in Samson. The victory has been achieved within the provinces of sin and death as much as in those of annunciation and life.

The Chorus confirms the inward illumination and "reviving motions" it too has enacted in the play. No longer bereft of God, purged of the doubt and despair that in a Christian tragedy are equivalent to Aristotle's "pity and terror," it knows that the champion for God has received the most exalted favor in being given his incredible championship by God, who as to the Son at Jordan, "to his faithful Champion hath in place / Bore witness gloriously" (ll. 1751–1752). The action has revealed God's uncontrollable intent—that larger action that shines through individual agons, whether of Adam, Samson, or Christ. The spent "passion" of the final line therefore refers not only to Aristotelian *pathos* but also, obliquely, to Christ's Passion. If God is reciprocally alien to the alienated, He is reciprocally "heroic" to the Christian hero. Benediction reaches out to the fictional but *"true experience"* (l. 1756—italics added). In this somewhat startling last-second pronouncement, Milton insists upon the verity of the tragedy: it is no fable even in Aristotle's sense, but instead is the enactment of deepest and most direct truth, for the sake of the audience. The audience has participated in the answers of both God and a "hamartious" martyr to the baffling question of the center: "God of our Fathers, what is man!" And as Samson quit himself like Samson, so the entire human Chorus with active knowledge new "acquist" can similarly be dismissed in a Nunc Dimittis like that with which Eve closes *Paradise Lost*. All the actors "quit" the agon only by being acquitted, purged, redeemed within it.

Perhaps we should make the circle just with a final consideration of the question of tragedy. *Samson Agonistes* seems to me more conventional than some of the questions that are formulated about it. It encourages neither of two questions about the hero: the excessively backward-looking one, Is he St. Samson? and the excessively forward-looking one, Is he either an unregenerate sinner, or a futile character anticipating those of Beckett? He seems to me a proto-Christian tragic hero. Because he is involved in a general action, the tragedy is shared by the Chorus, Manoa, and the audience. Although *Samson Agonistes* has some of the characteristics of recent drama, it preserves much that is best in Greek structure and Christian implication. The axiom "All is best, . . ./ . . . ever best found in the close" (ll. 1745, 1748), together with the image of the phoenix, seriously intimates the Apocalypse as well as present catharsis and the restoration of Israel, thereby impressing massive order beyond that of the immediate artistic action. To the question whether or not *Samson Agonistes* is a tragedy, perhaps the only answer finally is a paraphrase of Dr. Johnson's reply to the question about Pope: If *Samson Agonistes* is not a tragedy, where is tragedy to be found?

Bibliography of Works Cited

Adamson, J. H. "The War in Heaven: Milton's Version of the *Merkabah*," *JEGP*, LVII (1958), 690–703.
Allen, D. C. *The Harmonious Vision*. Baltimore, 1954.
——. "Milton and the Descent to Light," *JEGP*, LX (1961), 614–630.
——. "Milton's Eve and the Evening Angels," *MLN*, LXXV (1960), 108–109.
——. "Symbolic Color in the Literature of the English Renaissance," *PQ*, XV (1936), 81–92.
Arthos, John. "Milton's Sabrina, Virgil and Porphyry," *Anglia*, LXXIX (1962), 204–213.
——. *On "A Mask Presented at Ludlow-Castle."* Michigan University Contributions in Modern Philology, No. 20. Ann Arbor, Mich., 1954.
Auerbach, Erich. *Scenes from the Drama of European Literature: Six Essays*. New York, 1959.
Barker, Arthur E. "The Pattern of Milton's Nativity Ode," *UTQ*, X (1941), 167–181.
——. "Structural Pattern in *Paradise Lost*," *PQ*, XXVIII (1949), 17–30.
Broadbent, J. B. *Milton: Comus and Samson Agonistes*. London, 1961.
——. *Some Graver Subject*. London, 1960.
Brooks, Cleanth, and J. E. Hardy, eds. *Poems of Mr. John Milton: The 1645 Edition, with Essays in Analysis*. New York, 1951.
Bryan, Robert A. "Adam's Tragic Vision in *Paradise Lost*," *SP*, LXII (1965), 197–214.
Bush, Douglas. *John Milton*. New York, 1964.
——. "Virgil and Milton," *CJ*, XLVII (1952), 178–182, 203–204.
Campbell, Lily B. "The Christian Muse," *Huntington Library Bulletin*, VIII (Oct. 1935), 29–70.

Carpenter, Nan Cooke. "The Place of Music in *L'Allegro* and *Il Penseroso*," *UTQ*, XXII (1953), 354–367.

Chambers, A. B. " 'Goodfriday, 1613. Riding Westward': The Poem and the Tradition," *ELH*, XVIII (1961), 31–53.

——. "Wisdom and Fortitude in *Samson Agonistes*," *PMLA*, LXXVIII (1963), 315–320.

Cirillo, Albert R. "Noon-Midnight and the Temporal Structure of *Paradise Lost*," *ELH*, XXIX (1962), 372–395.

Coffin, Charles M. "Creation and the Self in *Paradise Lost*," *ELH*, XXIX (1962), 1–18.

Colie, Rosalie L. "Time and Eternity: Paradox and Structure in *Paradise Lost*," *JWCI*, XXIII (1960), 127–138.

Cope, Jackson I. "Fortunate Falls as Form in Milton's 'Fair Infant,' " *JEGP*, LXIII (1964), 660–674.

——. *The Metaphoric Structure of Paradise Lost*. Baltimore, 1962.

Corcoran, Sister Mary. *Milton's Paradise with Reference to the Hexameral Background*. Washington, D.C., 1945.

Cox, Lee S. "The 'Ev'ning Dragon' in *Samson Agonistes*: A Reappraisal," *MLN*, LXXVI (1961), 577–584.

——. "Food-Word Imagery in *Paradise Regained*," *ELH*, XXVIII (1961), 225–243.

Daiches, David. *Milton*. London, 1957.

Daniells, Roy. *Milton, Mannerism and Baroque*. Toronto, 1963.

Diekhoff, John S. *Milton's Paradise Lost*. New York, 1946.

Dyson, A. E. "The Interpretation of *Comus*," *E&S*, n.s. VIII (1955), 89–114.

Eliade, Mircea. *Cosmos and History*, tr. Willard Trask. New York and Evanston, Ill., 1959.

Empson, William. *Milton's God*. London, 1961.

Ferry, Anne D. "The Authority of the Narrative Voice in *Paradise Lost*," in *In Defense of Reading*, ed. R. A. Brower and Richard Poirier. New York, 1962. Pp. 76–93.

——. *Milton's Epic Voice*. Cambridge, Mass., 1963.

Finney, Gretchen L. *Musical Backgrounds for English Literature: 1580–1650*. New Brunswick, N.J., 1962.

Fish, Stanley. "Further Thoughts on Milton's Christian Reader," *CritQ*, VII (1965), 279–284.

——. "The Harassed Reader in *Paradise Lost*," *CritQ*, VII (1965), 162–182.

Fixler, Michael. *Milton and the Kingdoms of God*. Evanston, Ill., 1964.

Fox, Robert C. "Satan's Triad of Vices," *TSLL*, II (1960), 261–280.

Frye, Northrop. *The Return of Eden.* Toronto, 1965.

——. "The Typology of *Paradise Regained,*" *MP,* LIII (1956), 227–238.

Giovannini, G. "Historical Realism and the Tragic Emotion in Renaissance Criticism," *PQ,* XXXII (1953), 304–320.

Gohn, Ernest S. "The Christian Ethic of *Paradise Lost* and *Samson Agonistes,*" *Studia neophilologica,* XXXIV (1962), 243–268.

Gossman, Ann. "Milton's Samson as the Tragic Hero Purified by Trial," *JEGP,* LXI (1962), 528–541.

——. "The Use of the Tree of Life in *Paradise Lost,*" *JEGP,* LXV (1966), 680–687.

Haller, William. " 'Hail Wedded Love,' " *ELH,* XIII (1946), 79–97.

Hanford, James H. *A Milton Handbook.* 4th ed. New York, 1954.

Hardison, O. B., Jr. *The Enduring Monument: A Study of the Idea of Praise in Renaissance Literary Theory and Practice.* Chapel Hill, N.C., 1962.

Harrison, Jane E. *Prolegomena to the Study of Greek Religion.* 3d ed. Cambridge, 1922. (Reprinted New York, 1959.)

——. *Themis.* Cambridge, 1927. (Reprinted Cleveland, 1962.)

Hassan, Ihab. "The Literature of Silence," *Encounter,* XXVIII (Jan. 1967), pp. 74–82.

Hollander, John. *The Untuning of the Sky: Ideas of Music in English Poetry, 1500–1700.* Princeton, 1961.

Hughes, Merritt Y. *Ten Perspectives on Milton.* New Haven and London, 1965.

Hunter, William B., Jr. "Holy Light in *Paradise Lost,*" *Rice Institute Pamphlet,* XLVI (Jan. 1960), 1–14.

Huntley, Frank L. "A Justification of Milton's 'Paradise of Fools' (*P. L.,* III, 431–499) ," *ELH,* XXI (1954), 107–113.

Huntley, John. "A Revaluation of the Chorus' Role in Milton's *Samson Agonistes,*" *MP,* LXIV (1966), 132–145.

Hutton, James. "Some English Poems in Praise of Music," *EM,* II (1951), 1–63.

Jayne, Sears. "The Subject of Milton's Ludlow *Mask,*" *PMLA,* LXXIV (1959), 533–543.

Kermode, Frank, ed. *The Living Milton.* London, 1960.

——. "Milton's Hero," *RES,* n.s. IV (1953), 317–330.

Klein, Joan. "Some Spenserian Influences on Milton's *Comus,*" *Annuale Mediaevale,* V (1964), 27–47.

Knox, Bernard M. W. "Sophocles' *Oedipus,*" in *Tragic Themes in Western Literature,* ed. Cleanth Brooks. New Haven, 1955.

Kristeller, Paul O. *Eight Philosophers of the Italian Renaissance.* Stanford, 1964.

Krouse, F. Michael. *Milton's Samson and the Christian Tradition.* Princeton, 1949.

LeComte, Edward S. "New Light on the 'Haemony' Passage in *Comus*," *PQ,* XXI (1942), 283–298.

Leishman, J. B. " 'L'Allegro' and 'Il Penseroso' in Their Relation to Seventeenth-Century Poetry," *E&S,* n.s. IV (1951), 1–36.

Lewalski, Barbara K. *Milton's Brief Epic.* Providence, 1966.

——. "Structure and the Symbolism of Vision in Michael's Prophecy, *Paradise Lost,* Books XI–XII," *PQ,* XLII (1963), 25–35.

Lewis, C. S. "A Note on *Comus*," *RES,* VIII (1932), 170–176.

——. *A Preface to Paradise Lost.* London, 1942.

Lloyd, Michael. "The Two Worlds of 'Lycidas,' " *EIC,* XI (1961), 390–402.

MacCaffrey, Isabel G. "The Meditative Paradigm," *ELH,* XXXII (1965), 388–407.

——. *Paradise Lost as "Myth."* Cambridge, Mass., 1959.

MacLure, Millar, and F. W. Watt, eds. *Essays in English Literature from the Renaissance to the Victorian Age, Presented to A. S. P. Woodhouse.* Toronto, 1964.

Madsen, William G. "The Idea of Nature in Milton's Poetry," in *Three Studies in the Renaissance: Sidney, Jonson, Milton.* New Haven, 1958.

Mahood, M. M. *Poetry and Humanism.* London, 1950.

Martz, Louis L. *The Paradise Within.* New Haven and London, 1964.

Miller, Dorothy D. "Eve," *JEGP,* LXI (1962), 542–547.

Mueller, Martin E. *"Pathos* and *Katharsis* in *Samson Agonistes*," *ELH,* XXXI (1964), 156–174.

Nelson, Lowry, Jr. *Baroque Lyric Poetry.* New Haven and London, 1961.

Newmeyer, Edna. "Beza and Milton: New Light on the Temptation of Learning," *Bulletin of the New York Public Library,* LXVI (1962), 485–498.

Nicolson, Marjorie H. *John Milton: A Reader's Guide to His Poetry.* New York, 1963.

Oras, Ants. *Milton's Editors and Commentators from Patrick Hume to Henry John Todd (1695–1801): A Study in Critical Views and Methods.* New York, 1964.

Orgel, Stephen. *The Jonsonian Masque.* Cambridge, Mass., 1965.

Otis, Brooks. *Virgil: A Study in Civilized Poetry.* Oxford, 1963.

Panofsky, Erwin. *Studies in Iconology*. New York and Evanston, Ill., 1962.

Patrides, C. A. "Adam's 'Happy Fault' and XVIIth-Century Apologetics," *Franciscan Studies*, XXIII (1963), 238–243.

——. *Milton and the Christian Tradition*. Oxford, 1966.

——. "Milton and the Protestant Theory of the Atonement," *PMLA*, LXXIV (1959), 7–13.

——. "*Paradise Lost* and the Theory of Accommodation," *TSLL*, V (1963), 58–63.

Pecheux, Mother M. Christopher. "Abraham, Adam, and the Theme of Exile in *Paradise Lost*," *PMLA*, LXXX (1965), 365–371.

——. " 'O Foul Descent!': Satan and the Serpent Form," *SP*, LXII (1965), 188–196.

Pope, Elizabeth M. *Paradise Regained: The Tradition and the Poem*. Baltimore, 1947.

Radzinowicz, Mary Ann N. "Eve and Dalila: Renovation and the Hardening of the Heart," in *Reason and the Imagination*, ed. J. A. Mazzeo. New York and London, 1962. Pp. 155–181.

Rajan, B. *Paradise Lost and the Seventeenth Century Reader*. New York, 1948.

——. "The Shattering of the Leaves," *SP*, LXIV (1967), 51–64.

Ricks, Christopher. *Milton's Grand Style*. Oxford, 1963.

Robb, Nesca A. *Neoplatonism of the Italian Renaissance*. London, 1935.

Robins, Harry F. *If This Be Heresy: A Study of Milton and Origen*. Urbana, Ill., 1963.

Saillens, Emile. *John Milton*. Oxford, 1964. (Saillens' authorized translation of *John Milton, poète combattant*.)

Samuel, Irene. *Dante and Milton*. Ithaca, N.Y., 1966.

——. "The Dialogue in Heaven: A Reconsideration of *Paradise Lost*, III, 1–417," *PMLA*, LXXII (1957), 601–611.

——. *Plato and Milton*. Ithaca, N.Y., 1947.

——. "*Purgatorio* and the Dream of Eve," *JEGP*, LXIII (1964), 441–449.

Schultz, Howard. "Christ and Antichrist in *Paradise Regained*," *PMLA*, XLVII (1952), 790–808.

——. "A Fairer Paradise? Some Recent Studies of *Paradise Regained*," *ELH*, XXXII (1965), 275–302.

Scott-Craig, T. S. K. "Concerning Milton's Samson," *Renaissance News*, V (1952), 45–53.

Sellin, Paul R. "Sources of Milton's Catharsis: A Reconsideration," *JEGP*, LX (1961), 712–730.

Shawcross, John T. "The Balanced Structure of *Paradise Lost*," *SP*, LXII (1965), 696–718.

——, ed. *The Complete English Poetry of John Milton*. New York, 1963.

Sims, James H. *The Bible in Milton's Epics*. Gainesville, Fla., 1962.

Sirluck, Ernest. "Milton's Idle Right Hand," *JEGP*, LX (1961), 749–785.

Spitzer, Leo. *Classical and Christian Ideas of World Harmony*. Baltimore, 1963.

Steadman, John M. " 'Bitter Ashes': Protestant Exegesis and the Serpent's Doom," *SP*, LIX (1962), 201–210.

——. "Eve's Dream and the Conventions of Witchcraft," *JHI*, XXVI (1965), 567–574.

——. "The God of *Paradise Lost* and the *Divina Commedia*," *Archiv*, CXCV (1959), 273–289.

——. "Heroic Virtue and the Divine Image in *Paradise Lost*," *JWCI*, XXII (1959), 88–105.

——. " 'Like Turbulencies': The Tempest of *Paradise Regain'd* as Adversity Symbol," *MP*, LIX (1961), 81–88.

——. "Miracle and the Epic Marvellous in *Paradise Lost*," *Archiv*, CXCVIII (1961), 289–303.

——. "*Paradise Regained:* Moral Dialectic and the Pattern of Rejection," *UTQ*, XXXI (1962), 416–430.

——. "Tantalus and the Dead Sea Apples (*Paradise Lost*, X, 547–73)," *JEGP*, LXIV (1965), 35–40.

Stein, Arnold. *Answerable Style: Essays on Paradise Lost*. Minneapolis, 1953.

Summers, Joseph H., ed. *The Lyric and Dramatic Milton*. New York and London, 1965.

——. *The Muse's Method*. Cambridge, Mass., 1962.

——. "The Voice of the Redeemer in *Paradise Lost*," *PMLA*, LXX (1955), 1082–1089.

Svendsen, Kester. *Milton and Science*. Cambridge, Mass., 1956.

Thorpe, James, ed. *Milton Criticism*. New York, 1950.

Tillyard, E. M. W. *The Miltonic Setting*. London, 1947.

——. *Studies in Milton*. London, 1951.

Tung, Mason. "The Patterns of Temptation in *Paradise Regained*," *Seventeenth-Century News*, XXIV (1966), 58–59.

Tuve, Rosemond. "George Herbert and *Caritas*," *JWCI*, XXII (1959), 303–331.

——. *Images and Themes in Five Poems by Milton*. Cambridge, Mass., 1957.

Van Kluyve, Robert A. " 'Out, Out Hyaena!' " *American Notes and Queries*, I (1963), 99–101.

Waldock, A. J. A. *Paradise Lost and Its Critics*. Cambridge, 1947.

Watkins, W. B. C. *An Anatomy of Milton's Verse*. Baton Rouge, La., 1955.

Wilkenfeld, Roger B. "Act and Emblem: The Conclusion of *Samson Agonistes*," *ELH*, XXXII (1965), 160–168.

Williamson, George. *Milton and Others*. Chicago, 1965.

Woodhouse, A. S. P. "The Argument of Milton's *Comus*," *UTQ*, XI (1941), 46–71.

——. "*Comus* Once More," *UTQ*, XIX (1950), 218–223.

——. "Pattern in *Paradise Lost*," *UTQ*, XXII (1953), 109–127.

——. "*Samson Agonistes* and Milton's Experience," *Proceedings and Transactions Royal Society of Canada*, sec. 2, ser. 3, XLIII (1949), 157–175.

——. "Theme and Pattern in *Paradise Regained*," *UTQ*, XXV (1956), 167–182.

Wright, B. A. *Milton's Paradise Lost*. New York, 1962.

Yates, Frances A. *Giordano Bruno and the Hermetic Tradition*. Chicago, 1964.

Index

Each of Milton's major works is listed separately. Particular themes within the works are subindexed under the titles of the works. Similarly, for selected characters subentries appear under the character's name.